To Stuart
Merry Christmas 2002
Love MAM ++

Military Classics

THE GREAT ESCAPE
Paul Brickhill

THE WHITE RABBIT
Bruce Marshall

Contents

THE GREAT ESCAPE

Paul Brickhill

To the fifty

INTRODUCTION

S everal days ago I was given the manuscript of this book to read. I took it home and Eleanor and I, becoming engrossed in it, sat up all one night poring over what Paul Brickhill has written. 'Whew!' she said when we had finished. 'Did all this really happen?'

The manuscript was on the floor between us and I was staring out the window.

'Yeah,' I murmured. 'It really happened.'

And that is the only introduction this book actually needs: Yes, it really happened. But because every man mentioned in this book was a friend of mine, because I have shared pitifully small rations with them, fought lice with them, baited the Germans with them and because many of them are now dead, I am grateful for this chance to point out that they did not die for a senseless reason.

This book is many, many things. It is the story of a project, a project conceived in the minds of, and carried through to success by, a group of ragged, starving scarecrows who, despite all privations, never lost sight of their sworn duty.

There is something demoralising about being taken a prisoner of war. At first it stuns the mind and one is overwhelmed with a feeling of helplessness, and hope is only a dim, dim shadow. The new prisoner is sorely tempted to sit back quietly, co-operate with his captors and thus make life comparatively easy for himself. In fact that is the philosophy the Germans were constantly trying to drive into our minds. They offered us many alluring inducements in the form of extra privileges and rations to 'behave,' to co-operate and to give up our vexing escape attempts.

But it is the duty of any officer in time of war, should he have the bad fortune to be taken prisoner, to do all in his power to escape. If escape is impossible it then becomes his duty to do everything within his means to force the enemy to employ an inordinate number of soldiers to guard him, to do all he can to harass the enemy and to convince his captors that they have caught a very large, very active and troublesome bear by a slippery tail. If the carrying out of this duty can be heavily spiced with a rollicking, ribald sense of humour and a sharp sense of the ludicrous such as is possessed by most Americans and British then this duty becomes more a game than a duty, a game to be entered into with fiendish glee. And as such it was considered by all the thousand-odd officers whom the Germans had corralled in the North Compound of Stalag Luft III during the war.

By the time the Americans began arriving in the North Compound the escape, sabotage and harassing organisations were already well organised. There was considerable doubt in the minds of the more prison-wise British as to just how helpful the Americans would prove to be in this game of cloak and dagger with the Gestapo. The average Briton of course prides himself on being part of 'perfidious Albion' and the British contingent was doubtful that the Americans, with their vaunted background of Dan Beard-Boy Scout-Fair Play training, could turn their minds from this pabulum and take an effective part in activities that required a completely Machiavellian attitude.

However, the British obviously overlooked the fact that an American only has to be sold on the idea that his cause is just and he is capable of anything. (The American Indian and the Panama Canal are two points in proof.) And it was not long before all the subversive activities of the camp were taking on a rowdy, fresh air of hubba-hubba that was leaving the Germans completely bewildered. As soon as the Americans got over the initial shock of being prisoners they started robbing the Germans blind of anything they could possibly use, lying through their teeth to their captors with all the persuasiveness of a European diplomat and, if need be, were quite capable of slipping up behind a guard with a ready loop of piano wire – to the constant terror of the reprisal-fearful British. They began showing even the wily

British some new and improvised tricks in waging an undercover, unscrupulous war.

But this book is a whole lot more than a hilarious story about a group of food- and sex-starved men playing grim practical jokes on a race of square-headed people who are devoid of any sense of the ridiculous. It is the story of achievement against impossible odds. And it proves something that I believed then and know now – there is nothing that can stop a group of men, regardless of race, creed, colour or nationality, from achieving a goal once they agree as to what that goal is. The aftermath may be sheer, stark tragedy – that lies with the gods – but the point is, men, working together, can accomplish anything. This book – and the episode about which this book is written – proves it.

In its essence this is the story of a group of men – and of one man, Roger Bushell, who was the colourful leader. And yet through it all runs the theme that even in death man can triumph over any obstacle. To my mind this is also the story of a Tower of Babel. The fact that this tower was in reverse and happened to be a tunnel is a minor point. What was important then – and is more so now – is that this Tower of Babel was successfully erected. It proves something important. In one magnificent gesture the seventy-six ragged, verminous men of all nationalities who climbed out of that stinking hole in the ground in Silesia on that windy March night in 1944 thumbed their collective nose at the entire Third Reich and all it stood for. They triumphed, through the only means left to them, over an idea that was rotten from the core out. And they proved for all posterity that men, working together, can dig a damned deep hole in the ground – or build a shining Tower of Babel.

George Harsh
New York

FOREWORD

Prison camp life would not have been so bad if:

(a) It weren't such an indefinite sentence. At times you couldn't say you wouldn't still be there (or worse) in ten years.

(b) The Germans didn't keep dropping hints that if they lost, Hitler was going to shoot you anyway, just to even the score.

(c) You could get enough food to fill your belly again. Just once.

So we spent a lot of time trying to escape. It is a melancholy fact that escape is much harder in real life than in the movies, where only the heavy and second lead are killed. This time, after huge success, death came to some heroes. Later on, it caught up with some villains.

You learn to escape the hard way. It took us three years to become proficient – from the first primitive tunnels to the deep, long ones with underground railways, workshops and air pumps, forgery and compass factories, and so on. Above all we learned how to 'destroy' sand and to hide everything in our little compound from the Germans constantly searching us.

The British had a start on the Americans because they were there first. Then the Yanks joined us and took to the escape business like ducks to water.

One got used to living in a microscopic world where life lay in working patiently for that brooding genius, 'Big X.' I suppose it is romantic now. It wasn't then. Life was too real, grim and earnest.

They were all real – Rubberneck, the humourless and coldly efficient German; 'Big X,' the South African; Walenn, that charming Englishman;

Ker-Ramsay, the dour Scot; Harsh, the rambunctious Yank; Sage, another Yank, also rambunctious; Floody, the Canadian who looked consumptive (and still does); Cornish, the baby-faced Australian; Pohe, the dark Maori; Minskewitz, the Pole with the Uncle Sam whiskers; Staubo, the handsome Norwegian; and all the others, too numerous to mention, even in the narrative that follows. No one ever noticed a nationality tag.

The Germans tried to play off the British against the Americans and vice versa, and in the end they took the Americans away and segregated them in another compound. We got along too damn well together.

Of my own part in the show – little enough to say. I am a sort of Boswell, not a hero. I was a cog in the machine, boss of a gang of 'stooges' guarding the forgers, who had to work in an exposed position by windows to get enough light. Walenn, the chief forger, and I invented the 'cloak and dagger' stooging system that gave them warning. It was rather complicated, but it never let us down – and that was the main thing. It just meant being on the job all the time, but there was nothing else to do anyway.

And when I finally drew a privileged position for the actual escape, 'Big X' debarred me and three or four others on grounds of claustrophobia, a correct, if infuriating, decision. A few weeks later I was deeply grateful.

With the exception of the fake passport photograph of Ed Tovrea, the photographs in this book were taken by the methodical Germans. Some pictures, like the views of 'Harry,' formed a part of the official record. Others, including all the group pictures, were taken by the camera fans among our captors; often they gave us prints of their work – unhappily not so good as it might have been.

A couple of years after it was over, a friendly German interpreter sent prints of about half of those used in the book to our old leader in the camp, Air Commodore Massey, who kindly lent them to me. The rest of the photographs were preserved in one way or another by George Harsh, Col. A. P. Clark, Lt. Col. Jerry Sage, Capt. Donald Stine, and Ed Tovrea, to all of whom I am indebted in more ways than one.

The maps and drawings printed throughout the text are by Ley Kenyon and were made from sketches Kenyon did at the camp as a diversion from his regular work as one of Tim Walenn's star counterfeiters.

Since the war I've twice been back to Germany to dig deeper into the story, being lucky enough once to get into the forbidden Russian zone and fossick once more round the scene of the crime. After the hangman's job was done in 1948 I went through several thousand pages of unpublished reports, getting all the German side of the affair as well as a lot more of our own. And then I searched out the important survivors and filled in the few gaps left.

So here it is, as nearly the way it happened as I can make it.

Paul Brickhill

PRELUDE

Roger Bushell had just turned thirty when he reached Dulag Luft, the reception camp for Air Force prisoners. He was a big, tempestuous man with broad shoulders and the most chilling, pale-blue eyes I ever saw. In his early twenties he had been British ski champion, and once in an international race in Canada he had come swooping downhill like a bat out of hell and taken a bad spill over a boulder. The tip of one ski caught him in the inner corner of his right eye and gashed it wickedly. After it had been sewed up, the corner of his eye drooped permanently, and the effect on his look was strangely sinister and brooding.

It was on 23 May, 1940, that he had led the twelve Spitfires of his squadron in over the coast between Dunkirk and Boulogne. Down below, men in sweaty battle dress were digging in on the beaches and spilling blood on the sand from the bombs. There weren't many RAF fighters about because there weren't many RAF fighters, and most of them were over on the rim of the battle trying to stop the dive-bombers from getting through.

Forty Messerschmitt 110's had slid down toward the Spitfires, and five of them picked on Bushell. He steep-turned and they overshot and pulled up. As he saw the last one sliding above, Bushell straightened out, pulled up, and was almost hanging on his propeller when his stream of bullets hit the German. Smoke poured out of the Messerschmitt's port engine, and it turned on its back and went straight down.

Another Messerschmitt was coming at Bushell head-on. They were both firing; everything was red flashes, and then Bushell shot inches above the German and saw the German behind shoot steeply up, flick into a stall, and spin down, smoking. Bushell was on fire too, smoke pouring into his cockpit. His engine seized and the smoke cleared away.

Gliding down, he picked a field, and as he slid the Spitfire into it on its belly flame spurted under the engine cowlings. He had cracked his nose on the gunsight and scrambled out with blood pouring down his face. Watching the plane burn while he fished for a cigarette, he judged he was in British-held territory and with an luck would be back in his squadron in a couple of days.

A motorbike came pelting down a lane and turned in at the far end of the field. Bushell waited placidly for it, and then he saw that it wasn't a crash helmet that the rider was wearing but a coal-scuttle helmet, and a moment later he saw the gun pointing at him.

If the Germans had realised what a troublesome man they had caught they would possibly have shot him then. It would have paid them.

Though he was a squadron leader in the RAF, Roger Bushell had been born near Johannesburg, and at the age of six he could swear fluently in English, Afrikaans, and Kaffir and spit an incredible distance. Later he acquired public-school polish by being educated in England at Wellington. His housemaster when he first went there summed him up very neatly in a letter to his mother: 'Don't worry about him. He has already organised the other new boys. I know the type well. He will be beaten fairly often but he will be well liked.'

At Dulag Luft the Germans put him hopefully in solitary confinement to soften him up for interrogation, but that was not an enormous help because Bushell had been a barrister with a talent for suave belligerence, and they got nothing out of him except a rather acid charm. They turned him loose then in the compound, a bare patch of earth a hundred yards square with three long, low huts surrounded by mountains of barbed wire, searchlights, and machine guns, and inhabited by an unhappy band of men trained to fight but shut up behind barbed wire while their country awaited invasion.

The senior man, Wing Commander Harry Day, had been shot down five weeks after the war started, flying a Blenheim on a suicidal, lonely daylight reconnaissance over Kaiserslautern. He'd flown as a youngster in the first war, and now he was greying, a tall, stringy, vital man with a lean face (the type they call 'ravaged') and a hooked nose. There was a wild streak in him, and prison camp didn't help it. He was capable of a sort of austere introspection, and then it would vanish in a mood of turbulent gaiety. He could be steely and frightening, and then sometimes that wry mouth of his would relax in a gentle smile.

'The Artful Dodger,' Major Johnny Dodge, had been born an American (his mother, Mrs Charles Stuart Dodge, was a daughter of John Bigelow, US Minister to France under Abraham Lincoln). In the first week of the 1914 war, the Dodger, a smooth-cheeked youngster of twenty, sailed to England to get into the fight as soon as possible. Five years later he was a colonel with the DSO and MC When things started again in 1939 the Dodger's friend and family kinsman, Winston Churchill, soon had him back in the army and the Dodger was trapped a few months later with the BEF in France, down the coast from Dunkirk.

Now, in his forties, he swam miles out into the channel to intercept a ship, missed it, swam back, was caught, escaped, then was caught again by the Luftwaffe and always thereafter stayed in Air Force prison camps (when he wasn't escaping). Tall and courtly, the Dodger had an incredibly charitable nature and a strange insulation from fear. I don't say that extravagantly. I think fear didn't bother him. Bushell was like that and so was Wings Day.

So was Peter Fanshawe, a Fleet Air Arm lieutenant-commander, regular RN in character as well as fact – fair-haired Fanshawe, whom you couldn't call Peter because he was so Royal Navy, but very sound and hard to get to know. Jimmy Buckley was also a Fleet Air Arm lieutenant-commander, more hard-boiled than Fanshawe. There were the dependable Mike Casey, Paddy Byrne, and a lot of others. In the subtle hierarchy of character, independent of rank, Bushell was soon one of the leaders in the common ambition to escape. He, Wings Day, and a dozen others started digging tunnels. They had a lot to learn about it. The first one they started under Paddy Byrne's bed, cutting a trap door in the floor. The Germans had a lot to learn about finding tunnels too, so they got away with a lot they shouldn't have, burrowing into the wet earth with their hands, hauling the dirt back in basins, and dumping it under the hut. It was pitch-black down in the rat hole, and they did it all by touch, working in long woollen underclothes so that dirt stains on their uniforms wouldn't give them away.

The first tunnel was just under the wire with about eight feet to go to freedom when they ran into a spring and water gushed up and flooded them out. They started another tunnel in another direction. The Germans found it. Winter closed in and the escape season was temporarily over. You can't hike two hundred miles over snow without much food and no shelter to a friendly border.

As spring softened the country they started a fresh tunnel under a bed in Wings Day's room, and this time there were no serious hitches. By July it was eighty feet long, under and past the wire with only a couple of feet to dig up. And after all that, Roger got away the night before they made the break.

The prisoners were taken into an adjoining field for exercise, and in a corner of this field a goat lived in a tumble-down shed. A mock bullfight between the goat and the prisoners drew the guards' eyes (as it was meant to), and Roger crawled into the shed. There had been a lot of debate as to how he would get on in the shed. Buckley started the old gag by saying, 'What about the smell?' and Paddy gave the stock reply, 'Oh, the goat won't mind that.' And, as it happened, the goat didn't mind at all. There was no fuss and after nightfall Roger crawled out and was away across the fields.

The next night there was a great din from a midnight party in one of the huts in the compound, and while the guards pondered on the merriment from behind their machine guns, Byrne dug out the last couple of feet of the tunnel and seventeen shadows emerged at the far end and snaked off into the wood under cover of the party noise.

Getting out of a camp is only half the battle; they learned this bitterly. They were all caught – most of them on the following day. The Dodger was snared trying to cross a bridge where there happened to be a guard. Wings Day stayed out three days till a couple of woodmen bailed him up with a shotgun. He had roughly tried to convert his uniform to look like civilian clothes, but you want a dark night to get away with that sort of thing.

Roger had crushing luck. He got away to the Swiss border and was within thirty yards of the frontier in a little village at night when a border guard stopped him. Roger pretended he was a slightly drunken skiing instructor going home after arranging a skiing match in the village. The guard was friendly and believed him but said he'd better come along to the station for formal check. Knowing what that would mean, Roger charmingly agreed and suddenly bolted around a corner and was away with a couple of bullets chasing him. He thought he was completely clear when he found he'd run into a cul-de-sac with high walls all around it, and back he was brought to punitive solitary confinement in a Frankfurt jail and then to Dulag.

Still, it had been valuable experience and the prisoners had tasted blood.

It was a good lesson for the Germans, too. They 'purged' Roger and the Dodger and all the others who had escaped to a new camp at Barth, up by the shores of the Baltic. Within the next year, forty-eight tunnels were started there; but water lay only about four feet under the surface so the tunnels had to be very shallow, and the Germans used to collapse them all by driving heavy wagons around the compound.

Apart from the normal fervent wish to get out of prison and back home to the war, there was plenty of other motive for escaping. The Geneva Convention lays it down that captured troops are to be properly fed. The German idea of proper feeding wasn't much more than a formality; they fed us on about ½d. a week. If you've ever known hunger – not gnawing appetite, but real hunger – you'll understand part of the reason for POW reluctance to endure German hospitality. In his first year in the bag, Roger lost nearly forty pounds.

After a few months there, he and some others were herded into cattle trucks for transfer to another camp. Roger and some others levered up the floor boards in their truck, and bodies began to slip through into the night. One man went under the wheels, had both legs cut off, and died immediately.

At night, in a siding near Hanover, Roger and a Czech officer in the RAF, Jack Zafouk, slipped out, reached cover, and set off for the Czech border, where Zafouk's brother lived. Jumping a couple of goods trains, they reached the brother, who gave them money and the address of a friend in Prague, who took them in and sheltered them.

For a week they both had to keep inside in the friend's flat. Zafouk didn't dare to go out because old friends might see him, and Roger had to stay in because he couldn't speak Czech. The host contacted the underground and arranged for their escape through Yugoslavia, but just as they were setting out the Gestapo broke the escape chain and executed the members.

Still shut in, Roger and Zafouk waited weeks till another underground chain arranged to pass them along to Turkey. They got to the Czech border when the Gestapo broke this chain too, and they narrowly escaped back to Prague. Czech patriots shot the Gestapo chief Heydrich about that time, and hell broke loose in Czechoslovakia. There were many executions and tortures besides Lidice.

And many spiteful betrayals. One morning the bell of the flat rang sharply. The Czech host, his son, and daughter were all out. Roger and Zafouk kept quiet and didn't answer the bell, but the door was burst open, five Germans pushed in, and in a few moments they were off to the Gestapo cells.

Zafouk was interrogated for a week and then sent to another camp. Roger was taken to Berlin, to a Gestapo cell. The Czech family was shot.

Meanwhile, other escapes were going on; that is, escapes from prison camps. No one yet had succeeded in getting back to England. At Barth, a primitive escape committee was organised to co-ordinate escape work. Wings Day nominated Jimmy Buckley as first chief. A genuine cloak-and-dagger atmosphere was creeping in. They called it the 'X organisation' for security reasons, and Jimmy Buckley was officially labelled 'Big X.'

The Germans became escape-conscious too, and 'ferrets' appeared in the compound – German security guards dressed in overalls and armed with torches and steel spikes to probe for tunnels. Then they dug sound detectors into the ground around the barbed wire to pick up sounds of tunnelling, and like clockwork they found tunnel after tunnel.

But there were still other ways of escape. One man dressed himself as a ferret and walked openly out of the gate at night. Others hid in trucks that brought food into the compounds. A Swiss commission (the Protecting Power) came to inspect the camp, and while they were in the compound a team dressed in makeshift civilian clothes walked out in their place. Pat Leeson dressed himself as a sweep with a dirty face and a cardboard topper like the German sweeps wear and walked out of the gate while the real sweep was in the compound.

Another reluctant captive was Douglas Bader, that phenomenal man who'd lost both his legs in an aircraft crash in the early thirties and went flying with tin legs to get a string of victories, wing commander's rank, a DSO and Bar and DFC and Bar. He'd collided with a German fighter in a scrap over France and had a leg trapped immovably in his damaged cockpit. So he took his leg off (the only time he ever appreciated losing his real ones) and baled out. The RAF dropped a new tin leg for him and, mobile again, Bader was so intractable that the Germans took him out of the camp and put him into a prison hospital.

A few days later, Bader sneaked into a working party of British soldier prisoners being taken to a near-by airfield for labour. He stayed four days with them there looking for a chance to jump into a plane and take off for home, but before he could make it the working party was paraded one morning and a German security NCO who knew Bader appeared and put the finger on him. They packed him off to Kolditz Strafelager, the punishment camp for the naughty boys.

In England, the RAF air offensive was getting into full swing and a lot of good men were being shot down. Mostly they died, but some landed alive and were captured, and the number of prisoners was growing. To cope with them, the Germans built a new camp at Sagan, a town of about 25,000 in Germany's dust-bowl, Silesia, about halfway between Berlin and Breslau. It was up toward the Polish border and a long, long way from any friendly or neutral territory. The Germans called it Stalag Luft III, and by that name now it is notorious. We called it Goering's luxury camp, but that was sardonic. In the spring of 1942, a couple of hundred prisoners were purged to Stalag Luft III from Barth and other camps.

Among them was a fellow with the DFC, a persistent escape fiend. While crates containing equipment were being loaded on the train at Barth, a German interpreter said archly to the prisoners doing the loading, 'Be careful of those crates. Maybe an escaper is nailed up in one.'

The boys all dutifully said, 'Ha ha, how funny that would be,' knowing very well it *was* funny because the DFC man was nailed up in one of them. He broke out on the journey and got away for a day or so but was caught and sent to Kolditz Strafelager.

When the others reached Sagan they found it about as grim as they'd expected – six low drab wooden barrack huts in a patch of sand surrounded by a double barbed-wire fence nine feet high. Spaced about a hundred yards apart just outside the barbed wire, the 'goon-boxes' stood up on their stilts about fifteen feet high so that from the little huts on top the sentries behind their searchlights and machine guns could look down into the compound with clear vision and an unrestricted field of fire. (They were called goon-boxes because every prisoner in the Third Reich referred to the Germans as Goons.)

About thirty feet inside the barbed wire ran the warning wire on its little posts about eighteen inches high. It was there to keep prisoners away from the fence, and it certainly did. If you put a foot over it, you could be reasonably sure of several bullets from the nearest trigger-happy sentry.

The night the first party arrived at Sagan, Wings Day and two others dressed up in RAF uniforms they had converted to look like German Luftwaffe uniforms (all the guards were Luftwaffe) and tried to bluff their way through the gate. The guard wasn't fooled, and they were marched off by a reproachful Kommandant for fourteen days' solitary in the cooler. The cooler, like Grannie's castor oil, was the German universal remedy for intransigent POW behaviour and, like Grannie's castor oil again, solitary is not funny. Even the Germans, incidentally, called it the 'cooler,' an expression they picked up from us.

There were many more reluctant guests in the new camp. Jimmy Buckley had been purged there too, and he started up the 'X organisation' again. Before long there were several tunnel syndicates worming out under various huts and a variety of other schemes too.

Bravest of them was a brilliant idea of Ken Toft and 'Nick' Nichols. Nichols was a good-looking Californian with a crew cut; a cool, composed and deliberate individualist if ever I saw one. He'd been in the American Eagle Squadron, with the RAF, and been shot down early in 1942. Nick didn't seem to have any nerves, which was just as well for the kind of job that he and Toft pulled. They had a theory that halfway between the goon-boxes there should be a blind spot hidden from the sentries by the long line of thick, coiled wire. If they could get to that spot across the lethal area from the warning wire, they could cut their way through in safety (?). If the theory was right they had a slim chance of getting through the wire (probably to be caught soon after). If they were wrong, a probable bullet each.

Four goon-boxes had a view of the warning wire at the chosen spot, so Jimmy Buckley laid on four elaborate diversions. At a given signal, a prisoner yelled to the sentry in one box to ring up for an interview with the Kommandant. In front of the next, two men staged a spectacular (sham) fight and one of them was knocked out while the sentry gaped at them. Another prisoner hailed the sentry in the third box and asked permission to get a ball that had been tossed over the warning wire. By the fourth, a man was doused with a bucket of water while the sentry looked on and laughed.

And in the vital five seconds Toft and Nichols crossed to the fence and crouched down by it. A hundred men held their breath (including Toft and Nichols), but the theory worked. They weren't seen. Nichols had a pair of crude wire-clippers made from a couple of hunks of metal. Strand by strand they worked their way through the wire till they were through. At another signal, four more diversions were repeated in front of the sentries, and Toft and Nichols ran the few yards into the cover of the woods. It would be nice to report that they got back to England, but they were caught soon after and slung into the cooler for the punitive solitary.

The tunnellers in the new compound were soon running into complications. The Germans had built the huts in the middle of the compound and cleared the ground on the far side of the wire so there was well over a hundred yards to tunnel to get to cover outside the wire. The soil was sandy and collapsed easily, and one by one the tunnels were found. One was very shallow and a horse pulling the ration wagon stuck his hoof through it, to the grief of the diggers, the joy of the Germans, and the surprise of the horse.

'Piglet' Lamond, a slight, toothy little New Zealander, won fame with his brilliant 'mole' idea which generally shortened the distance necessary to tunnel. We had been digging a sump by the ablutions hut, only about five yards from the wire, and it was Lamond's idea to tunnel from the sump. When it was about seven feet deep he tunnelled a hole in the side toward the wire, covering the entrance by hanging a coat over it. After a few days he had a little tunnel about twenty feet long, and one evening he and two others crawled into it. We buried them there alive, filling up the pit with rocks and gravel. Lamond's idea was to tunnel the remaining few yards in the one night and surface just outside the wire before dawn.

They were all stark naked, carrying their clothes in bundles, and there was just room for them to lie one behind the other, with a few feet to spare behind.

Lamond in front did the tunnelling; the other two shoved the sand back, filling up the tunnel behind them. They were only about four feet down and stuck pointed sticks up through the surface for breathing holes. It was pitch-dark down there and stiflingly foul. No one had done this sort of thing before, and it was just a theory that they could get enough air to keep them alive. For all they knew they might gradually lose consciousness and suffocate.

Prisoners watching from the nearest hut saw steam rising out of the air holes and prayed that the hundführer and his Alsatian dog who patrolled the compound at night wouldn't notice. The 'moles' lost track of time after a while. Their watches stopped because of the sand, and in any case the air was too foul for a match to light. They were thinking they might be far enough to dig up and away when Lamond saw light filtering down through an air hole. It was day.

They lay sweating in the foulness all day. The tunnel was just as wide as their shoulders, and they could hardly twitch a muscle. When no more light came down the air hole they still waited a few more hours for wandering Germans to go to bed, and then they tunnelled up the few feet and found themselves just outside the wire.

After tramping through the woods to the Oder River eight miles away, Piglet found a rowboat and they set off downstream toward the Baltic, hundreds of miles away. Within a few hours the boat was reported missing, and a policeman downstream on the watch for it picked them up at gunpoint.

To stop this sort of tunnelling nonsense the Germans dug an eight-foot-deep ditch between the warning wire and the fence. Three men crawled nervously out of their hut one night, dodged the searchlight beams, snaked under the warning wire, dropped into the trench and started to dig a blitz 'mole' tunnel like Lamond's. They only had about

twenty feet to go to get outside the wire, but they didn't push enough
sand out of their entrance hole into the trench. No matter how tightly
you pack it, sand that is dug out fills up a third as much space again in
its loose form. Before they reached outside the wire the sand they had
passed back had filled in all the tunnel behind them and they could
pass no more back. So they were trapped – couldn't go forward,
couldn't go back. All they could do was to dig up, and when they
surfaced it was dawn and they were caught, feeling rather foolish out
there by the wire.

The Germans very quickly filled in their anti-escape trenches and
took new, and much more efficient, precautions, burying microphones all around the wire, as at Barth. Over in the *Kommandantur*
(the German administrative compound) men sat with headphones
plugging in to each detector in day- and night-long watches.

Buckley heard about it and he and the tunnelling experts, Wally
Floody, 'Crump' Ker-Ramsay, Johnny Marshall, Peter Fanshawe, and
others had a conference at which they decided to dig two tunnels
thirty feet deep to get out of the range of the microphones. If one
tunnel was found, they might break out from the other. They made
camouflaged trap doors in the floors of two huts, and then came the
master stroke! They dug two shallow camouflage tunnels about thirty
feet long and stopped them there. Halfway along each of these they
made a second camouflaged trap in the floor and under this sank a
shaft twenty feet vertically and started the real tunnel from there. If
the Germans found the shallow dummy tunnels they probably
wouldn't find the secret deep shafts, and the diggers could burrow
down to the real tunnel from another direction. They were learning,
growing in cunning.

The ferrets did find one of the dummy tunnels, and then, by
accident probably, hit upon the hidden trap door in it and that was the
end of that one. The other tunnel forged ahead, the tunnellers hacking
at the crumbling face in stinking darkness, passing the sand back in a
metal washbasin drawn by plaited string. Special dispensers hid the
sand under the hut and carefully raked it over so it did not seem
obvious.

They devised a crude form of ventilation for the deep tunnel. Short
sticks were fitted into sockets in each other like a fishing rod and

pushed up through the soil till they broke through the top, twenty feet up. A POW sentry (always known as a stooge) lay upon the sand above to hide the stick as it pushed through, and then he camouflaged and protected the hole with a stone. Stinking air filtered up through these little holes. They made conditions just possible for working below, but only just. After a couple of hours of blind digging at the face, men crawled painfully back up with splitting heads and retched up green vomit. Pretty often it was dry retching because on German rations you didn't have much to bring up.

Johnny Travis, a dapper little Rhodesian, had been a mining engineer until he was trapped for three days 4,000 feet down a gold mine once by a fall of rock. He had bad claustrophobia from that, but he still used to go down the tunnel and work close to screaming point for a couple of hours, then come up to vomit. The sand was so crumbly there were frequent falls and there was always a number two digger close behind to haul you out by the legs if you were buried. It was grim.

Buckley noticed that Travis was a minor genius with his hands, making baking dishes from old tins, and shaving brushes from hunks of wood and bits of string. He pulled Travis out of the tunnel and started him making escape equipment – fat lamps from old tins with fuel made from margarine boiled to extract the water, and wicks made of pyjama cord. He made shovels for the diggers from bits of metal from old stoves and filed down broken table knives for chisels. (Buckley got the bits of file from bribing German guards.)

As the tunnel lengthened, the air got so bad they couldn't go on. Buckley commandeered an old accordion from one of the prisoners, and they used this to try to pump some air in. Then Marshall, Travis and some helpers designed a rough pump from a kit bag, with old boot leather for valves. It was just finished when someone fell on it and smashed it. He made another, and the Germans found it before it could be smuggled below. He made another, and it pushed just enough air into the tunnel to enable them to carry on.

The level of the dispersed sand was rising too noticeably under the hut so they dug a short tunnel back to the adjoining hut and started putting sand under there. The main tunnel was steered under the kitchen hut to disperse more sand there, but they were disappointed to find that there was no room underneath. There was a huge fall under that hut, and Wally Floody was nearly suffocated under half a ton of sand. It shook him up.

Then the Germans found the shallow dummy tunnel. All of us held our breath, but the Germans missed the secret trap door in it. They destroyed the dummy tunnel, so Floody and Crump dug a new dummy tunnel from another room and sank another secret shaft to link up with the main tunnel again. They didn't know the burrowing had undermined the hut foundations, and the weight above collapsed the new dummy tunnel as Floody was crawling naked along it. Ten feet of it came down along his body but by a miracle he had his face just over the trap door to the secret shaft and could breathe. The tunnel team dug madly for an hour and got him out. He was lucky.

They dug another shallow dummy tunnel, sank another deep shaft and at last made contact again with the main tunnel.

They'd been working for months now, and the X organisation was slowly growing all the time. Tim Walenn and a couple of men who'd been artists before they became airmen started a little factory for forging papers and passports. Tommy Guest organised a tailor shop to convert uniforms into rough civvy clothes. More metal workers and carpenters joined Johnny Travis. The tunnel pushed on till it was over three hundred feet long; less than a hundred feet to go now, but the sand was rising blatantly under the new dispersal hut.

A gang of ferrets raided the hut one morning, cleared everyone out, and almost took it apart. Underneath they found fresh sand over the exit of the dispersal tunnel, dug down to the trap door, and traced it right back to the deep shaft. They blew up the lot.

Buckley, Wings Day, the Dodger and others were purged to Schubin, a camp up near Bromberg, in Poland. In the train going there the dogged Dodger prised up a floorboard in his cattle truck and jumped out. A guard saw him and a posse jumped off the train and persuaded him to come back at pistol point. Paddy Byrne got out too. Also caught.

Within a week of arriving at Schubin, Buckley, Wings and company were tunnelling from one of the lavatories, and this time there was no hitch. The tunnel was 150 feet long when they surfaced outside the wire, and nearly forty men got out through it.

It wasn't discovered till *Appell* (counting parade) next day, and even then the Germans nearly missed it. Normally we paraded in five ranks for appell, but that morning some sections paraded in fours. The German officer had nearly finished counting when he noticed some of the fives he was counting were not fives but fours, and his blood pressure nearly sprayed out of his ears.

Five thousand troops turned out for the search, and before long the escapees had nearly all been caught. Wings Day was out for a week till a Hitler Youth boy spotted him hiding in a barn, and the local Home Guard winkled him out with shotguns.

Two they never caught and this was tragedy. Jimmy Buckley and a Danish lad in the RAF got to Denmark and started out in a little boat from the Zealand coast. Five miles across the water lay Sweden and freedom. No one ever found out exactly what happened. Maybe they were rammed, or shot, or just capsised. The Dane's body was found in the sea weeks later. They never found Buckley.

Late in 1942 Roger Bushell arrived in Sagan. The Gestapo had grilled him for several months, trying to pin charges of sabotage and spying on him, but Bushell's tough and nimble brain had kept him clear of the firing squad. They would probably have shot him in any case if Von Masse, chief censor officer at Stalag Luft III, who knew and liked Bushell, hadn't heard that the Gestapo was holding him. Von Masse's brother was a *Generaloberst* (colonel-general), and he used this influence to have Bushell handed back to the less lethal custody of the prison camp.

In Prague Bushell's Czech host had given him a smart, grey civilian suit, and it never occurred to the Gestapo, who dealt mainly with civilians, to take it from him. Roger wore a tattered old battle dress back to Sagan and carried his suit with him, wrapped in paper. Von Masse met him when he got to the camp, and Roger went for him with bald-headed fury over the way the Gestapo had treated him. Von Masse apologised.

'Don't blame us, please, for what the Gestapo do,' he said. 'They're not the real Germany.' He added warningly: 'What I particularly want to say is that you're lucky to get back this time. You won't get away with it again. I'm telling you that if you get out once more and they catch you I think they'll shoot you.'

'If I get out again they won't catch me,' Roger said, and went off into another tirade about the Gestapo, upsetting Von Masse so much that he forgot to search him – which was what Roger had banked on. He brought his suit into the compound, planning to use it on his next break.

This was a changed Roger – not the old boisterous soul who thought escape was good, risky sport like skiing. When he skied he used to take one course straight down at uniform, maximum speed, swearing like a trooper. Now he was moodier, and the gaze from that twisted eye was more foreboding. In Berlin he'd seen the Gestapo torturing people, and he did not tolerate Germans any more. By now he'd been behind the wire nearly three years, and his frustrated energy was focusing on the people responsible. He cursed all Germans indiscriminately (except Von Masse), but inside it was a clear, cool-headed hatred and it found sublimation in outwitting them.

With Buckley and Wings Day gone, he took over as Big X.

CHAPTER I

I t looked like a long war, and the Germans were building a new compound at Sagan. In the pine wood across the *Kommandantur*, gaunt Russian prisoners had felled some trees to clear a patch and workmen were putting up the long, wooden huts.

'You will be happier there,' said Hauptmann Pieber, the lageroffizier, who had stopped by the wire to welcome Roger to Stalag Luft III. Pieber, who had known Bushell at Barth, was a kindly little man with duelling scars on his cheeks and a sentimental heart. If he'd been lageroffizier in hell and had seen you brought in screaming he'd have blinked tenderly behind his glasses and wished you a felicitous sojourn.

'Most of you will be going to the new compound,' he added. 'It will be a happier new year for you. You will have taps in your huts and even lavatories.'

'A change,' said Roger sarcastically, 'is as good as a holiday. When are we moving?'

'I think March,' Pieber said, and Roger, eyeing the snow that hung on the ugly wire, was thinking of summer, the escape season.

He called on Wally Floody, and they collected Fanshawe, Crump Ker-Ramsay, and the others.

'If the bloody Goons don't rupture themselves, we'll be in the new compound by spring,' he said. 'We're going to get cracking on schemes now. My idea is to dig three major tunnels simultaneously and get about five hundred men on the job. The Goons might find a couple of them but we ought to make it with at least one. What d'you think?'

The conference lasted two hours with all of them shooting out ideas, some wild, some good. When it broke up they had the basic points decided – three tunnels thirty feet deep with underground railways and workshops, mass forging of passes, a tailor shop, mass-produced compasses and maps, and a huge intelligence and security organisation. A year ago it would have seemed impossible, but they had been learning the hard way for a long time and now they knew what they could do.

Roger took the details to Massey, the senior British officer, and the group captain, resting his game leg on his bunk and drawing on a pipe, listened with satisfaction but made a disturbing suggestion.

'Look, Bushell,' he said. 'You've been out twice now and nearly made it. The Gestapo think you're a saboteur and would be happy to get something more on you. Lie low for a while and leave it to the others. I don't want you getting a bullet in the back of the head.'

'I won't, Sir,' said Bushell. 'This is going to be a long job, and if we get out they'll have forgotten about me. I'll worry about that when the time comes if you don't mind.'

'You'll be worrying before then if they think you're working on tunnels. You'll be off to Kolditz,' Massey said.

'They're not catching me this time.' Roger was quite confident. 'We're flat out for security, and I don't think there'll be any slips.'

Massey looked at him doubtfully and then said, 'Well for God's sake be careful. I think you'd better keep in the background as much as you can and try and look like a reformed character. Stick to the brains part of it, and as far as the actual work is concerned I'll see you have the whole camp behind you. Let me know of anything or anyone you want, and I'll make it an order.'

He said it a little wistfully, resigned to the fact that he had no chance of escaping himself. He'd won his MC flying in the first war, but had smashed his foot when he'd been shot down then. The same foot had been damaged again when he got his DSO in Palestine in the thirties, and he'd bent it a third time when he bailed out over the Ruhr in this war. He shouldn't have been flying really, but he wanted to make one last trip before they made him an Air Commodore. Now, when he could move, he hobbled with a stick, his foot swaddled in an old flying boot.

Roger collected his specialists, and one by one he walked them miles around the circuit while he told them what he wanted. The circuit was a beaten track around the compound just inside the warning wire. You could walk there for hours till you were numb and didn't worry about home or the war or even the more important things like sex or liquor. You could also talk there without being overheard. The ferrets had a habit of hiding under the huts or in the roofs or outside the walls at night with ears agape.

Pounding the circuit Roger told Tim Walenn he wanted two hundred forged passes, and Tim, who never swore and was the politest man I ever met, pulled on his great long moustache and said, 'Jesus!'

'Maybe he'll help you,' said Roger ruthlessly. Walenn said earnestly he didn't really think it could be done, as all the printing on every pass had to be hand-lettered, but Roger said flatly he wanted them and wouldn't argue.

He told Tommy Guest they would need eventually two hundred full outfits of civilian clothes, and Guest, appalled, said it was impossible. Apart from the materials and manufacturing, there would be nowhere to hide them till a tunnel was ready.

'Make your own materials,' Roger said. 'Most of the boys who get out will have to convert their own duds to civvies. I want you to co-ordinate the thing; make some yourself and show the rest how.'

'And how do we hide all this stuff?' Guest asked, resisting to the last.

'We'll fix that when the time comes,' Roger said.

Al Hake, phlegmatic Australian, lifted his thick black eyebrows when Roger told him he wanted two hundred compasses. He said he'd see if he could get a mass-production line going.

Roger told Des Plunkett he wanted a thousand maps, and Plunkett said he'd be quietly confident if he could get some jellies to make a mimeograph.

Travis nearly had a fit when Bushell described all the railways, air pumps, pipe lines, and underground workshops he had in mind. He said he'd start tooling up.

Roger had another conference with Massey, and Massey went to the

Kommandant and suggested a few POW working parties might go over and help in the new compound. A good co-operative spirit, thought the Kommandant, and benignly agreed. So the working parties were marched over, and with them, in the guise of innocence, marched Roger, Floody, Crump, and 'Hornblower' Fanshawe. They mapped the layout of the new camp, tramped out distances, measured angles and more distances by rough trig, and surveyed the area outside the wire. Back in their own compound they put it all together and worked out where to dig the tunnels and how long they would have to be.

One of them showed such interest that a kind German surveyor showed him most of the plans, and the prisoner limped back to the old camp stiff-legged and thoughtful. Down the leg of his pants he had a stolen copy of the underground sewage system. They looked it over back in the compound, and there were two beautiful, tailor-made tunnels leading out to near-by drainage areas. If only the pipes were big enough, it looked like happy days. Roger didn't take anything for granted, and the tunnel chiefs carried on their planning.

Wally Valenta was training men who spoke German for the intelligence branch. Day after day, 'Junior' Clark, George Harsh and Tom Kirby-Green padded around the circuit devising security on a scale they'd never tried before. Security was going to be one of the keys to the whole thing. Clark was chief of security and known as 'Big S.'

On the face of it, proper security looked impossible. There were going to be half a dozen Germans in the compound all the time wandering around with torches and probes. We had to hide the proposed forgery and map factories, compass and clothing factories, metalwork and carpentry shops, the sand we dug out and the tunnel traps . . . We even had to hide the security stooges themselves because nothing stuck out to the ferrets' eyes more than some character self-consciously sitting around in the same spot every day and all day trying to watch, give signs of approaching ferrets, and look innocent all at the same time.

Junior Clark and George Harsh were both Yanks of totally different types. The Yanks were just getting going in Europe, and a lot of them were being chopped down as they experimented with the dangerous business of daylight bombing. The ones who didn't die were being trundled dolorously behind the wire to join us, and there were about a hundred of them with us at that time. Clark was a gangling red-headed youngster in his twenties and already a lieutenant colonel. George Harsh was well into his thirties and as grey as a badger. He looked like a Kentucky colonel and was a wild, wild man with a rambunctious soul. He'd joined the RAF a couple of years earlier and had been shot down as a rear gunner over Berlin. Tom Kirby-Green was a big, black-haired Englishman who looked like an overgrown Spaniard.

Roger controlled every phase of the growing organisation, holding daily conferences with the departmental chiefs, presiding over them as charmingly incisive but slightly sinister chairman. He had a mind like a filing cabinet, and that was one of the reasons he was so brilliant at organisation. Once he'd chosen his man for a job, he never roughly interfered with him. He listened to his problems, made suggestions, and when they'd thrashed it out and a decision had been made, he gave the man concerned full brief to carry it out. With that twisted eye taking everything in, he was a potent influence enveloping every detail of the planning. He wandered around in a battered old RAF tunic, scarf around his neck and hands in pockets, a tall, brooding figure, with that steady and disconcerting gaze. Every day he went to Massey, and they talked over the master plan.

By the end of March, the new compound was ready. So was the X organisation.

We moved on April Fool's Day, a straggling line of seven hundred scruffy prisoners carrying all our worldly possessions. Most of us wore all our clothes, festooned ourselves with cooking pots, plates and mugs, and the gadgets made out of old tins, and carried cardboard Red Cross boxes with what food we had and a few beloved personal things like photographs and nails and bits of string. Mother wouldn't have known us. There weren't enough razor blades to shave every day so some of us were shaven, some had felonious stubbles, and a few had beards ranging from the farcical to the flamboyant. Here and there a bottom peeped pale and unashamed out of obsolete pants, and the air was blue to the noise of happy cursing. A change, as Roger had observed, was as good as a holiday.

Henceforth the old home was known as east compound and the new

THE GREAT ESCAPE | 33

one was north compound. First the Germans searched us, but no more efficiently than usual. People clustered around and harried them, passed articles from one to another, and the result was mildly chaotic. No one lost anything of importance. Roger, amazingly enough, got his grey suit through. Travis brought all his tools, and Walenn had no trouble with his forging pens and inks. Then the screen of tommy-gunners ranged up on each side and escorted us the four hundred yards to the new home.

North compound was as innocent of luxury as we'd expected. There were fifteen bare wooden huts in three rows in the northern half, and the rest was a patch of stump-studded, loose grey dirt for recreation and appell.

The compound was about three hundred yards square and right around it ran two fences about nine feet high and five feet apart, each strung with about twenty close strands of rusting barbed wire. In between them great coils of barbed wire had been laid, so thickly in parts that you could hardly see through it. Some thirty feet inside the main fence ran the warning wire. Just outside the northern wire lay the *Vorlager*, containing the sick quarters and the long, grey concrete cooler with its barred windows. Another double fence of spiked wire sealed off the other side of the vorlager. The entrance to the compound was on the north side, so there had to be a gate in each fence and each was guarded.

Every 150 yards behind the fences the 'goon-boxes' stood up with their watchful sentries, and at night more sentries patrolled the fences and another hundführer prowled inside the camp with his dog trained to go for a man's throat if necessary.

Woods completely encircled the compound; not pleasant green woods but gaunt pines with skinny, naked trunks, packed close together in the dry, grey earth. They were everywhere you looked, monotonous barriers that shut out the world and increased the sense of Godforsaken isolation. Just outside the wire the Germans had cut the trees back for about thirty yards so there would be no cover for escapers and so that any tunnels would have to reach a hundred feet beyond the wire.

The huts were divided into eighteen rooms about fifteen feet square, each to be bedroom, dining room, and living room for eight people,

THE NORTH COMPOUND OF STALAG LUFT III

and three little rooms for two, reserved for those who could pull enough rank to deserve them. Furniture was elementary – double-decker bunks, a deal table, stools, lockers, and a stove in one corner on a tiled base. The bunks consisted of four corner posts with planks screwed along the sides and across the ends at two levels. Short, flat boards rested across the side planks, and on these one laid one's palliasse – a bag of woven paper that looked like hessian, and stuffed with wood shavings.

These flat bedboards were about thirty inches long and six inches wide. If they'd been specially designed for shoring tunnels they'd have been just that shape and size!

Each block had a washroom with a concrete floor, a lavatory, and a tiny kitchen with a coal stove that had two burners on top and a little oven. There were to be over a hundred men in the block, and they had to do all their cooking on that little stove. Actually there was a kitchen block in the compound, but that could just cope with boiling water for the brews and sometimes boiling potatoes (if there were any) or making soup.

We got by with cooking on the little block stove because there wasn't much to cook. German rations allowed a very thin slice of bread, margarine, and ersatz jam for breakfast, a couple of slices for lunch, and a couple for dinner, probably with neither margarine nor jam. Usually there were a few potatoes and once every three weeks a little minced horsemeat. Occasionally there were some vegetables or barley or sauerkraut. If Red Cross parcels were coming in (thank God they mostly did after the first couple of years), there would be an evening meal of bully beef or Spam and extra luxuries like chocolate, coffee, cheese, and jam.

There was a mad rush for rooms, and as there weren't enough prisoners to fill the huts yet, there was a wonderful lot of space, almost enough to swing a stunted cat. That day and the next three days were chaos – on the German side too – while everyone was getting organised, and the X organisation took advantage of it. Escape fever hit the camp.

CHAPTER II

————————

Roger first settled the question of the drainage pipes. Within an hour a willing bunch of prisoners gathered for an open-air meeting as a diversion, and in the middle of them someone whipped off a manhole noted on the stolen drainage chart and Shag Rees, a nuggety little Welshman, slipped into it. He was up again in a minute with a dirt-streaked face.

'The bastards,' he said. 'You couldn't pull a greasy piglet through them.' He indicated with his hands a circumference of about six inches, and there was a low moan. Roger cut it short.

'Can't expect the Goons to be stupid all the time,' he said. 'Let's get on with the other things.'

There were a few hungry Russian prisoners still in the compound under guard clearing away the last of the spindly pine trees they'd cut down, and trucks loaded high over the cab were taking the branches and foliage away. The road out went past three of the huts, and before you could say 'Hitler is a *Schweinhund*,' furtive shapes were crawling up on the roofs of those huts under cover of the near-by trees. As the trucks rolled past, shapes hurtled through the air and crashed down out of sight into the loaded branches. There were so many trying it that a man about to jump had to look carefully to see there wasn't already a man who had jumped from the previous hut looking up from the branches, making frantic signs for him to wait for the next truck and not brain him with his boots as he came down.

But every truck was searched at the gates, and one by one the prisoners were winkled out, and with much show of jovial regret from the Germans locked in the cooler for the traditional two weeks' solitary. A couple, however, burrowed deep into the branches and got away (to be caught soon after). The Goons took to probing the branches with pitchforks, and when a would-be escaper caught a couple of prongs in the bottom, the rest turned to other methods.

Ian Cross climbed under one of the trucks and hung on to the chassis. A few moments later, the chief German ferret, *Oberfeldwebel* (staff sergeant) Glemnitz, had a word with the driver, and the truck shot off like a rocket across a patch of the compound studded with tree stumps. We held our breath waiting for Cross to be mashed to pulp, and then the truck stopped and Glemnitz walked up and leaned under.

'You can come out now, Mr Cross,' he called. 'We have your room ready in the cooler.'

'You see,' said Roger, watching Cross marching lugubriously off, 'how bloody careful we've got to be. Secrecy is the key.'

Glemnbitz was the arch-enemy. We didn't exactly like him, but we certainly respected him. He was a droll fellow in a sardonic way, with a leathery face you could crack rocks on. He didn't wear overalls like the other ferrets but was always in uniform complete with peaked cap and the dignity of rank. A good soldier, Glemnitz, efficient and incorruptible, too good for our liking.

Griese, his second in charge, was the other dangerous ferret, a lean *Unteroffizier* (corporal), with a long thin neck and known, naturally, as 'Rubberneck.' He was smart but he didn't have Glemnitz's sense of humour.

'Cherub' Cornish, an angelic little Australian, didn't shave for two days, borrowed an old Polish greatcoat that reached to the ground, rubbed dirt into his face, and slipped among the last group of Russian prisoners leaving the camp. At the gate a bovine guard counted them and scratched his head. Fifteen had come in and sixteen were going out. He reported this phenomenon to the *Herr Hauptmann* (captain), and Pieber, more in sorrow than in anger, plucked Cherub from the tattered ranks despite the truthless but virtuous vows of a gaunt Russian who claimed that Cornish was an old pal from Smolensk.

As the cooler door closed on Cornish, the escape fever was over and the organisation settled down to the real stuff.

Roger appointed a 'Little X' and 'Little S' in every block to co-ordinate the work in their blocks. Conk Canton, built like a pocket battleship with a great aggressive jaw, became Roger's adjutant; Crump, Johnny Marshall, and Johnny Bull were the tunnel committee under Floody. Fanshawe was sand dispersal chief. George Harsh had charge of tunnel security. They all met in conference nearly every day.

One tunnel, Roger had decided, was to go from Block 123 out under the western wire to the woods beyond – an obvious choice as it was as near the wire as any hut. It was also on the far side of the compound to the German camp and the farthest hut from the gate, which meant more seclusion and more warning of any snap search. It also meant it was going to be a hut the Germans would suspect, but you can't have everything.

'We're going to call this one 'Tom,'' Roger told the attentive committee. 'They're all to be known by their names, and by their names only. If any bastard in this camp ever utters the word tunnel carelessly I'll have him court-martialled.'

The second tunnel was to go from 122 because it was an inside hut and not likely to be so much suspected. It was to be known as 'Dick.' The third one was to go from Hut 104 by the northern wire. This meant an extra hundred feet to go under the second boundary wire, but that also meant the Germans wouldn't regard it as a likely site. Roger named it 'Harry.'

Roger, Floody, and the other tunnel kings surveyed the three huts to find sites for the trap doors, a most important part of the business because it was usually the traps that gave tunnels away. So the traps had to be perfect, and this was a headache because the Germans had built the hut floors about two feet above the ground so they could crawl underneath to see if anyone was tampering with the soil of the Fatherland. They made one mistake, though, because they made solid brick and concrete foundation walls right around under the wash-rooms in the huts and also under a little square of each living room where the stove stood. The ferrets couldn't crawl into these areas, so they were the logical spots for the traps.

By 11 April, Roger and Floody had picked all trap sites. 'Tom' was to be in a dark corner of the concrete floor by a chimney of 123. 'Dick' was to start from the washroom of 122, and 'Harry' was to drop under a stove in one of the end big rooms of 104.

Minskewitz, who was the trap expert, was a short, wiry little Polish officer in the RAF, with a little grey goatee beard which he was always tugging lovingly. The German workmen had left some cement in the compound, and Minskewitz used some to cast a concrete slab about two feet square in a wooden mould. He reinforced it with bits of barbed wire left lying around and sank a couple of lugs in the sides, almost flush but protruding just enough for a couple of pieces of fine wire to be looped around them. He hid it under a palliasse to dry while he chipped a slab out of the concrete floor of 123, exactly the same size as the slab he'd made.

Stooges kept watch for ferrets outside while he handled his chisel like a surgeon and, when he'd finished, his home-made slab fitted the hole perfectly and could be lifted on and off with the wires on the lugs. The wires themselves folded down into the cracks when the trap was in position, but you could fish them up in a moment with a knife blade. In position, the slab rested on a padded frame beneath, and the cracks all around were lined with cement paste and dusted with dirt.

It was such an extraordinary precision job that Roger and Floody took Massey over to see the site for 'Tom' and Massey examined the corner and said, 'Seems a good spot, Bushell, but how are you going to camouflage it when you've chipped a hole there?'

'We have, Sir,' Roger said, and Massey got down, holding his game foot out, and peering hard could just see the outline. He shook his head in wonder.

'It's just extraordinary,' he said.

I wouldn't have believed it possible myself if I hadn't been taken in the same way.

Minskewitz, tugging on his beard, said cautiously, 'I seenk it will do.'

For 'Dick,' Minskewitz devised one of the most cunning trap doors in the history of prison camps. In the middle of the concrete floor of 122 block's washroom was an iron grating about eighteen inches square through which overflow water ran into a concrete well about three feet deep. A foot up from the bottom a pipe led off to carry the water away so there was always a foot of water in the well up to the edge of the pipe.

Minskewitz took off the iron grating while the stooges watched outside, bailed out the water, and mopped the well dry with old rags. He chipped away one wall of the concrete well laying bare the soft earth behind just ripe for tunnelling. He cast a new slab to fit where the broken wall had been, slipped it in, sealed the cracks with soap and sand, put the grating back on top, and sloshed water down till the well was again full to the outlet pipe. The ferrets didn't have a hope of finding 'Dick' unless they had second sight, and they didn't have that.

With practice it took only a minute or two to take the grating off, bail out the well and lift out the slab. Later on, when the shaft was dug beneath, the diggers would vanish into it, the slab and grating would be replaced, and water poured into the well so they could work happily below for hours without a stooge on top.

Floody, Canton, Crump, and Marshall had already started to sink the shaft under 'Tom's' trap. It was to go straight down for thirty feet so that when the tunnel was burrowed out at the bottom it would be out of range of the sound detectors around the wire.

Then Crump started 'Harry's' trap. In Room 23 of Block 104, he heaved the stove off the square of tiles on which it stood, took up the tiles one by one, and recemented them on a wooden frame that Travis' carpenters had made. He hinged this on as a trap door in place of the former solid tile foundation.

Under it he found solid brick and concrete to get through to reach the earth. Someone had souvenired an old pick head which the Russian workmen had used, and Crump fitted a baseball bat in it for a handle and bashed into the brick and concrete. It kicked up a hell of a ringing noise, exactly like a pick biting into brick and concrete, and it was obvious Glemnitz and Rubberneck and every ferret within half a mile would be galloping up inquisitively at any moment.

Half a dozen diversionists gathered outside the window hammering at bits of tin and wood making innocent things like baking dishes as noisily as they could for a couple of days while Crump sweated with the pick, until he had cleared a way to the earth. Crump was a good man with a pick, a wiry stocky character with a square red face and red hair.

Half a dozen of the tiles on the trap had been cracked, and it wasn't good enough for him.

'It looks too suspicious,' he said at a meeting of the committee, and they searched the camp till they found some spare tiles in the kitchen block and replaced the cracked ones. To muffle some of the hollow sound if the ferrets should tap on the trap, he fitted a removable grill that covered the top of the shaft just underneath and piled blankets in the little space. Minskewitz put the same sort of grill under 'Tom's' trap and, as 'Tom's' concrete slab sounded more hollow than 'Harry,' he made little bags of sand to stow on the grill.

'HARRY'S' TRAP DOOR

It was a good moment when Floody reported to Roger that the last of the traps was finished. It had been the riskiest part of the scheme because if he'd seen chunks of flooring torn up, even Dopey, the dimmest of the ferrets, would have guessed that something was wrong. When Crump was making 'Harry's' trap, the floor was up for about ten days and covered with a spare palliasse when a ferret wandered near by. It would never have passed undetected in later days, but in the first weeks of the north camp occupation the ferrets were not well organised and the gamble came off.

Only a few dozen people in the whole camp knew where the trap doors were. A lot of the rest didn't even know what huts they were in. That was how good the security was. Yet nearly everyone was working in some way on the X organisation. A couple of days after we moved into the compound, blank sheets of paper had been pinned up in all huts with such headings as 'Volunteers for cricket or softball teams will please put their names down here.' Little X in every block went around interviewing everyone who signed to see if he had any useful skill, from languages to mining and needlework.

Anyone who could sew went to join Tommy Guest's tailoring section. Artists went to Tim Walenn's forgery factory, miners into the tunnels, engineers to Johnny Travis' department, and so on. The rest became stooges or penguins, the penguins being the people who dispersed the sand from the tunnels. Most, of course, became stooges, doomed to hour after hour of skulking and spying on ferrets and warning of their approach to any danger area.

Junior Clark had the compound divided into two sections, 'D' for danger zone and 'S' for safe. 'S' was the east half of the camp where the gate was. The rest was 'D' zone, where the tunnels and factories were. As soon as a ferret penetrated into 'D,' he was tailed, and if he got within fifty yards of an exposed tunnel or factory, work was packed up right away till he wandered off again.

Down by the gate, the 'Duty Pilot' sat with his runner, watching everyone who came into the camp, noting on his list the time they came in and the time they went out. He sat there every minute of every day without a break, never moving till the next man came to relieve him. All over the camp there were warning points to relay his sign messages. Near him was a little cement incinerator, an innocent-looking Red Cross box, and a coal scuttle. If the coal scuttle alone was lying carelessly on the incinerator, it meant there were only a couple of administrative German staff (pretty harmless) wandering about. If the Red Cross box was tossed up too, it meant ferrets in. There were various combinations and positions.

Over by the back of 110, a man lounging on a stool with a book kept his eyes on the incinerator, and if the box and scuttle position flashed a danger sign he got lazily up and rearranged some shutters. Across by a corner of Block 120, a man casually blew his nose, upon which George Harsh, looking out of a window of 123, put his head around the door and said pithily, 'Ferrets. Pack up.' And then the trap was on in seconds, the wires folded down, and sand and cement paste smoothed into the cracks.

Every factory had its own stooges watching in case a ferret got through the general screen. There were nearly three hundred stooges altogether rostered in shifts. The organisation needed them all.

The whole scheme was taking shape so smoothly that Roger one morning said thoughtfully to Floody and George Harsh, 'You know, this time it might really be home for Christmas for some of us,' and for once they didn't laugh.

CHAPTER III

Floody had dug only six inches into the dirt under 'Tom's' trap when he came to the yellow sand. The grey dirt was only a thin layer over the surface of the compound, and everywhere underneath was the bright yellow subsoil. Whenever the ferrets saw it they knew there was a tunnel, and the heat was on till it was found. With three tunnels going, there would be about a hundred tons of yellow sand to disperse, about as easy as hiding a haystack in a needle. It was the worst enemy.

'You'll never get a tunnel out of here,' said Glemnitz once, 'till you find a way of destroying sand.'

Fanshawe had been thinking solemnly about this for a long time. 'You don't have to destroy it,' he said (to the committee, not to Glemnitz). 'You ought to be able to camouflage it.'

Everyone, he said, ought to dig gardens outside the huts so the yellow sand would be turned up naturally. Glemnitz couldn't be very suspicious of that. He'd watch them, but if the level of the gardens didn't rise he wouldn't suspect any tunnel sand was being dumped there.

'We can save the grey sand of the garden topsoil and mix a bit of tunnel sand in the gardens,' Fanshawe explained. 'Then we can spread the rest of the tunnel sand in the compound and sprinkle it with the grey stuff we've saved from the gardens.'

'Sounds possible,' Roger said, 'but how are you going to spread the yellow stuff without being spotted? It'll look pretty bloody obvious.'

Fanshawe had done his heaviest thinking about that. 'With trouser bags,' he said cryptically, and out of his pockets he dragged what can only be described as a gadget. It consisted of the two legs cut off a pair of long woollen underpants, and to the tops he'd tied each end of a piece of string. He explained that you looped the string around your neck under your tunic and the underpants legs could then hang suspended down inside the legs of your trousers. He had a pin stuck in the bottom of each trouser bag and a string tied to each pin. Those strings, he explained, led up inside the trousers to the pants pockets.

'I don't usually wear these things,' he said apologetically. 'It's just an idea. You fill the bags with sand at the traps and you wander around the various spots and then you pull the string in your pockets; out come the pins and the sand flows out of the bottom of your pants. If you're not a complete clot the ferrets'll never see a thing.'

For a conservative citizen like Fanshawe, RN, the idea was indecently brilliant.

'By God, we try it immediately,' said Roger.

'I have already,' said Fanshawe. 'It works.'

The penguins (there were about 150 of them) made themselves trouser bags complete with pins and string, cutting up long underpants with sadistic joy. Our clothes came through the Red Cross, and they, bless their maternal hearts, thought mainly of long woollen underpants. They were the only things we had plenty of. It's bad enough rusting behind barbed wire thinking of Dorothy Lamour without the final degradation of long underpants. You feel so hopelessly celibate.

In the deepening hole under 'Tom's' trap, Floody and Marshall were scraping the yellow sand into metal jugs and passing them up to Minskewitz, who acted as 'trapführer' for 'Tom.' Minskewitz had blankets spread around the hole so none of the yellow stuff would be left on the floor. He had the trap door drill down to a fine art, and whenever George Harsh stuck a warning head around the corner he had the men out of the hole and the trap back on and sealed in a shade under fifteen seconds. Beside him in the corner he kept his tin of dirt and cement paste to seal the edges. The penguins took it in shifts, walking up with their trouser bags, stopping a moment by the trap while Minskewitz filled them, and then wandering casually out into the compound.

Jerry Sage, the lanky Yank from Washington State, organised the dispersal diversions as though he were planning the invasion. A tough curly-headed fellow with a permanent ferocious grin and pointed ears, he'd been a paratroop major in North Africa, and the Germans had only cornered him after he'd been walking about behind their lines for two weeks sniping at people with a tommygun.

For his diversions he used to get about forty men having unarmed combat drill – a milling mass of bodies, dust rising in all directions, and the penguins in the middle being flung over someone's shoulder with the sand dripping out of their pants. The yellow stuff was shuffled into the sand, and the grey soil from the gardens sprinkled over any parts that showed. Sometimes Sage had volley-ball games going with a mob standing around cheering, and the sand was shuffled in among them. More sand was poured down the deep privy pits.

A curly-headed Australian called Willy Williams, who was supply chief, stripped some of the double-decker bunks and smuggled the bedposts over to 123. When Floody had sunk the shaft about five feet he stood four of these posts in the four corners of the shaft, bolted them together with cross braces, and slid bedboards in behind as a solid wall. After he'd packed sand as tightly as he could behind the lining boards, that part of the shaft framing stayed rigidly in position while he dug down another five feet and put in another section. He framed the whole shaft like that, and as they got deeper he nailed a ladder in one corner.

When it was about fifteen feet deep Johnny Marshall took over 'Tom' with three or four selected diggers, and Floody went to start 'Dick's' shaft with another team. It was strange that these two could work so well down tunnels; they were both so tall. Floody was lean as a beanpole with a large, rather sensitive mouth and eyes sunk back in his head making him look solemn and ill. Johnny Marshall lived a lot on his nerves, very intelligent and good-looking, a little thin on top and with perfect white teeth.

They dug fast because the sand was crumbly, but they would rather have dug through hard clay. Even in clay you could dig as much as the dispersers could handle and clay was safe. The sand wasn't. It collapsed if you winked an eye at it; and it had to be solidly shored all the way. Even so, there were a lot of nasty falls, dangerous things thirty feet down a rat hole when a couple of hundred pounds of earth slips away and can smother you.

Just before sand falls like that, it gives a faint crack and there's a shaven second to get out of the way. No one ever spoke much down below. You were too busy listening.

'Tom's' shaft was thirty feet deep in a couple of weeks. 'Dick' reached the same mark a few days later, and over in 'Harry,' Crump was getting down to the twenty-foot level. Marshall and his gang started to excavate the working chambers at the base of 'Tom.' They dug a little chamber about five feet long where a shaft man could store his gear and assemble the tunnel-shoring frames. On another side they dug a similar chamber to store sand in when it came back from the tunnel until the dispersers could handle it; and on the third side they made a chamber six feet long for the air pump and pumper. The fourth side was the west side, facing the wire – the tunnel side.

Crump left 'Harry' to help Floody dig the workshops at the base of 'Dick.' They were down there one day with Canton shoring the pumping chamber when they heard a crack in the shaft and Canton looked up and saw a broken bedboard sticking out of the frame about twenty-feet up. Sand was pouring through the gap, and, as he shielded his eyes from the cascade, there was a rending sound up there; a frame burst out with the pressure behind it, and as the sand crashed down, the shaft framework began to twist and break up.

By some miracle the ladder held, and Canton was going up it like a rocket with the other two right behind. Canton and Crump shot out of the top and turned to grab Floody just in time. The sand had reached his waist and he was pinned and couldn't heave himself any higher while the sand mounted. They were just able to heave him free. When he'd got the sand out of his eyes, Floody swore for five solid minutes. He had an imaginative vocabulary. 'Dick's' shaft was full to just below the top.

Floody found Roger out on the circuit and told him the news. Roger said one exceptionally rude word and was calm again. I've watched Roger flare up in passion over some little provocation, but when big things went wrong he had this bitter calm.

'How soon can you start digging it out?' he asked.

'Crump and Conk are on it,' Floody said.

*

They had 'Dick's' shaft dug and framed again in four days. Leaving Johnny Bull to carry on, Floody and Crump went to hack out the chambers at the base of 'Harry.'

Wings Day arrived at north compound that day. The Kommandant at Schubin had been severely reprimanded after the tunnel break there, and when Wings was caught the German gave him a solid stretch in the cooler and purged him to Stalag Luft III as soon as he could. Nothing could have pleased Wings more. He stalked through the gates under the usual tommygun escort, looking more like a hungry and unfriendly hawk than ever, and asked the way to Roger's room.

It was an epic meeting. Roger told him briefly what was going on and, without telling him what was there, suggested he go and live in 104, Room 23. He took him across and Wings walked in and saw the open trap with Floody and Crump just climbing out.

'Oh God,' he groaned, 'not here,' and dashed off to find a peaceful room. It wasn't that he didn't like tunnels any more, but when you live in a room with a tunnel, the tunnel is the boss. The stooges are always about, inside the room and out, and there is usually a diversion team standing by to beguile any ferret who gets too close. If you live with a tunnel, you can't walk into your own room when you want to, or out again either. You're a servant to a great ugly hole in the ground.

Crump went back down 'Harry' with Johnny Bull to put the last touches to the workshop chambers, and at the bottom, with his ear cocked, he was thinking of his narrow squeak in 'Dick' when he heard the sinister 'crack' again. He and Johnny Bull shot out of the trap above like champagne corks with dust puffing up behind them as the sand thundered down. When it had settled, they found all the chambers and half the shaft full. Doggedly they started digging it out.

Jerry Sage had a victory that week. A few hundred yards away there was an *Arbeitskorps* camp, and every morning the good young Nazis tramped to their work along the road outside the wire with shovels over their shoulders, just like a newsreel, always smartly in step and singing Nazi marching songs. Jerry got two hundred men every morning smirking offensively through the wire singing with horrible voices the marching song from *Snow White and the Seven Dwarfs*, the one that goes, 'Heigh-Ho, Heigh-Ho, it's off to work we go,' and after four days the Germans changed their route.

CHAPTER IV

In a gaggle of men noted for beard stubble, shaven skulls, and
general spectacular scruffiness, Travis stuck out like Beau Brum-
mel. He'd got his RAF uniform through in a Red Cross parcel, and
he pressed his pants every night under his bunk and ironed his tunic
with a tin of hot water. He polished his boots, wore a silk scarf,
brushed his hair and begged, borrowed, or stole enough razor blades
to keep his pink face as smooth as a baby's bottom. He had a theory
that if he went around looking immaculate the ferrets would never
bale him up in the compound, as they sometimes did to people, to
search for things no model prisoner should have, even to the extent of
looking into embarrassing parts of the body.

The idea seemed to work because they never tackled him, which was
just as well because he was in the middle of tooling up the engineer's
section and usually was a walking toolshop, with pliers and chisels and
hacksaw blades stuffed in his pockets. He had nearly a dozen tin
bashers and woodworkers now. One of the ace carpenters, Digger
McIntosh, had been shot down and badly burned on the suicide raid
on the Maastricht Bridge in France in 1940 when the Germans first
broke through. He was just going into his fourth year in the bag.
Another, Bob Nelson, had been shot down a hundred miles behind the
German lines in the desert and walked right back to the lines, keeping
alive by licking the dew off rusty gasoline cans. He'd been within three
hundred yards of safety in our lines when a German patrol caught him.

Valenta's intelligence men had bribed a couple of pliable guards to bring in some bits of file and hunks of apparently useless metal, and the engineers sat hour after hour filing away till they had a couple of cold chisels, a couple of wood chisels, screwdrivers, wirecutters, and even a augur they filed out of a thin rod of steel. McIntosh made a winding frame for this so they had a drill for boring. They filed thin metal strips into blades and knives and fitted some of them in wooden frames so they had planes and spokeshaves.

Some of the knives were so good you couldn't tell them from the genuine article, but they didn't get that way by accident. Travis spent ninety hours filing one of the knives he made. Their fingers were getting into shreds until Guest's tailors made some gloves for them. It wasn't humanity so much as necessity, because when you don't get enough to eat, sores take a long time to heal. One of the Germans brought in a broken gramophone spring, and they filed teeth on it, strung it on a wooden frame, and made a saw.

Willy Williams got a lot of materials within the camp: bedboards and wall battens and soft metal tie-bars off the angles of the huts. He had men pulling nails and screws out of the huts till it was a wonder some of them didn't fall down.

Every second day, a gang of about thirty ferrets and guards poured into the compound after morning appell, threw everyone out of one of the blocks, put a screen of tommygun men around it, and searched the thing from top to bottom, turning everything upside down, sticking their dirty fingers into the sugar and barley to see that nothing was hidden in them, and emptying palliasses on the floor. They used to do a different hut each time and take about three hours on the search, leaving behind chaos and usually all the things they were trying to find, such as Travis' tools.

Ted Earngey, 'Little S' in 110, cut out bits of the inside of books so the chisels and pliers fitted flush inside and were never noticed unless the book was opened; and the ferrets, fortunately, never went in for literature.

The outer hut walls were double, with about four inches in between, and in the little end room opposite Roger's, Digger McIntosh moved a wall out about nine inches so neatly you'd never know anything was wrong unless you measures the room dimensions (and I don't think the ferrets even knew the room dimensions, except that they were exceedingly small, which we knew a damn sight better than they did). Digger put a concealed trap door in this wall and Earngey parked a lot of material behind it. Digger did the same to another wall in 120.

He made concealed trap doors in the double walls of other rooms, so Roger Bushell had a dozen equipment hide-holes throughout the camp. One was in his own room.

Travis was always short of a good hammer till the honey wagon, a great horse-drawn cylinder on wheels like a neolithic oil tanker, trundled into the compound one day to pump out the earth latrines. A stooge sidled up to it while a couple of diversionists staged a fight on the other side to entertain the moustachioed old peasant who drove it. At the height of the battle, the stooge yanked out of its socket the great iron spike that held one of the wheels on the hub, and retreated. The fighters patched up their differences, the driver went on with the pumping, and then giddyapped his horses to take his load away.

At the first corner, down by 101, the wheel came off, the cart wobbled for a moment, and crashed on its side, spilling unspeakably.

Watching from afar, Travis balanced the iron spike in his hand. 'It'll make a bloody good hammer,' he said, holding a handkerchief to his well-scrubbed nose 'but I'm not quite sure it was worth it.'

It was about this time we were building the camp theatre just beyond the ends of blocks of 119 and 120. Under the parole system the Germans had lent tools for the work, and it was galling for Travis to see all the tools he wanted so close at hand; but the parole system was inviolate and no one ever broke it.

They didn't wait to finish tooling up before they started on the three air pump for the tunnels, working in a room of 110 that had been set aside as a library and with stooges at the windows and doors watching for ferrets. Travis and Jens Muller, a Norwegian, had designed a new-type pump with accurate working drawings of every part, and in the library the engineers were hammering and bashing, filing and sawing at bits of tin and wood, kicking up a great racket.

There were eight of them in there one day just after appell, going hammer and tongs (literally), the floor littered with verboten tools and gadgets and wood shavings, when three ferrets heard the din and crept up under cover of 103. A stooge spotted them and relayed the alarm, and in the ten seconds it took the ferrets to get to the library window everything was out of sight in the wall panels and the shavings swept under a blanket. The ferrets looked in and saw two bored prisoners hammering out a baking dish with the heel of a boot.

It was a fairly close shave all the same. Bushell sent for Jerry Sage and that urbane and tolerant character, the Artful Dodger.

'I think, Roger,' said the Dodger, 'that if you want a really noisy diversion this time we ought to have music while you work.'

Every day after that about a hundred prisoners gathered outside the library window and raised their voices in community song, accompanied within by the muffled anvil chorus and without by a lean and lugubrious Yank called Tex – on a leaky accordion.

The singers all thought it was part of the camp social programme for their benefit, and one day a squadron leader stuck his head sourly through the library window and said, 'For Christ's sake, keep quiet in there. I can't hear myself sing.'

With new purges, the camp was now about eight hundred strong, but only about a dozen knew everything that was going on. The rest knew little more than the job they were doing themselves. It was safer that way. They wouldn't talk if they couldn't talk, and it only needed a couple of words to wreck everything. Even the diversionists, most of them, knew how they were diverting and whom they were diverting, but not why they were diverting him. 'X' told every new prisoner that no matter what silly sight he saw in the compound he was to ignore it and carry on as though nothing were happening.

'It's like this,' Russell in 103 said to a new prisoner. 'If you see me walking around with a tree trunk sticking out of my arse, don't stare. I'll be doing it for a good cause.'

The three pumps were finished in about ten days and smuggled down the shafts. The bellows were kit bags ribbed with wooden frames carved out in arc sections, mortised, glued, and screwed in circles and fitting tightly inside the bags. The tops of the kit bags were sealed around a wooden disk, and they had fully automatic double inlet and outlet valves of leather-lined blades of wood working off a spring-loaded camshaft (the spring coming from a set of chest expanders).

The pumper sat in front, grabbed the handle of the pump, and pulled the kit bags in and out like a giant accordion, as though he were rowing. The bags folded in and out on runners. When the pumper pushed, air was shoved out of the exhaust valves and when he pulled, it sucked in through the inlet valve.

The pumps weren't any good without air pipe lines, but the engineers had been making these out of powdered milk tins from Red Cross parcels, collected after use by the 'Little X's.' The tins were about four inches in diameter, and the engineers peeled off the bottoms, leaving a clean metal cylinder. Where the lids had fitted, the tins were a shade smaller in circumference, and this section fitted very neatly into the base of the next tin. The joint was wrapped tightly with paper and was strong and airtight enough because once the pipe lines were laid they were never touched. They made yards and yards of the piping and smuggled it down the shafts.

AN AIR PUMP

The intake pipes for the three tunnels led from airbricks in the foundations well under the huts and camouflaged so the ferrets crawling under there wouldn't notice. To get to an airbrick for 'Dick,' Floody tunnelled about ten feet through rubble under the washroom floor. The pipes then led down to the intake valves on the pumps, and another pipe led from each exhaust valve to the spot where each tunnel was to start. Above in the shaft an outlet pipe led off underground to the nearest chimney.

Crump and Floody tested every pump by holding a piece of smouldering rag in front of the airbrick where the inlet pipes started. The man down below kept pumping, and after a while the black fumes came puffing from the outlet pipe. They examined the piping in between but there was no trace of any leaking fumes.

From that moment on, the trapführers shut the traps on top as soon as the diggers went down. They could work indefinitely below then, sealed and safe from prying eyes above. As the pumper worked, fresh cool air from under the hut flowed into the bottom of the shaft, and the stale air, rising as hot air always does, drifted up through the outlet pipe into the chimney, drawn beautifully by the chimney whenever there was a breeze on top.

Sometime about the third anniversary of the day he was shot down, Roger Bushell was sitting on his window sill, leaning against the frame with his hands in his pockets, staring moodily across the hot compound when Valenta came in.

'You're early,' said Roger. 'The others won't be here for half an hour.'

'They'll be here in a few minutes,' said Valenta. 'That new ferret's in again.'

'What's he doing?'

A little grimly Valenta said, 'He dived straight under 122 with a torch.'

'Christ!' Roger got sharply to his feet. 'They're testing 'Dick's' pump.'

'It's all right,' said Valenta. 'George got everyone in the block stamping around their rooms. There'll be so much noise underneath the ferret won't hear a thing. George signalled the boys to pack up just in case. They're coming across.'

'We'll have to watch that,' Roger said frowning. 'You can hear the pumps under the hut sometimes through the inlet pipes. This new ferret's a pretty keen type. What's his name?'

'Don't know yet. Haven't made contact.'

'He'd better go on the danger list with Glemnitz and Rubberneck,' Roger said. 'I'll spread the word. We might as well christen him 'Keen Type.''

Floody and the others drifted in in twos and threes, and after a while Block 'X' stuck his head around the door, gave the all clear, and the committee was in session. Floody reported all the pumps were working.

'All set to go,' he said. 'We've got over thirty good underground men in three teams for each hole. Marshall's taking 'Tom,' Johnny Bull'll be on 'Dick,' and Crump and Muckle Muir will have 'Harry'.'

'How much can you do in a day?' Roger asked.

Floody said he thought they could dig ten feet in each tunnel, and Roger turned to Fanshawe.

'What can you disperse, Hornblower?' he asked.

'Not that much,' Fanshawe said bluntly. 'For all three we might manage six feet a day each . . . that's without too many risks.'

'We don't want *any* risks,' Roger said.

'I don't think we have to be rigid about it just yet,' said Floody. 'We can dig what we can and store it in the dispersal chambers. The penguins can get rid of what they can, and then we'll know how much we can dig next time.'

The first shifts were down that afternoon. The traps were closed on top, and in the sooty glow of fat lumps they were gently scraping away the sand that started the tunnels themselves. A man was sitting in front of each air pump pushing and pulling rhythmically on the bellows so that cool air from under the hut panted out into the base of the shafts and the lamps flickered now and then as the draft from a powerful thrust caught them. Black fumes from the lamps rose wispily into the gloom at the top of the shaft and were sucked into the outlet pipes and out the tops of the chimneys.

Every half hour the pumper changed places with the digger so that one set of tired muscles could take a rest and another set could be brought into play on a different task.

The digger excavated a space a little larger than the tunnel was going to be, and after about nine inches of forward progress he selected four matched bedboards with tongues and slotted ends from the workshop chamber. First he laid the baseboard, about two feet long, then an upright side board leaning slightly inward. On top he held the roof board which was only about twenty-two inches long, then fitted the other side board in and packed sand tightly behind each board. As the tunnel section tapered slightly toward the roof, the weight of the earth above held the whole frame rigidly, and there was no need for nails or screws.

Under the baseboard he dug a little channel about nine inches deep, and into this he fitted the air pipe line, wrapped more tarred paper around the joint, and packed the sand in tightly around it so the pipe line was airtight and safely out of harm's way under the floor of the tunnel.

They worked steadily for several hours packing the sand they excavated in the dispersal chambers and taking things very carefully this first day so there would be no blunders. They did roughly three feet in each tunnel. The stooges reported to the trapführers about half-past four, and when they had given the 'all clear' the trapführers opened up and the diggers scuttled up the ladders. A few minutes later, after a scrub under the tap, another brushdown and combing the sand out of their hair, they were on appell.

The next shifts reported as soon as appell was over. This was the dispersing shift, and it meant that the traps had to stay open while the sand was being hauled out. It came up in metal jugs hauled on a rope, and as the first jugs came up in each shaft the controllers signalled the first of the penguins. A penguin reported to each trap, his trouser bags already in place inside his pants. He stood on the blankets on the floor so no sand would be spilled, his bags were filled, and he strolled out into the compound where Jerry Sage and the diversionists gave him cover.

One by one the penguins reported, collected their sand, and disposed of it. Then they strolled back for their next turn. The controllers sent them in by several different routes to every trap door so no ferret would notice the same men doing the same thing several times in one night.

By nine o'clock nearly half a ton of yellow sand had vanished into the grey dust of the compound, the tunnellers came up from below, and the traps were shut till the morning.

Morning appell was at nine-thirty. It lasted about twenty minutes as usual, and by ten o'clock all the traps were open again and the duty shift was slipping underground. Johnny Marshall was first down 'Tom' and knew there was trouble as soon as he put his foot on the bottom of the shaft and felt it squash into soft sand. He lit the fat lamp and saw the mouth of the infant tunnel nearly blocked with sand that had cascaded out into the base of the shaft.

The top boards of a couple of the first box frames had collapsed in the mouth of the tunnel, and several hundredweight of sand had crashed down. Just as well no one had been under it. Marshall felt a little dread as he realised that directly above the spot of the fall stood the chimney of the block inside the trap, a dead weight of about five tons. The crumbly sand below was so undermined that the whole thing was liable to come crashing down and wreck everything, including anyone who happened to be down there.

His number two digger joined him at the bottom of the shaft, saw the damage, and had the same thought.

'I should think,' said Marshall, 'that the chimney is held up just now purely by sky-hooks and the grace of God. You'd better go up on top again and give me plenty of room to clear this up.'

He got a blunt refusal and the two of them set to work to patch up the damage, making nervous jokes about the glories of a martyr's death. They cleared away the mess, fitted new double-strength shoring, and through a small gap in the side of the shaft packed sand for hour after hour into the great domelike cavity left by the fall above the roof of the tunnel. When it was done, they carried on where they'd left off the previous day, burrowing into the blind face of the tunnel to win a few more feet.

After evening appell, the penguins got rid of most of the sand dug during the day, but not quite all. The Keen Type was in the compound again. He was a short man with blond hair, a long sharp nose, and a tight little mouth, and he tramped tirelessly up and down and around the huts, in one and out the other end, and then darted to the next. He had a sharp, suspicious eye, and every trap had to be closed a couple of times as he entered the area. Once he came almost at a trot out of Block 109, turned straight for 123, and walked in the door. The trapführer had had about seven seconds' warning.

The penguin controller had been sitting on the ground a few yards away directing his penguins by signs. He half got to his feet as the Keen Type bowled into the hut and then he sank back, his palms sweating a little. There was nothing he could do.

Keen Type just missed his promotion. He was three paces from the alcove where the trapführer was lowering the heavy concrete slab over the mouth of the shaft when a door burst open, a body came hurtling out pursued by shouts of wrath from behind and crashed headlong into him. They both went down on the floor, the Keen Type underneath. He tried to get up, but the body was lying heavily on him, groaning.

Several people came out of the room and gathered about, helping both to their feet and brushing them down. George Harsh was holding his knee, his face twisted in pain, and trying to apologise. The ferret didn't understand English, and Harsh made signs that he didn't understand German. Someone offered to translate, and in a prolonged three-sided conversation George reviled himself for his clumsiness. The ferret was too winded to be impressively angry, and eventually, with a rather icy smile, he walked on.

The trapführer had had time to replace the trap, camouflage it, and smoke a cigarette.

'Thanks, George,' he said, 'it was nicely timed.'

Harsh was swearing too much to listen. He really had hurt his knee.

CHAPTER V

$\mathbf{V}$alenta had put Axel Zillessen on to the Keen Type. Axel wasn't his real name, but the one he'd chosen to use if he ever escaped from the compound so that he could travel as a Swede. He got everyone to call him Axel so he'd get used to answering to it. Actually he was a wool buyer from Bradford, a tall young man with a slightly hooked nose and kinky hair; and with a charming and infectious enthusiasm, Axel could talk the leg off an iron pot almost as fluently in German as in English.

The next time Keen Type came in the duty pilot's runner went and told Axel, and Axel strolled into the dusty compound where Keen Type was patrolling. He passed him a couple of times without speaking and on the third time gave him a casual greeting and they exchanged a few words about the weather. The same thing happened the next day. The third day they spoke for about five minutes.

Keen Type came in every day, and as soon as he did, the runner warned Axel. By the end of the week, Axel and the ferret were walking up and down together chatting for an hour. Gradually they got on to the war, Axel staying always on neutral ground, regretting the bombing and the suffering on both sides.

'It's ridiculous,' he said. 'Here are we, two ordinary people talking as civilised people, and if I put a foot over the warning wire you have to shoot me.'

The Keen Type laughed.

'I have shot no one yet,' he said mildly.

'But you would!'

'Only in the leg,' said the Keen Type, 'and with regret.'

'That doesn't make it any more civilised.'

'The bombing is not very civilised either' – this rather resentfully.

'We didn't start it,' said Axel, and veered off what could only be a bitter subject. 'What are you going to do after the war?'

The ferret laughed without humour. 'Why worry now? I don't think it's ever going to end, and if it does I probably won't see it.'

'Look,' said Axel, 'when it's over we're going to need the co-operation of Germans who weren't mad Nazis. You won't be an enemy then.'

The ferret considered the delicate implication but did not answer. Neither did he think to deny, as normally he automatically would, the clear inference that Germany was going to lose.

Axel took him to his room for the first time next day for a cup of coffee. 'X' gave the room a little extra ration for this, and whenever they wanted hot water for a brew they could claim time on the stove, no matter how many other pots were on it.

The others in the room, Dave, Laurie, Nellie, and Keith gave Keen Type casual welcome. He sat among them with a hot brew, a biscuit, and a cigarette. It was more comfortable than padding around the dust of the compound, and it was interesting to hear the British and American point of view. It is a soldier's privilege – his only one – to grumble, but you couldn't grumble in the German Army unless you were tired of life and wanted to go to the Russian Front. Keen Type had a lot that he hadn't been able to get off his chest, and now he had a sympathetic and safe audience, and he spoke with more and more freedom.

'What can we Germans do?' he said, after a week, sitting with his coffee and nibbling a piece of chocolate from a food parcel. 'Against Hitler and the Gestapo – nothing.'

'I'll tell you what you can do,' Axel got up and sat down on the bunk beside him. 'You can realise that the war is lost, and nothing you do can help that. The sooner it's over the better. We're not going to be enemies forever. Start regarding us as friends now.' He added quietly, 'We won't be forgetting our friends.'

The duty pilot checked the Keen Type into the compound just after appell the next morning, and the runner slid off to warn Axel. Then he saw that the Keen Type seemed to be following him so he shied off. The ferret went straight into 105, knocked on Axel's door, and put his head around the corner. 'Keen Type here,' he said with a friendly grin. 'Can I come in?'

He stayed a couple of hours, and then he excused himself, saying he'd better put in an appearance in the compound or Glemnitz would be wondering what he was doing. He was much more leisurely this time in his patrolling. He reported to Axel's room every day after that for a brew, and when he reluctantly went out into the compound again he had a new benevolence. After a while Roger took him off the danger list.

Valenta had detailed a German-speaking contact to every ferret and administrative German who came into the compound. The contact made friends with his man, fed him biscuits, brews, and cigarettes, and listened sympathetically to his grumbles and worries.

Funny people, the Germans. When you got them in a bunch they were all Nazis (they had to be), but when you got the little people by themselves and worked on them for a while they didn't have any morale underneath. Inside they seemed naked and defenceless. You could bribe 90 per cent of them – including the officers – with a little coffee or chocolate.

In a way, I don't think you could blame them. Valenta's contacts were like white ants, nibbling away a little at a time at the German faith in victory. Hitler had said that if you tell a big enough lie, people will believe it, but he rather overlooked the fact that once the lie is exposed, everything else you've said is also disbelieved. It wasn't hard to get a German thinking that Hitler wasn't the angel of virtue, and then the rest of his edifice of wishful faith came tumbling down.

The contacts sympathised with their Germans that they had to fight Hitler's war, lamented with them about Gestapo persecution, and poured out a stream of irresistible logic to show that Germany could never win.

'Why then,' they said, 'regard us as enemies? Soon, you will want us as friends.'

The talking wasn't only one-way. Delicate steering had the ferrets talking about the security measures they planned, about conditions in Germany, details of the area around the camp. Dozens of little snippets were picked up, and Valenta, who had done an intelligence course at Prague Staff College, put them all together with Roger.

Soon they knew all the paths around the camp, how far the woods stretched, and the layout of Sagan town. They had timetables of all trains out of Sagan Station and the prices of all tickets. They knew what foods were ration-free, where the Swedish ships lay in Stettin and Danzig, what guards were around them, what guards covered the Swiss frontier and the Danish frontier, and a thousand other handy hints on how to get out of the Third Reich.

Some of the most useful information was gathered by Bill Webster from the German officers. Webster was an American, though born in South Africa and educated there and in England. He was always impeccably dressed and had a man-of-the-world air about him that encouraged the Germans to believe he would never do anything so vulgar as to engage in escape activities.

Bill did nothing to disabuse them of this belief. Whenever one of them dropped in on him he would graciously make his visitor welcome, and a pleasant chat would follow. Ultimately they would get around to lamenting the disruptions the war had caused – disruptions especially galling to men of the world like themselves.

'It is all so insufferable,' the German would say.

Bill would give a heart-felt sigh and nod his head.

'Even I must now have a special pass to visit Berlin,' the German would continue.

This, Bill would say politely, was an outrage.

And so on. By the time the tête-à-tête was over, Bill would know all about the special pass, the trains to Berlin, and conditions in the city.

Bill also interrogated all the newly-arrived prisoners to get from them every scrap of information about conditions outside that would be useful in an escape. This sort of work was going on in all the compounds, and we were pretty successful in exchanging the information.

'Why do you make such a bloody mess when you search the huts?' Axel asked the Keen Type.

'We have to be thorough,' said the ferret. 'Germans are always thorough. We have to take everything apart or we are in trouble with Glemnitz. And if we waste time putting everything together again, we are in more trouble with Glemnitz.'

'You never find anything.'

'Orders,' said Keen Type virtuously, 'are orders.'

'Orders don't say you have to make a bloody mess wherever you go,' said Axel, who'd reached the stage where he could be a little stern with the Keen Type. 'Last time you people went through my room, you pinched half the wood-shavings out of my palliasse, and it was spread all over the floor. It took me half an hour to clear up.'

'It wasn't me,' the Keen Type said apologetically. 'I will do your room myself next time.' He added reproachfully, 'You must not forget that you are our prisoners. Do not expect too much.'

'Don't forget you'll be our prisoners one day,' Axel said, with flippant menace, though the Keen Type did not need much reminding. Axel had been wedging the thought into his mind for a couple of weeks.

'It'd help us all,' Axel went on, 'if we knew when we were going to be searched. We could have things a little more orderly, and you wouldn't have to waste so much time going through all the mess. Be a help to you too.'

'You ask too much,' said Keen Type, shaking his head in fright at the thought.

Axel carefully brought up the subject again the next day, but it was a fortnight before he got Keen Type to tell him what huts were to be searched in the next few days, and after that it was easy. Roger nearly always got at least a day's notice of searches, and it was just a question of smuggling verboten stuff out of the hut next on the list, usually to the hut that was last searched. That was the safest spot of all. Once the ferrets had searched a hut it was usually immune till all the other huts had been searched and its turn came up again. It suited us.

'There's madness in their method,' said Roger with satisfaction.

The contacts got more than information out of their German friends. There were a lot of things we wanted, and a prisoner's opportunities for shopping are limited. If Plunkett wanted maps or Travis wanted some tool, Roger passed it on to Valenta, and Valenta told his contact men. Once a contact had his German well trained, it wasn't difficult.

A bearded young man called Thompson worked in the kitchen block and was practically blood brothers with the little German clerk who checked the rations there. He was a nice little German who'd been a juggler in a circus before the war and travelled around the world a couple of times as a steward on boats and had no illusions about any nation, including his own.

Sitting over a brew one day Thompson had a tantrum and smashed his cup on the floor.

'I'm going nuts in this place,' he moaned. 'I'll be no bloody good when the war's over. I'll be wire-happy in a strait jacket.'

'I would rather be here in your shoes than at the Russian Front,' said the little German philosophically. 'You are better off than some. There's an old Arabic proverb that says, "I cried because I had no boots till I saw a man who had no feet."'

'I'd rather be flying again,' Thompson said dolefully, 'even if I did get the chop. At least I wouldn't be sitting on my arse all day being useless and thinking too much. I want something to do.'

'You can study your German,' said the little clerk grinning. 'Your grammar sometimes amazes me.'

'Reminds me too much of being in here,' said Thompson. 'I'd like to take up drawing again. I used to do it at school, and it was very soothing.'

The little German nodded approvingly.

'Only I haven't got any bloody thing to draw with,' said Thompson plaintively. 'Look, could you get me some drawing paper and nibs and Indian ink?'

The German looked doubtful. 'You're not allowed to have pens,' he said.

'They'll never know. I won't leave them around, and if the ferrets did find them, they'd only confiscate them. They only cost a couple of marks, and I could pay you with some coffee and chocolate.'

The German promised to think it over, and Thompson prodded him for a couple of days till one day the little clerk produced three drawing nibs, a little bottle of ink, and a dozen sheets of cartridge paper. He was nervous about it but went off happily with some cigarettes and coffee stuffed in his pockets. Thompson delivered the drawing materials to Tim Walenn in his forgery factory.

'It was a piece of cake,' he said. 'I'll get him to bring in some more in a couple of weeks.'

The first time was always the hardest, but once a man had done it, overcome his scruples, and found it easy and profitable, he did it fairly readily the next time until it became a habit.

There was a very young *Obergefreiter* (private) who was persuaded to bring in a pair of pliers and was paid very generously in chocolate. His contact explained apologetically that he had to draw the chocolate from his room mess and had to account for it. Would the obergefreiter mind signing a receipt for it. Just a formality. Why no, the obergefreiter wouldn't really mind at all, pocketed the chocolate, and signed on the dotted line.

He came to regret it. Later he brought in passes, money, files, maps, tools, and even some German uniform buttons and badges. It was much better than having his receipt handed over to the *Lageroffizier* and getting a bullet for trading with the enemy.

Bit by bit the stuff came in through all the contacts – pliers and hacksaw blades for Travis, inks and nibs and pens for the forgers, a magnet for Al Hake and his compass factory, bits of cloth and thread and buttons for the tailors, two prismatic compasses so the tunnels would go straight, German marks in dribs and drabs till 'X' had quite a bank roll socked away. Also radio parts.

German news was a wee bit angled in their favour, and it was nice to hear from home. A couple of radio operator–air gunners assembled a compact and very powerful receiver. Travis made a hide-hole for it in Hut 101 by ripping a lavatory off its base and sinking the set in the floor below. The lavatory was set back on its base and looked as respectable as any lavatory can look, but the bolt heads holding it down were dummies. A couple of shorthand writers listened to the BBC every day and took it all down. With stooges posted, it was read in all huts. The BBC has never had a more appreciative audience. Nor, I imagine, will they ever have again.

But you couldn't bribe all Germans. Glemnitz and Rubberneck were so obviously incorruptible that I don't think anyone ever tried them. I don't think I ever heard anyone ever refer to Glemnitz without saying

'That bastard Glemnitz,' but there was no hatred in the term; it was almost an expression of respect because he was a good soldier, even if he was a German. Rubberneck was always called a bastard too, but with Rubberneck we meant it. For all the sinuous length between his head and his shoulders, he was a stiffneck, rank-conscious and with a dangerous temper.

There were a lot of good Germans in the camp. They were all Luftwaffe, just ordinary *Soldaten*, with wives and families and homes, and when you take the nationality tag off ordinary people they're pretty much the same all over the world. It wasn't till later that the Gestapo and SS came into the picture.

The Kommandant had been wounded seven times in the 1914 war, and now he was just over sixty, still as straight as a young lad. He was an *Oberst* (colonel), and his name was Von Lindeiner. He was a lean, good-looking man with composure in his face, always immaculate in the Prussian tradition, the Iron Cross on his left pocket, tailored tunic, extravagantly cut riding breeches and black riding boots.

Within the limitations of war, he and Massey were friends. Even if Von Lindeiner had been a petty tyrant, Massey would have tried to keep on reasonable terms for the concessions he could worm out of him for the camp; but as it was, it was an association based on mutual respect.

Von Lindeiner had once been a personal assistant to Goering, and Goering had put him in command of the camp because he knew him to be firm but humane. There wasn't much that was humane about Goering, but he had been a brilliant operational pilot in the 1914 war, and we gathered he had a soft spot in his heart for Air Force prisoners. I can't say any of us returned the feeling, and in any case Goering himself lost it when the bombing got under way.

Von Lindeiner was very correct. It is military etiquette in a prison camp for a captive officer to salute a captor officer and be saluted in return. But you must never salute without a cap on (except in the US), and there were only a few caps in the whole of the north camp. So whenever Von Lindeiner came into the compound, the bare-headed prisoners who passed him would nod politely, and the impeccable Prussian would salute the scruffy prisoner who, like as not, had a great hole in the seat of his pants and a two days' stubble because he'd been using the same razor blade for a month. It was an intriguing situation, a touch of ritual and civilised sanity.

And next day the Kommandant would issue a routine order emphasising to all guards the necessity to shoot anyone who poked his nose over the warning wire. (Not many of the guards needed prompting. The bombing was hurting them too much.)

Pieber was another good German. Actually he was Austrian, but that didn't count. A lot of people said Pieber was two-faced, and perhaps he was. His brotherly love was half opportunism, but the other half was due to a kind, if not very stout, heart. He liked to be on good terms with everyone.

CHAPTER VI

Roger went in search of Travis and found him in his room filing a broken knife into a screw driver.

'Can you make me a rifle?' he asked, and Travis stared at him.

'It's for show, not for shooting,' Bushell explained.

'What sort of a rifle exactly?'

'German one. Imitation. We've got a new show on. D'you remember the time just before we moved they took a mob out from East Camp to be deloused?'

'Yes,' said Travis. 'Someone on a new purge came in with wogs all over him.'

'That's it,' said Roger. 'I think we can put on a couple of unofficial ones. We've got to have some Goons to go as escort. Guest is making the uniforms. You're going to make their guns.'

'They'd have to be terribly good to pass the gate *Postens*, Roger,' Travis said slowly. 'I don't know that we can do it.'

Roger swivelled his twisted eye on him. 'I want them in a week,' he said, and walked out.

Travis, McIntosh, and Muller tried to put on paper an accurate plan of a German military carbine and found they didn't have a clue about the detail and dimensions. Muller went and got Henri Picard out of the forgery factory. Picard, a young Belgian, was one of the best artists in the camp. Muller's idea appealed to him, and he went away and cut a rough pair of callipers out of a piece of tin.

Coming off appell that afternoon Muller started chatting to one of the guards, and Picard stood just behind very carefully measuring with his callipers the width and depth of various parts of the carbine slung over the guard's shoulder. Then he stood beside him and calculated the length of the rifle, noting where the barrel came to about the height of his head and where the butt finished by his thighs. For the next day he cautiously trailed several guards drawing in rough detail parts of the gun.

Travis had noticed that about one in every three hundred bedboards was made of beech instead of pine, and Williams toured every hut and swiped every beech board he could find. The boards weren't thick enough to make a rifle, so they sawed and carved out each rifle in two halves, glued them together, and clamped them to set in vices made out of reinforced ping pong net-posts. They carved out in wood the parts that were supposed to be metal, barrel, breech, and bolt, and rubbed and polished them with a lump of graphite brought in by a tame German till they looked like blue gun metal. The wooden parts that were really wood they stained with tan boot polish and rubbed and rubbed till it looked perfect.

The clips around the barrels Muller made from strips cut off a metal jug; he used bent nails for the sling clips and belts for the slings. Muller didn't think the polished wooden barrel looked quite perfect enough, so he melted down silver paper from cigarette packs into lead and cast a proper barrel end in a soap mould. He polished it with graphite until it was perfect.

By happy chance, the grey of Luftwaffe uniforms was almost identical with RAF grey-blue, and Tommy Guest used old RAF uniforms to cut out several unteroffiziers' uniforms. Six of his amateur tailors hand-sewed them.

Muller made the little eagles that went on the lapels and the belt buckles by casting melted silver paper in soap moulds, carving the eagles in the mould himself. The belt buckle was perfect. One of the contacts got his Goon to take off his tunic on a hot day while he drank his daily brew and Muller stealthily pressed the buckle into the soap to make his mould. Guest cut a bit off the tail of a terrible old shirt of Kirby-Green's to make the colour patches on the uniforms.

Tim Walenn produced several beautifully forged gate passes (the originals had been brought in by a tame guard). The 'unteroffiziers' would have to show the passes to get out of the camp with their party, and Walenn's staff had hand-lettered them, working nonstop on the job for about a week. He took the passes to Roger.

'Which is the real one?' he asked.

Roger peered at them for a while. 'They're bloody good, Tim,' he said. 'I don't think I could pick them apart.'

'As a matter of fact,' Tim said, 'they're all forgeries.'

And the day it was all done and thirty-two men were getting their last briefings for the break, the German unteroffiziers came in without rifles. They all had pistols instead, in holsters on a belt. It was a new order. Unteroffiziers weren't going to carry rifles any more, and there had to be an unteroffizier on the fake delousing party. An ordinary *Gefreiter* (private) wouldn't be allowed to escort a party out of the gate.

Roger really lost his temper this time, and for two days he was quite unbearable. Travis and Muller weren't much better.

One of Tommy Guest's men had been a handbag maker in private life, and Roger put him to work making imitation pistol holsters out of cardboard. He marked the cardboard to give it a leathery grain and rubbed it with boot polish, and you couldn't tell the result from a real holster. McIntosh made a couple of dummy pistol butts out of wood and fixed them so they peeped coyly out of the holster flaps.

Roger planned the break in two phases. First, twenty-four men escorted by two 'unteroffiziers' were to march out of the gate (they hoped) ostensibly bound for the delousing showers. Ten minutes after they were clear, Bob Van Der Stok, a Dutchman in the RAF who spoke perfect German, was to march out a party of five senior officers for a 'special conference' with the Kommandant.

Roger, Wings Day, and the committee hand-picked the people to go, selecting men who'd been working hard for 'X' and who'd been behind the wire for a couple of years or more. Roger himself toyed with the idea of going, but Wings and the others energetically talked him out of it. As Wings pointed out, there was a very fair chance of the alarm being given quite quickly, in which case many of them probably wouldn't get very far, and if Roger was caught again so soon after the last time, he knew what to expect.

'Wait till you can get out through 'Tom,'' Day said. 'You'll be out of the area by train then before they wake up to it.'

Roger reluctantly agreed, partly because he was banking so much on 'Tom.' Floody wanted to go on the delousing party too, but Roger vetoed the idea, and they had a short, sharp argument. Arguments with Roger were often sharp and always short.

'We need you here for the tunnels,' he told Floody flatly.

'God, I'm sick of tunnels,' Floody groaned. 'I seem to spend my life down a stinking hole in the ground. I want a change.'

'Look, Wally,' Roger said. 'We're just getting somewhere now, and everything's going like a bomb. Don't spoil it. We'll get 'Tom' out in a couple of months, and then you can go for your life, but *not* now. You're needed here.'

'But I'd be back,' said Floody, spreading his hands appealingly. 'They'd catch me. Nothing surer. I'll go on the delouser now, and in two days I'll be back in the cooler. Then I can have a nice rest for a fortnight and come back fit. How 'bout that?'

'No,' said Roger.

It was just after two o'clock on a warm afternoon that twenty-four men fell in outside 104, carrying bundles wrapped in towels, presumably to be dumped in the steam delousers. It would be too bad if the gate guards inspected them because they contained uniform jackets and pants converted to look like civilian clothes and little packets of concentrated food cakes made from oatmeal and bread-crumbs, milk powder, chocolate, and sugar. In the pockets were maps and a little German money. Two 'unteroffiziers,' holsters at their waists, formed them into three ranks, and they straggled off toward the gate laughing and joking with the fake heartiness people show as they climb into the dentist's chair. The atmosphere was a little electric. Roger and the envious Floody felt it a hundred yards away where they sat by a corner of a hut, unobtrusively watching.

The party stopped at the first gate, and one of the 'unteroffiziers' showed his pass. The guard hardly even looked at it, and then the big barbed-wire gates were swinging open. They marched to the next gate, the guard looked casually at the pass, and in a few moments they were walking out into the road that curved into the pine wood. It was practically an anti-climax.

Three hundred yards down the road without a German in sight they turned sharply and vanished into the trees, then broke into a run for half a mile. Deep into the woods they changed into their travelling clothes and split up into ones, twos, and threes.

At a quarter-past two, Van Der Stok walked out of 110 with the second party and headed for the gate. Goodrich, the senior, was an American colonel of about forty, with a red, rough face and barrel chest. Beside him walked Bob Tuck, slim and elegant, a Battle of Britain ace with a DSO and three DFC's; then Bill Jennens, RAF squadron leader and compound adjutant with a voice like a drill sergeant and a face like a lump of uncarved granite. The other two were the lanky 'Nellie' Ellan, who looked after the camp radio, and a Polish wing commander.

Van Der Stok showed his pass at the first gate, and they walked through. At the next, the guard was a little more conscientious and turned the pass over and looked at the back. (We found out later it was only a week before that the Germans had put a new mark on the back of the gate passes in case they were ever copied.) Van Der Stok's pass didn't have the mark, and the guard looked suspiciously up at him. It was only then that his brain slowly grasped the fact that he had seen this man walking around the compound as a prisoner. He raised a shout and a dozen German soldiers came clumping out of the guard-house.

Van Der Stok bowed disarmingly and raised his hands.

Broili came over from the kommandantur in response to an urgent message. He was chief security officer, a plump little major with shiny black hair, given to monumental anger when prisoners escaped and patronising politeness when they failed to. He greeted the little group jovially.

'Mr Van Der Stok,' he said roguishly, 'you are improperly dressed. Ah, it is too bad, gentlemen,' (with a happy grin) . . . 'the fortunes of war. Perhaps you will have better luck next time.'

He congratulated the guard on recognising Van Der Stok, and the guard put his foot right in it.

'I thought it unusual, Herr Major, that two parties should leave the camp so close together,' he said smugly, and Broili looked suddenly older.

'Two parties?' he asked in a voice of doom, and the guard told him.

'*Mein Gott, sechsundzwanzig,*' shrieked Broili, and with a terrible look at Van Der Stok and Goodrich he ran for the guardhouse phone.

The Kommandant reached the gate within two minutes and strode in followed by Broili (sweating), a dozen guards from the guardhouse and a screen of ferrets. The ferrets and guards ran ahead shouting, '*Appell! Appell!*' Pieber ran in flapping his hands. He went straight to Bill Jennens' room to get him to hurry everyone along for appell and stopped foolishly in the door when he remembered Jennens was with Goodrich, Van Der Stok, and the others in the cooler. Through the trees from the kommandantur marched nearly a hundred jackbooted and helmeted troops carrying rifles and tommyguns. They moved into the huts clearing everyone out.

Block 'X's' went quietly through their huts and out in the compound telling everyone to take his time. There would be an identification parade to discover who was missing and the longer it took, the better chance the delousing party would have to get clear. The prisoners were all moving like snails, and Pieber found Wings Day.

'Please,' he said. 'Efferybody on appell quickly, and we will have no shooting. The Kommandant is most angry.'

Von Lindeiner's face was the colour of a storm cloud. He stood apart from everyone watching the eight hundred men dawdling. Glemnitz stood apart, too, his mouth shut in a hard line, and you could see the jaw muscles sticking out at the sides. Rubberneck, as usual, showed more outward signs than anyone. He was very red in the face, his forehead creased and his mouth drooping as though he'd been found in a girls' school without his pants. No one laughed because he had a pistol in his hand.

Eventually we formed up by blocks in the usual hollow square and stood there seven hours. Pieber counted us twice, and it didn't check so he counted again and then started the business of the individual photograph check.

Army and Navy officer prisoners of the rank of colonel or above, and every British or American pilot, no matter what rank, was classified as 'important prisoner,' and the Germans filed their photographs and fingerprints. One by one a ferret called us by name and checked our faces with our photographs. It wasn't easy. Not many looked as they were when they were shot down. Everyone was thinner and many had beards or shaven heads.

It had been hot when we went on appell, and most of us had only shorts on. About four o'clock a thunderstorm broke and the rain bucketed down for an hour. None of the Germans had topcoats. Von Lindeiner looked as though he wasn't even aware it was raining. He stood by the photographs, implacable and still, and soaking wet. You had to hand it to him. As darkness closed in about nine-thirty, it was all over, and we were allowed, shivering but satisfied, to go back to the huts.

None of the twenty-six made it back to England. Within three days they were all caught but three, Morison, Welch, and Stower.

In the bundles they carried out of the gate Morison and Welch had fake German uniforms they'd made for themselves. They donned them in the woods and got to a near-by airfield where they sneaked into an old Junkers training plane. They were just starting the engine to fly to Sweden when a German pilot came along – quite unsuspectingly – to fly the plane. He thought Morison and Welch were ground crew. They couldn't speak a word of German but saluted madly, wound the starting handle for him and the German took off, leaving them on the ground grinding their teeth. They crawled into another plane, found it didn't have a starting handle, so they marched boldly into a hangar, took a starting handle from the locker of another plane there and were just starting up their chosen aircraft when a German sergeant stormed up and asked them what the hell they were doing.

'Well,' said Morison casually in English, knowing the game was up, 'we thought we'd borrow this, actually, and go home for the weekend.' The sergeant looked faint, but soon recovered. The Germans wanted to try them for sabotage and kept them in jail for weeks, but finally purged them to Kolditz Strafelager.

Tough little black-haired Johnny Stower was nearly caught in the first half-hour of the escape. A guard questioned him a mile from the compound, but Stower had a forged pass from Walenn showing that he was a Spanish worker. He bluffed his way past and walked sixty miles to the Czech border, across fields and through woods, keeping away from the roads.

In a border town he made friends with a Czech innkeeper who gave him civilian clothes and money, and Stower went on by train to a spot near the Swiss border. He set out at night to walk across and actually walked into a narrow salient of Swiss territory, but not knowing just where he was he walked out the other side back into Germany and was caught by a frontier guard. After a few grim weeks in a Gestapo prison, he came back to us. It was tragic luck. Later, we realised how tragic.

Conk Canton had had bad luck too. He got into a train at Sagan Station, and as the train started a German officer got into the same compartment. Canton recognised him as a German doctor from the kommandantur and quickly hid his face behind a paper. He stayed that way for several minutes wondering how he could get to another compartment without being recognised when he felt an insistent tap on the knee. It was impossible to ignore it. He had to look over the top of the paper inquiringly, and there was the German doctor looking at him tolerantly.

'I'm sorry, Canton,' he said. 'You'll have to come back with me.'

Around dusk, at lock-up time a few days after the delouser, three men in German uniforms and with rifles over their shoulders marched out through the compound gate, after perfunctorily showing their passes. There was nothing wrong with the passes. They all had the new mark on the back, and the three men vanished into the night.

Unfortunately two of them ran into Glemnitz on their way to Sagan Station, and the shocked and enraged Glemnitz recognised them as two prisoners and arrested them. The third man, Cochran, was picked up on a train a few hours later. It was bad luck, but at least Travis' dummy rifles hadn't been completely wasted.

CHAPTER VII

By the time the tunnels were about twenty feet long, Muller, Travis and McIntosh had the underground railways ready. Gone were the days when a man hacked away a basinful of sand at the working face and inched his way a hundred feet backward with it to the shaft to empty it, and then crawled up to the face again.

The trolleys had to stand up to a lot of work, so Travis used the beechwood bedboards to make the chassis. He had a trolley for each tunnel, and each one carried two detachable wooden boxes for the sand. Each wheel was three disks of beechwood screwed tightly together (the inside disks being larger to make the flange that held and guided the trolley on the rails). He screwed strips of metal from old food tins around the rims for tyres and used metal rods off the stoves for axles. They turned in wooden bearings greased with margarine.

For the rails, Willy Williams went around the blocks tearing off the beading battens that lined the walls and the ceilings of every room. The carpenters split them lengthwise to make strips about an inch wide, half an inch thick, and a few feet long, and nailed them to the floors of the tunnels about a foot apart. The trolleys ran very smoothly on them, pulled each way by ropes made of plaited string tied to both ends.

Tunnelling now was falling into a smooth routine. Each tunnel had about twelve permanent diggers on its staff, divided into shifts of four. Immediately after morning appell, Block X looked under the hut and in the ceiling to make sure no ferrets had hidden themselves away during appell, and when everything was clear the stooges kept guard while the trapführer opened up and the shift of four went below. He shut the top, dismissed all except one of the stooges, and everything was safe on top till reopening time just before afternoon appell.

Down below, one of the shift squatted in front of the pump and started the rhythmic rowing action. Two men whipped off their clothes and changed into filthy long woollen underclothes. One of them lay on his belly on the trolley and wheeled himself up to the working face with a dog-paddle motion of his hands. The other hauled the trolley back by the rope and paddled himself up to the face. The fourth man back at the base of the shaft hauled the trolley back, clipped the sand boxes on, and the rear man in the tunnel hauled it back up to the face.

There was no room to turn around in the tunnel or lie side by side. Digger No. 1 lay full length and dug into the face, and as the sand piled up by his head, he pushed it down past his hips until Digger No. 2 (lying facing the other way – toward the shaft) could scrape it toward him and load it into the boxes on the trolley. When the boxes were full, he tugged the rope and the man in the base of the shaft hauled it back, whipped the boxes off, and emptied them into kit bags stacked in the dispersal chamber. He put the boxes back on the trolley, tugged the rope, and Digger No. 2 hauled it back to the face.

The man in the shaft spent most of his time finishing off the slots and tongues cut by the carpenters in the ends of the bed-boards stored in the workshop chamber. When a new shoring frame or piece of air pipe or fresh fat lamp was needed, Digger No. 2 sent a note back on the trolley, and back came what he wanted.

They worked without a break below till evening appell. If they wanted any lunch, they took it down with them. Mostly they didn't. Lunch was usually a slice of black bread and a couple of potatoes; at its best it still tasted like black bread and potatoes, and seasoned with sand it was even worse.

Now and then they switched jobs to ease the muscles and the tedium. Digging was the worst. You had a fat lamp by your head, you sniffed the fumes all day, and when you came back up again you did nothing but spit black. The pumps relieved this a lot. At the end of the air line there was a transferable nozzle which led up over the shoulder of the digger, gave him plenty of fresh air, and kept sand out of the air pipe itself. When another section of pipe was being fitted, the nozzle was taken off, the new pipe laid under the floor, and the nozzle put back.

Lightly-built diggers changed places by one lying flat and the other crawling over him, but with hefty characters like Tom Kirby-Green, they had to wheel themselves back to the shaft to change over. It was surprisingly warm below, and the diggers were in a constant sweat.

Sometimes a ferret wandered near the trap, and then the alarm tin in the shaft gave a soft rattle. Everyone froze where he was because sometimes muffled sounds of work below could be heard on top. They lay there without moving until the tin rattled again as the ferret moved away and they carried on.

The warning tin hung from the roof of the dispersal chamber. There were a couple of little pebbles in it and a string from it led up the shaft through the hut floor not far from the trap. It needed just a gentle tug from the stooge above whenever a ferret was approaching to rattle the pebbles.

About four-thirty the tunnellers changed into their ordinary clothes below and tried to comb the sand out of their hair. Above, the stooges drifted along to keep guard, and a German speaker stood by to lure away any ferret hanging about the trap areas. When they got the all clear the trapführers opened up, the tunnellers came out, and the traps were shut. The tunnellers washed off any telltale sand in their huts and went on appell with everyone else.

After appell Block X's searched the huts again, the duty stooges kept watch, the traps were opened, and the second shift went below. They laid new rails, replaced any shoring frames that needed it, swept surplus sand out of the tunnels, and checked the fat lamps and the pump.

Travis had made two spirit levels, and every evening they carefully checked the levels of the tunnel floors to see that they really were on the level. It wouldn't have been so bad if they'd risen slightly (though not too much). They certainly didn't want them to go any deeper. The evening shift also checked for direction. Through the tame Germans the organisation had two little prismatic compasses of the Wehrmacht infantry type. They only gave rough checks. The close checks were done by holding a fat lamp by the wall of the tunnel at the face and sighting along the same wall from the base of the shaft.

Then the tricky part started. If everything was clear, the traps were kept open and the kit bags of sand excavated during the day were hauled to the top by a rope sling. One by one the penguins stopped by, collected their sand, and wandered off. As soon as the last bag of sand had been emptied the underground men came up and the traps were shut for the night.

In the morning the third shift took over for the day's tunnelling, and so they went in rotation, each shift working two days out of every three.

You needed stamina and steady nerves to be a digger. It was a heavy strain to lie for hours on one elbow carving away at the sand face with an outstretched arm, and you had to carve carefully if you didn't want a hundredweight of sand collapsing in your face. There were minor falls every day and sometimes bigger ones.

A mixed lot, the diggers. They came from nearly every British colony, from America and France, Poland, Norway, the Argentine, and Czechoslovakia.

From Wales, there was Shag Rees, the little man with thick black hair and a nose that had been broken so often it was getting to be a habit. His friend, 'Red' Noble, was a red-headed Canadian, built like a navvy with a slow, gentle drawl and nearly always a half-grin on his face. He and Shag used to like baiting Rubberneck, and so they weren't always available because they spent a lot of time in the cooler.

HOW THE TUNNELLERS WORKED

Major Davy Jones was American, mostly known as 'Tokyo' because he flew on the famous American raid in 1942, when General Doolittle led them off from a carrier and they bombed Tokyo and prayed they had enough fuel left to fly on to China. A few of them made it, and Davy finished up among the Chinese guerrillas. He got to the Middle East after that and was shot down on his first trip. A short but singularly violent operational career! He came from Oklahoma, a wild and lanky creature with jet-black hair, who looked like a hawk-eyed Indian.

Piglet Lamond was the little New Zealander who had dug his way out in the spectacular 'mole' tunnel from East Camp. Danny Krol, a little Pole about five feet tall, used to be a sabre champion. He had a clean-cut face, straight hair brushed back, and the most perfect physique in miniature I ever saw.

Jean Regis, a Frenchman in the RAF, was dark and hairy and built like a gorilla. Regis was tireless. He used to sit pumping for four hours at a stretch and break into a tirade of French curses if you tried to give him a relief.

'Muckle' Muir, a tall, fair-haired Scot, had a huge handle-bar moustache that he grew to keep the sand out of his nose.

Ed Tovrea's father was a big meat magnate in Arizona, and Tovrea, a good-looking youngster of about twenty-one, had been shot down on one of the first American Spitfire squadrons in England.

Buck Ingram was a big, tough Yank from Idaho with thick black hair and glinting eyes.

Johnny Staubo, the Norwegian, should have been in Hollywood. He was really a good-looking man, over six feet tall, with beautifully chiselled features and Nordic blond hair. He used to play Davis Cup tennis.

'Scruffy' Weir, another Canadian, had been flying without goggles the night he was shot down, and the plane caught fire. His helmet and oxygen mask saved most of his face but the fire caught him around the eyes, and the skin had healed thick and smooth like parchment, but was scarred purple and red.

The black-haired Birkland, also Canadian, was distinguished by a little fringe of beard around his jowls.

They all had their little peculiarities. Davy Jones had no nerves and a blind faith that a tunnel would never fall on him. Later he found out. Whenever Scruffy Weir dug, the tunnel used to take a diving turn to the left. Crump used to curse him every second day for going off course, but Scruffy kept making diving turns. Birkland used to veer to the right nearly every shift, so Crump always rostered him to dig after Scruffy to even things out. For a long time, Birkland insisted on working stark naked below, and to see him, sweat-and-sand-stained, reversing down the tunnel was an unnerving sight. Floody noticed he was getting sand-scarred on the knees and elbows and made him wear the hated long underpants and vests. The sand scars looked too obvious.

When each tunnel was about thirty feet long, Floody changed the shoring system to conserve wood. Instead of solid framing all the way, they spaced the frames about a foot apart and laid boards over the tops.

Williams had already made three levies on bedboards throughout the camp, demanding a certain number from every room. Every bed now had about three boards missing, and the palliasses, which were never very comfortable, sagged in the gaps. You got used to it in time. Some of the rooms had double floors, and Williams sent his carpenters under the huts to rip off some of the lower floor boards. They sawed them into lengths of about eighteen inches and took them below to shore the tunnel roofs between the box frames.

With the new shoring the face had to be dug forward about two feet before they could put in a new box frame and line the roof, and the falls of sand immediately became worse. No matter how carefully you scraped the concave archway overhead, the stuff cracked and fell nearly every day. There was hardly ever enough warning to get clear; just the little cracking noise and down it came, usually burying the digger from head to hips and leaving a dome overhead.

Sometimes a couple of hundred pounds of sand fell and then number two worked fast, grabbed his half-entombed mate by the ankles and hauled him clear, sand in his eyes and ears and choking in his nose and mouth.

Nearly always the fat lamp and air line were smothered, and they were left in stifling blackness. Unable to write a note, number two trolleyed himself back to the shaft and returned with another lamp, by which time number one would probably have coughed the sand out of his nose and mouth so he could breathe again. You'd know if he could breathe by the curses.

The last four feet of the tunnel would be blocked with sand. They dug out the nozzle of the air line, emptied the sand out, and refitted it.

About a third of the sand that had fallen they sent back on the trolley, and then, with just enough room to work in, number one box-framed the area of the fall. He left a little gap in the roof through which he packed sand for half an hour till the dome above was filled in. Then he boarded over the gap and carried on tunnelling. The exasperating thing about a fall was that, no matter how tightly you crammed it, you could only pack about two-thirds of the amount that fell back in the dome. The rest was so much extra sand to be dispersed.

One of Travis' men relieved the fat-lamp situation a little. He'd been an electrical engineer, and he went around every hut rearranging all the electric-light wiring. When he'd finished, he had about forty bits of cable from a foot to ten feet long. He spliced them all together, tapped the power lines behind the walls, and installed electric lights in all the shafts and for the first few feet of the tunnels. It wasn't any good during the day because the power wasn't on, but it was a great help to the evening dispersing shifts.

On a good day when there weren't too many ferret alarms or falls, each tunnel crawled forward about five feet. Often it was less, but by early June 'Tom' was sixty feet long and the other two weren't far behind.

That wily man Glemnitz stopped Conk in the compound one day. 'Ah, Mr Canton,' he said affably, 'how many tunnels are you digging now?'

'Just above fifty at the moment,' Conk said facetiously, and passed on.

A few minutes later Glemnitz encountered Floody and asked the same thing.

'Why should I tell you?' Floody said. 'You wouldn't believe me.'

At an 'X' committee meeting a couple of days later it came out that Glemnitz had been asking dozens of people the same question. He had gone to every room in one block saying it.

'The cunning sod,' Roger said. 'I'll bet he's checking all the different answers and reactions to try and get some idea if there's a tunnel going.'

He sent word around the compound that if Glemnitz spoke to anyone he was to ignore him completely.

CHAPTER VIII

The Russian prisoners came back about 10 June. About a hundred of them surrounded by German tommy-gunners deployed into the wood outside the south fence and started chopping the trees down. Convoys of trucks came and carted the trunks and foliage away, and in four days the edge of the wood had slid back fifty yards.

Massey found an excuse to see the Kommandant, and Von Lindeiner told him they were building a new compound.

'It is for the Americans,' he said. 'We are going to segregate you.'

'Surely that's not necessary,' Massey objected. 'We speak the same language. They're our allies, and we get along very well together.'

'I think,' Von Lindeiner said dryly, 'that is what the High Command had in mind. It is their order.'

Massey sent for Roger, Goodrich, Clark, and Wings Day and told them.

'It's no good my working on the Kommandant,' he said. 'If it's an *Oberkommando* order, that's all there is to it. He turned to Goodrich. 'You see what it means,' he said. 'If they finish the compound before we finish a tunnel, your chaps are going to miss out.'

Goodrich asked if any date was fixed for the move to the new compound.

'Von Lindeiner either didn't know or wouldn't say,' Massey said. 'I myself think it should be about two months.' He looked inquiringly at Roger. 'What about it, Bushell?'

'The obvious thing, Sir, is to concentrate on one tunnel for the time being. 'Tom' is the most advanced. We'll go flat out on it.'

'What are the chances?' asked Goodrich.

Roger said confidently, 'We can do it if we're lucky. We might need a bit of luck because we might have to cut a few corners.'

He told the committee the new programme without hesitation. In view of the dispersal bottleneck there was no point in going ahead with 'Dick' or 'Harry' at the same time. Selected diggers could do up to twelve feet a day. Fanshawe guaranteed the penguins could handle that much. More would mean risks.

That night, Minskewitz scraped out the soap that sealed the edges of 'Dick's' trap and put in cement. Crump cemented 'Harry's' trap solidly all around so that it was again part of the floor.

Roger and Floody picked the fifteen best diggers and split them into three shifts to work 'Tom.' They included Lamond, Cornish, and Rees because they were short and wiry, tailor-made for underground work. They left off some of the big fellows like Kirby-Green. There was nothing wrong with Kirby-Green's work but he had such massive shoulders he occasionally knocked a box frame out of plumb and caused falls. Roger put all the American diggers on the team.

'Whether we break 'Tom' or not,' Goodrich said, 'I want to take as many experienced men to the new compound as possible. Some of the boys might get homesick.'

There were Americans on every factory, and they didn't need much teaching. The ones with Travis could do anything with their hands.

Crump, Marshall, and Johnny Bull took over as the three shift bosses on 'Tom,' and Floody was overseer (and digger as well – all the shift bosses dug). Though he was tall and hefty, Roger himself insisted on going on one of the digging teams. He was tired of using only his voice.

They pressed forward ten feet the next day, and Fanshawe got rid of it all without trouble. The following day Floody was half buried in another bad fall that left a dome four feet high over the tunnel roof. His number two pulled him out by the ankles, and they were an hour and a half reframing and packing it. That day they made only eight feet.

There seemed to be a hoodoo on Floody for falls. His ear was so sharply cocked for the crack of falling sand that he could reverse down a tunnel nearly as fast as he could run. Tokyo Jones still had the blithe confidence that he'd never be buried. Floody sent him up to the face next day, and Jones had made about two feet forward and was just putting in the top board of the frame to shore the roof when about two hundred pounds of sand crashed down, and he just had his feet sticking out. Floody was able to pull him out and, when he'd got his breath back and finished cursing, the American got grimly and silently to work clearing the sand.

'I never knew anything would keep you so quiet so long,' said Floody, amused, and Jones looked back over his shoulder, the whites of his eyes standing out in the lamplight in his dirty, sweaty face.

'The meek shall inherit the earth,' he said. 'Boy, I certainly inherited some that time.'

Floody was buried again the following day, and this time the sand tipped the hot fat lamp against his leg and held it there. His number two pulled him out nearly screaming, a great patch of red and blistered flesh on his thigh. They had run into such a soft patch that they started box-framing all the way again.

By the end of the week, 'Tom' was 105 feet long, and Floody, Crump, and Marshall built the halfway house. Floody wanted halfway houses every hundred feet. Beyond that distance the rope hauling the railways tended to scrape against the shoring and there was too much danger of knocking frames out.

They made the halfway houses about ten feet long and about six inches wider and higher than the main tunnel using longer boards for the shoring. It was a staging post, and no rails were laid in it. Two extra men lay there, with just enough room to turn around. As the trolley came back from the face, one man lifted the sand boxes off and passed them to the next man who put them on a second trolley and sent them back to the shaft. Travis had the second trolley ready as soon as the halfway house was finished.

Measuring below by string and above by trigonometry, Floody estimated that the halfway house was just about under the wire. About thirty yards on was the edge of the wood, and Roger agreed with him that about seven yards inside the wood was a safe enough spot to break out.

'We ought to be there safely in a fortnight,' Floody announced to the committee, 'then we're going to have a very tricky job to dig straight up about twenty-five feet.'

'Why can't we slope gradually up from where we are now?' asked Marshall. 'We'd only have a few feet to go vertically then, and it'd save a hell of a lot of time.'

'I've been thinking of that,' Floody said, 'but I don't think it'd work. Too risky. If a trolley full of sand gets away on a downhill slope, it'll smash everything.'

'I don't see why a trolley should get away,' said Marshall. 'We're out to save time, aren't we?' Marshall was the obstinate one. When he got an idea he hung on to it like a leech.

'If a rope breaks,' said Floody, 'you can kiss your tunnel goodbye. The trolley'll tear half a dozen frames down, and you'll get twenty feet of sand collapsing. Over that distance it'll probably fall for a hell of a height, and you'll have twenty tons blocking the works. The trolley might run on and bring down a bloody sight more than that.'

'Put double ropes on,' said Marshall. 'The time's the important thing. If we don't get it finished, the Yanks are going to miss out and be pretty sore, and I don't blame 'em.'

Pulling on his moustache, George Harsh said seriously in his Georgia accent: 'What about the guys down below if a trolley gets away and brings everything down?'

'I tell you there's no need for a trolley to get away,' Marshall said.

'A man's only got to lose his grip on the rope,' said Floody. 'You can take all precautions, but it can happen. There'll be a couple of blokes trapped, and they won't have a chance.'

'I'll take a chance on that,' Marshall said.

'So will everyone,' said Roger gently, 'but that isn't the point. If we have to take a chance, we can. The thing is, do we have to?' He turned to Floody.

'No,' said Floody. 'I'm bloody sure we can make it in time my way.'

'Then that's it,' Roger said. It wasn't often he came into the technical arguments, and when he did it was always at the end with a decisiveness that settled it. Marshall fought tooth and nail for his ideas, but when the decision went against him he accepted it, muttering for a few minutes sometimes, but then resigning himself to it. He was an old regular, had been in the Air Force for donkey's years, and was always bubbling with high-strung enthusiasm. Outside tunnel work his only relaxation in the camp was playing the oboe, and his roommates wouldn't let him do much of that.

In Block 106 Jerry Sage and Davy Jones had been sitting up all night for two nights running. Their vigil was by the light of a fat lamp around the kitchen stove where a great covered pot was bubbling. Out of the lid of the pot stuck a long thin tube made out of bits of jam tin rolled around a pencil. There were yards of the tube; it angled down from the pot into a tin of water where it curled around and around and then stuck out through a fat-sealed hole in the bottom. Every few seconds a globule of colourless liquid dripped and fell with a glistening splash into a jar on the floor. The Fourth of July was approaching, and through one of Al Hake's stills the Americans were preparing for it.

The camp was drier than Prohibition ever made the US Once a year the Germans produced a few barrels of a liquid which mocked the traditions of German beer and was compared detrimentally with the natural product of the horses that pulled the honey wagon.

For state occasions the substitute was raisin wine and its by-products. About a dozen men saved all the raisins and sugar from their Red Cross parcels for several weeks and tipped them into half a barrel of water with a fermented raisin as a starter. For three weeks it bubbled like a witch's cauldron, and when all the raisins had fully fermented the pulp residue was strained through a towel. The sludge that came out was courteously called raisin wine. It had phenomenal alcoholic ferocity and would lubricate one good party, leaving a feeling of impending doom in the morning.

The fastidious ones double-distilled it into raw spirit, and one of the Poles, who had been a chemistry lecturer at Kraków University, used to make from it an imitation rye whisky in return for a share in the party. He poured in some viscous stuff that looked like honey and added a little white powder. He would never say what they were, which was probably just as well. The spirit turned a pale amber, and if you couldn't remember very clearly what rye whisky tasted like, it wasn't a bad substitute. When July fourth dawned, a dozen American syndicates had gallons of the stuff prepared.

They started toasting the day as the sun edged up behind the pine trees, and half an hour later hell broke out in the British blocks as Paul Revere came riding through, followed by forty whooping Indians. Paul Revere was Jerry Sage, in a paper tricorne hat and long woollen underpants for knee breeches. He threw Bushell out of bed, and Roger, grinding his teeth slightly, took it quietly, largely because Sage and Harsh were sitting on him. He was rostered for the tunnel that day and went below after appell with a wistful glance at a bottle of hellbrew that Sage was brandishing.

The party went on all day until about three o'clock a senior officer suggested they should ease off in case some exuberant soul wandered over the warning wire. Half a dozen senior British and American officers threw him into the firepool, clothes and all. Goodrich, with bland apologies, leaned down and offered to help him out and the man in the pool dragged Goodrich in too. Goodrich climbed out and threw Wings Day in, and within five minutes everyone had been thrown in the pool.

After they had climbed out, someone noticed a body drifting sluggishly on the bottom of the pool. They hauled it out, laid it flat, and started squeezing the water out with artificial respiration until you could almost hear the ribs cracking. The body stirred after a while and eventually sat up with a wan smile. 'The water wouldn't hold me up,' he said foolishly.

George Harsh wagged a solemn finger at him. 'It's the faith you lack,' he boomed, and vanished in the direction of his hut.

He was back again in a minute with a blanket draped around him in biblical style. Standing on the edge of the pool, he raised an arm for silence and intoned: 'Thou shalt have faith and walk upon the waters.' He took a firm pace forward, and the water closed ruthlessly over him.

They pulled him out, and he stood in dripping dignity, wrapping his cloak around him.

'I got two steps,' he lied shamelessly, 'but my faith gave out.'

CHAPTER IX

'Tom' had gone fifty feet past the halfway house when one of the penguins slipped up. He was a little careless, pulling the pin out of his trouser bags on the fringe of a crowd around a volley-ball game instead of in among them. It only needed a little slip. Glemnitz was prowling about and saw the yellow sand before it was covered up. He didn't say anything at the time. Glemnitz never signalled his punches.

Every ferret was in the compound next morning, and they turned over all the gardens. In several of them they found more yellow sand than should have been there. Roger and Valenta watched them and saw Glemnitz and Rubberneck walk out, grim and thoughtful.

Roger sent for the committee.

'Glemnitz knows there's a tunnel,' he announced. 'Now there won't be any peace till he finds it. It's going to be a race, and we're on the dirty end of it. They'll be searching every hut, and that means they'll be concentrating on all the concrete floors. There's nothing more we can do about 'Tom's' trap. Maybe it'll hold, maybe it won't. Dispersing is going to be the toughest part. Glemnitz'll be watching the compound like a hawk.'

'If he knows there's a tunnel, why worry so much trying to hide the sand?' someone asked. 'We're not giving anything away they don't already know.'

'You bloody stupid clot,' Roger turned on him. 'They'll identify the penguin traffic and trace it back to 123. Use your brains, for God's sake.'

'Have you seen the guys in the goon-boxes?' said Harsh. 'Every son of a bitch has got his field glasses up watching all the time.'

'Probably marking the numbers that go in and out of every block,' Roger said. 'I want an immediate restriction on traffic in and out of 123.'

'You can't stop it all,' someone said.

'I don't want to stop it all,' Roger said cuttingly. 'That'd be just as fishy. I just want the camp to know they're not to go to 123 during dispersal hours. There ought to be about enough penguin traffic to make it look natural. There's one thing we've got to keep in mind. Glemnitz doesn't know how many tunnels there are or how advanced they are, and he won't have the faintest idea everything is so organised. He mustn't get to thinking it's anything more than a little effort of a few blokes. If he does, he'll turn the whole bloody camp inside out. He mustn't find anything more.'

'Well, what about the dispersal areas?' Floody asked. 'It's going to be bloody risky putting it in the compound.'

'We can put some in the gardens they found the first lot in,' Roger said. 'I know the Goons. They won't think of looking there again. For the rest, we'll just have to have bigger and better diversions.'

Sage said he'd get the whole goddam camp out.

Glemnitz, Rubberneck, and a dozen ferrets searched block 106 the next morning and nearly took it to pieces in the process. It was one of the three blocks along the western wire. The others were 107 and 123.

About 11 a.m. three heavy wagons drove in and careered around the compound, mostly along the sides of the huts, trying to collapse any tunnels by weight. They wrecked half the camp gardens, but tunnels thirty feet deep were safe from that sort of thing.

Next morning they searched 107 for five hours. The Keen Type had had an attack of cold feet and wouldn't tell Axel Zillessen what huts were next on the list, but Blind Peter could have made a pretty good guess. There were no shifts down 'Tom' that day. With the ferrets busy on 107, Minskewitz spent the morning carefully cementing the edges around 'Tom's' trap. Very thin cement, so it would dry quickly.

We came off appell next morning and found the screen of tommy-gunners around 123, the ferrets inside. Roger, Floody, and Crump couldn't bear to watch and walked silently around the circuit all morning. At two o'clock the ferrets came out carrying a few nails and some wire – all they'd found in the way of illicit property.

They searched another block the next day, and that morning the stooges on the routine searches found ferrets hiding in the roofs of two blocks. They'd climbed up there while we were on appell and had their ears glued to the ceilings. There was no point staying up there after being spotted, and the embarrassed ferrets dropped out of the man-holes and walked off.

Outside the south wire the first huts of the new compound were nearly finished. They were prefabricated and went up quickly. With all the ferret activity there had been no tunnelling for three days. Time was getting short.

Roger went and talked it over with Massey, Goodrich, and Wings Day. The senior men, less experienced in tunnelling, never tried to throw their rank about and interfere, but they shouldered responsi-bility where they could help on policy matters. They advised Bushell to take the calculated risk.

Roger sent a special security warning around the camp that night. In the morning Minskewitz chipped the new cement away from the edges of 'Tom's' trap and Floody took a shift down. They dug ten feet during the day, but the penguins, working very cautiously, could get rid of only three-quarters of it.

Birkland was walking round the circuit that evening and saw a ferret moving in the wood outside the compound. As he watched, curious, he saw the ferret slip down behind a pile of branches on the edge of the wood. Birkland stood there for a quarter of an hour but the ferret didn't come out again. He went to Roger's room.

'I think we've got a peeping Tom,' he said, and Roger collected Clark and Harsh and went to look. From an angle by the recreation ground they could just make out a vague shape behind the branches. They wandered around the circuit and spotted two more piles of branches on the edge of the woods. One of them was right at the spot where 'Harry' was eventually intended to surface. For half an hour they watched quietly from a hut window and saw a ferret crawl away from behind one of them into the woods. He was carrying a case that looked like field glasses.

At two o'clock in the morning Pieber and half a dozen guards came into the compound. The people sleeping in 101, nearest the gate, were the first to find out. There were hoarse shouts of '*Raus! Raus!*' and the trampling of jackboots in the corridor. Doors were flung open, and everyone was hauled out of his bunk and paraded outside the rooms. Pieber counted them, and the guards searched the rooms.

Pieber did the same in every block, and to several hundred blinking, tousled men he was a very unpopular man. A dour and muttering Crump told him irritably that he didn't have a hope of finding anything, and Pieber made an unfortunate essay into English.

'You think I know damn nothing,' he said indignantly. 'Actually I know damn all.'

He didn't find anything. 'X' had not worked at night since a snap 2 a.m. appell at Barth the previous year had found men working on a tunnel.

In the morning, Glemnitz found more freshly dispersed sand in the gardens by 119 and walked straight out of the compound. At eleven o'clock a long column of about a hundred fully armed troops marched in and went straight to the western side of the compound. They turned everyone out of 106, 107, and 123 and posted tommy-gunners to cut off that area of the camp. The Kommandant drove in in a staff car with Broili and a little civilian with a bony face. The civilian seemed to be on equal terms with the Kommandant and Broili was being very respectful.

A wagon drove up, and the soldiers unloaded picks and shovels. Glemnitz marked out a narrow strip between 123 and the barbed wire, and about forty men set to work digging. By three o'clock they had a long trench four feet deep. Rubberneck and ferrets Herman and Adolf took some thin steel rods about five feet long out of the wagon and began sinking them into the floor of the trench. They hammered them down almost to the hilt hoping to hit against the roof boards of a tunnel. Von Lindeiner and the civilian stood watching them. So, from a distance, did we. Floody was making insulting remarks under his breath. The ferrets would have needed probes five times as long to get anywhere near 'Tom.' Roger was standing with his arms folded, watching, not saying anything.

When the ferrets had sunk a probe as far as it would go and struck nothing but yielding sand, they pulled it up and tried a foot further on. Once they hit something about four feet down and there was a rustle of excitement among the Germans. Half a dozen shovellers got to work, slinging the sand over their shoulders out of the trench, the sweat pouring off them. As they reached the obstruction, the Kommandant leaned over the trench. It was a rock. Floody nearly had hysterics.

Just before appell, the Germans gave it up. The guards filled in the trenches and made a dignified withdrawal. It was another day lost on the tunnelling, and that night Roger learned from a kitchen Goon that the bony-faced civilian was second in command of Breslau *Kriminalpolizei*. Sagan was in the Breslau Gestapo and Kriminalpolizei area.

'We're up in the big stuff now,' Roger told the little gathering in his room. 'They must be pretty sure we've got something big on to call the coppers. From now on anything can happen.'

'Well, it's just a bloody race then,' someone said. 'We'll have to cut a few corners.'

'That's exactly what we can't do. It's too late for that,' Roger said. 'Don't you see the implication? If they get any more evidence they'll go crazy and bring in a few hundred troops or something. You'll find yourselves sleeping out in the dirt while they tear up all the hut floors. We can't afford another slip.'

Colonel Clark suggested that everything might be closed up for a few weeks till the fuss died down. He added quietly, 'As far as the Americans are concerned, it's more important that the tunnel be saved rather than risk it now in the hope that we can use it before we move.'

'Hell no,' said Floody. 'You've put in a hell of a lot of work. Don't miss out.'

'We'll have our own tunnels going in the new compound soon,' Clark said.

'Too late to close up now anyway,' Roger, as usual, put his finger on the vital point. 'The Goons'll go on hunting till they find something, and the longer they go on the more chance they'll have of finding 'Dick' and 'Harry' as well.'

'Let 'em find 'Dick' or 'Harry',' said someone, 'and they'll probably stop looking.'

'We're not giving anything away,' Roger snapped. 'We're going on with the original plan. The only thing is we've got to do it without leaving any more traces or we'll have the damn Gestapo in. Glemnitz mustn't find any more sand.'

And then Fanshawe achieved fame.

'Why not,' he said, 'put it down 'Dick'?'

It was so simple.

One of the northern blocks was searched in the morning and a shift was down 'Tom' again. In the evening the penguins carted all the sand to the washroom of 122 where Mike Casey passed it below in jugs. Crump and two helpers dumped it at the far end of 'Dick,' taking out the box frames and trolley rails as they filled it in. They took the frames and rails across to use in 'Tom.'

They made twenty feet in two days without much trouble from the ferrets. Glemnitz seemed to be ignoring 123 and was concentrating on the other huts. They were searching a new hut every day, and the ferrets were diving under the blocks looking for sand. Willis-Richards saw Glemnitz himself disappear under 119 and took a cup of tea and a piece of black bread and laid them by the trap door in the base of the wall.

Leaning down, he called cordially into the darkness, 'Oberfeldwebel, *do* come and have some tea. It must be very hot and dirty under there.'

A wall trap door on the other side of the hut opened and Glemnitz crawled out and walked away, his hard-bitten face flushed a delicate pink.

That evening, the duty pilot reported that Rubberneck had come into the compound soon after appell and had not been checked out. The stooges crawled under the floors and up under the roofs of every block, but there was no sign of him. And then someone reported they'd seen him go into the kitchen block. The lageroffizier used a little office there, and a stooge found it was locked. We went around the block and closed all the blackout shutters (they couldn't be opened from the inside). At dusk, Rubberneck emerged glowering from the door and stalked out of the compound with a dirty look at the duty pilot sitting on the steps of 112 as he passed.

A tame ferret reported the next day that Rubberneck had gone straight to Glemnitz and asked him to throw all the duty pilots into the cooler. Glemnitz refused because, he said, a new team of duty pilots would only watch the gate from various windows and he'd rather have them out in the open where he could see them.

Glemnitz never did quite know what to do about the duty pilots, and as there was actually nothing effective he *could* do he tolerated them philosophically as an innocuous irritant. He even went so far as to be light-hearted about them. Coming in the gate one afternoon a couple of days after the Rubberneck incident, he walked straight up to the DP and grinned benevolently.

'Put me down,' he said. 'I'm in.'

The DP courteously entered his name.

'Who else is in?' asked Glemnitz affably.

'No one,' said the DP, and Glemnitz's smile died.

'Show me that list,' he said. The DP hedged for a while, but there was no way out and he handed it over. Glemnitz read it grimly and handed it back.

'You can mark me out again,' he said; 'I have some business,' and he walked back out of the gate and over to the kommandantur where he found Rubberneck, the ferret Adolf, and another new ferret in their barrack blocks. Would they please explain, asked Glemnitz, why, if they were listed for duty till 5 p.m., they had been marked out of north compound at four o'clock.

Four days' cooler for Adolf, four for the new ferret, and two weeks' extra duty and confinement to barracks for Rubberneck. (Oh frabjous day in north compound!)

CHAPTER X

Partly because he couldn't do anything about the duty pilots, Glemnitz sent in a team of men with axes and saws and they started felling all the pine trees that had been left around the huts. The trees were almost all down in about three days, and the compound looked naked without them.

From outside a watcher could obviously see any movements around the huts. Clark and Harsh spread the word that all factory and tunnel stooges were to watch from inside the huts if possible. If they had to be outside the huts they were to try to change position every day. Clark sent a standing patrol around the circuit watching the little piles of branches that the ferrets had stacked by the edge of the woods. The ferrets were still spying from them, and he broadcast a warning to all stooges that they were to consider themselves under observation all the time.

'Tom' was going ahead nicely, from eight to ten feet a day, and Floody estimated that in two days they would be under the edge of the wood. He and Roger met after appell to discuss a way of digging straight up without the sand falling in on them when Clark stuck his head through the window.

'Come and look at this,' he said, and took them over to the western fence by 123. Men were swarming along the edge of the wood with axes and saws, and a tree was falling every five minutes. They were working like beavers, and in three days the edge of the wood had moved back about thirty yards. There the woodchoppers left it for the time being.

The tunnellers and other people in the know surveyed it with frustration and fury. 'Tom' was just over two hundred feet – and still now a hundred feet short of the shelter of the trees. Pieber told Valenta they were going to build a new compound on the spot.

'Bloody funny coincidence,' Roger commented acidly. The only thing to do was dig on. That was unanimous. Breaking out where they were in the open was a permissible risk for one or two, but not for a big show involving a hundred.

The dispersal problem was raising an ugly head again. Sand had been pouring out of 'Tom,' and 'Dick' was full now to the base of the shaft. Roger refused to let them fill the shaft because he wanted it for an equipment store and underground workshop. He wouldn't let them touch 'Harry' either. If 'Tom' was found, he wanted 'Harry' as it was.

The ferrets were rooting around the gardens and the dust of the compound every day, and it was too risky to dump more than small amounts of sand there. It was Roger's idea to store it.

'Everyone keeps Red Cross boxes full of junk under their bunks,' he said. 'Why not put sand in the boxes and stow them under beds all over the camp?'

'We won't get away with that for long,' Conk said.

'Put 'em in a couple of the unlikely blocks they've just searched,' Roger said. 'They'll be safe there for a couple of weeks. That ought to give us time.'

Floody backed him up, and Block X's went around collecting Red Cross boxes. That evening the penguins picked up sand from 'Tom' in boxes and stowed them under bunks in 101 and 103 which had both just been searched.

They got away with it for five days, and 'Tom' shot ahead nearly fifty feet. The atmosphere in the compound was rather electric. Floody had scrapped the idea of a second halfway house as a refinement he couldn't afford, and they went hell for leather all the way. Then Glemnitz sprang a surprise search on 103 and a ferret found the boxes of sand. Glemnitz stormed out of the compound, and the wagons were in half an hour later trundling around each side of 103, wrecking the gardens again.

One of the ferrets (we learned this later) remembered seeing a couple of prisoners coming out of 123 with Red Cross boxes. He told Glemnitz, and the wagons rumbled over and wrecked the gardens around 123 too. Glemnitz wandered thoughtfully through the block, but apparently decided that the two searches it had already had were enough and wandered away again. Red Cross boxes, after all, were a common sight in the camp.

Von Lindeiner issued an order in the afternoon that no more of the boxes were to be taken into north compound. The rest of the day passed quietly and tensely, but in the evening Roger sent Minskewitz across to seal down 'Tom's' trap with cement again. He had decided 'Tom' had gone far enough. It was 260 feet long and still 40 feet short of the wood, but it was about 140 feet outside the wire and clear of the pools of light around the goon-boxes.

Roger – and most of the committee agreed – thought it was reasonably safe in the circumstances to break out at that point and crawl to the edge of the wood. It was too dangerous, and in any case there was no time, to try to go any further. Across the south fence the last hut of the new American compound was up, and the roofers and painters were at work. The barbed wire was strung around the fence, and the goon-boxes were in position. As far as the contacts could learn, the Americans would move within two weeks.

Floody thought it would take about four days to dig up to the surface. Fanshawe was worried about dispersing the sand, but said he'd fix it somehow, even if he had to eat the stuff.

'You don't have to worry for a couple of days anyway,' Roger said. 'I want to shut things down for three days and try to divert Glemnitz somewhere else. There's a faint chance we can get him to think the whole thing might conceivably be a hoax. There won't be any convincing him, but it might relieve the pressure a bit.' He turned to Jerry Sage. 'I want a big gang of stooges,' he said, and explained his idea.

Sage went down to his block, 105, stamped into the corridors, and bellowed, 'I want fifty volunteers right away.' He knocked on all the doors and repeated it. After a while two or three men appeared.

'Where the hell is everyone else?' Sage demanded.

It appeared that everyone else was either peeling spuds, playing cards, reading, sleeping, or just not in a volunteering mood. Sage barged into the first room, and there were knocking and trampling sounds. A couple of bodies came hurtling through the window, followed by a couple more. A fifth man escaped through the door. Sage went from room to room, his progress marked by thuds, noises of running, and more bodies tumbling out of windows. 'When I call for volunteers,' he bawled, 'move!'

When he'd infiltrated about fifty people into 103, he handed each man a Red Cross box, and at short intervals he sent them walking in twos and threes across the compound to 119. Rubberneck noticed them within ten minutes and stood off at a distance watching. He had a word with Adolf, and Adolf went out of the gate at a fast walk.

Glemnitz was striding into the compound in a quarter of an hour followed by a dozen guards and half a dozen ferrets. Poker-faced, he marched them straight to 119; they hustled everyone out of the block and searched it for four hours.

One of Valenta's contact men, a reliable-looking soul who placidly smoked a pipe, took Glemnitz aside that evening and told him he was being ribbed. He hinted vaguely that there was actually no tunnel, and that the whole thing was a camp stunt to pull the German legs and tie up their men for weeks searching fruitlessly for something that wasn't there. For the next two days a couple of contacts trailed Glemnitz and Rubberneck, and now and then flashed sardonic grins at them. One of them made the mistake of laughing openly at Rubberneck, and the sensitive Rubberneck lost his temper and had him sent to the cooler.

The bluff campaign partly fooled Glemnitz. Only partly. He was sure there was a tunnel – he took that for granted – but he thought the Red Cross boxes being taken out of 123 might have been a blind, like the Red Cross box trail out of 103. He had a night conference with the ferrets. Herman, flushed with victory, told his contact about it later.

Glemnitz thought there was probably a tunnel in one of the huts along the north fence. It was a less obvious spot than 123, and he had great respect for POW cunning. He ordered searches of 104 and 105, and then at the last moment he changed his mind and ordered one last search of 123. Floody was sending a shift down that morning to start digging up for the surface, but when we came of appell the cordon of guards was around 123.

Floody walked grimly over to 110, collected Bushell and George

Harsh, and they took up position in a room of 122, standing silently by the window, watching, getting occasional glimpses of the ferrets as they moved about inside 123. For two hours they stood there, frozen-faced, and hardly exchanged a word. Bushell said briefly once, 'If we get away with it this time, we'll make it. They're bound to concentrate on the other huts.' There was something about the tension in that room like the heavy stillness before an electrical storm, and it spread to other people in the camp. Nearly everyone now had a fairly accurate idea of what was going on. Many months' work by many people, many hopes, were hanging on this, and for two hours, time seemed to be motionless, as though it, too, were waiting.

About eleven o'clock Herman was jabbing his probe around the concrete floor by the chimney listening for hollow sounds when the spike suddenly stuck in the concrete. Herman, startled, wiggled it and pulled it out with a jerk. A little chip of concrete came away with it. Herman was short-sighted, and it was only when he got down on his hands and knees that he made out the faint outline of the trap and let out a shout of wild triumph.

Glemnitz was beaming with a loathsome joy. Even Rubberneck looked happy. They stood in the doorway of 123 waiting for Von Lindeiner and Broili. Behind them the trap was still unopened – because they didn't know how to – but they had scraped the edges clear, and a ferret had gone for a sledge hammer. A group of us stood about twenty yards off eyeing them stonily and then gave it up and wandered away rather than give them any more satisfaction.

When Von Lindeiner came, they smashed the trap in, and Rubberneck went down the shaft and looked up the tunnel. He wouldn't go into the tunnel. Only one ferret ever had the nerve to do that, a grinning little grey-headed fellow with a flat face called Charlie Pfelz. Charlie was everyone's friend, including the prisoners'. He was always stationed at east camp.

Glemnitz sent for him, and Charlie came over and vanished into the tunnel with his torch. It took him half an hour to go right to the end and crawl back again, and Glemnitz's grin slipped a little when Pfelz bobbed up again, still grinning, and told them how close the tunnel had been to success.

Bushell was in a vile mood all day but snapped out of it toward evening, and he, Wings Day, and the committee had a three-hour session to plan the next move. It was a dispirited gathering. Roger said he wanted to keep the other two tunnels sealed until all the fuss had died down.

'No risks at all from now on,' he said. 'I know if we don't get on to them soon it'll be winter. That's OK by me. I'd rather keep them safe through winter than risk losing them.'

Depression comes easily in prison camp. Some of the older prisoners had been working on tunnels for three and four years, and they were still stuck behind the wire, becoming obsessed, a few of them, with the hopelessness of it all.

'It makes you wonder,' Tovrea said to Crump, 'whether we'll ever break one of these things out.' Tovrea would be one of the experienced tunnellers going to the new American compound.

'Don't let it bother you,' Crump said. '"Tom's" only the ninety-eighth one they've found.' Crump had been keeping score since 1941.

There was a mass meeting in the camp theatre the next afternoon.

'As most of you know,' Bushell announced, 'we started this project with three separate schemes, knowing we might lose one or two – and prepared to lose them – to make pretty sure of succeeding with at least one. We've still got two up our sleeves, and the Germans probably think we've shot our bolt. We're going to lay off the other two for a while to make sure they think this. Then we're going ahead. I don't think they can stop us this time.'

Wings Day hit the best note. 'The Kommandant,' he said, 'wants to retire as a general. It's our job to see he's retired – but not as a general.'

After the first flush of joy, the ferrets didn't quite know what to do about 'Tom.' Usually they flushed out tunnels with a hose, but 'Tom' was too long and too strongly shored. Finally Von Lindeiner rang the Army engineers, and they sent along a tiny little man with a happy but cretinous face. He pottered about 'Tom' for two days and laid gelignite in it. Everyone cleared out of 123 and waited expectantly while the little man pushed the exploder. He wasn't a very good engineer. The charge roared out of the tunnel up the shaft. A great mass of 123 roof flew into the air, the concrete floor disintegrated, and the chimney ponderously tilted on one side. The little man went away in disgrace, and workmen came in to repair 123. Even in death, 'Tom' had done his part for the war effort.

Glemnitz made the mistake of talking too loudly in the compound to a ferret, and one of Valenta's German-speakers overheard him saying that he didn't think there would be any more trouble in north compound because the prisoners must have used every scrap of available wood to shore the tunnel. If they ever tried another big one in the future, he would notice bedboards gradually disappearing.

Roger heard about it within an hour and sent Willy Williams around every room organising the biggest bedboard levy yet. Within two days he had collected nearly two thousand and stored them down 'Dick' and behind false walls. Roger reasoned that if Glemnitz considered he'd broken the major effort he wouldn't be watching bedboards for a while. When he *did* start checking them again, he'd be reassured by the fact that none were disappearing. Meanwhile the tunnels could be shored from the hidden stocks.

Roger set an example by giving up every one of his bedboards and persuaded Bob Tuck, who shared his little room with him, to do the same. He got Travis to make them both a string bed – a net of plaited string slung between the side frames of the double-decker bunk. For once Travis' handiwork failed. Roger climbed into his top bunk the first night, the string gave way, and he crashed through onto Tuck below. The weight smashed Tuck's strings, and they both went through onto the floor. It took them all the next day to mend them both so they would hold.

A week later the Americans were marched out to their new compound, laying bets they would break a tunnel out before us. Jerry Sage and Junior Clark, and a lot of other good men went with them. Though he came from Atlanta, George Harsh stayed with us because he'd been in the RAF Apart from the fact that he was such a fanatical watchdog, it was good to have him around because he was such a character, pulling at his great grey moustache, glaring furiously at the Germans, and mumbling ingenious American curses.

He used to sit on the edge of his bunk, massaging his moustache, dreaming about food, and after a few minutes he'd explode, 'Goddam, I'm a hungry sonofabitch. Why did I ever pull that rip cord!'

'How were you shot down, George?' a new boy asked him, and George eyed him gloomily.

'I was sitting on a barn door over Berlin,' he said, 'and some bastard shot the hinges off.'

Glemnitz also went with the Americans. Von Lindeiner had detailed him to look after security in their new compound, and we hardly ever saw him in north camp after that. We grieved not.

Actually it didn't help. Rubberneck was as smart and more unbending. He also wanted to be a feldwebel instead of an unteroffizier and started riding the ferrets hard. He threatened the Keen Type with the *Ostfront* for loafing in Zillessen's room, and the Keen Type wasn't much good with information after that. Instead of slackening off after the break, the ferrets were more of a nuisance than ever.

Smarting after his four days in the cooler, Adolf found a new conscientiousness and began haunting the forgery factory wherever they went. He was a sombre little man with a thin face, a blue chin (what there was of it), and a black toothbrush moustache that gave him a faint, caricature resemblance to that other, more notorious, Adolf – hence the nickname. Roger had toyed with the idea of opening the tunnels again after a few weeks, but with the ferrets so keen and one tunnel already gone, he decided to hold off indefinitely. All the other factories worked steadily on.

CHAPTER XI

With a nice feeling for gentle and ironic humour, Tim Walenn gave his factory the code name of 'Dean and Dawson,' after the British travel agency. Getting around the Third Reich was largely a matter of having a fistful of permits and passes, and one couldn't go far, particularly by train, without having to submit them to the cold eyes of the Gestapo or *Sicherheitspolizei*.

Walenn had that methodical and precise nature which, if you didn't know it before, is essential for good forging. He had a smooth, unruffled face – and hid most of it behind a spreading, Jerry Colonna-type moustache which revolted every artistic feeling in the compound. Artists liked to work with him because he was so unfailingly courteous.

His first efforts in east compound were faking gate passes and simple travel permits in the form of typewritten sheets. A tame Goon had produced the originals from the kommandantur and Walenn hand-lettered copies with such incredible care and accuracy it was impossible to tell them from the originals without looking very closely. Gordon Brettell was one of his first assistants, and no one ever figured out how Brettell came to be a good draftsman. He was a dark, tough customer with a thickset jaw and had been a racing driver before the war.

He had tested one of the passes just before the move into north camp. Wangling his way into a working party, he had drifted into one of the half-built huts and hidden in some palliasses. Pieber searched the camp for him, even fussed about the spot where he was hiding, but didn't find him, and at night Gordon sneaked away from the empty compound. He was only picked up through back luck. At Chemnitz he asked for a ticket to Nuremberg, not knowing that Nuremberg was verboten territory because of a recent bombing. And the Gestapo collared him. He had one of the passes saying he was a French worker. The Gestapo accepted it, but Gordon's French wasn't good enough to confirm it and he did three weeks' solitary before coming back to us.

The Gestapo never woke up to the fact that the pass was hand-made. Walenn had gone to such pains over it that he'd even hand-lettered strikeovers, as though some of the letters had been mistakes and been typed over with the right one. Others he did as though the shift key hadn't completely returned, showing part of the capital of one letter slightly above the line and the top of the lower-case letter slightly below.

The factory grew, and more artists joined the gang. One of them was a curly-haired little man who smoked a pipe nearly as big as his head – Dicky Milne, DFC and Bar, who'd been fighter wing commander at Biggin Hill before he was shot down. Henri Picard, the Belgian youngster with the Croix de guerre, was the man who had got the German rifle measurements with home-made callipers for the delousing break. The most distinctive, in appearance anyway, was Alex Cassie. No one could look like Cassie without working hard at it. He had a great thatch of long ginger hair that fell over his eyes like a Skye terrier and little tufts of ginger beard sticking out of isolated spots around his jaw.

One of the forgers was an American, Donald Stine, a very quiet, slim, dark lad with a crew cut. He was a beautiful artist who also made many drawings and paintings of camp scenes and personalities. Ley Kenyon, tall, fair Englishman, was another magnificent artist who became a forger.

They started working in north camp in an empty room in 120 until Adolf, suspicious of the stooges outside the block, started hanging around and walking up and down looking in the windows. One of Dean and Dawson's occupational hazards was that they had to sit by a window so they could get enough light for the finicking work. Adolf nearly caught them a couple of times, but they were just able to cover the work before he reached the window.

Adolf was getting too dangerous, so Walenn moved the factory to a room in the kitchen block next to the room where the camp orchestra practised. They worked there with peculiar noises in their ears. It wasn't a very good orchestra. They took the duty stooge into the room with them. He sat on a high stool looking over their heads out of the window at a little chair standing beside 122. If a ferret approached, a man sunbaking by 122 moved the chair; the stooge muttered a sharp 'pack up,' and the work was covered in a moment. The only time Walenn ever lost his gentle courtesy was if he saw the stooge take his eyes for a second off the chair by 112. When the orchestra finished practice, the forgers packed up too, and the stooge walked out with the musicians, carrying a violin case. He took it over to 104 when Pengelly opened it, took out the forged papers, and stowed them behind a secret wall panel.

Bit by bit, mostly through Valenta's tame Goons, Walenn built up his stock of originals. He had an *Ausweis* for being on Reich property, gate passes, two types of *Urlaubschein* for crossing frontiers, about three different forms of travel permit, and a French worker's identity card.

Once when Pieber was away on leave, a new hauptmann came in as lageroffizier. He didn't understand POW morality very well and was induced to take his tunic off and sit down in a room for a brew one day. It wasn't till he got outside the compound that he found his personal identity card missing. He was in an awkward spot. He couldn't very well report that the prisoners had stolen it because the Kommandant would have given him, figuratively speaking, a disciplinary kick in the seat of his well-cut breeches.

He chose the lesser of two evils, and in some embarrassment and as politely as he could in the circumstances, he asked the squadron leader who had been his host if he would be good enough to arrange the return of his card. He couldn't very well be rude about it because the squadron leader would have blandly denied all knowledge of it, and there would be nothing the hauptmann could do about it without getting in hot water himself. The squadron leader said he would do what he could, and two days later handed the card back. Walenn didn't want it any more. He had a very accurate copy of it.

The *Soldbuch* of the ordinary soldaten was easy to get hold of. The soldbuch was a combination pay-book and identification card, and the very young obergefreiter who had signed the receipt for the chocolate used to hand his soldbuch to his contact when he came into the compound.

'But you *must* let me have it back when I go out,' he pleaded.

One of the complications about the soldbuchs and a couple of the other passes was that they carried a photograph of the bearer. The meticulous Tim told Roger that they must get genuine photographs of the people who were to use them.

'We'll have to get a camera, that's all,' said Roger, and passed it on to Valenta. Valenta told the contact, and the contact put it up to the young obergefreiter who nearly passed out with fright on the spot and pleaded to be excused this time. Valenta, a little conscience-stricken, went to Roger.

'We can't ask the poor little Goon to do this,' he said. 'He's liable to be shot if he does.'

'Tell him,' said Roger grimly, 'he's liable to be shot if he doesn't.'

The little Goon brought in a tiny camera. Later he brought some developing and printing materials and Chaz Hall, the compound meteorological expert, set up a little studio in his room. Tommy Guest supplied imitation German uniforms and civilian clothes for the sitters.

Forging was a slow business. Some of the documents were covered with line upon line of close print; others had a background of fine, whorled lines almost like a banknote, and it all had to be reproduced with fanatical care and accuracy with pen and ink or brush and paint. Tim scrapped any forgery that he didn't consider to be nearly perfect. One careless line would wreck a little document that a forger might have been working on for days.

One of the urlaubscheins used to take a skilled forger, working five hours a day every day, a whole month to make. Altogether, Dean and Dawson eventually turned out about four hundred documents. It was a little hard to believe. They had fifty forgers and stooges on the job three to five hours a day for a year. All the phony documents were endorsed by official Nazi stamps, bearing the eagle and swastika and the titles and signatures of various police branches. Tim used to paint the designs on rubber boot heels, and Al Hake, the compass maker, carved them out with bits of razor blade.

As well as passes, Tim used to fake letters for escapees to carry. If a man got out, say, as a French worker, Tim would give him a little bundle of letters in French bearing loving bits of gossip from his 'wife' back in Cherbourg or somewhere. They were rather convincing. One of his favourite stunts was the letter of authorisation. These, hand-'typed' on a business firm's letterhead, authorised their employee, Herr So-and-So, to travel to Stettin or Danzig or some such strategic place. Stettin or Danzig were both favourite spots because neutral Swedish boats docked there, and if you could stow away on one of them your troubles were nearly over.

From tame Germans Tim got a couple of actual letterhead sheets to copy. If he wanted something different, he designed it himself. He produced an imposing embossed letterhead purporting to come from a near-by Focke Wulf factory. Gordon Brettell did the embossing by pressing a toothbrush handle on the back of the hand-painted 'print' against a pad of paper. It looked quite genuine.

One of the documents was a travel permit in the form of a typed foolscap sheet. They did a few laboriously by hand, but each one took ages. Valenta got Thompson working on the little German juggler in the kitchen, and he agreed to help. Tim gave him one of the sheets, and the little German took it out of the compound in his boot. He sent it to Hamburg, where his wife had a typewriter, and she typed stencils of the form and sent them back to her husband, who delivered them to Tim.

Travis made a tiny printing press with a roller made of a carved piece of wood covered with a strip of blanket. Brettell and Cassie made printing ink from fat-lamp black mixed with neat's-foot oil, and they ran off dozens of the forms.

Getting the right quality, thickness, and colour of paper for some of the passes was a constant problem. They used to tint paper with water-colour backgrounds, and for some of the better-quality paper Tim ripped out the flyleaves of a few Bibles. The soldbuchs and a couple of the other identification ausweises had stiff linen-faced covers. The forgers glued tracing linen over thin cardboard, tinted it the right colour, and painted the lettering over it. You couldn't pick them from the originals.

On some of the originals, the eagle and swastika stamps were embossed, particularly over the identification photographs. Jens Muller cut out a mould of the stamp in soap and cast a replica in lead from melted silver paper. Travis made a stamping machine with a centring device, and that difficulty was overcome.

Rubberneck began to hang around the kitchen block so Tim put muslin over the windows of the forgery room, ostensibly to keep out flies. They went on working there till Adolf whipped around the corner one day and, before they could cover the work, he was peering in at them through the muslin. Apparently he couldn't see very clearly because he wandered away again, but Tim thought it was getting too hot and moved the factory across to the church room in 122. The padre raised eyebrows and voice in protest, but Roger claimed it was all God's work in a good cause, and as there didn't seem to be any specific ruling on this point in church dogma, the forgers kept going to church every day to indulge in a little Christian counterfeiting.

It wasn't long before the wretched Adolf was hanging around again. He must have noticed the stooges because he kept wandering around 122 looking in the windows, and a couple of times every day the forgers had to cover up in a hurry and sit around innocently while Cassie gave an imitation of a lecture in psychology until Adolf went away. Tim thought it was getting too hot again and moved across to the library in 110. Travis, who'd had his engineers there, moved down to the bottom of 'Dick's' shaft. There wasn't much room there, but it was quiet and safe for such noisy pursuits as tin-bashing and filing.

The other departments didn't seem to be troubled so much by security. Des Plunkett, a nuggetty little man with a fierce moustache, had a staff of map tracers dispersed in various rooms throughout the camp. Through the contacts he had collected all sorts of information about the surrounding country, and his local maps showed all the quietest paths away from the area. His general maps illustrated the escape routes down through Czechoslovakia to Switzerland and France and through the Baltic to Sweden.

Tracing was too slow to do all the maps he wanted, so he got a contact to scrounge some invalid jellies through a German in the hospital block in the kommandantur. He cut them up, soaked them in hot water, and wrung them through a handkerchief, tasting the fruity solution that streamed out until it was no longer sweet. Having extracted the sugar from the mess in the handkerchief, he had the straight gelatine, which he melted, poured into flat trays made from old food tins, and there, when it set, was his mimeograph.

He drew his maps for reproduction with ink made from the crushed lead of indelible pencils (strictly verboten, but the tame Germans supplied them). After pressing the maps on the mimeograph, he ran off hundreds of copies. Tim Walenn used his mimeograph sometimes for his forged papers.

Tommy Guest also dispersed his tailors in rooms throughout the compound. Cloth was his main trouble. Mostly he took old uniforms to pieces and recut them along civilian lines. He got bits of cloth smuggled in from outside and sometimes used the heavy linings from old greatcoats. The only jackets and trousers ever issued in the compound came through the Red Cross, and they were either rough old Polish uniforms or the unlovely stuff they issued (and still do) to RAF 'other ranks' – made of heavy serge. Guest had a couple of people shaving the serge nap off with razor blades to fine the cloth down, and then he dyed it – with beet-root juice, or a boot-polish solution, and once or twice in dyes made from the covers of books soaked in water.

He made himself a stock of paper patterns of various sizes by cutting them out of sheets of German newspaper. It greatly simplified the business of reshaping clothes. If he didn't have time or cloth to make you a suit himself, he would – if he was in a very good mood – lend you his paper patterns. He usually did the cutting for the difficult suits himself.

One man who wanted to try to hack his way through the wire at night had the idea of travelling outside as a German railwayman and asked Guest if he could make him a porter's uniform. Guest ran a ruler over him.

'Come back at one o'clock for a fitting,' he said.

The man reported back at one, had his fitting and collected the finished uniform, complete with cap, at 5 p.m. He would probably have got a long way in it if the searchlights hadn't picked him up on the wire as he was trying to cut through.

Al Hake had his compass production line in a room in 103. He made the compass casings out of broken gramophone records, heating the bits till they were soft as dough and then pressing them in a mould. Artists painted the points of the compass accurately on little circles of paper, and they fitted neatly into the base of the casings. He sank a gramophone needle into the centre of the base for the needle pivot. The direction needle itself was a bit of sewing needle which he rubbed against a magnet.

With great delicacy he soldered a tiny pivot socket to the centre of the magnetised needles. (The solder came from the melted joints of bully-beef tins, and he dug resin for the soldering out of the pine trees, and after the trees were cut down, out of the resinous wood of the huts.) Valenta got him some luminous paint for the needles so they could be used at night without the danger of striking matches.

Glass for the compass tops he took from bits of broken window. If there weren't any broken windows handy, he broke one himself and then cut the pieces into circular disks under water so the glass wouldn't crack or chip. He made a little blow lamp out of a fat lamp and some thin tubing rolled out of old food tins. Through the tube he blew a gentle jet of air against the flame, playing it around the rim of the compass case, and when it was melting soft he pressed in the glass and there it set, tight and waterproof.

He was finishing one a day, and they were so beautifully done you'd have thought they were bought in a shop. I think the neatest thing about them came from the inscription he had carved in the bottom of the mould for the casings. When you turned the finished compass over, there on the base was professionally engraved, 'Made in Stalag Luft III.'

As they turned their stuff out – maps, compasses, clothes, and forged papers – Roger dispersed them behind the false walls and down in 'Dick.' It occurred to him that though the Germans searched the huts with Teutonic, but not particularly imaginative, thoroughness, they never thought to search the huts of the outside earth latrines, so he hid a lot of the bulky clothing up in the roof of one of them.

They kept two or three of Tommy Guest's creations, including a

German uniform, behind a wall panel in the room which Chaz Hall and Cornish used as a passport photograph studio. It was safer to have them right on the spot. Hall produced a striking shot of 'Unteroffizier' Roger Bushell of the Luftwaffe, looking out of the picture with that sinister drooping eye. Later Roger had one taken as a businessman, and that was the one he eventually used on his passes.

Von Lindeiner flatly refused to allow any communication with the Americans in their new compound, so Massey put a semaphore signaller in an end room of 120, standing well back from the window so that he was outside the field of view from the goon-boxes. The Americans spotted him in about two minutes, and put their own signaller in a window. They chattered away every day for half an hour exchanging compound gossip. He used to send the BBC news over for a while, but the Yanks didn't take long to get their own radio going.

Ellan, our radio man, was collecting more stuff through the contacts with an eye to making a transmitter if the need should ever arise. One had to be a shade prudent about that. If Rubberneck came across a transmitter or the signs thereof, the other seven in his room could look forward with confidence to a bullet in the back of the head, preceded by a little gathering in a sound-proof Gestapo room to discover what had been going on.

Johnny Travis made them a bolt hole by putting a tall locker against the thin wooden wall in Ellan's room and another locker in the same spot in the next room. He put detachable panels in the backs of the lockers and another detachable panel in the wall so that stuff could be passed through in emergency.

The summer lingered on, and the weather stayed good for escaping. That was probably why Rubberneck kept the ferrets up to the mark. He got the idea (only too justified) that a foolish little ferret known as 'Young 'un' had been wooed from the path of duty. I don't think Rubberneck ever proved that 'Young 'un' brought in contraband, but he had him sent to the Russian Front, and even the Keen Type smartened up after that. The Ostfront was the bogeyman.

The woodchoppers came back and cleared the rest of the wood outside the west fence, and a new compound started to go up there. That ruled out 'Dick' for good, except as workshop and store, leaving only 'Harry.' Roger kept it sealed down. He wouldn't risk his last tunnel while Rubberneck was so active. Autumn was suddenly on us, and Roger faced the fact that there was no chance of breaking out 'Harry' safely before winter and that they would have to wait till the spring.

'Don't get the idea we're sitting back till then,' he said. 'We want 'Harry' finished by the time the weather's right again.'

He was moody and irritable in the next few weeks, and it was worse when a man came in on a new purge whom Roger had known before he was shot down. The new man had been an engine mechanic on his squadron. Now he was a squadron leader. Bushell never did take kindly to rusticating in a backwater while the rest of the world went ahead.

He found some relief for his frustration in the camp theatre, taking parts in nearly every play – and playing them brilliantly. One couldn't have a personality and ego as powerful as Bushell's without being a good actor. Sometimes he was difficult to live with, but he was mostly forgiven that except by a few who experienced his wrath. Bushell's way with the lazy or the foolish was blunt and lacerating, and yet he had enormous charm. He was two people, really – one ruthless and autocratic, and the other the generous playboy.

'He's got killer's eyes,' Travis said, 'but he's a helluva nice chap.' They weren't killer's eyes. That was only the effect of the ski gash. They were brooding. There had been a hint of it when he was first shot down.

He wrote to his old adjutant in England, 'That devil, the human mind, makes one go crazy at times. The hardest part here is being out of things.'

And to his mother in South Africa, 'The most tiring job is doing nothing.'

At the time he was learning Czech, Danish, and Russian, as well as acting, teaching German, and playing rugger. Massey and Wings Day encouraged his activities because it helped to lull German suspicions. They never ceased regarding Roger as a marked man, though. Valenta had had his contacts very delicately spreading the word that Roger was a reformed character, had given up tunnelling as hopeless, and was content to wait for the end of the war. Rubberneck came to believe it almost completely, and Roger certainly gave the impression of a man living a blameless life. He recovered his spirits after a while and was the playboy again. That was about the time he and Canton raided Travis' room and emptied their sugar bowl. They filled it with sand and put a thin layer of sugar over the top. There was a roar of dismay from Travis' room at brew time that night. They suspected Bushell immediately and tackled him. Roger turned on his best declamatory barrister's manner.

'The bloody Goons,' he roared in outraged sympathy. 'They must have pinched it during appell. I'll tear a strip off Pieber for that.'

'I'm not so sure it was the Goons,' said Travis, suspiciously.

'Must have been,' said Roger indignantly. 'Who else but the Goons would think of putting sand in its place?'

'You're a hell of a barrister,' Travis said, eyeing him flintily. 'No one's mentioned sand yet,' and Roger bowed his head in shame.

'It was for raisin hooch,' he said disarmingly. 'I was going to invite you.'

CHAPTER XII

Roger still found time for escape work. With 'Harry' still sealed down, he organised 'wire jobs.' Anyone who wanted to try it applied to the committee and had to convince Roger he had a sound travel plan and had made up a good enough story about himself to pass casual police checks on trains and roads. The committee gave him a little money, ausweis, compass, maps, clothes if he needed them, and a pair of wire-clippers.

The man waited for a stormy night or an air raid when the boundary lights were turned off, then crawled out of his hut, prayed he wouldn't strike the hundführer, made for the boundary wire, and tried to cut his way through.

A couple of dozen people tried it before winter set in, but there were too many guards and searchlghts. One or two got clear, but only for a night or two. The usual form for wire jobs was out of the hut, up to the wire, and down to the guard-room with hands up and pistol in the back, then into the cooler.

Jacky Rae, a New Zealand Spitfire pilot, decided that the reason most wire jobs failed was because on a dark night the guards were always on their toes around the wire by the huts. He thought there was a better chance of making it if one could get to the wire on the far side of the appell ground where the guards wouldn't be expecting anyone.

The area was swept by searchlights, but there was a slight dip in the ground across the appell ground where the Germans had been thinking of making a road. Rae and a Canadian called Probert got out of their hut one night and crawled on their bellies along the dip, the searchlights flashing just above them. They were so careful it took them seven hours to crawl 250 yards, but they finally made the wire and then only had about two strands to go when a guard picked them up.

The Kommandant was so angry at their audacity he gave them a month each in the cooler. Probert had claustrophobia and couldn't stand it. He got out of his cell to go to the toilet one day and made a dash for the cooler door, but a bullet got him in the shoulder before he made it. It was months before he recovered enough to return to the compound.

Travis made the wire-clippers for these jobs out of tie bars which he ripped off the huts. He riveted them together like scissors and filed cutting notches in them. It was very soft steel, so he hardened the metal himself. In a home-made forge he heated the clippers till they were red hot, poured a few grains of sugar on the metal around the cutting notches, and heated it up again so the carbon in the sugar was baked into the metal. Then he plunged it into cold water, and the steel came out hard enough to cut wire. It was the same technique he used for making his cold chisels.

As the weather got colder, even the most incurable optimists faced the fact that it was too late now for any Second Front in 1943, and people, with varying degrees of patience, resigned themselves to another year of prison. Some who had been behind the wire for three and four years were developing little eccentricities – 'wire-happy' was the polite name for it. One man became convinced he was General Smuts and insisted the people in his room call him 'Sir.' The German doctors took him away for treatment.

There was another one who cut his wrists on two occasions with a razor blade to finish it all, but there is no privacy in prison camp and he was seen bleeding and it was stopped. The Germans took him away to sick quarters, but he got out of his bed one night and climbed up on the roof where a guard spotted him, challenged him and, as he ran across the roof, caught him with a burst of machine-gun fire.

Another one was to be taken away by train for treatment, but at Sagan Station, as the train came in, he wrenched himself away from the guards and jumped onto the tracks right in front of the engine which had no time to pull up. Over in the east compound, a man could suddenly stand it no longer, jumped over the warning wire, and ran for the fence. He was tearing his hands to pieces on the barbed wire when the machine guns put him out of his anguish forever.

It was about this time in east compound that Eric Williams and two of his friends escaped through the most brilliant and ingenious tunnel yet devised.

They made a vaulting horse with covered-in sides and parked it every day by the warning wire in exactly the same place. While a team of men had vaulting drill over it, Williams and his colleagues, who had been carried to the spot inside the horse, were tunnelling underneath. Being able to start by the warning wire instead of under a hut gave them a couple of hundred feet less to dig to freedom. After weeks and weeks of dogged and courageous work, they broke through outside the wire one night and all three of them got back to England by way of Sweden. That effort (described in Eric Williams' brilliant book, *The Wooden Horse*) is already acknowledged as one of the classic escapes of history.

By the middle of 1943, Germany was finding it hard to cope with the millions of prisoners and slave labourers within her borders. Himmler was pressing Hitler to give him full control of all prisoners of war. In October, Keitel, Chief of the High Command, issued the 'Igel Order,' which laid it down that all prisoners in transit henceforth should be chained.

About two months after Italy fell, Von Lindeiner sent some workmen in to fix a loud-speaker in the compound so we could be dosed with German radio. They were stringing up several hundred yards of wire to connect it to the master set in the vorlager and while they worked dumped a couple of reels of wire behind them. Roger got the news in the theatre where he was rehearsing and sent Canton off with a gang of diversionists to collar some of the wire. They hid behind a near-by hut, planning a disturbance to divert the workmen while one of them sneaked up and grabbed some of the wire.

At that moment the compound gate opened and Red Noble wandered in, carrying his blanket over his shoulder, just out after his latest spell in the cooler for trying to sneak into a hut that was being searched. He wandered up the dusty path, and a quiet gleam came into his eyes as he spotted the wire about fifty yards in front. Changing course just a fraction, he scooped up a coil of wire, tucked it under his blanket, and walked on. The workmen, ten feet away, didn't notice a thing. A minute later, two of Canton's men started fighting, and the workmen downed tools to watch. The fight didn't last long. Neither did the other reel of wire.

That night it was all smuggled down 'Dick.' There was over eight hundred feet in the two coils – more than enough to light 'Harry' when work started again.

The committee's joy was tempered with doubt and worry.

'There'll be a hell of a row,' Floody said. 'Rubberneck will know bloody well why we've taken it, and we might be starting a new bunch of searches just when we're getting them to relax a bit.'

Roger, strangely enough, wanted to take a chance.

'I don't think he'll necessarily assume we've got anything going underground,' he said. 'He knows we'd pinch the stuff on principle anyway, and in any case I think 'Harry' is pretty safely stuck down. It's worth taking a risk. It'll be pretty handy if we get away with it.'

As usual, Roger got his way and, as it happened, the foolish workmen were too frightened to report that they'd lost the wire. Later they were sorry they didn't.

A German general came in to look us over that week, a great plump character with red slashes down the side of the riding breeches, a large bottom, and white lapels on his greatcoat. He drove into the compound with Von Lindeiner in a big shiny Mercedes and about a hundred scruffy prisoners clustered around to gape at that strange sight from another world, a motorcar. Von Lindeiner, knowing his prisoners, told them to keep their distance, but that jolly and benevolent extrovert, the general, wouldn't hear of it.

'Ach no,' he said. 'Let them see how Germany can make motorcars. My chauffeur will keep watch.' And away they marched on their inspection, Von Lindeiner still looking doubtful.

The chauffeur didn't know much about prisoners either. He did his best, but as soon as he hauled a man out of the door there were half a dozen more scrambling in the other doors, looking in the tool kit and crawling underneath. A couple of the German speakers started firing questions at him about the car, offered him cigarettes, and others milled around him, smiling, innocent and admiring.

They drifted away after a while, with admiring comments, the general's gloves, his torch and map case, all the portable tools in the tool kit, and a German Army handbook they found in the glove box.

I do not know what happened later between the general and the chauffeur, but I expect it was a fairly testy and one-sided conversation. The chauffeur probably caught the next train to the Ostfront, but there were no reprisals in the compound. The general, it seems, was too embarrassed to make any official fuss because the book that vanished from his glove box was a secret military handbook – and generals are not supposed to lose such things, particularly to enemy officers.

Von Lindeiner came into the compound the next day and had a private talk to Wings Day (Massey was in hospital having his foot treated).

'We know you have all these things,' Von Lindeiner said. 'Let us not argue about that. If you will return to us the book, we will say nothing about the other things and no further action will be taken. But we must have the book. You understand the situation.'

'I am most surprised to hear about this,' Wings said politely (and not very truthfully). 'I will have some inquiries made, and if one of my officers has forgotten his principles in his zeal, I will see what can be done.'

Von Lindeiner withdrew, a little prickly.

There wasn't any point in hanging on to the book. The German speakers had been through it thoroughly, and it was only one of those fatuous military tomes that lay it down oracularly and pompously that if you have your right arm shot off above the elbow you may salute with your left arm.

It was Roger's idea to have a special boot-heel stamp cut for the book and, after this had been applied, Wings handed it back to Von Lindeiner. I'd love to have seen the general's face when he got it back. The boot-heel stamp was right across the cover – 'Passed by the British Board of Censors.'

Snow fell heavily, early in December. It was too cold to be outside, so some of the stooges looking after the factories stood out like sore thumbs as they loitered around the same spots in the snow day after day, and it didn't take long for Adolf's watery eyes to fasten on Dean and Dawson's stooges at each end of 110.

'Adolf, it would be bloody Adolf,' muttered Tim, ruffled for once. He was getting an obsession about Adolf, who was tramping around the block every day, a quaint little figure with earmuffs and a blue nose, looking impassively through the windows. His expression never changed. Neither did his tactics. As soon as he saw the stooges, he was circumnavigating the block. The forgers were getting warnings four or five times an afternoon, and there was a mad rush to cover the work and look innocent while one of them stood up and held forth as though he were giving a lecture. It didn't matter what he said. Adolf didn't speak English.

He took to walking into a couple of the rooms, and that meant they had to shoot the stuff into the wall panel, damaging some of the work before the ink was dry and wasting time while they sorted it out again afterwards.

So far, the stolid Adolf had been immune to any approaches from the contacts, but Tim got a contact to beguile him into a Christmas raisin wine party. They poured a couple of potent slugs into him, and he began to thaw and talk, his nose turning from blue to a luminous pink.

'You have some tricks going on in Barrack 110,' he said solemnly after a while. 'I know. I have seen your postens outside. They are always there, and they give warnings when I approach.'

That gave Walenn an idea.

'Take the stooges away,' he said. 'Adolf will think work has stopped there and won't worry us.'

'Oh . . . risky,' said Cassie doubtfully.

'No more than it is now,' Tim said. 'We're giving ourselves away and losing a hell of a lot of time.'

We decided to give it a try and told the stooges to take a holiday. Adolf's attentions stopped immediately. It was miraculous. The forgers were happy; the stooges were happy (stooging in the snow in leaky boots and on poor food is not funny), and presumably Adolf was happy too.

For a week they went forging ahead with no interruptions from Adolf or anyone else. They got twice as much work done, and it was easier on the nerves. Then one afternoon Henri Picard looked up and saw Adolf's bony face peering through the window.

'Oh hell,' he said.' Look!'

There was a paralysed silence, and then Tim quietly said, 'Go on working as though nothing is happening.'

Adolf continued to peer through the window, but the cold outside and the warmth of the room inside had condensed moisture on the window and it was running down the glass, blurring it so that Adolf couldn't quite make out what was going on. He must have thought they were writing letters or studying, because after a minute his face vanished. There was a mad rush in the room, and in a few seconds all the documents were shoved behind the wall panel and the forgers had dispersed, but Adolf never came in to investigate.

'The stooges have got to go back, obviously,' Tim said.

'Correction,' said Cassie. 'The stooges have got to go back – but *not* obviously.'

The problem was how to hide them so they could cover all approaches to the library room and still be able to give the pack-up in time. Hiding stooges from the ferrets also usually meant, to a certain extent, hiding the ferrets from the stooges. The ferrets, if they suspected a hut, had a habit of approaching it under cover of another, then darting around the corner and up and down, peering through the windows.

We worried over this one for a couple of days because Dean and Dawson were so exposed there couldn't be any slips. Eventually we worked out a real cloak-and-dagger system which sounded very complicated.

The library room was midway along the western side of 110 with a door to the corridor and two windows facing west to be covered. One stooge stood by a window in an end room of 103, facing the northern end of 110, so he could see down both sides and around the near end. Another stood by an east window of 109, facing the library room so he could see past both ends of 110. The third stooge stood in the window next to the library (he couldn't go in the actual library itself because the forgers were all around the windows). This third man could see anyone approaching from the west, and the outlooks of all stooges overlapped for double security.

HOW THE STOOGES PROTECTED
THE FORGERS

When the stooge in 103 saw a ferret approaching, he opened his window. The man in 109 immediately saw this and put a folded paper against the window. The stooge next to the library caught the signal, knocked on the wall, and the stuff was out of sight in a few seconds.

With no stooges in sight, Adolf stopped hanging around 110 again. Occasionally he and other ferrets had a routine peek through the block but there was no deliberate concentration on it, and the stooges always warned in time.

Roger wrote home, 'It can't last much longer. This is definitely our last Christmas in the bag.' Grimly true for him.

On the last day of the year, the 'X' chiefs threw a raisin wine party in 110, and by evening appell the world was sweetness and light. Canton and Bob Tuck charitably got on each side of a prominent tunneller and carried him on appell, his legs making walking movements about six inches above the snow. They held him up, swaying, in the ranks but when Pieber came past counting, the tunneller swayed out of their grip and staggered to one side.

'Please stop moving,' said Pieber severely. 'I cannot count you properly.'

'Tisn' me moving,' said the tunneller, focusing desperately. 'T'syou.'

There weren't any more raison wine brews after that. For two reasons.

A young squadron leader went to a hooch party in another block, and early in the morning, hours after lock-up, he felt so good he decided to slip out of the window and crawl back to his own block. He hadn't gone far when the hundführer's dog caught him and was mauling his arm when the hundführer himself walked up and emptied his pistol magazine at him. He was a rotten shot. Only one of the five bullets hit the man, low down in the stomach, and he lived, but hooch was banned after that.

The ban was hardly necessary. Freezing weather had brought sharper hunger and people wouldn't spare a single raisin for a brew. The only vegetable from the Germans was sauerkraut. For weeks everything was sauerkraut, and the charm and novelty of sauerkraut are as fleeting as an English summer. A certain American summed it up when, for the tenth time in ten days, they handed him his sauerkraut ration.

'Jesus Christ,' he muttered disgustedly. 'The same yesterday, the same today, and the same forever more.'

The compound dust was frozen hard under a foot of snow, and most of us tried to keep warm by going to bed during the day. It was no time for escaping and Rubberneck knew it. The rest of the ferrets were very glad to be invited into rooms for a brew, out of the cold.

CHAPTER XIII

That, reasoned Roger, was the time to open up 'Harry' again. It was about 7 January, when he called the committee together.

'The idea is a blitz campaign,' he said. 'If we can finish 'Harry' in a couple of months while the Goons aren't expecting it, we can seal it again and break as soon as the weather's right.'

'What about dispersal, for Pete's sake?' Floody asked. 'We can't get rid of the stuff while the snow's about.'

'That's what the Goons'll be thinking,' Roger said. 'We've got to find some way of doing it now. Anyone got any ideas?'

They talked about it for an hour and got nowhere. There didn't seem to be any way of doing it. If they packed it under the huts, it would be found. If they stored it up in the roofs, it would probably be found there too. Likewise if they hid it, as before, in the rooms, once the ferrets found sand, the hunt would be on again till they located a tunnel. And 'Harry' was the last hope. They wouldn't risk it.

Canton suggested digging a small tunnel as a blind and letting the ferrets find it but that only meant more sand dispersal. Also, as Roger pointed out, they might find 'Harry' instead. Now that the new compound was up outside the west fence, the north side was the only practicable tunnel route. That would mean tougher searches of the northern blocks, including 104. He closed the meeting and told them to go away and think of something.

Crump and Fanshawe stood talking for a while outside 110, and Fanshawe suddenly said, 'What about the theatre?'

'Under it!' said Crump. 'God, I was just thinking of that.'

'Is there any room?'

'Bound to be. It's a sloping floor.'

They ran back inside and told Bushell, who was peeling potatoes. He put them down with a dawning glint in his eye and said slowly, 'I really think you've hit it. That floor's a couple of feet high.'

'It ought to be safe,' Crump said. 'I don't think the sods have ever bothered to search it properly.'

'They can't.' Roger was grinning. 'Not underneath anyway. We didn't put any trap doors in the walls.'

The theatre people weren't happy about the idea. They thought if the Germans found sand under their floor they might shut the theatre down and put a stop to camp entertainments.

'Escape is more important,' Wings Day said, and issued a tactful but uncompromising order that the theatre was to be used for dispersal.

Travis fixed a seat in the back row of the auditorium so that it tipped back on hinges, and under it he cut a trap door in the floor. Fanshawe slipped below with a fat lamp and found there was enough space to disperse more sand than 'Harry' would ever yield.

Immediately after appell on 10 January, Floody, Pat Langford ('Harry's' trapführer), and Crump started chipping the cement away around 'Harry's' trap. They thought they could get it done in about twenty minutes, but Crump had made such a good job of it that it took them two hours. They lifted the stove off the tiled square, the trap swung up easily, and they clambered below carrying a fat lamp each, wondering nervously what they would find. 'Harry' had been shut for three months, and tunnels need constant maintenance to stay in good order.

Crump had made a good job of 'Harry.' The air was still fresh down there because he had left the by-pass valve open on the pump. He crawled up the tunnel, finding a little sand had seeped through here and there, but only four shoring frames had twisted out of plumb and he chalked them to be replaced later. Floody found the kit bag bellows on the pump had rotted, and that afternoon Travis went down with a couple of carpenters and fitted new bags. The pump seemed to be working stiffly, and Crump reported from the face that not much air was coming through.

'I guess there's a blockage in the air line somewhere,' Floody said gloomily. There was nothing to do but unearth the line till they found the damage – the stickiest job possible because it meant reefing up floor boards with the risk of the frames above sinking and starting dangerous falls. Luckily they found the worst trouble in the first few feet, near the tunnel mouth. Some of the tins of the airline had buckled and sand had leaked in. They replaced them and the pump worked normally again, but Crump found jets of air hissing up through several floor boards and they had to take out more boards, dig down, and seal the leaking tins with fresh tarred paper. It was a long and exasperating job and took several days.

On 14 January, Floody was able to take the first full shift down for digging. He trolleyed up to the face and ran his finger gently down the sand. It was fine and felt fairly firm so he knew he could space his frames about a foot apart and board them on top. He dug ten feet that day, and the sand flooded back to the shaft where Crump packed it in kit bags.

After appell, the evening shift laid fresh rails, and about 8 p.m. Langford opened the trap for the first dispersing. It had never been so easy to get rid of the sand, because it was the off season for escape, Massey had persuaded Von Lindeiner to let the prisoners walk about between the blocks till ten o'clock. Covered by darkness, there was no need to use the trouser bags.

As each penguin reported to the trap, Langford hauled up a kit bag of sand on a sling, and the penguin swung it over his shoulder. George Harsh signalled the all clear from the corridor, and the penguin nipped swiftly out of the hut and across the path into the door of 109 opposite. He reported to a controller's room there, and if ferrets were about he slung the bag under a bunk and waited. If it was all clear he moved out of the far door of 109 with his sand and walked around 120 through the snow straight into the theatre. Fanshawe, by the trap, passed the kit bag below.

A faint glow was coming out of the trap where, down below, a dozen dirt-stained men in long underpants were crawling on their bellies by the light of a couple of fat lamps. In turn each one took a bag and wriggled to the side of the floor and emptied it, packing it down as hard as he could. The penguin took an empty kit bag back with him, folded under his coat.

Over in an end room of 112, the duty pilot kept a team of runners, and if any German – ferret or otherwise – came into the camp, he sent one man to tell George Harsh who it was and where he was heading, and two more to tail the German. One of them kept him in sight all the time and periodically sent the other to tell George his latest movements. George sat most of the time in the room across the corridor from 'Harry's' trap, knowing at any time where every German in the compound was. If a ferret headed for 104, George slipped across and warned Langford.

Langford had a drill for closing the trap and could do the whole operation in just over twenty seconds. Closing the trap itself was easy enough, but there was more to it than that. First, a quick warning to the people below to keep quiet, then he slipped the grill in position and used blankets to muffle the hollow sound. The trap came down, and he slipped the extension flue off the stove, moved the stove back on the trap, and slipped on the usual short flue. Langford always had the stove burning red-hot so any ferret prowling about the room would be discouraged from moving it to investigate the tiled base.

'Harry' was electrically lit all through at night, the stolen cable being taken right up to the face, tacked to a corner of the tunnel roof. It made work much easier, though the day shift still had to use the fat lamps because the power wasn't on. They were getting rid of so much sand that Floody sent down a couple of extra workers on the night shift to keep on digging. Fanshawe dispersed it all, and in a week 'Harry' had gone forward fifty feet, and Crump and Floody built a halfway house. It was on the same lines as in 'Tom,' about seven feet long and two feet six inches square. They called it Piccadilly, and it was just about under the cooler.

Sound travels through loose sand, and Shag Rees swore he could hear the jackboots rasping on the concrete floor of the cooler.

'I ought to know,' he said. 'I know the bloody sound well enough.'

Roger insisted on going down and working a couple of shifts. He was in grim good spirits again, obsessed with the prospects of escape.

'There'll have to be at least one more halfway house,' Floody told him. 'I think we can probably leave it at that. We've done just over 100 feet now, and I'd say there's another 250 to go.' That was across the rest of the vorlager to the far fence, under the road and the grass verge to the shelter of the woods.

George Harsh was getting greyer every day. There was a little ginger-haired ferret called Rudy, and his contact lived in 104. It had never mattered a great deal before but now Rudy went on the late ferret shift and came in after appell every evening. He made a beeline for his contact's room and sat down to talk, smoke his contact's cigarettes, and get his brew. He sat there for hours behind the closed door, while the trap was open down the corridor and penguins went traipsing by, lugging their sand. For a time George considered making the contact move to another block, but dropped that idea because he knew Rudy might still haunt 104 to scrounge cigarettes from his other friends in the contact's room.

'We'll have to let Rudy stay,' he gloomed to Floody, pulling agitatedly on his moustache. 'I guess we can take enough precautions.'

Rudy was always given the chair farthest from the door, and his contact and at least two others always sat between Rudy and the door. Outside, George had a stooge standing hour after hour with a cooking pot, and if Rudy ever got up in a hurry to go, there would have been a loud scraping of feet in the room, and as Rudy opened the door, he'd have been bowled over by the stooge bringing in the pot. George also always had one of Valenta's German speakers loafing in the door of the kitchen, and if Rudy or any other ferret wandered in at short notice, he would hold him up with half a minute's conversation while Langford went through his trap drill.

'Harry' was nearly two hundred feet long when the full moon came. The sky stayed clear, and for a week the moon-glow off the snow filled the compound with a soft radiance.

'It's too risky,' Fanshawe told Roger. 'It looks like day outside. The penguins'll be spotted in no time. They could see them from the goon-boxes.'

Roger, impatient and irritable, gave the pack-up order, and there was no tunnel work for a week. Every day he went along to Chaz Hall and asked what the weather would be that night, and every day Hall gave him the same answer, 'Bloody moon. No cloud.'

Crump used the time to make new ropes for the trolleys, as the old ones were rotting. Williams had been saving up string from the parcel store, and Crump took on the exasperating job of making three hundred feet of four-ply plait, the long ends constantly tangling so that he had two men standing behind him clearing it.

The moon faded and digging started again. Floody made a new record of twelve and a half feet in one day. Then they ran into a soft patch and Floody was buried again, badly. A couple of hundred pounds of sand slipped from the roof, and Floody was nearly unconscious from the force and weight of it. Crump had a little trouble dragging him clear, yelled back, and Canton came crawling up from the halfway house. Together they dragged Floody out, and he recovered quickly and insisted on staying to clear the mess.

There were other falls, too, just as dangerous. A bedboard slipped out of a pile at the top of the shaft, fell nearly thirty feet, and got Cooky Long on the head as he was coming out of the tunnel. They brought him up concussed, green and sick, and he was two days in his bunk.

A day or so later a metal jug fell from the trap and hit Floody on the head – luckily not a direct hit from the rim but a glancing blow on the side, otherwise it would have split his head open. As it was, he had a wicked contusion, and his head was in bandages for days. He told Pieber he'd tripped and cannoned into a door, and Pieber was very sympathetic.

Langford dropped a bedboard and nearly brained Crump, who cursed him for a couple of minutes.

'I suppose you think I bloody well did it on purpose.' Langford called down, and then apologised. Langford lived in the trap room and ruled it with a rod of iron. The trap was his baby. Nerves were getting very frayed. The volatile Johnny Marshall had a couple of outbursts; in fact everyone did, even the limping, good-natured Johnny Bull.

By 10 February, they had finished the second halfway house. It was nearly under the outer wire and Crump named it Leicester Square. There were about 130 feet to go for the woods, and Johnny Marshall again wanted them to start digging gradually up so they would finish near the surface. Floody opposed him, and there was a heated debate in the committee. Roger settled it by saying they would dig straight on. On a long uphill haul, he still wouldn't trust the trolley ropes.

Wings Day was doing an occasional digging shift on 'Harry.' Floody wouldn't let him dig too often because Wings, like Roger, had a notorious record as far as the Germans were concerned and was supposed to keep in the background as a sort of over-all controller, lending his advice whenever it was needed.

Pop Green was another one of the old brigade who wouldn't be out of it. Pop had won an MC in the 1914–1918 war and got into this war as a tail gunner by lying about his age. He was about fifty and had been one of Fanshawe's penguins since the days of 'Tom.' He still insisted on being a penguin and used to collect his kit bag of sand weighing about fifty pounds from Langford and stagger down the corridor with it. Fanshawe tried to make him take an easier job and Pop refused in terms that hadn't been used to Fanshawe since his midshipman days.

Pop shared a little room with the Dodger at the end of 104 – next to the room which sheltered 'Harry's' trap. Bushell thought it would be a good idea to help divert any suspicion if they boldly had Pieber in to tea, nonchalantly rubbing shoulders, so to speak, with the trap. It was a fair assumption that if the Germans were invited in they would tend to believe that nothing sinister could be going on in that area. So Pieber was invited; and about the time he was due to arrive, the Dodger, that amiable and nerveless Anglo-American, sighted the Kommandant striding majestically in the compound; so he invited the Kommandant too, and the four of them spent a pleasant half hour in innocuous chit-chat with the trapdoor only 10 feet away behind a wooden partition. The duty shift of tunnellers was down below and George Harsh was standing by to see that nothing went wrong, glowering, tugging on his grey moustache and muttering curses.

At the end of February, Himmler had another victory in his campaign for more ruthless treatment of prisoners. Keitel issued the order known as 'Stufe Roemisch III.' It said that every escaped officer prisoner, other than British and Americans, was to be handed over on recapture to the Gestapo. Recaptured British and American officers were to be kept in military or police prisons, and the High Command would decide in each case whether they were to be handed over to the Gestapo. The recapture of the officers must be kept secret, and they were to be officially reported as 'Escaped and not recaptured.'

*

We came off appell one morning and found the tommy-gunners around 104, Rubberneck and the ferrets inside. Floody, Crump, Harsh, and Roger walked around and around the circuit telling each other airily that Rubberneck didn't have a hope, and all of them feeling butterflies in their stomachs. Rubberneck came out three hours later, looking his usual lugubrious self.

Adolf was making himself a nuisance again. He came in on the late shift and wandered restlessly all over the camp and in all the blocks, causing a near-panic in 104. The German-speaker delayed him in the corridor and Langford got the trap closed, but dispersing was held up and George Harsh had bitten his fingernails right down and went around muttering horrible threats. Adolf was still the friendless one. No contact was able to inveigle him into his room for a brew. Adolf might exchange a few words with them, and then he shut his stolid mouth and gloomed off.

It seemed like an Act of God when, for no accountable reason, he suddenly developed a friendship for a tall red-bearded Scot called Jim Tyrie who spoke fluent German. Tyrie took him into his room in 103 for a brew, and Adolf settled down there comfortably for a couple of hours. He went back the next night and made it a habit.

Valenta had cultivated Walter, the bookführer, a thin obergefreiter with glasses who came in the compound nearly every day and often helped Pieber count the appell. He was harmless, rather a gentle type, and he told Valenta that Rubberneck was getting the idea there was a tunnel somewhere in the compound.

'What in winter?' Valenta said innocently, fishing for more. 'Where the hell does he think we can hide the sand?'

Walter shrugged and spread his hands expressively.

'I would not know,' he said. 'It is nothing to do with me. I think you can expect more searches.'

'Where?' asked Valenta, and Walter nodded toward 110.

Roger cleaned out his wall panel that night. There wasn't much bulky stuff in it, but there were some lists of names. He hid most of them behind a panel in another block, but, a little carelessly (unusual for Roger) he carried the rest in his pockets.

There was no search next morning but halfway through appell Rubberneck walked on to the appell square with half a dozen guards.

They split up and approached various squads, one of them being the inhabitants of 110. Roger, conscious of the papers in his pockets, had a sudden instinct of what was going to happen and his heart was bumping a little. He shoved his hands in his pockets and muttered out of the corner of his mouth, 'Conk, stick around.'

Canton, Piglet Lamond, and McIntosh moved up close to him, and as they did so, Rubberneck and Eichacher, an English-speaking German, reached the squad. Eichacher had a word with Bob Tuck, who was at the front, and then turned and called, 'Squadron Leader Bushell, please. Come out and follow me.'

As he shouldered forward in the crowd, Roger pressed the papers into the hands of those around him, and they passed them on to others down the line. Rubberneck didn't notice a thing.

In 104 squad, another ferret had called out Floody and George Harsh, and they marched, a forlorn little group, across the square. Rubberneck stopped by Wings Day.

'*Komm!*' he said.

Half a dozen armed guards fell in around them, and they were marched off to their huts, Rubberneck stripped them all naked and searched them, finding nothing. Poker-faced, he let them go and marched out of the compound.

Walter had been right. Rubberneck searched 110 the next morning and, probing above a window in a room on the east side he sprang a secret wall panel. It was empty. No. Not quite. Rubberneck pounced on a little piece of paper lying in it. There was some writing on it. He passed it to Eichacher.

'What does it say?' he asked.

'It says,' Eichacher translated a little nervously, ' "Sorry. Too late!" '

It wasn't a very wise thing for the roomführer to do. Rubberneck was a bad man to goad, and judging by his next move, he was ready to do anything to unearth the tunnel he was beginning to suspect.

Floody called Bushell out of his room.

'For God's sake, come and look at the circus.'

In the vorlager just outside the fence a little procession was walking along the wire. Rubberneck was there, Broili in his shiny black boots, one or two other German officers, and a few ferrets. Leading them was an old man in a cloth cap and a ragged corduroy jacket. He held a rod in front of him and was looking at the ground over his drooping moustache.

'What the hell . . . !' Roger said.

'A bloody diviner.' Floody was hugely amused. 'Ever heard of a tunnel diviner?'

'I never thought I'd live to see the day,' Roger said, shaking his head.

The old diviner had started opposite 101, and now he was opposite 103. A couple of times he stopped and cocked an eye pensively at the sky while the rod gently waved in his hands. Once he turned back a few paces, Rubberneck and Broili stepping devoutly aside, watching, it seemed, a little self-consciously because Rubberneck was swivelling an occasional eye sideways at the compound. A few prisoners stopped on the circuit and gaped at them open-mouthed.

'No, I never heard of a tunnel diviner,' Roger said after a short silence, 'but I think we ought to be in this. The old boy might imagine he's found something and start a panic.' He moved down to the wire, Floody after him, and they muttered to the spectators by the warning wire. A few seconds later, groans and catcalls started to rise, followed by wild, shrill laughter. People came running up to see what all the excitement was, and the chorus of derision swelled. Rubberneck wouldn't look across any more, but his face was scarlet. The old diviner looked up in offended dignity, then Broili spoke to him and he dropped his eyes again.

But he was a rattled man. He doddered on, passing over 'Harry' opposite 104 without a tremor, dithered for a while round 105 (where there was nothing), and continued on to the end of the compound, followed behind him by the Germans and along the warning wire by a hundred derisive prisoners. He tried again on the return journey but the ectoplasm didn't seem to be working. It was the first time the ferrets had ever tried diviners.

And the last.

'It's not really funny,' Roger told the grinning committee later. 'It means we're going to have that sod Rubberneck on our tails. Everyone's got to be doubly careful from now on.'

Harsh sent out a special security warning and threatened he would personally bash to a pulp any stooge who slipped up or anyone talking about escape where they might be overheard. Langford noticed the white-washed cement facing on the wall behind 'Harry's' trap was a little scarred where the open trap had leaned against it. He carefully 'whitewashed' it again with a solution of foot powder, smearing it on with a shaving brush.

As a further blind for himself, Roger took on another part with the camp theatre. In addition to his escape work and his language classes, he started rehearsing every night the part of Professor Higgins in *Pygmalion*. The fact that Rubberneck had still suspected him enough to search him personally was making him very cautious.

CHAPTER XIV

Roger expected Rubberneck might put on a couple of snap appells during the day. That had happened once at Barth when the Germans suddenly ran into the compound and a couple of people down a tunnel didn't have time to get up again. The count showed they were missing, and the tunnel was found because of it. He sent an order around that in the event of a snap appell, everyone was to dawdle as much as possible, and Floody fixed an emergency procedure for the men underground.

The timing was uncanny. A score of guards marched in for a snap appell in the early afternoon a couple of days later. If the fools had done it properly they might have trapped the day shift underground, but with boneheaded Teutonic thoroughness they had to go through the usual bullshine routine of falling in by the gate, numbering off from left to right, and then dismissing to clear the prisoners out of the huts. Harsh saw them from 104, and Langford went through the new drill. He had the trap up in a moment and called down the shaft the one word, 'Ferrets!'

At the bottom, the shaft man flashed a torch up the tunnel and the diggers dropped what they were doing and trolleyed back hell for leather, Langford just had the trap in position again as the jackboots sounded in the corridor and the voice was bellowing, '*Raus! Raus! Alle rausgehen!*'

Early in March, SS General Mueller, Berlin Gestapo chief, issued the 'Kugel Order.' It was an extension of the 'Stufe Roemisch' order. Kugel

means bullet, and the new order said that recaptured escapee officers,
other than British and Americans, were to be taken in chains to
Mauthausen Concentration Camp.

Mauthausen was instructed that prisoners transferred to them under
the 'Kugel Order' were not to be entered on the camp books but taken to
the underground cells and either gassed or shot, whichever was con-
venient.

About that time security police visited Sagan and had a conference
with Von Lindeiner about counter-escape measures. They hinted to Von
Lindeiner that prisoners who escaped in future might suffer very harsh
penalties. One of them suggested that reprisals might even consist of
shooting people in the camp. (To one of his officers, Von Lindeiner later
remarked that if he was ordered to shoot prisoners, he would take his own
life.)

Von Lindeiner sent for the senior officers, doctors, and chaplains in all
the compounds and asked them to put a stop to all escape activity.

'It's not worth it, gentlemen,' he said. 'The public temper outside is
running very high, particularly against the Allied Air Forces, and
escapers may suffer harsh consequences. The war may be over in a year
or two . . . it is not worth taking unnecessary risks now.'

It was a pity he could not have been more explicit. A captive officer
cannot give up the idea of escape just because the enemy asks him not
to.

Walter, the bookführer, told Valenta that Rubberneck was going on
fourteen days' leave on 1 March. That was in three days. The
committee could hardly believe their luck.

'We can finish it before he's back,' Floody said exultantly. 'I'm
bloody sure we can if we really get down to it. Then we can seal up and
wait for the weather.'

He reckoned there was just over a hundred feet to go and then they
could dig straight up under the trees.

Floody's joy was premature. Rubberneck struck the day before he
was to go on leave. We were on morning appell when thirty extra
guards marched on to the square. Broili and Rubberneck were with
them, and Broili went from squad to squad calling out names. One by

one the men he called walked suspiciously out of the ranks, and the guards closed around them. Floody was one of them. So was George Harsh (still in pyjamas). Fanshawe was another. There were nineteen of them, including Bob Tuck, a couple of diggers, and Jim Tyrie, the man with the beard who had kept Adolf out of the way for the past vital fortnight.

Broili marched them down to 104, giving Floody, Harsh, and Fanshawe some nasty moments wondering if they had located 'Harry.' They hadn't, but they spent two hours searching them, and then, without giving any of them a chance to go to their rooms to get their few belongings, they marched them out of the gate to a compound at Belaria five miles away.

It was a stunning parting pick from Rubberneck. Three key men lost without warning at the critical moment! No one knew how they'd chosen the nineteen. Some of them were completely harmless types who had nothing to do with 'X,' and about a third of them were fairly important workers. It was a wonder they didn't take Bushell, but apparently his outside activities had really convinced Rubberneck that he was a reformed character. (Walter later revealed that the ferrets had gone through all the identification photographs and picked out those they suspected might be on escape work. Why they suspected them we never did find out.)

Floody, Harsh, and Fanshawe were seething when they were taken away. They'd been slogging on the tunnel for nearly a year; they would all have been certainties to get out, and now this . . . right on the point of success.

Later they felt rather differently!

Crump took over the next day as chief tunnel engineer, and with Rubberneck away they dug like furies. There were eight men down the tunnel on every shift now; two at the face, two in Leicester Square, two in Piccadilly and the frame cutter and pumper in the shaft. The sharp-eared Shag Rees got a shock when there was a sudden rumble right overhead, and he cringed back expecting the whole roof to come crashing down . The rumble passed and he realised it was a heavy cart above. They were under the road.

There were almost no falls over the last stretch. With Rubberneck away everything seemed to go smoothly, and there was still plenty of room for dispersal under the theatre. In nine days they dug nearly a hundred feet. Rubberneck was due back in five days. On the tenth day they built the whole of the last halfway house, ten feet long. Crump trolleyed backward and forward trailing a long piece of string, checking the measurements. 'Harry,' from shaft to face, stretched for 348 feet.

The surveyors had said it was 335 feet to the edge of the wood. Crump crawled out of the trap that night feeling that the whole thing was unreal. It didn't seem possible that they were really inside the trees as they had planned nearly a year ago.

'The ground falls away outside the fence,' he said to Roger. 'If the mathematical marks are right, we've only got about twenty-two feet to go up. Barring the unforeseen, I'll guarantee it before Rubberneck gets back.'

He already had the framing for the outlet shaft stored below. Travis had been working on the sections for a week. It was to be solid box-framing around four bedposts.

Digging up was tricky and dangerous. The sand kept clumping down, and as Crump fitted the sections of the framing he roofed over half the top to minimise the falls and scraped the sand down on the open side. Then he changed the roof to the other side. They fixed the ladder in sections as they burrowed up and stood on it to dig. It was backbreaking work.

Just before appell on the fourteenth, Crump came to pine roots and gathered he had only three feet to go. His idea was to stop about two feet from the surface and roof it firmly. With two feet of earth it wouldn't sound hollow if anyone walked on it above. To break out they could remove the roof and hack the two feet of soil away in a couple of minutes. It could drop to the bottom of the shaft, and they could leave it there.

He came up for appell and told Johnny Bull, who was doing the evening shift:

'Test it to see how far you can go. I think you ought to be able to put in two more frames and leave it at that.'

Bull vanished up the tunnel after appell. He was back twenty minutes later shaking with excitement.

'There's only six inches of dirt there,' he said. 'By Christ it's lucky I tested it first. I'd have broken right through.'

SECTIONAL VIEW OF 'HARRY'
1. Trap door under heating stove
2. Vertical entrance shaft 3. Storage chamber 4. Putting finishing
touches on bedboards for shoring
5. Wooden sandboxes 6. Air-pump
chamber 7. Air pipe buried under
tunnel floor 8. Man on trolley
9. Wooden rails for trolley 10.
Halfway house No. 1 ('Piccadilly
Circus') 11. Halfway house No. 2 ('Leicester Square') 12. Exit shaft 13. Coon-box
14. Cooler 15. Hospital 16. Sound detector under inner barbed wire 17. Warning wire

He'd stuck a metal rod up into the sand, and after six inches' penetration there was no more resistance. He went back and roofed it strongly, packing the sand above the roof as tightly as possible so it would be solid above if anyone trod on it.

At a quarter to ten they were all crawling out of the trap; still with that feeling of unreality, unable to believe it was the last shift and 'Harry' was finished. They brought up all the unused bedboards and pipe-line tins, the dispersal bags, the tools, and spare shovels, even the sand boxes off the trolleys, and either burned them or stored them down 'Dick.' They weren't going to need them any more. It was hard to believe that too. Langford stuffed the muffle blankets very carefully under the trap and lowered it.

'Well that's it, you old bastard,' he said, sounding deeply satisfied. 'Next time you come up you'll be useful.' He added soberly to Crump, 'It's none too soon, you know,' and pressed a foot gently on one corner. It made a little knocking noise as it rocked.

'Warped as bloody Hitler,' Langford said. 'It won't matter so much now.' He spent the next half hour cementing it down around the edges, completely sealing it as he had done twice before. Then before he went to bed he scrubbed the floor. (He scrubbed the floor every day after that, sloshing water all over it. It wasn't fanatical cleanliness. The water made the boards swell, and they filled in the last vestige of crack around the edges of the trap.)

Crump went over to tell Roger it was all done. Roger was staying away from the trap area as much as possible now, not because he wanted to, but because of the time Rubberneck had searched him. He knew he was probably still suspect, and Massey and Wings were insisting he didn't take any chances. He'd been rehearsing as Professor Higgins that night. He and Crump sat quietly for a few minutes, not talking much but conscious of a feeling of elation, and Crump drifted off to sleep still trying to convince himself it was fact, not fiction.

Rubberneck was back in the compound in the morning. He didn't waste much time. Just after lunch a squad of ferrets and guards ran in the gate and headed at a fast trot for 104. Rubberneck loped down the corridor throwing the doors open so he could see anything that might be going on before they had a chance to cover up. He cleared everyone out, and the ferrets went through it for four hours. It was the worst four hours we had known and oh, the blessed relief when Rubberneck walked out again as solemn as ever.

'There's nothing to be smug about,' Roger warned that evening in the library room. 'Rubberneck's obviously got it into his head there's something in 104, and we probably won't get away with it next time. I don't see that we can risk a next time.'

'Well, we can't break it now,' someone said. 'Not in this snow.'

'We damnwell can if we have to' – Bushell was speaking roughly at that meeting.

'Doesn't give the hardarsers much chance,' said Marshall.

'Johnny, they haven't got much chance any way,' Roger said. 'You know as well as I do they'll nearly all be caught. We can't lose 'Harry' just because conditions are tough. It isn't only to get people home, it's to muck the Goons about too and get them to divert troops to look for us.'

Roger had thought of just about everything. There were, he said, four factors he wanted for the night of the break: (1) no moon, (2) a wind to cover up noises, (3) reasonable weather, and (4) no Rudy in 104. He had three days in mind – the twenty-third, twenty-fourth, and twenty-fifth of March. They were the three most moonless nights for the next five weeks. Almost immediately he ruled the twenty-fifth out.

'It's a Saturday night,' he said, 'and that means Sunday timetables for most of the train travelling.'

They talked it over for two hours and didn't reach any hard and fast decision. Crump and Langford sided with Roger in breaking out as soon as possible. They didn't think the trap would stand up to another search.

'We'll work toward the twenty-third or twenty-fourth,' Roger said, 'and see how the weather turns out.'

He had worked it out that at the most about 220 people might be able to get through the tunnel on the night of the break. That meant 'no joy' for most of the 'X' workers. There were about 600 of us who had taken part in the project in the various departments.

Roger and the committee picked 70 names from among those who had put in most work and those, particularly the German speakers, who had most chance of getting home. They put the rest of the names in a hat and drew out another 130, and then Roger approved another 20 names of deserving people who hadn't drawn a place. They were all to go in the order they were drawn.

The lucky ones were told to get ready, and the committee appointed marshals to help them. Each marshal was allotted ten men, and it was his job to see they had everything they needed. For a start they concentrated on seeing that each man had a fake name and a fake personal background so he could answer questions if he was picked up and interrogated. The marshals carried out mock interrogations on them, firing questions about their home life, where they were going and why, and then doubling back on questions to see if they gave the same answers. They found out what each man wanted in the way of ausweises, money, civilian clothes, compasses, food, and maps.

The marshals held mannequin parades of all the men in their charge, the would-be escapers dressed in their escape kit parading up and down while the marshals ran their critical eyes over them to correct anything that looked unnatural. A ferret passing a window nearly stumbled across one of these parades – and would have if the strutting models hadn't dived under bunks and into corners to get out of his field of vision. Roger was furious when he heard about it and threatened unseemly forms of mutilation against any marshal or stooge who gave the game away.

The whole organisation was buzzing with activity. They had several thousand marks in the kitty by this time, enough for about forty people to travel by train. The rest of them would have to 'hardarse' across country by foot. Most of them planned to strike down to Czechoslovakia, where they would have a chance of contacting friendly people. The border was only sixty miles to the south, though there was a mountain range in between. Johnny Vesley, a Czech in the RAF who knew the area, lectured the hardarsers in batches on how to go about it, and Johnny Stower, who had got to the Swiss border after the delousing break, lectured them on his experiences.

Roger himself checked all the train travellers' stories and gave them all the information Valenta's men had been able to collect on timetables and routes. He gave general lectures to everyone on German customs. Marshall and Crump spoke to them on how to get through the tunnel without coming to grief.

Travis' engineers had switched to the production of metal water-bottles. They cut old food tins into sheets according to patterns, and a team of solderers, drawing heavily on stocks of bully-beef-tin solder and resin got to work with home-made blow lamps and turned out little flat flasks by the score.

Plunkett had his mimeograph going and rolled off something like four thousand maps, from local maps to strip maps of routes.

Stooges all over the camp were working overtime, and by the grace of God, no slips were made that week. Rubberneck was still prowling about as alert as ever, but nearly all the huts had been cleaned out and the stuff was down 'Dick.'

Al Hake shut down his compass production line. He had about 250 of them stored down 'Dick.'

Guest's tailors kept on working to the last day, and by that time they had hand-sewn nearly fifty complete suits; and most of them would have been a credit to some of the tailors I have met. They were mostly for the train travellers who had to look the part. A lot of the hardarsers were converting old uniforms. It didn't matter so much if they looked as though they were wearing hand-me-downs. However smart they were when they left, they were going to look pretty scruffy after a few days' trekking. Guest showed them how to shave the nap off the cloth and dye it, lent them his paper patterns and gave them civilian-type buttons.

For some months past 'X' had been making a levy on the Red Cross food parcels, and in a room of 112 half a dozen cooks were mixing 'fudge,' the concentrated escape food. It was the recipe of David Lubbock, a naval type, and was a compound of sugar, cocoa, Bemax, condensed milk, raisins, oats, glucose, margarine, chocolate, and ground biscuits. The beaten mixture looked like old glue, and it was taken across to the kitchen block where Herrick baked it into cakes, or rather bricks, and packed it into flat cocoa tins. Lubbock had worked it out that one four-ounce tin held enough calories to last a man two days. The difficulty was to get it down past the ribs, where it tended to stick tenaciously. The train travellers were each allowed four tins, and the hardarsers could take up to six.

Massey gave a final warning to those who had drawn a place for the tunnel and told them he had been informed that the German population was becoming increasingly hostile, particularly toward the Allied Air Forces.

'If you are caught, some of you may not be treated very well,' he said. 'I do not think the Germans would dare to take extreme measures, as you are protected by the Geneva Convention, but do please avoid any provocation.'

Roger spoke to a few of us who hadn't drawn a place.

'I can promise you plenty of entertainment later,' he said. 'Once they find there's been a mass break under their noses, it'll be a case of *"après nous, le déluge."* '

In between his lectures and rehearsals, Roger drew up the scheme to get the 220 people into 104 on the night of the break without exciting the ferrets. It was two and a half times more than the block was supposed to hold, and they had to be hidden when the Germans came around to lock up. Everyone in 104 who wasn't escaping was allotted a bunk in some other hut on the night of the break.

Rudy's contact moved out immediately to another hut and told Rudy he'd had a row with his roommates because they didn't like the idea of associating with a German. Rudy cut them dead after that.

Roger knew well enough the ferrets had periodical checks on people moving between the blocks to see if any unusual activity was going on. He put traffic checkers around 104, and for two days they logged the numbers of people who normally moved in and out. From their figures Rogers worked out a timetable and routes to control people moving to 104 on the night of the break.

Dean and Dawson had the hardest job of all because everyone's papers had to fit his stories. The forgers were working full pressure filling in fake names and particulars, sticking on the photographs that Hall and Cornish had taken in their studio, and stamping them. All told they had about four hundred forged papers of various kinds. Everybody was to have at least one, and many were taking two. Men with elaborate identities like Bushell and some of the German speakers had up to half a dozen, including letters of credit and incidental forged personal letters just for effect. Tim had a folder for each man.

Meticulous as ever, he wouldn't risk leaving them in the wall cupboards, but insisted on hiding them down 'Dick.' It was damp down there now, so Travis made four large metal cans with sliding lids which were quite waterproof when smeared with margarine. The forgers were working on the papers morning and afternoon, and Tim wouldn't even leave them out during lunch. They had to go back down 'Dick.'

The stooges reported to 'Dick' every morning after appell. Mike Casey lifted the iron grating in the middle of the washroom floor, baled out the well, scraped the soap off the edges of the slab, lifted the slab out. Tim went down, got the cans, and while he was carrying them to the workroom under a box of potatoes, Casey replaced the slab, sealed it again with soap, ran the water into the well, and put the grating back. At midday the forgers broke off for a spell because they found they couldn't keep going all day without botching the work. Tim took the cans back to 'Dick,' and Casey went through the complicated procedure of opening up and closing again. An hour later, after lunch, he did the same again while Tim collected the cans, and again about four-thirty, just before appell.

The forgers worked till their heads were splitting and the points of their nibs and brushes and the letters they were forming seemed to jump and wriggle and blur under their eyes.

Most of the escapees were going as foreign workers coming from nearly every country in Europe. Tim was going as a Lithuanian.

'And what happens, please,' asked Marcinkus, who really was a Lithuanian (in the RAF) 'if the Gestapo get hold of you. How much Lithuanian do you know?'

'None,' said Tim, 'but then I don't suppose the Gestapo bloke would know any either.'

The snow still lay six inches deep on 23 March, but there was a hint of mildness in the air and the white carpet was wet on top and a little squashy underfoot. The bush telegraph had sent a whisper around the compound that the break might be in a couple of days, but most people didn't believe it. It was too tough for the hardarsers.

There was a committee meeting in the morning at which Chaz Hall said he thought the weather would hold fine.

'Looks like the thaw's starting just in time,' Roger said. 'We'll wait and see how it is tomorrow. If the weather keeps like this, I'm all for getting cracking, but we don't decide until we have to.'

'I'll have to know as soon as possible,' Tim cut in. 'We've got to cut a date stamp and stamp all the papers.'

'I've got to know too,' Crump said. 'I must know by lunchtime on the day of the break. I've a lot to do to get 'Harry' ready.'

Marshall was concerned again about the cross-country men.

'Some of the poor devils'll freeze,' he said.

'I'm sorry, Johnny, but it just can't be helped,' Roger said. 'I wish to God we could do something about it, but if we wait till next no-moon period, we're about certain to lose everything.'

'What about putting out a few of the train travellers and then closing up again?' Marshall asked.

'No,' said Roger. 'We'd lose the tunnel, and a few people getting out won't upset the Goon as much as a mass job.'

He thought about it all day, and after afternoon appell he went to Wings Day and they walked round the circuit in the gathering dusk.

'We've got to go tomorrow,' said Roger, 'but I hate having to make the decision. Bloody few of the hardarsers'll have any chance.'

'They wouldn't have much chance even if there wasn't any snow,' Wings said. 'You know yourself what their chances are . . . a hundred to one. If things get too tough out there they don't have to freeze to death. Once they know they can't make it, they'll have to give themselves up.'

'You think I'm right then?'

'Look,' Wings said, 'it's an operational war. Don't forget that. It isn't just a question of getting a few people home. It's just as important to mess the Goons about. Most of the boys will be caught anyway, but if we get a good team out there'll be a flap all over Germany, and we'll have done something useful . . . more useful than getting a few back home.'

'All right,' said Roger. 'Thanks.'

After dinner he went across to the theatre for the dress rehearsal. *Pygmalion* was to open in two days for a four-day season. Roger stood and watched them. McIntosh was playing Professor Higgins. He'd understudied Roger for the past three weeks just in case.

The twenty-fourth dawned fair, and by appell the sun was well over the pine trees, unchallenged in a clear sky. The surface of the snow was glistening, and it was quite mild.

They met at eleven-thirty in Roger's room. It was one of the shortest meetings on record, certainly the tensest. There were only a few words spoken. After the last man came in there was a dragging silence. People were looking up at the ceiling or sitting with their arms folded on the bunk, staring at the floor. Roger looked at Langford.

'How do you feel about it?'

'I won't guarantee the trap another month. I can't . . . not with that wobble.'

'Crump?'

'I think I can speak for all the tunnel men,' Crump said, 'including those who are hardarsing. I don't think we could take it if we lost everything now. Morale'd go for a burton.'

'Right. Tonight's the night,' Roger jumped energetically to his feet. 'Get cracking.'

CHAPTER XV

The entire camp must have known about it within five minutes.
You could feel the tension. It was absolutely electric.

Langford and Crump made a beeline for 'Harry.' Langford
chipped the cement away, and Crump and one other tunneller went
below and trolleyed up to the far end with a load of blankets. Crump
nailed one blanket as a curtain across the end of the last halfway house
at the foot of the exit shaft, and nailed another about three feet back in
the halfway house. They were to act as light traps and silencers when
the shaft was broken through. They nailed blankets to the floors of all
the halfway houses so that people could crawl over them without
getting their escape clothes dirty.

Crump tore more blankets into strips about six inches wide,
doubled them over, and nailed them on the railway lines over the first
and last fifty feet of the tunnel so the trolleys would run silently. Travis
came down with the board platforms he'd made for the trolleys and
nailed them on so the escapers could lie comfortably on them with all
their kit.

Up in the compound, there was a sort of ordered chaos as the 220
made their final preparations. So many things had to wait till the last
day in case the ferrets stumbled across them. 'Little X' in every hut
called together the men in his block who were going out and handed
them their water bottles, fudge, compasses, maps and money. He also
told each one the exact minute he was to leave his room and where he
was to report to the controller. They went back to their own rooms

and started sewing all their special kit into extra pockets inside their clothes. A lot of them had made little fat-lamp heaters for brewing cocoa on the trek across the snow-clad country. They kept inside the huts as much as they could so the Germans wouldn't notice too much rushing about.

The stooges were on duty that day in scores. Tommy Guest raided his secret clothing stores and passed the suits out to the lucky ones.

Dean and Dawson, as usual, had the most hectic time. Tim had asked Al Hake the previous night to start cutting the date-stamp out of a rubber heel, and it was ready by the time the decision was made. The forgers went to work stamping all the papers and then they sorted them all and distributed them.

Crump had to come up from below for five o'clock appell.

'Still got a hell of a lot to do,' he told Roger.

'Can you make it by eight-thirty?' Roger asked.

'I think we might just,' said Crump. 'Have a bloody good try anyway.'

He and Langford were back in 104 as soon as appell was over. The stooges searched the block as usual in case any ferrets had hidden there and gave the signal. Langford swung the trap up.

'The last all clear,' Crump said and scuttled below. He seemed a little sad about it. Crump and Canton were barred from the escape this time because Massey wanted a nucleus of experienced tunnellers left in the camp for the future.

Carrying a little box of electric-light globes (filched from the huts), Crump made his way slowly along the tunnel, taping the cable in the roof about every forty feet and fitting extra globes. He trolleyed back to the base, praying that they'd all work, and clicked on the switch. The tunnel lit up like Blackpool illuminations. It was rather a thrill to see the blaze of light stretching into the distance.

He trolleyed slowly back along the tunnel looking for damaged frames, found four side boards twisted out of line, and carefully started replacing them. Darkness had settled over the compound, and people were sitting restlessly in every room trying to talk of innocent things and thinking only of the tunnel.

At six o'clock there was an early dinner party in Travis' room. Half a dozen people present were hoping it would be their last meal in prison camp – Bushell, Lamond, Van Der Stok, Armstrong, McIntosh and Osborne. Travis had made an enormous pile of bully-beef fritters mixed with flour he'd milled by grinding barley under a bottle and seasoned with garlic. To follow he had a great bowl of 'barley glop' – barley boiled like rice with milk powder, sugar, and raisins. He pushed a massive plate of fritters over to Roger.

'If you can get outside that,' he said, 'it'll keep you going for a week.'

There wasn't much conversation. Roger ate methodically, trying to relax. He'd been working like a machine all day on last-minute details. Someone broke the silence and asked him how he felt about it.

'OK,' he said laconically. 'I'll make it this time.' He must have felt the silence and known what they were thinking because he pushed the plate away and grinned easily.

'You don't have to worry,' he said. 'They won't be getting me this time. I think I know the score pretty well now.'

At five to seven a man in a rough black suit got up from his bunk in a room in 107 and pulled on a greatcoat that seemed to bulge in a few directions. Richards was one of the hardarsers, and with a grin that was a shade too tight and on one side to be natural he shook hands around the room.

'Good-bye, you bastards,' he said. 'Sorry I can't stay. See you in London after the war.'

'See you looking out of the bloody cooler window in a couple of days, you mean,' said the roomführer. 'Good luck, old boy. Don't get your feet wet.'

Richards picked up a folded and tied blanket, and at seven o'clock sharp he walked out of the south end of the block and down the path into the end of 109 away from 104. He went into room 17. A stooge was standing at the window, and Wings Norman was sitting at a table with a list.

'On time,' said Norman. 'You're first. You can go right away.'

Richards turned and walked down to the north end of the block. Another stooge was standing there and ten yards away across the path was the door of 104.

'OK, said the stooge. 'All clear. On your way.'

Richards walked straight out across the path and into 104.

Torrens, block commander for the night, was standing in the doorway of the hut kitchen with a list in his hand.

'Richards?' He ticked the name off with a pencil and pointed to a door. 'Room six. Get into a bunk and stay there. Keep fairly quiet and talk about the weather . . . if you have to talk.'

Richards went in and lay down. He tried to relax but couldn't. He was fairly tingling with wakefulness.

At thirty-second intervals all over the compound, farewells were being said, doors were opening, and men in bulky great-coats walked out and went by a dozen circuitous routes to 109 where they reported to Norman. In ones and twos he sent them at intervals across to 104 where Torrens ticked them off on his list and set them to the rooms allotted to them.

Stooges were bringing Norman reports every couple of minutes as to the position of every German in the camp. Luckily it was a quiet night, and after a time only Rudy was in, firmly ensconced in his contact's new room in 112. He was enjoying himself. Everyone in the new room seemed terribly friendly, and that very decent fellow, his contact, had given him half a bar of chocolate. The sat there a long time, smoking cigarettes and talking.

Outside in the corridor three men were loafing by the stove, a German speaker and two stooges. If Rudy had come out, the German speaker would have started a conversation. One of the stooges would have gone to warn Norman, and the other would have tailed Rudy.

So far it was going like clockwork and 104 was filling fast. There were ten stooges standing beside the windows, watching into the darkness and edging back out of sight as the fingers of the search-lights came probing past. The stooge at the north window could see the goon-box over the roof of the cooler. 'Harry' would break somewhere among the dark trees almost directly behind. Outside the fence he watched two greatcoated sentries pacing their beats. One patrolled slowly from the goon-box down to the guardroom by the gate and back again, and the other paced in the other direction from the goon-box to the west fence. They would be more of a danger than the man up in the goon-box swinging his searchlight with his back to the exit.

About a quarter to eight, Torrens had his bad moment. The door of

104 opened and he saw a German unteroffizier walk in and stride down toward him, jackboots clumping heavily on the boards.

There were three escapers in their civilian clothes in the corridor, and they scuttled in panic into the nearest room. Torrens, petrified for a moment, recovered and headed down the corridor toward him to try to stop him, head him off, do anything to get him out of the block. He had a shattering, sick feeling that everything was lost, and then he saw it was Tobolski, the Pole.

A controller had forgotten to warn him that Tobolski was going as a German, in one of Tommy Guest's home-made uniforms. The uniform was a terrifyingly good imitation, with all the right swastikas and eagles and badges on it. If you compared it with a German uniform by daylight, you could see that the colour was a shade bluer than the German grey.

Tobolski apologised, and Torrens, weak with relief, waved him into his allotted room. The people in that room nearly died when Tobolski opened the door and walked in. Tobolski was travelling with Wings Day, who had converted a Fleet Air Arm tunic into a double-breasted civilian coat and had a pair of grey trousers and a cloth cap. They planned to make for Stettin and stow away on a Swedish ship.

In Room 23, Roger, Marshall, and Johnny Bull were standing with Langford by the trap waiting for Crump to finish up below. Langford had pulled a couple of lockers out from the wall, blanking off the trap area from the window, and he had the blackout shutters closed.

Massey limped in to wish them au revoir and Godspeed. He didn't say much. The atmosphere was too tense. A week earlier a board of doctors had told him he was going to be repatriated soon because of his injured foot.

'I can't tell you how proud I am of you,' he said quietly. 'I'm hoping you will get to London before me, and you know how much I'll be looking forward to meeting you there.'

He shook hands. 'Now I'll get out of your way and give you a clear run,' and he limped off down the corridor and into the snow.

At eight-thirty Crump was still somewhere in the tunnel. Marshall and Langford were fidgeting restlessly, but Bushell, vivacious and bright-eyed, was talking gaily. A little too gaily. He looked very smart in the grey lounge suit that he'd saved from Prague, a black overcoat (an RAF coat dyed with boot polish), and a dark felt hat he had somehow scrounged through a contact. His papers described him as a French businessman, and, carrying a little attaché case filled with his kit, he really looked the part. His travelling companion was the Frenchman, Scheidhauer, a lieutenant in L'Armée de l'Air attached to the RAF Scheidhauer knew people in Alsace and Paris, and they planned to link up with an escape chain in France.

Up by the trap the minutes dragged like hours, and even Roger was getting restive. They were behind schedule already. Langford climbed down the shaft and met Crump as he trolleyed back to the base.

'For God's sake, how much longer?' he asked.

'All OK except the new rope on the end trolleys,' Crump said. 'Bull and Marshall can fix them on when they go up. Save time.'

Langford went back up and reported, and at eight-forty-five Bull and Marshall clambered down the ladder. Crump handed Bull the new trolley ropes and quietly shook his hand.

'Good luck,' he said. 'Wish to God I was going with you.'

Bull lay flat on his belly on the trolley and paddled himself up to Piccadilly. He tugged on the rope, and Marshall hauled the trolley back, climbed on himself, and Bull hauled him up the tunnel. Bull went ahead to Leicester Square to fix the trolley rope.

Roger was next down the shaft, shaking hands with Crump. He hauled the trolley back, climbed on, holding his case out in front of him, tugged the rope, and Marshall hauled him along.

One by one, in strict order, men were clambering down the shaft and shooting up the tunnel on the shuttle service. There is a terrific sensation of speed rumbling up a tunnel on a trolley with your nose about three inches from the floor.

Eventually seventeen men were in position underground and everything was ready to open up. In the end halfway house lay Johnny Bull and Marshall, side by side. Just behind, overlapping their feet, lay Bushell and Scheidhauer, then Valenta and Stevens, who were to follow them out, and Dowse who was to haul the next bodies up. In the tiny space they were packed like sardines. In Leicester Square a man was lying on the trolley, another man waiting to go next and a hauler. In Piccadilly, the same. At the base of the shaft there was a man on the trolley, Langford waiting to go next, the pumper, and Crump, in charge of operations.

It was about half-past nine when Roger set the ball rolling, speaking quietly as though it were an everyday occurrence, 'I think you can have a shot at it now, Johnny. Everyone ought to be in position.'

Bull grunted and crawled carefully through the blackout blankets. A couple of seconds later they heard him clambering up the shaft in the darkness. After he had opened up, Bull was to lie outside the hole in the trees to control the first people out. They were to climb up the ladder and stop just below the top so he could feel their heads in the darkness. When it was all clear, he would give them a gentle tap on the head, and out they would go. He had landed that job partly because he was travelling third class by train as a workman, and it didn't matter if he got his clothes dirty opening up and lying in the snow.

Down below the remaining six lay quietly, breathing slowly and deliberately because the air was thick and heavy. In the heat and the crush they were all running with sweat. They could hear Bull scraping at the roof boards at the top of the shaft with the special trowel that Crump had left there earlier in the day. Travis had carved it out of wood because it would be quieter than the metal ones.

He seemed to be scraping away up there for hours and the minutes dragged endlessly. They could hear him grunting a little now and then. Johnny Marshall crawled through the blankets and called softly up the shaft:

'How long?'

'Can't loosen the damn top boards,' Bull whispered down. 'They're wet and they've jammed. Must be swollen with water.'

He worked on in the darkness, standing precariously on the ladder and trying to lever out the unseen, tightly packed boards that roofed the shaft, the sweat running off him.

Time dragged, and down through the tunnel and up in the hut nerves were stretching tight. Everyone was thinking that something must be wrong but had no idea what it could be, and imaginations were running away with some of them. Crump was looking vainly up the tunnel trying to see what the matter was. He noticed the air by the tunnel roof getting thick and hazy and told the pumper to give it all he had.

People kept on calling down from the trap asking what the hell was wrong. They should have opened up at nine o'clock. It was now ten o'clock.

Marshall, up at the end, looked at his watch and saw that Bull had been up there half an hour.

'For God's sake go and see how he's getting on,' Roger said, his voice a little strained.

Marshall went through the blankets again and, as he did so, he heard Bull coming down the ladder, and a moment later he stood beside Marshall at the bottom, breathing heavily.

'You have a go,' he gasped. 'I'm done in.'

With hardly an inch of space to move it, Marshall laboriously stripped off his smart suit and climbed up the ladder in his long woollen underpants. He couldn't risk getting into a first-class train compartment with his clothes streaked with dirt. At the top he hooked an arm around the ladder and tugged at the roof boards. He kept at it for ten minutes before he felt one shift just a fraction, and then he worked at it madly and felt it loosen bit by bit. In another five minutes it came away and then the others came easily.

Marshall eased himself sweatily down the ladder again, wiped his face on his shirt-tail, and started to dress while Bull went aloft and gently scraped away the last few inches of soil covering the top. Cramped in the halfway house the others heard the music of the sand as it pattered down to the floor of the shaft.

Bull felt his little shovel suddenly move unresistingly and knew he was through, and then the cool air was caressing his upturned, sweating face. He scraped a widening hole and in a minute he could see the stars above – a glorious sight and an epic moment – and he hoisted himself up the last two rungs and stuck his head up into the open.

He got the shock of his life. The surveyors had blundered. 'Harry' was too short! Instead of being a few yards inside the wood, he saw that he was out in the open, ten feet short of the dim line of trees. He looked back at the compound, and the full tragedy of the situation hit him. The goon-box was only fifteen yards away, a stilt-legged monster outlined against the glow of the searchlight. He could see the German guard's shoulders and his ugly square helmet as he peered over the rail into the compound, swivelling the beam of light.

Bull felt naked out there. He ducked his head and softly felt his way back down the shaft. Crawling behind the blankets, he broke the news. There was a stunned silence.

'God, we can't be short. We can't be,' Marshall said. 'Right out in the open?'

'Go and look,' Bull said tiredly. 'You'll see.'

All of them felt the sick dismay. It looked as though everything was a flop . . . six hundred men working every day for a year . . . the escape fever of those who had been behind the wire for up to five years. They couldn't quite grasp the reality of it.

Bushell recovered first.

'Could you be seen from the goon-box?' he asked.

'Couldn't be certain,' Bull said, 'but I think you would sooner or later. It's dark all right but a man couldn't lie on the snow for long. He'd show out against it so bloody plainly.'

'Well, we can do two things,' Roger said. 'Either go ahead now and get as many out as we can before we're caught or put a couple out and let 'em close up the outside. Then we can dig on a few more feet, put up another shaft and break next no-moon period . . . if we get away with it that long.'

They talked it over in whispers for a few minutes, shying away from the idea of postponing everything. Worse than the anticlimax was the probability that Rubberneck would find the tunnel. They all knew about the wobbly trap.

It was Roger who thought of the vital factor.

'We can't put it off now,' he said. 'All the papers are date-stamped. They won't be any good next month, and we won't get far without them. We've got to go tonight.' He paused and then went on slowly, thinking as he talked.

'We've got to have a new way of getting people out without a man lying by the hole in the snow. Someone's got to control it from outside somehow.'

And funnily enough it was the ferrets who gave the answer.

'Just a minute,' said Johnny Bull, with dawning inspiration. 'About ten feet from the hole right by the edge of the wood, I saw one of those spy nests the ferrets put up while we were digging 'Tom.' Put the controller behind that.'

'Pretty remote control,' Roger commented.

'Tie a rope to the ladder,' Bull said, his voice rising in excitement. 'The controller holds the other end. When it's all clear, he gives a couple of tugs and the bloke crawls out.'

It was so obviously the solution that Roger agreed on the spot.

Cramped against the side of the halfway house, he fumbled through the buttons of his greatcoat to a pocket and brought out a pencil. Inching over onto his back, he began to write the new procedure in scrawling print on the wall:

'Pause at the top of shaft. Hold signal rope tied to top rung. On receiving two tugs, crawl out. Follow rope to shelter.'

He spoke to Dowse.

'Warn everyone coming through of the new procedure. Make sure they understand. Tell your relief hauler to do the same when he comes through and make sure he tells the man who relieves him.' He spoke generally, 'Everything clear?' and there were quiet grunts of satisfaction.

'Well, here we go,' said Bull, and crawled out through the blankets and up the shaft, carrying a long coil of plaited rope. He tied one end to the top rung and cautiously stuck his head out of the hole to get the lay of the land. It seemed to be clear, and he gently eased himself onto the snow and crawled noiselessly till he was behind the shelter of the ferret fence, paying out the rope as he went. The snow fell wet and the crust broke through easily.

The sentry in the goon-box was still looking into the compound. He did not seem to be worrying about the woods behind. Probably he never thought to look there. His searchlights roamed over the vorlager, up and down the fences, and then joined the beams from the other goon-boxes playing over the huts and the churned-up snow in the compound.

Bull heard a man approaching from the west and then saw him dimly, a German soldier walking along the wire, the barrel of his slung rifle sticking up behind his shoulder. He walked to the sentry tower, stamped his feet once or twice and walked back. A few moments later the other sentry came into sight in the other direction, reached the goon-box, and turned back. Neither of them seemed to be glancing toward either the woods or the compound, but just tramping in frigid unhappiness up and down, up and down.

Over the top of the sheltering brushwood, Bull could see the black outline of the hole in the snow. When he lowered his head it narrowed, and he thought that from the eye level of the sentries it would not be very obvious. He waited a while to see what would happen, and shortly the two sentries appeared again, one shortly after the other, and then turned and tramped away.

As soon as they were out of sight, he tugged sharply twice on the rope and a moment later Marshall snaked over the edge of the hole, keeping low, and crawled on his belly, keeping one hand on the rope till he was beside Bull. Marshall stayed with him a while, his eyes getting accustomed to the dark. He put his lips close to Bull's ears and whispered, 'Doesn't seem too bad.'

'No,' Bull answered. 'I think we might get away with it.'

The wire patrollers came into sight again.

'I have to wait till they're both out of sight before I can get anyone out,' Bull said. 'It's going to make it a bit slow.'

'No help for it,' Marshall whispered. He waited till the sentries were out of sight again. 'Well, see you in London.' He felt for Bull's hand. 'Good luck, Johnny.' Then, picking up the rest of the coil of rope, he crawled off into the darkness of the wood, paying out the rope behind. About sixty yards inside the trees, he came to the end of the rope and tied it to the trunk of a tree, pulling in the slack. He gave it a couple of tugs to let Bull know he was in position and waited.

Back at the ferret fence, Bull tugged on the shaft line, and Valenta crawled out and joined him behind the brushwood.

'Marshall's up there,' Bull said, and Valenta crawled off, keeping the rope running loosely through one hand so he could receive signals if Germans came close. If he felt a tug he was to freeze on his belly in the snow, and wait till he got two tugs, the all clear.

He joined Marshall at the end. A couple of minutes later, Bushell arrived.

'Doesn't look too bad,' Roger whispered. 'I think it'll be all right. Off you go. See you back home. Good luck.'

Marshall and Valenta crawled another hundred yards deeper into the woods before they stood upright and walked swiftly away. Marshall had his compass cupped in his hand, and they followed the luminous needle, heading north. Less than half a mile through the woods lay

Sagan Station. They were catching a train down through Hirschberg to Czechoslovakia, where Valenta had friends.

Bushell was joined by Scheidhauer and they waited, sheltering behind two trees by the end of the rope, till Stevens, the South African, reached them. Then they headed north after Marshall and Valenta while Stevens waited for his partner.

So it went on.

CHAPTER XVI

Back in 104 the tension had been nearly intolerable. The first men had been up at the far end for over an hour and there wasn't a sign of anything happening. People kept calling down the shaft to Crump, asking what was wrong, and Crump, harried and fearing the worst, called back in a strained whisper, 'For Christ's sake wait, will you. How the hell do I know what's happening?'

Shortly after ten o'clock the lock-up guard went around the camp as usual, shutting and barring all the hut doors. He never bothered to look into the huts as a rule. He walked up to 104, and the stooges held their breath while he slammed the doors shut, slipped the bar in position, and walked off. It helped relieve the tension a little.

Torrens set up a table outside the trap room and stationed himself there for the night. Now that the huts were locked and only the hundführer would be left in the compound, the overflow of bodies in the rooms moved into the corridor. First of all Torrens ordered a dozen of them to lay blankets all over the corridor floor to muffle the sound of anyone moving about. Everyone took his boots off.

The corridor was an amazing sight; bodies lying all over the floor, Tobolski in his unteroffizier's uniform stepping daintily in his socks over people in rough suits, and plus fours; odd types in berets and cloth caps, sitting up beside blanket rolls and makeshift suitcases, smoking and trying to look natural – and looking, in fact, like refugees from the underworld.

At quarter-past ten Crump felt cold air on his cheek. He turned and peered up the tunnel, and there was no mistaking the cool draft sweeping past his face. A great exhilaration swept over him, and he lifted his head and whispered up the shaft, 'They're through. They've broken through. Tell Torrens.'

Torrens came and leaned over the trap.

'You're sure?'

'Yes,' Crump called throatily. 'You ought to feel the draft down here. They should start moving soon. Warn the next man, but don't send him down till I tell you.'

They waited nearly a quarter of an hour, and it wasn't till half-past ten that the man on the trolley at the base felt the rope tug as the hauler in Piccadilly signalled. He tugged back and went rolling softly up to the halfway house over the blanket-deadened rails.

Crump called up, 'Next please,' and a few seconds later a bulky shape was moving down the ladder.

The trolley was back in a minute, and another man lay his belly on it and waited.

Gradually the movement got under way.

Torrens had two runners by his desk to carry instructions. As one escaper crawled down the shaft Torrens sent a runner to warn the next man on the list to be ready in five minutes. The man struggled into his kit, whispered farewells around the room, and was ready to go when the runner came back for him.

He went to the door by the trap and waited till Crump called for him. Davidson, at the trap with another list, checked his name and gave him the patter: 'All right, now sit down here on the edge of the trap. Feel that ledge a foot below with your feet. Stand with your right foot in the far corner. Feel the top rung of the ladder with your left foot. Got it? All right now, let it take your weight. It's quite strong. Turn your body and down you go.'

At the bottom Crump showed them how to lie on the trolley and hold their kit. When they reached Piccadilly the hauler there had the trolley from Leicester Square, and the escaper crawled on, rolled along on the next stage, and changed trolleys again for the last lap.

The haulers were all experienced tunnellers like Noble and Rees and Birkland, so that everything underground would go smoothly. As each hauler pulled ten people past him, the eleventh, twelfth, and thirteenth men successively relieved them, and the old haulers continued on down the tunnel and out. The controller outside the hole behind the ferret fence got twenty men out, and then the twenty-first relieved him, and so on.

It wasn't long before Crump realised that they were falling badly behind schedule. Barring hitches, Bushell had aimed at getting a man out every three or four minutes, but the first hour soon settled those hopes. Only six people were called in that hour. The suitcases were the trouble, and it looked as though they were going to be the trouble for some time.

The first thirty-seven were all going by train, and they nearly all had suitcases, made mostly out of cardboard or plywood and rubbed with boot polish. Nearly all of them found trouble in handling the cases on the trolleys. Some of them dropped them and some got the corners dangerously wedged against shoring frames. Trying to hold them out in front, several men overbalanced on the trolley platform, lifted the wheels and derailed them. The derailing was the worst.

The tunnel was so cramped that the men on the trolleys couldn't do anything about getting the wheels back on again. The hauler would feel the rope tighten and then jib altogether, and usually he knew what the trouble was. He had to crawl down the tunnel and get the man on the trolley to take his weight on his hands and toes while he fitted the wheels back on the rails. Then the hauler crawled backward to his halfway house, started hauling again, and like as not the trolley would be derailed again before it reached him.

Crump turned once to see who was next and was surprised to see not a man but a suitcase. In fact, not so much a suitcase as a trunk. Behind it grinned a strange face which he recognised after a second or two as Tim Walenn without his great moustache, which he had shaved off for the occasion.

'Where the hell d'you think you're going with this?' Crump demanded with a blend of wonder, exasperation, and amusement.

'Home, I hope,' Tim said soothingly, 'but I expect to the cooler, actually.'

'You'll never bloody well get that thing through,' Crump said.

'Don't worry. I'll cope.'

'Not a hope,' said Crump. 'Can't be done,' and they argued for a couple of minutes.

In the end Crump sent the case up on the trolley by itself, and Tim followed after.

Nerves were affecting a lot of them. Even some of the veteran diggers who had been riding on trolleys for months found themselves fumbling and getting stuck.

Rockland and Muller, the two Norwegians, went through very smoothly, Muller with a parting affectionate glance at the pump he had designed. They both looked very smart in plus fours. Neely, a Fleet Air Arm man, was another who went through smoothly.

A little after midnight the men in the hut heard the sirens and groaned. There had been no air raid alarms for a fortnight, and Roger was praying that this would be a free night too. As the wail of the sirens died, the stooges at the windows heard faintly the rumble of the first bombs dropping on Berlin, sixty miles away, and almost in the same moment a German over in the kommandantur switched the power off, and all the lights went out.

Down in the tunnel it was Stygian, terrifying blackness, and everything stopped at once. Further progress was impossible. In the halfway houses, the confinement, the stuffiness, the fear of moving in case of a fall combining with the blackness gave rise to claustrophobia, and nerves were at snapping point again.

Wings Day, who had just been about to set off for Piccadilly, stayed and helped Crump light the fat lamps stored in the shaft and took them up on the trolley with him. His nerves seemed steady as a rock, and Crump watched with thankfulness as he receded into the tunnel, a moving, flickering pool of light.

Wings carried the lamps right through the tunnel, leaving one in each halfway house. When he got to the far end he found the hauler there had vanished. When the lights had gone and his relief did not arrive the hauler had apparently thought that something had gone wrong or that the Germans had entered the hut and found the tunnel, so he decided to leave. It was just lucky that Wings was experienced. He hauled through his partner and stayed to pull the next hauler up before he continued on his way. By the time men were moving slowly through again, a good thirty-five minutes had been lost, and, but for Day's coolness, the time lost would have been a lot more.

There was one cheerful side to it. The camp boundary lights and searchlights were off too, leaving everything in blackness, and the guards by the wire were watching closely all the time into the compound, looking for optimists trying wire jobs in the darkness. The exit controller took advantage of it to speed up the departure.

The stoppages had already dislocated the plans of most of the escapers. The train travellers all had certain trains to catch and apart from four or five of the early ones they had all missed them. Some were able to catch later trains, but the delay meant the wouldn't be as far away as they had hoped to be when the alarm was raised.

Up above it had been time for camp 'lights out' at midnight and Torrens ordered 'lights out' procedure. All the blackout shutters were opened (they had to be, because it was the usual practice), all the fat lamps were doused, and everyone in the rooms had to stay in a bunk. No movement was allowed except in the dark corridor, and there was little enough movement there. The whole floor was covered with bodies huddled in blankets trying to snatch a few minutes' sleep before their turn came.

Not many were sleeping. They were too keyed up. Nearly all of them were hardarsers, and they knew they weren't going on any picnic. The trek across snow-clad country would beat most of them, and there were bound to be a few Gestapo beatings.

By the windows the stooges saw the hundführer and his dog several times within a few yards of the window of Room 23. The stooge whispered a warning, and everyone froze out of sight but the German never came near enough to look in.

Crump had had his fingers crossed for hours praying there would be no falls but about one-thirty the luck gave out. Tom Kirby-Green was halfway between Piccadilly and Leicester Square when he moved position slightly on the trolley and the rear wheels rose and came off the rails. He tried to squeeze himself off the platform and back to fix it, and his burly shoulders caught on a damaged box frame and tore it out. The roof collapsed and down came the sand, bringing down about three more feet of roofing and more sand crashed down.

It was a bad fall. In two seconds Kirby-Green was buried from legs to shoulders and the tunnel was blocked. Wrapped in all his escape kit the big man couldn't move, but luckily his head was clear and he could breathe.

Up in Leicester Square, Birkland, who had been hauling him, felt the rope tighten and stop. Looking down the tunnel he could not see the dim light of the fat lamp in Piccadilly and knew that the tunnel was blocked. He crawled down to the accident and slowly pulled Kirby-Green clear, then made the big man crawl over him up to the halfway house. Birkland started patching up the tunnel, working like a sweating madman in almost total darkness, feeling where the boards had come away and then probing for them in the fallen sand.

It was a dangerous job in the darkness, with a constant risk of more sand coming away, burying him alone there and wrecking the tunnel. As far as he could judge there was already a dome about three feet high over the fallen roof. He got the side boards in place again and then some of the roof boards and started packing the fallen sand on top. It was a solid hour before he had finished, soaked in sweat and sand and breathing heavily with exhaustion.

Just as he was finishing the sirens wailed again, sounding the all clear and over in the kommandantur a German switched on the current and the tunnel was flooded with light. The cable, luckily, had survived the fall. Birkland found himself, as usual, left with a pile of sand that could not be packed back above the roof. He did the only thing possible and spread it out over the floor of the tunnel for several feet between the rails, then crawled backward to Leicester Square, and the shuttle service started again.

About a quarter to three the last of the suitcase carriers went through, and the rate speeded up a little as the blanket brigade started. They all carried a single blanket rolled and tied tightly and slung on a string around their necks. It left their hands free so they could hold themselves more steadily on the trolley.

There were still too many stoppages. Some of the men hadn't tied their blanket rolls as they'd been shown, but had made them too long and the ends jammed between their shoulders and the walls of the tunnel. They had to keep freeing themselves every couple of feet and one man took seven minutes to go a hundred feet. Others had the string too loose about their necks so that the blankets dangled under the platform of the trolley, caught under the wheels, and the next thing they knew the trolley was derailed and they were nearly strangled.

Some of them had so much food and spare kit packed around them that they looked like swollen editions of Falstaff, and down at the base of the shaft Crump ruthlessly went through their corpulent forms emptying out their accessories till he thought they were lean enough. The Dodger was one of his victims. He was swaddled in so much stuff that he looked like a cocoon, but, courteous as ever and with only the most considerate of protests he submitted to Crump's reducing treatment and then went trundling smoothly through. Pop Green was another, but after Crump's merciless fingers had done their work he, too, went through with only minor trouble.

Men had been moving for over four hours now. There were less than three hours to first light and less than fifty had reached the far end. Now the hardarsers were going through, the procedure outside was altered slightly. At the end of the rope in the wood, men waited until a party of ten had assembled, one of whom had been specially briefed on leading them through the wood, around the west side of the camp, past a French and a Jewish compound, and on to a little dirt road leading south toward Czechoslovakia.

The numbers had just passed the half-century mark when Cookie Long stuck on the trolley within twenty feet of Piccadilly. Bob Nelson, who was hauling, tried to pull him gently through, but a box frame suddenly dragged away and the sand crashed down, burying Long. He was able to drag himself off the trolley and crawl up to the halfway house and Nelson crawled down to the fall. It wasn't quite as bad as the first one, but working flat out it took him half an hour to clear it.

Two more prisoners were stuck soon after that but eased themselves through without further falls. As the fifty-seventh man was being hauled in the middle section a trolley rope broke, and there was another hold-up while it was mended.

Crump climbed up to the top and saw Torrens.

'Not much more than two hours to go,' he said. 'We won't make the hundred at this rate. We'll have to do something drastic. Blanket rolls are causing most of the trouble so from now on blankets are out. They'll just have to take their great-coats and nothing more.'

'It's a bit desperate,' Torrens said.

'It's got to be desperate,' said Crump.

The hardarsers took it with good grace. The wakeful ones padded up to the desk and asked what their chances were of getting out. By this time Crump knew they wouldn't be able to beat the century and told most of them to go back, forget about it, and get some sleep.

He dived back down the shaft, and without the blanket rolls, the rate immediately speeded up. Then there was another fall in the second section, and Cookie Long, who had relieved Nelson hauling in Piccadilly, crawled up to the scene. It wasn't a bad one, and working in the usual mad sweat he fixed it in about twenty minutes. There wasn't any more serious trouble after that, and men began to go through comparatively swiftly, as swiftly, that is, as the exit man at the far end could dare to signal them out.

About four o'clock, Roy Langlois, Number 60, went through and relieved the exit man behind the ferret fence. Lang had signalled two men out of the exit, when guards started to tramp along the road only about seven or eight yards from the hole. They were going past in ones and twos and didn't seem to have anything in particular on their minds. Lang puzzled about it for a while and then realised that it was guard-changing.

It meant another hold-up. For the next twenty minutes guards were strolling back along the road after being relieved, and Lang only got about two people out in that time. Then the last sentry tramped past, and the exodus from the hole quickened once more.

At half-past four, Lang jerked his head up in fright as he heard the sentry suddenly start shouting in the goon-box. He wasn't looking into the compound now but leaning over the side, and for a terrifying moment Lang thought he had been spotted.

He saw the guard wasn't talking to him but calling to one of the sentries patrolling the wire who was approaching. The patroller climbed up into the goon-box, and the searchlight sentry clumped down the steps, and to Lang's horror turned straight across the road toward the hole.

Langlois' heart was choking him in his throat. The German kept coming straight toward him in the gloom. He was right on top of the hole, and then he casually turned away as though he wasn't worried about it. A bare four feet from the black opening in the snow he squatted down, busying himself with one of the less dignified functions of man. The exit was just to his side and he took absolutely no notice of it. Lang, a bare ten feet away, burrowed face down in the snow wishing to God his heart wouldn't thunder so loudly, couldn't believe it was real.

The German must have been blind – what actually happened, of course, was that he'd been looking through a searchlight beam for hours and couldn't see a thing in the darkness after the dazzle. A broad black trail of slush led away from the hole showing where the prisoners – the ex-prisoners – had crawled away, and out of the hole itself Lang could see, against the glare of the searchlight, a thick column of steam rising, a peculiarity of all newly opened tunnels.

For five minutes the guard crouched there communing with Mother Nature, and then he hitched up his pants, strolled casually back to the goon-box, and clumped up the steps. The patroller who had taken his place clumped down and resumed his monotonous walk, and Lang breathed again for the first time in five minutes.

Back in 104, Torrens had ticked off Number 83 down the shaft. They were going through fairly smoothly now, and there were few hitches. Crump looked at his watch and climbed up the shaft to check on the light outside. It was still dark, but he knew it couldn't last much longer and he lingered by the window, trying to keep his eyes away from the searchlights and fix them on the wood to see if the trees were becoming clearer.

About five minutes to five he thought there was a shade more light coming off the snow and imagined he could see the trees across the wire in a little more detail. He called Davison over.

'I think it *is* getting a bit clearer,' Davison said.

'Right. About time to pack up,' Crump said. 'Get the next three down and that's the lot. If we can get 'em all out of the way without being seen, the Huns won't know a thing till appell, and the boys'll have an extra four hours before the hunt's on.'

Davison hurried the next three down – Michael Ormond, a tough New Zealander who used to play glamorous girl parts in the camp theatre, Muckle Muir, and Tim Newman. Newman was just vanishing up the tunnel on the trolley when a rifle shot cracked across the snow. It came from outside the wire in the direction of the tunnel.

CHAPTER XVII

J ust before ten to five, a big burley air gunner called Reavell Carter
climbed out of the hole, went crawling past Lang, and followed the
rope into the wood to the rendezvous tree. He was to lead the next
party of ten through the trees to the road running south from the
camp.

A couple of minutes later Oggy Ogilvy, a Canadian, emerged and
snaked past Lang toward the tree. Next was Mick Shand, New Zealand
Spitfire pilot. Len Trent (Squadron Leader Trent, VC, DFC), who
followed him, had just crawled clear of the hole when the sentry who'd
been patrolling the east beat along the wire came into sight again. For
some unknown reason, he was walking on the near side of the road,
along the edge of the wood. No sentry had done that yet. If he kept on
going he must walk across the hole.

Lang could make out the buttons and cross belts over his greatcoat
and went even colder than his long vigil in the snow had made him. He
tugged sharply twice on each rope and Shand, halfway to the tree
behind him, and Trent, just outside the hole, froze where they lay. The
Germans kept steadily on. He was ten yards away, and Lang felt his
eyes were sticking out like organ stops. The German was seven . . .
six . . . five yards away, and still he came on and still he hadn't seen
anything. He seemed to be looking dead ahead and not at the ground
at all.

His boots were crushing methodically through the snow, left, right,
left, and then he put a boot down within a foot of the edge of the hole

and still didn't see it, and his next foot missed by a couple of inches treading on Trent, lying doggo and quaking by the hole. Still the guard didn't see him. It was unbelievable.

He took another pace – and then he came out of his coma. He must have noticed the slushy track the bodies had made through the snow. A little muttering came out of him as he swung toward it, and in the same movement he shrugged the rifle off his shoulder and into his hands. Then he must have seen Shand lying on the track. He lifted his rifle and was about to fire when Reavell Carter, who could dimly see the drama from the tree, jumped into sight waving his arms.

'*Nicht schiessen, Posten!*' he yelled. '*Nicht schiessen!* ('Don't shoot, sentry! Don't shoot!')

His sudden appearance gave the German the shock of his life, and his rifle jerked upward as he fired. The bullet went wild. So did the quiet woodland scene. Shand bounced up from where he lay on the track and made a crouching dash for freedom, dodging in and out of the pine trees. Ogilvy jumped up from behind the far tree where he had been burrowing into the snow and did the same thing, tossing away excess kit as he ran.

As they vanished among the dark trees, Reavell Carter came forward – there was nothing else he could do – and then, right beside the paralysed guard and still unseen, Trent slowly rose to his feet. The guard saw him, jumped about a foot in the air, and stood rooted again, staggered with shock. He was a simple peasant type and quite speechless.

A second later, Lang – with no option – also stood up behind the ferret fence about ten feet away. The guard, seeing him, could only shake his head unbelievingly, and then he saw the hole in the ground right at his feet, and his mouth opened and shut like a fish.

For about three comical seconds he stayed paralysed, and then he recovered, whipped out a torch and shone it down the hole. Just below the surface, hanging on to the ladder, was Bob McBride, who was to have been next man out, the eightieth.

The sentry fished up his whistle and blew it shrilly, then found enough presence of mind to point his rifle at McBride and beckon him out. McBride crawled sheepishly out, and the sentry covered the four of them with his rifle. He was making hoarse speaking sounds, but no one knew what he was saying, least of all, probably, the sentry.

Lang heard the guard up in the goon-box frenziedly telephoning the German guardroom, and along the road from the guardroom by the gate a couple of hundred yards away a horde of German soldiers came running. The man in the goon-box yelled to them, and they fanned out into the woods. The sentry prodded his rifle at the four and nodded meaningfully down the road. They turned, hands in the air, and trudged off.

Back in 104, a hush had followed the shot. Around the trap the silence lasted perhaps three seconds as the people in the room, frozen into the attitudes they had been in, looked at each other. Crump said quietly, with magnificent understatement, 'That appears to be a shot.'

'That was indeed a bloody shot,' someone else said, his voice sharpening as he spoke.

'Christ!' Crump was the first to move. 'Someone's got it. Davison, get the blokes back from down the tunnel.' And as Davison slipped down the ladder Crump spoke to Torrens in the doorway.

'Get everyone in the hut to start destroying their papers and all their incriminating kit.'

He darted over to the window but could see nothing. The cooler was in the way of the tunnel exit. He crossed back to the trap, knowing that most people in the tunnel wouldn't have heard the shot and would still be travelling through. As he was vanishing into it a stooge from the front room called out that a mob of Germans had come out of the guardroom and were running along the wire toward the exit of the tunnel.

As it happened, the people in the end halfway house *had* heard the shot. Denys Maw, Number 81, had been just about to crawl into the exit shaft when right above his head, and echoing down the shaft came the shattering crack of the rifle. One awful thought flashed through his mind. 'The bastards! They've known all along and they're plugging each bloke as he crawls out.'

He realised immediately that couldn't be or they'd have heard it before. The guards must have just found the hole. Maw turned back into the halfway house where two other people, the hauler and the next man out, had reached the same conclusion.

'Let's get to hell out of here,' he said, and the other two needed no persuading. One man lay on the trolley and propelled himself back to Leicester Square, and then the trolley was hauled back and the next man paddled himself down. Maw hauled the trolley back and set off on the return journey himself.

So the shuttle service was reversed as the men started to scurry like moles back toward the compound. For a few minutes, however, the people in the first section of the tunnel still didn't know the flap was on, and they did not find out till people started to scuttle back from the far end. Meanwhile Crump and Davison, at the base of the shaft, were trying to inform them.

Peering up the tunnel, Crump could just see the trolley up by Piccadilly with Newman's bulky shape lying on it. He howled; 'Come back! We've been spotted. Pass the word along.'

His voice was muffled in the long, narrow space, and the man on the trolley could just hear a faint voice but didn't know what it was saying. A vague, muffled shout came back to Crump in reply.

'Come back! Come back!' Crump howled again. 'It's all up. The tunnel's been found.'

Again the muffled answer. It developed into a shouting match, and neither man could make out what the other was saying. Crump grabbed the trolley rope and tried to haul it back with Newman still on it, but Newman would have none of it. He was on his way out, and he wasn't coming back for anyone. He grabbed hold of the rails and held the trolley firmly. Crump shouted again and hauled back more strongly. He heaved and heaved, and then the rope snapped.

Crump realised there was no point crawling up the tunnel after him. People at the far end would soon find out the game was up and come pouring back, and he would only block the exodus if he crawled up. Newman sensed that the rope had broken and began to realise something was seriously wrong. He was just able to twist his head over his shoulder to look back and saw Crump beckoning frantically in the mouth of the tunnel. Crump, with enormous relief, saw him begin to paddle the trolley backward, and in a few seconds Newman emerged feet first into the shaft.

'What the hell . . .' he started, red-faced and sweating.

'Tunnel's spotted,' Crump snapped. 'Someone's been shot out there. Duck up to the block.'

As Newman went up the ladder Crump tossed the trolley into the dispersal chamber. With the rope gone, it was better out of the way. He looked up the tunnel again and saw a body crawling down. Soon a face stuck out into the shaft and the man scrambled out, perspiration pouring off him. He'd come all the way from the end halfway house.

'We're spotted,' he said superfluously. 'I think the ferrets are coming down. There's someone just behind me.'

More sounds in the tunnel. Mike Ormond appeared and breathlessly hauled himself out. 'They've found us,' he said. 'Ferrets are coming along.'

One by one they came crawling down the tunnel, panting and sweating, and as each one emerged he burst out excitedly, 'Look out! There's a ferret just behind me.'

Each time it was only another prisoner, but Crump felt his scalp prickling. The last three back were Red Noble, Denys Maw, and Shag Rees. Shag had been hauling in Leicester Square and had had a nasty moment. When he heard Maw returning from the far end, Shag didn't know whether it was a prisoner or a ferret. He took the light bulb out of its socket in the halfway house and squeezed himself against the wall in the darkness to get out of the way of any bullet that came whistling down. Unable to stand the tension any longer, he called, 'Who's that?'

Maw answered reassuringly and said he was the last man. Back they scuttled toward 104, Shag expecting a bullet at any moment. When they emerged at the top Crump closed the trap door and moved the heavy stone back over it. He and Davison picked all the blankets off the floor and tossed them on the bunks, then slid the lockers that had shielded the trap back against the wall.

Crump went out into the corridor and thought for one frightened moment the block was on fire. There were a dozen fires in the corridor and more in the rooms as people burned their papers and maps, and the hut was full of smoke and lit palely by little flames. They crushed some of their compasses and tried to hide others and their German money in palliasses. They tore civilian buttons off their converted clothes and either hid or burned them.

A few leapt out of windows – strictly against orders – into the lightening compound and dashed back to their huts. The guard in the goon-box by the cooler sent a couple of bullets whistling after one of them, and the practice stopped.

Everyone was suddenly still, looking at the door of the hut. They heard the bar withdrawn, and the door opened and in walked the hundführer and his dog. The dog looked unconcerned but the hundführer stood there a moment uncertainly, eyeing everyone warily. He was a simple soul and didn't quite know what to do. Rather half-heartedly he told a few people to go into the rooms, and they largely ignored him. Wandering up and down the corridor, he collected greatcoats off the hooks and piled them in a heap by the hut door. The Alsatian knew what to do. He lay on the coats and went to sleep.

The hundführer could think of nothing more. He sat down near the coats and contemplated his toes.

Now that the show was over the tension had relaxed and about 140 prisoners sat around in the rooms, talking, laughing, and letting off steam. They knew they would be searched soon and probably sent to the cells on bread and water, and after a while the main occupation was eating escape rations. The stuff was too concentrated to get much down and before long no one could swallow another mouthful. In Room 23 Crump heard a faint scratching and scuffling under the trap door. The ferrets had arrived. As they had found their own way there, Crump decided to let them find their own way out again.

In the guardroom by the gate, Von Lindeiner was standing in front of the four men caught at the tunnel mouth. He was red-faced, shouting at them, and little flecks were flying off his lips. They stood up straight at attention and kept quiet, unable to make out much of what he was saying. He was nearly incoherent. Lang caught one part.

'So, you do not want to stay in this camp' – Von Lindeiner's voice was high and shaky. 'You wish to be out so the Gestapo will get you. They will shoot you – get rid of the lot of you.'

He went on in that strain. No Kommandant, to a prisoner, is a good man, but I think Von Lindeiner was. At least as good as a Kommandant could be in Hitler's Germany. It was not his fault if he could not give us enough food, or if someone went wire-happy and was shot by a trigger-happy guard. And he knew the tunnel was going to break him and that his own arrest could not be far off.

About six o'clock the first helmeted German column came tramping through the trees from the kommandantur into the compound, roughly seventy of them, in full riot squad kit. This time they were carrying mounted machine guns as well as tommyguns. They fanned out through the compound, closing the shutters around every window, and then formed a silent ring around 104. Four squads set up machine guns on tripods covering the hut doors.

Von Lindeiner walked into the compound, very upright and moving fast, staring straight ahead, still red in the face. Broili was just behind him, pale in contrast and almost running to keep up. And then the Kommandant's adjutant, Major Simoleit and Pieber, who was looking owlishly solemn. Rubberneck came running up, and behind him marched another squad. As Von Lindeiner stalked up to the hut, the guards all stiffened to attention. There was a succession of salutes, a rattle of boot-clicking, and all the ferrets drew their revolvers.

Several guards threw the doors open and clumped inside yelling the old familiar 'Raus! Raus!'

One by one the prisoners started to emerge, half expecting the chatter guns to open up on them. Snow was just starting to fall, and about a dozen ferrets were waiting for them. As each man came out a ferret grabbed him and made him strip naked in the snow, even to his boots. The ferrets closely examined every garment, and anything that looked as though it had been modified to look like civilian wear or could remotely be an aid to escape they tossed on a pile to one side. A lot of the boys lost their pants and were left standing up in their woollen long johns. It began to have a faintly funny side but not so that you'd burst out laughing.

Simoleit came running agitatedly out of 104, streaked past the prisoners in the snow, and headed toward 101. He was a dapper little man shaped like an undernourished gorilla, and his back view, running in breeches and boots, looked absurdly bandy-legged. He burst into Bill Jennen's room and breathlessly announced that Unteroffizier Pfelz had gone down the far end of the tunnel an hour before and they couldn't find the entrance trap to let him out. He would suffocate – die. Herr Major Jennens was to come at once and get him out.

Big rough Jennens was still in his bunk. Slowly, stretching and yawning, he roused himself and demanded what the hell Pfelz was doing down the tunnel. (It was amazing what Jennens got away with by shouting and banging his fist. He was always doing it, and the Germans always respected him.)

Simoleit explained that Unteroffizier Pfelz had gone down to see if any more prisoners were left there. Would Herr Jennens be good enough to hurry. The Unteroffizier would be suffocating. Simoleit was hopping up and down in his distress.

Jennens leisurely dressed and leisurely followed Simoleit down to 104, where he found that Red Noble had taken pity on his old friend Charlie Pfelz and was lifting the trap door. Down at the bottom of the shaft a relieved Charlie blinked up at them and scrambled up the ladder. He went out, saluted smartly and told the Kommandant what he had seen. Then he grinned at Rubberneck. A big moment for Charlie. He loathed Rubberneck.

Von Lindeiner had his pistol in his hand now and so did the other officers as well as the ferrets. Broili's hand was shaking so much he probably couldn't have hit a barn door, but Rubberneck's hand looked remarkably steady, and the knuckles were quite white showing that he had already taken up the initial pull on the trigger. He was in a shocking temper, and his face was mottled red. Rubberneck, like the Kommandant, knew he was going to have a lot of explaining to do.

Shag Rees and Red Noble came out of the hut together, and when Rubberneck noticed them you could practically see his hackles rising. Red and Shag were his personal enemies. They had always given him trouble, and he'd sent them both to the cooler a couple of times. He rushed over as they were being searched, grabbed the shoulders of their coats, and pushed them around as he tried to tear the coats off.

Red and Shag both wrenched themselves away and swung defiantly out of his reach. A guard raised his rifle and squinted down the sights at Shag, and Rubberneck drew a bead on Red with his pistol. There was one of those long, deadly silences while the incident was on the verge of ending with a couple of shots, and then the barrels lowered slowly as the tension relaxed, and Red and Shag stripped in peace. The guard took their trousers and slung them aside, leaving them in their underpants.

Von Lindeiner had watched the incident, and his face went a shade richer in colour.

'Cooler,' he said curtly (funny how even the Kommandant used that word). Four guards marched Red and Shag off to the cells.

When the search was over, the prisoners stayed standing in the snow in three ranks, surrounded by guards. Some of them without coat or trousers were shivering. No one knew what was coming next, and there wasn't much humour left in the situation until Johnny Hutson, a fair-haired little Spitfire pilot from Kenya, relieved the atmosphere by making little mocking noises in his throat. Von Lindeiner saw and heard him.

'Cooler,' he said tersely, with a face like thunder, and the guards marched Johnny off.

There was a friendly feud between Hutson and a young London bombardier, a tousle-headed kid of about nineteen, not long out of school. He couldn't hide a grin as Hutson was marched off, and Von Lindeiner saw him too.

'Cooler,' he said again with the same black look, and two more guards marched Horace off; the grin now transferred to Hutson's face.

Von Lindeiner spoke to the prisoners near him. 'If there are any more disturbances here,' he said, 'I will personally shoot two of you.'

There were no more disturbances. Von Lindeiner meant it.

After a while, Eichacher brought out the identification photographs and checked all the men standing in the snow. Von Lindeiner left them standing there another two hours while they made a photo-graphic check of everyone else in the compound to find out who was missing.

When they reported to Von Lindeiner that seventy-six people had escaped, he walked, frozen-faced, out of the compound. Shortly after, the 140 were marched down to the gate, and there they stopped again. Pieber remained with them, in charge, and looked reproachfully through his glasses at them.

'Ah, shentlemen, shentlemen!' he said. 'You should not do this thing. It makes only trouble. The Kommandant is very cross; very angry indeed. I do not know yet what he will do with you. Ah, I would not like to be in the Kommandant's shoes.'

Shaking a disapproving head, Pieber turned sorrowfully away.

The Kommandant didn't know what he was going to do with them either. They waited there another half-hour in the snow, and then a runner came in and spoke briefly to Pieber. The little Austrian turned to the shivering men.

'You can dismiss,' he said briefly, and they turned and ran off to their huts where the rest of the camp was waiting impatiently to hear all about the night's doings.

Von Lindeiner had wanted to send them to the cooler, but there wasn't enough room.

CHAPTER XVIII

*S*hortly after six o'clock that morning, the telephone from Sagan had called Oberregierungsrat Max Wielen out of his bed in Breslau. He was area chief of the Kriminal-polizei, and as soon as he realised the extent of the break, he ordered a Grossfahndung. That was the nationwide hue and cry, the highest search order in Germany.

The German radio broadcasted the news, and thousands of troops and auxiliaries turned out to search. Gestapo and Sicher-heitspolizei worked through all trains checking papers, searched vehicles on the roads, patrolled the roads, checked hotels and houses and farms. The warnings went out to to all the SS, Army, and Luftwaffe troops in the neigh-bourhood, and out from their homes for miles around came the old men and boys of the Landwehr and Landwacht (a sort of Home Guard) to watch over the fields and lanes. Far away in ports like Stettin and Danzig, the Kriegsmarine co-operated with the Gestapo and Polizei to prevent any escapees slipping across to Sweden as stowaways. Around the Czech, Swiss, Danish, and French borders the Grenzpolizei were alerted. For a hundred miles around Sagan itself the country was thick with searching Germans.

It developed into the greatest search in Germany during the war up to that time. Wielen, that morning, appointed Kriminal Kommissar Dr Absalon to inquire fully into the circumstances of the break and furnish a report.

After getting out of the tunnel, Marshall and Valenta had walked cautiously through the woods for ten minutes until they emerged from the trees. Their direction had been good. In front of them was a narrow road and directly opposite, beyond crisscrossing railway lines shining dimly in the dark, they saw Sagan station. They walked up and down looking for the entrance to the subway which, they had been told, led under the tracks to the booking office and platforms. Unfortunately a shed had been built over the subway entrance as a shelter from the weather, and it was unrecognisable in the dark from the description they had.

For some time they searched for the subway which was right under their noses. A couple more dark shapes emerged from the woods and then two more. They couldn't find the subway either, and before long there were a dozen or so tramping up and down looking for it. A couple of times Marshall heard muffled curses and once, distinctly, an angry English voice asking where the hell the bloody subway was. By the grace of God no Germans heard.

In desperation Marshall and Valenta pushed open the door of the shed to see what was there. A couple of trains had come and gone already, and then they heard the air raid sirens. They couldn't see anything in the darkness of the shed, and while they were wondering what to do a German poked his head around the door and flashed a torch on them.

'What are you doing here?' he asked. 'Don't you know the siren has gone and you must go to the shelter?'

Valenta mumbled something at him in German, and they brushed past out into the road again. There was only one train left that they could catch. It meant a dubious change of trains later on, and in any case the train might be held up by the air raid. If the escape were discovered early, the train was bound to be searched.

'It's not worth the risk,' Valenta said. 'Let's strike down on foot for Czechoslovakia. I know the way, and I can get help there fairly easily.'

They turned back into the woods, heading for the road that skipped the western boundary of the camp, found the road, and followed it till they were out of the camp area. They tried then to walk parallel to it across the fields, but it was too slushy and they had to go back to the roads and take the risk of running into Germans.

Well before dawn they came to the Breslau *Autobahn* running about twelve miles south of the camp, crossed over it, and as dawn broke sheltered deep in some woods. They stayed there shivering with cold all day and too keyed up to sleep. At dusk they pushed on along a lane and walked through a small village. At the other end three men suddenly loomed out of the darkness, and before they quite realised it a shotgun was pointing at them.

Valenta tried to bluff it out, but they started firing questions at Marshall then. Marshall knew little German and tried to bluff it out as a French worker, but one of the Germans spoke better French and the game was up. The Germans were so obviously expecting to meet the escaped prisoners that they had no chance. The Germans marched them back to the village and phoned for police from Halbau. Marshall knew then there was no hope of bluffing any further and managed to tread his passes, maps, and compass into the snow.

An hour later a police car arrived and drove them to a small jail. They pushed them into a tiny cell about seven feet square, and there they found Humphries, a slim Australian called Paul Royle, and Shorty Armstrong, whom they had seen last the previous night in 104. All three had been caught in much the same circumstances. Jammed in the cell like sardines they found a little comfort in the common predicament. At least it was warm there in contrast to the weather outside. They chewed at their hard rations, talked for a while, and then slept, exhausted.

At dawn the cell door swung open and half a dozen tough-looking men in police uniforms called them out, pushed them roughly into a car, and drove them back to Sagan over the road they had walked. Not to the compound, but to the civil jail, where they were interrogated and pushed into a large cell full of three-tier bunks.

During Marshall's interrogation the phone rang in the little office, and he heard a guard who answered repeat in German into the mouthpiece, 'Yes, yes. Six at Hirschberg, yes, and four at Danzig.'

It wasn't hard to guess what it meant.

They found the big cell bug-ridden and cold. It was a little surprising not to be taken back to the camp cooler, and a vague disquiet was growing in them. The door opened again after a while, and in came Ogilvy, Chaz Hall, and two other escapees. Like Marshall and company, they had been picked up by patrols south of the autobahn and found the Germans too suspicious to be bluffed.

Three times more during the day the door opened and more escapees were shoved in. It was the same story. They had tried to walk across the fields, but the snow and slush had forced them back onto the roads and into the hands of the patrols. By dusk there were nineteen of them. The guards gave them each two slices of black bread for the day, but no blankets.

Wings Day and Tobolski found the booking office hall on Sagan Station half full of escapees. A couple of hours earlier they'd all been chatting in 104, and now they were walking around not recognising each other. Day brushed shoulders with Kirby-Green and Kidder, who were travelling together, and the South Africans, Gouws and Stevens, and none of them even winked at each other.

In the train to Berlin, Day sat apart from Tobolski, but they joined up later and felt safer when they walked among the crowds in the Berlin streets. They had the address of a Dane living in Berlin, found him at his flat, and stayed there overnight. In the morning they didn't like the look of the Dane's German girl friend and spent the next two days in a bombed-out cellar. On the Monday they went to the Stettiner Bahnhof for a train to the Baltic port, and on the platform a man sidled up to Day, showed a police pass, and asked for his identity card.

Day showed it to him, feeling the sweat starting up all over him and the detective glanced casually, handed it back, and walked off. 'Unteroffizier' Tobolski brazenly got his soldbuch stamped for leave at the R.T.O.'s office. They reached Stettin safely and after a day there made successful contact with some Frenchmen in a labour camp. The Frenchmen took them into their barracks and promised to find some Swedish sailors for them.

They were waiting there in the morning when four German police burst in, and the leader demanded at once, 'Where are the Englishmen?'

Day and Tobolski tried bluff for a while, but five minutes later they were being marched off with hands in the air and guns in their backs.

*

MAP SHOWING LOCATION OF SAGAN AND ESCAPE ROUTES

The Dodger, travelling with Werner, accompanied the party of ten 'workmen,' including Pop Green, going by train to Hirschberg and then down to Czechoslovakia. All wearing cloth caps and dirty clothes, they got out of the train at dawn at a little station just before Hirschberg, and there they split up.

The Dodger and Werner set out to walk to Czechoslovakia, but it didn't take more than a couple of hours to see that the snow was going to beat them. They went to Hirschberg Station that night, had a little trouble getting their tickets, but collected them eventually and were sitting in the carriage waiting for the train to start when the police came through, looked very closely at their passes and said, '*Komm mit.*'

Taken to Gestapo headquarters, they found half a dozen old friends, Jimmy James, Pop Green, and some of the Poles. The Gestapo had the Poles standing with their faces to the wall, forbidden to move. After interrogation, they handcuffed the Dodger and pushed him into a cell.

Plunkett, the map maker, and Dvorack lost their new freedom on the station at Klattau (Czechoslovakia) because they did not have the right type of leave pass. Danny Krol and Sydney Dowse were nabbed in a barn near Oels. The Gestapo caught Van Wyeermisch in Berlin.

Neely got to Stettin, where some French slave labourers hid him in a hut at the rear of a hospital where they tried to find him a ship to Sweden. They came back and told him that police were combing the whole town. Soon after that police descended on the hospital, and Neely got out the back way as they were coming in the front door. He got to the station, caught a train to Munich, and miraculously avoided all identification checks on the way, but they picked him up in Munich Station when he arrived.

Tim's passes were good enough for ordinary times, but in that enormous grossfahndung you needed more than good papers. The Germans rounded up several thousand people and threw them into jail. Some were innocent and later released. Many more were German deserters or wandering slave labourers. Some were criminals, fugitives from justice for a variety of reasons. The net that spread out from Sagan gathered them all in.

One by one the Sagan escapees were rounded up, and a fortnight after the break, out of the seventy-six who had got clear of the tunnel, only three were still free. The Germans never did find them. Two were already in England; the third was on his way.

CHAPTER XIX

*A*t Berchtesgaden, on the Sunday morning, twenty-six hours after the break had been found, Hitler received the first full Gestapo report on it and flew into one of the rages that were becoming more frequent with him. Staying at Berchtesgaden at the time were Himmler, Goering, and Keitel. The Fuehrer called them into immediate conference and ordered that no minutes were to be taken of the meeting. There is not much doubt that by this time he knew what he was going to do. He had reached the state of mind that could deal with the escaping prisoner problem by one method only.

Keitel later reported that Hitler was 'very excited' as he told them what had happened. Himmler immediately blamed Keitel for it. It would take, he said bitterly, 70,000 police and God knows how many working hours to recapture the escapees. Goering blamed Keitel, too, and Keitel in turn blamed Himmler and Goering, and a heated three-cornered argument developed in front of the angry Hitler. Keitel said they were Air Force camps and therefore Goering's ultimate responsibility. He would not, he said, endure any more reproaches in the presence of the Fuehrer.

Hitler squashed the argument.

'They are all to be shot on recapture,' he said flatly.

As tactfully as he could, Goering protested – not, be it said, on grounds of humanity, but of practical politics.

To shoot them all, he explained, would make it quite obvious that it was murder. Besides, there might be reprisals taken on German prisoners in Allied hands.

Hitler apparently saw the logic of this.

'In that case,' he said, 'more than half of them are to be shot.'

Keitel and Himmler held a private conference afterwards to plan the shootings, and later that day Keitel saw Generalmajor Von Graevenitz, his staff officer in charge of prisoners of war, and told him that more than half of the recaptured prisoners were to be shot.

Von Graevenitz, a regular Wehrmacht officer, was disturbed by the news. 'We cannot just shoot these officers,' he said, and the angry Keitel shouted at him, 'The time has come for an example to be made, or we will not be able to cope with escapes. This ought to be such a shock that prisoners won't escape any more. Every prisoner must be told about it.'

That night Himmler spoke to his second in command, Kaltenbrunner, in Berlin, and in the morning Kaltenbrunner issued the text of what has since become known as the 'Sagan Order.'

'The increase of escapes by officer prisoners of war is a menace to internal security. I am indignant about the inefficient security measures. As a deterrent the Fuehrer has ordered that more than half the escaped officers are to be shot. Therefore I order that Kriminalpolizei are to hand over for interrogation to the Gestapo more than half of the recaptured officers. After interrogation the officers are to be taken in the direction of their original camp and shot en route. The shootings will be explained by the fact that the recaptured officers were shot while trying to escape, or because they offered resistance, so that nothing can be proved later. The Gestapo will report the shootings to the Kriminalpolizei giving this reason. In the event of future escapes my decision will be awaited as to whether the same procedure is to be adopted. Prominent personalities will be excepted. Their names will be reported to me and my decision awaited.'

SS-General Mueller, Berlin Gestapo chief, and General Nebe, Kriminalpolizei chief, sent for Wielen, and that night they showed the Sagan Order to the Breslau police chief and sent him back with orders that Oberregierungsrat Scharpwinkel, Gestapo chief in Breslau, was to form an execution squad to dispose of the escapees caught in the area.

Scharpwinkel appointed one of his trusted lieutenants, Obersekretaer

Lux, to head the squad, and he and Lux chose half a dozen men to help him.

In Berlin, General Nebe told Mertens, his secretary, to bring him the record cards of the recaptured prisoners. He sat at his desk looking at them and sorted them into two piles on his desk. Mertens remembers him looking at one card and saying, 'Der muss dran glauben' ('He is for it') and putting the card on the bigger pile in front of him. Later, looking at another, he said, 'He is so young. No.' And he put it on the other pile.

Nebe marked the cards on the larger pile with red crosses. Mertens said he was grimly excited and behaved 'uncontrollably.'

Top secret teleprint messages went out to Gestapo bureaux which had reported recapture of some of the escaped prisoners. The first message said simply, 'In five minutes a message will be coming over which is for the eyes of the senior official of the bureau only. No one else will be standing by the machine when it comes over.'

A few minutes later the teleprinters tapped out the main message. It ordered the shooting of the officers being held, as laid down by the Sagan Order, and commanded absolute secrecy.

They arrested Von Lindeiner on the Sunday morning, on Goering's orders. He was confined to his room. Pieber reported later in the compound that he had gone to bed with a heart attack. That same morning Von Lindeiner heard that some of the escaped prisoners had been lodged in Sagan Civil Jail. He rang Dr Absalon and asked that they be returned to the camp. Absalon refused insultingly. He said he wouldn't take any orders from Von Lindeiner because Von Lindeiner had been relieved of his post.

About midnight on the Monday night the nineteen men huddled on the bug-ridden bunks in the big community cell at Sagan Jail heard tramping feet outside; the door swung open and in walked a collection of sinister-looking men who bashed them to their feet with tommyguns. The newcomers were all in civilian clothes, but it was a kind of uniform dress: they all wore heavy overcoats with belts and had black felt hats pulled down over their eyes. Marshall thought they looked like Hollywood's typical gangsters.

They prodded the nineteen outside and herded them into the back of a big covered-in truck which shortly moved off. Marshall thought they were being taken back to the camp, which was only a mile or so away, but the truck kept going, and he soon realised that they were on their way somewhere else. He thought it might be to another camp, and Valenta asked one of the guards who was sitting by the tailboard, nursing his tommygun and morosely surveying them. For answer he got a grunt and an ugly look. They could not see much outside the truck, and it was quite dark anyway so they just sat there quietly and not very happily.

It was nearly 3 a.m. when someone up by the tailboard said he thought he could see houses on each side, and soon he reported that they were running over a cobbled road and seemed to be in a largish town. The truck slowed and passed under what looked to be a stone arch, and a few yards further on it braked to a stop.

The guards piled out shouting 'Raus! Raus!' and formed a cordon around them as they dropped one by one over the tailboard. In the darkness they could dimly see they were in a cobbled courtyard surrounded on all sides by stone walls about three storeys high, pierced by little windows. There were bars over the windows. Evidently they were in a jail. Not so good!

At gunpoint, the guards herded them through a door, along gloomy stone corridors, and up a couple of flights of stairs. At the top they were pushed, four at a time, into tiny cells about six by nine feet. Three-quarters of the floor space in each cell was taken up by a wooden platform about a foot high. That was supposed to be the communal cell bed. Exhausted and hungry, the fours in each cell crowded together on the platforms for warmth and slept fitfully.

Crashing doors woke them at first light, and guards brought in their breakfast, a thin slice of black bread and a cup of ersatz mint tea, cold and horrible. No milk. No sugar. Funnily enough everyone was in fairly high spirits. They hadn't the faintest idea what was going to happen, and for the time being anyway, they didn't let it bother them.

They inspected the new quarters. Not much to see. Four bare stone walls of dirty white, a concrete floor, thick steel door, and high up in the walls a small window, heavily barred. Looking at the window they could see that the walls were nearly two feet thick. It wasn't very cold just then, and they relaxed on the wooden platforms and started yarning about their experiences since they crawled out of the tunnel. It was the first decent chance they'd had to talk, and in lighthearted accounts of their adventures their spirits rose further and they passed an uneventful, though hungry, day.

There wasn't room in the tiny cells for the usual bucket that served as a latrine in Nazi prisons, but if they banged long enough on the door a guard came eventually and took them to a bucket down the corridor.

The corridor reminded Paul Royle of a submarine – it was narrow, dank, and grey with the forbidding steel doors inset at intervals. The only people they saw for a while were drab-uniformed warders carrying bunches of enormous keys for the old-fashioned locks. All of them were unfriendly.

Later on a doddering old German and a little Polish boy, a slave worker aged about fourteen, came around and perfunctorily cleaned the cells out. Marshall tried to get the boy to talk, but he didn't seem to understand and the only thing he said, with a sidelong glance toward the door, was '*Deutschland Kaput.*' Supper consisted of two slices of black bread and a bowl of watery soup. They felt just as hungry afterwards.

Valenta was getting worried but trying not to show it. Only Marshall knew that Valenta had done intelligence work before he joined the RAF Valenta knew the Nazis rather better than the others. None of them slept well that night.

In the morning guards several times entered the cells and took out one prisoner at a time. No one knew where, or why, and nerves were getting a little edgy. In the afternoon a guard came and took Paul Royle out, escorted him downstairs, out into the courtyard, under the archway, and into the street. It was the first time Royle had walked openly in daylight in a street for four years, and after the confinement of the cells he felt exhilarated just to be looking at people and houses. It seemed a big town, and the guard, who was friendly enough, told him it was Goerlitz, about forty miles south of Sagan and not far from the Czech border.

They walked half a mile, and the guard prodded him into a grey stone building about four storeys high and took him up several flights of stairs and into an office where a villainous-looking interpreter with a strong American accent told him to stand up and answer questions. Behind a desk sat an elderly grey-haired man who put the queries through the interpreter.

The questions seemed harmless enough – 'Where were you heading?' 'What were your plans?' 'Where is all your equipment . . . compass and maps?' 'What sabotage directions did you receive?' 'What information were you to collect on the way?'

Royle answered simply and as disarmingly as he could. He denied, with a faint smile, that he had had any sabotage directions or intentions to collect information. He had just been four years behind the wire, he said, and he was sick of it. He suggested that the interrogator might feel the same if the positions were reversed.

The interrogator seemed like some sort of civil police official. He did not seem particularly hostile, and after a while he said to the interpreter, 'This man is obviously all right.' Royle knew just enough German to understand the words and began to feel a little better. The guard took him out after a while and back to the jail, but this time he was put in a different cell.

As every man returned from his interrogation he was put in a different cell, where he found other prisoners whom he had not seen since the night of the break. Evidently there were more of the escapees held there than the nineteen from Sagan Jail.

The interrogations went on for four days. Marshall had a bad time. The men who questioned him were much more hostile than those who saw Royle. As soon as he was pushed into the interrogation room, a heavy-featured English-speaking German got up from a chair, walked heavily across the room, stopped six inches from him, stuck his face out till it was almost touching Marshall's, and said ominously, 'You'll never see your wife and children again.'

Not an encouraging start but so obviously meant to intimidate that Marshall became very much on his guard and decided to play dumb. The interrogator behind the desk was a brisk, businesslike man who shot his questions out curtly. Marshall replied innocently to the same innocuous questions that Royle had been asked, and then the interrogator started insisting on knowing what Marshall had done with his papers.

'Papers?' Marshall asked, stalling and playing dumb as hard as he could.

'The papers you got in the camp,' the interrogator said dryly. 'You got papers, didn't you?'

'Heavens yes,' Marshall said. 'The *Voelkischer Beobachter* – that's Goering's paper, isn't it? – the *Deutsche Allgemeine Zeitung* and the . . .'

'No,' snapped the interpreter. ' Forged papers and identity cards. Don't be stupid. What did you do with them?'

Marshall looked surprised.

'Did the others have them?' he asked. 'Lord, I wish I'd had some. Where did they get them? How could they possibly have got hold of identity cards—' and he rattled on and on. He talked garrulously and aimlessly, misunderstanding some questions, deflecting others, and branching off onto new subjects, trying as hard as he could to give the impression of an amiable and voluble pinhead. It was the same when they asked him about maps. (He'd had several good detailed maps.)

'Map?' he said. 'Yes, I had a map. I made it myself from a war map of Europe in the *Voelkischer Beobachter*. It wasn't very good. I think that's why I was caught . . .' and off he went again on a long monologue.

The same with his clothes. He was wearing one of Tommy Guest's suits, and it was one of Guest's best efforts, dyed dark grey, and it had been topped off by a ski cap till they took his cap away.

'Of course you realise,' said the interpreter, 'you can be shot as a spy for wearing civilian clothes around Germany.'

'Oh, this is only a uniform I changed about,' Marshall said, beginning to feel uncomfortable. 'See, I recut it, put boot polish on it, and changed the buttons.'

'That's a civilian suit,' the interpreter said.

Marshall denied it again and tried to show where he had altered it. 'Bring in someone who knows about cloth, and they'll tell you it isn't a proper suit.'

The interrogator pressed a button on his desk, and his stenographer walked through the door from an adjoining room. The brusque man behind the desk pointed to Marshall and spoke to her in German, telling her, apparently, to examine Marshall's clothes. She stood in front of Marshall diffidently rubbing the cloth of his coat between bony fingers and looking at the seams inside. She was a gaunt, unhappy-looking woman, nudging the forty mark, with untidy grey hair and long features like a tired horse.

Covered by her head from the interrogator, Marshall smiled into her eyes, and faintly surprised, she smiled back. Turning to the man behind the desk, she said they were not proper civilian clothes but – demonstrating with her fingers – had seams where one usually found them on uniforms. She left the room, and Marshall answered more questions, but his diarrhoea of words exasperated the German so much that he slapped the desk with his hand and called the guard from outside, and Marshall was taken back to the jail.

After four days when everyone had been questioned, the prisoners were all depressed. They had no idea what was going to happen to them and could get no clues at all from the hostile wardens. Hunger was worrying them all the time, as they only got three or four thin slices of black bread a day and a little thin soup. By the fourth day there were hardly three words spoken an hour in any cell. There didn't seem to be anything more to say, and there was nothing to do except lie there and think about food and what might happen to them.

A warden caught one of them standing on someone's shoulders and looking out of the window. He hauled him roughly down and told them that the next man who looked out of the window would be shot. On the fourth afternoon, after all the sorting-out process of prisoners leaving one cell and being put back in another, Marshall found himself in the same cell as Royle, Ogilvy, and McDonald, a Scot with a patient and prematurely lined face.

In the morning they heard tramping along the corridor, and there was the sound of abrupt voices. Down the corridor cell doors were opening and there were sounds of shuffling feet as prisoners walked out. Ogilvy banged on the door till the guards came to take him to the latrine bucket, and on the way down he saw six of the prisoners being escorted out by several heavily armed men.

One of the prisoners was limping a little behind the others. It was Al Hake, and Ogilvy managed to whisper a few words to him. Hake said he had frostbitten feet. He thought they were going for another interrogation, and then the guards shouted angrily down the corridor and broke up the conversation.

'By God, they're plug-uglies,' Ogilvy told the others when he got back to the cell. 'Look like the same bunch that brought us from Sagan – same coats and black hats over their eyes. Must be Gestapo.'

One of them risked a bullet by standing up and looking out of the window and saw the six, surrounded by the guards, standing in the courtyard below. He watched as they climbed into the back of a covered truck, followed by the guards, and then the truck moved off and rolled out through the archway.

The next morning the four in Marshall's cell heard more tramping feet and shouting in the corridor and more cell doors opening. They heard another party shuffling down the corridor and, looking out of the window again, saw ten more of their prisoners below herded into a covered truck with guards. They sat around all day tensely waiting their turn, but no one came for them. That evening when the cell door opened and a warden brought in their cabbage water and bread Marshall saw a big 'S' had been chalked on the door.

'Good show,' he said. 'S for *Sagan*. That must mean we're going back to the camp.'

'Maybe it means S for *schiessen*' (shoot), said one of the others dryly, and there was a slightly hollow laugh.

That evening three Luftwaffe guards arrived in the jail and slept the night in the room opposite them. They told the four prisoners they were taking them back to Sagan in the morning. It was true. About 9 a.m., the cell door opened and the Luftwaffe guards escorted them down to the station and took them by train back to Sagan where they were pushed into the cooler for three weeks. This time it wasn't solitary confinement. The cooler was so full that everyone had company in his cell.

After a couple of days they found out who else was in the cooler – Rees, Noble, Baines, Hutson, Reavell Carter, Langlois, Trent, McBride, and several other naughty boys, but none of the sixteen whom they had seen taken away in trucks from Goerlitz Jail.

CHAPTER XX

It was curiously quiet in north compound for a week after the break. We woke up every morning waiting for reprisals, and none came. It was a faintly unnatural atmosphere as the days passed, and we wondered what was going to happen to us. And on the seventh day the Gestapo arrived to search the camp – about six of them, hard-faced citizens who walked into the compound and looked at us coldly.

They hadn't come across Air Force prisoners before, which probably accounts for their innocence. Presumably they'd only dealt with their own population and the nameless victims they collected in their dungeons – people too terrified and in no position to differ with them. We were, I suppose, privileged (if you could call it privilege). So long as we didn't stick a nose over the warning wire or make public reference to Hitler's ancestry, the Luftwaffe doled out the black bread and potatoes and didn't go around the compound squirting tommy-guns just for the hell of it. We were still under the Luftwaffe and generally outside the orbit of the Gestapo, and Goering wanted it kept that way.

The Gestapo curtly brushed aside any help from the ferrets and said they'd do the searches their own way. They let it be known, according to Eichacher, that they didn't regard the ferrets as being either intelligent or efficient.

They dumped their coats and hats in the entrances of the huts and prowled around the rooms, emerging now and then with some of the nails we'd pulled out of the walls or a lump of iron they didn't think we should have. These they piled beside their coats, and as they vanished again into the rooms one of the boys reached around the hut door and took away anything we particularly wanted to keep. I don't think it ever occurred to the Gestapo that anyone would do that to them.

It seemed to be so successful that he got a little more daring and swiped one of the Gestapo hats. A couple more people joined in the game, and the idea seemed to snowball. One of them, with more zeal than discretion, rummaged in the pocket of one of the Gestapo overcoats and rushed up to Canton a minute later, grinning all over his face. He pulled his hand out of his jacket where he had been holding it like Napoleon, and there he was holding a little automatic pistol.

Unbidden, a little squawk of horror came out of the onlookers' throats.

'For God's sake,' said Conk, 'put it back. Put it back. You're making it too hot. You'll start 'em shooting.'

Nervously the man replaced the pistol, and luckily for him he wasn't spotted. The Gestapo went off eventually, taking nothing we had particularly wanted to keep but leaving behind in the 'X' secret cupboards a hat, two scarves, some gloves, another torch, and some Gestapo papers. I imagine they were too embarrassed when they found out to do anything about it. Besides it would have caused German casualties. All the ferrets would have died, laughing.

They descended on the other compounds then, both British and American, and searched them, presumably more cautiously, but again finding nothing of importance. Lamentably they were faced with failure of their mission, an unthinkable disgrace; so, in Gestapo fashion, they decided to search their own people in the kommandantur.

And, behold! Success at last! They unearthed a little black-market organisation involving – you'll never guess – Von Lindeiner and Von Masse. A Luftwaffe major who flew transport aircraft used to bring in choice wines and foods from Denmark, and they had a little store of the stuff under the kommandantur cookhouse. We heard that a German who wasn't in on the game split on them to the Gestapo. Von Lindeiner was removed for court-martial.

The Gestapo got three more victims in their stay. They could not understand how we had obtained eight hundred feet of electric cable for the lighting system in 'Harry.' Being Gestapo, they could think of only one thing. Someone had betrayed the Reich. They looked through the inventories of the camp electricians and found that eight hundred feet of cable had been lost. Too late for the electricians to protest that the cable had been stolen from them while their backs were turned. The Gestapo, soaked in suspicion for years, took the two electricians and also the chief electrician, who had been too scared to report the loss of the wire, and they shot all three.

A new Kommandant arrived. His name, we heard, was Oberst Braune, but we didn't see him in north compound. The expected reprisals came a couple of days later. He shut the camp theatre, put on three appells a day, and refused to let us have Red Cross boxes or food tins. There seemed to be something wrong somewhere. These were only pinpricks. After thinking about it for a while we concluded that the new Kommandant wasn't going to extremes, probably, because his own personal reputation had not been affected by the break.

Rubberneck was still around, having successfully talked himself out of trouble. According to a voluble ferret, Rubberneck had claimed that we must have finished the tunnel months before and bided our time to break it. We couldn't have dug it recently because we couldn't have dispersed the sand. They had found none under the huts, and we couldn't have put it on the snow. It must have been dug at the same time as 'Tom,' said Rubberneck.

And how, inquired Dr Absalon, could so many people get into Block 104 on the night of the break without being detected? Rubberneck said we must have dug small tunnels from near-by blocks leading into 104. To prove it, he put on several surprise searches of the near-by huts, which proved, of course, nothing but gave time for official wrath to subside.

After the unfortunate effects of blowing up 'Tom,' they didn't quite know for a while how to destroy 'Harry,' but settled it finally by pouring sewage from the honey wagons down the 104 end, sealing it with concrete, and then blowing up the other end. Rubberneck resumed his patrolling of the compound with a churlish glitter in his eye, though no one bothered very much about that except the other ferrets who became more prudent in their lead-swinging.

We heard that Marshall, Ogilvy, Royle, and McDonald had arrived in the cooler. Jennens saw Pop Green and Poynter going into the cooler too. Then eight more were reported in the cells, having returned, it was said, from a town south of Sagan called Goerlitz. Next we heard Neely was locked up there. That made fifteen returned out of the seventy-six who had got clear of the tunnel. It was puzzling; hard to believe that only ten had been caught, considering the tough conditions for the hardarsers. We assumed that some had been purged to other camps – perhaps to Koldtiz Strafelager.

A fortnight after the break it seemed that things were more or less normal again. The thaw had come and people were pounding the circuit without their greatcoats, revelling in the crisp air. With spring we were expecting the invasion almost any moment, and invasion meant the end of the war. We were just beginning to understand that release, some day, might actually become a reality instead of a dream.

On a morning in early April, Pieber walked into the compound, went straight to Massey's room, and saluted politely. Would the Group Captain be good enough to wait on the new Kommandant in the kommandantur at 11 a.m., bringing his official interpreter.

'What does he want?' asked Massey. 'Is he going to announce more reprisals against us?'

Pieber's face was unusually solemn as he answered.

'I cannot tell you, Group Captain Massey, but it is something very terrible.'

That rumour spread round the compound. No one worried very much. There had been fifty rumours since the break, some of them much worse than this one, and anyway Pieber was an old woman!

Just before eleven o'clock, Massey was escorted out of the gate with his personal interpreter, Squadron Leader Wank Murray. They were kept waiting only a few moments in the kommandantur, and then they were shown into the Kommandant's office, a normal barrack room, but with a carpet, a leather chair, a large desk, and on the wall behind it the standard décor of Luftwaffe offices – photographs of Hitler and Goering.

Oberst Braune was standing behind his desk, a fairly tall man of about fifty with a lined, rather sad and patient face, fair, thinning hair and the Iron Cross, first class, on his left breast pocket. Usually, when the Kommandant and the Senior British Officer met officially, there was a formal handshake and the usual military courtesies. This time, no handshake. Braune gave a stiff, slight bow and indicated to the two officers that they were to sit on two chairs that had been placed by the desk. Simoleit and Pieber were standing beside the desk and looking at the carpet.

The Kommandant stood up very straight and spoke in German.

'I have been instructed by my higher authority to communicate to you this report . . .' He paused and Murray translated so far to Massey. Braune continued: 'The Senior British Officer is to be informed that as a result of a tunnel from which seventy-six officers escaped from Stalag Luft III, north compound, forty-one of these officers have been shot while resisting arrest or attempting further escape after arrest.'

Murray felt himself going red in the face. Unbelieving, he asked, 'How many were shot?'

'Forty-one,' the Kommandant replied. Murray slowly translated the passage to Massey.

Massey listened in silence and made almost no sign that he was hearing except that he stiffened slightly in his chair and the lines of his face tightened. At the finish he said briefly, 'How many were shot?'

Wank answered, 'Forty-one.' He felt his face was bright crimson and the scene in the room seemed unreal.

There was a long heavy silence. It dragged on and on as they waited for Massey to do something, and Massey just sat there looking unseeing in front of him. The tension was nearly unbearable when he raised his eyes slowly and turned them on Murray.

'Ask him,' he said, 'how many were wounded.'

Murray put the question to the Kommandant. The German looked uncertainly at a paper on his desk and then looked out of the window. He hesitated and then said, 'My higher authority only permits me to read this paper and not to answer any questions or give any further information.'

Massey said doggedly, 'Ask him again how many were wounded.'

The Kommandant looked painfully uncomfortable. He looked out of the window and then down to his desk, trying to make up his mind, and after another hesitation he slowly said, 'I think no one was wounded.'

'No one wounded?' said Massey, his voice rising a little. 'Do you mean to tell me forty-one can be shot in those circumstances and that all were killed and no one was wounded?'

'I am to read you this report,' the Kommandant said, 'and that is all I can do.'

Simoleit and Pieber had not taken their eyes off the carpet.

Massey asked for the names of the dead.

'I cannot give them to you,' Braune said. 'I have not got them. I have only this report which I am to read to you.'

'I would like to have the names as soon as it is possible to get them,' said Massey.

'Yes, I will do that,' the Kommandant answered, and then, after another little hesitation he added more quickly, holding a hand up, palm out in a slightly appealing way, 'I must remind you that I am acting under orders and may only divulge what I am instructed to by my higher authority.'

'What is this higher authority?' Massey asked.

Braune made a futile little gesture.

'Just higher authority,' he said.

'I require to know what has happened to the bodies so that I can arrange for burial and the disposal of their effects,' Massey said. 'I demand that the Protecting Power also be informed.'

The Kommandant said that this would be done. He would let the Senior British Officer have every possible scrap of information as soon as he received it, but reminded him again he was always limited in action by 'higher authority.'

He rose to his feet. 'I think that is all, gentlemen.' Stiffly the two British officers withdrew, and as they emerged into the fresh air again Massey said to Murray, 'Don't mention this dreadful thing to anyone till I have released it in the compound.'

Murray still felt his face was crimson. Neither man felt like speaking, and Massey's face was grimly set. On the way back to the barbed wire Pieber joined them. He seemed nervous and distressed, and said in a low voice, 'Please do not think that the Luftwaffe had anything to do with this dreadful thing. We do not wish to be associated with it. It is terrible . . . terrible.'

Pieber at times may have been a hypocrite, but he wasn't this time. He was a shaken man.

Half an hour later, back in the compound, Massey sent word around asking the senior officer in every room to report to the camp theatre for an announcement. With the order came a rumour that 'something dreadful' had happened. We were a little uneasy but it was only another rumour. We thought it meant reprisals were going to start in earnest – possibly we were going to lose Red Cross food parcels for a while. God knows that would be serious enough. German rations were just enough to ensure starvation in its most prolonged and unpleasant form.

About three hundred officers crowded into the theatre for the announcement. Massey walked onto the stage, waited a few seconds while the rustling died down, and then spoke without preamble.

'Gentlemen, I have just come from a meeting with the Kommandant in which he told me the unbelievable, the shocking news that forty-one of the officers who escaped from the tunnel on the twenty-fourth of March have been shot.'

There was a stunned silence. A lot of people felt suddenly sick.

Massey went on to describe the meeting briefly. He would announce the names of the victims as soon as they were available. Just now there was little more that he could say. There would be a memorial service on the coming Sunday.

Still in a stunned silence, we filed out of the theatre, and within two minutes the news had spread to everyone in the compound. Horror lay over the camp. Mass murder was something new in the quiet backwater of prison camp, however unpleasant the life was. A lot of us wouldn't believe it. 'I know the Huns are murderous bastards,' said a man in my room, 'but they've never been game so far to murder British or American people openly in mass, and I can't see their point in starting that sort of thing on relatively harmless prisoners.'

It about summed up the feeling. I suppose if the truth be known we wouldn't believe it because we didn't want to believe it. The mind builds its own defences. Most of us thought that the whole thing was a bluff, that the forty-one had been moved to another camp, and that we, believing they were dead, would be intimidated into stopping all escape activity. But there was no getting away from the fact that it had been officially announced. We held a memorial service, and every man in the compound sewed a little black diamond on his sleeve.

The Kommandant was afraid there might be some sort of demonstration or revolt and ordered all the guards to be more watchful than usual – more ruthless if they had to be. When some of us were a little slow getting into our hut at lock-up time, a sentry in a goon-box sent a spray of bullets over our heads and a couple more zipping around our feet, kicking up little spurts of dust.

The air raid siren went one afternoon, a lovely sound. We got more kick out of watching American Fortresses draw their vapour trails across the sky than we ever got out of a barrel of raisin wine. The Germans knew it and ordered that whenever the sirens went we must run into our huts and pull the black-out shutters across so we couldn't see anything. Some of us were a little slow getting inside when the siren went that afternoon, and one of the guards running in emptied his pistol magazine at us. He was a rotten shot, but several people sitting in their room in 109 jumped smartly out of the way when a couple of bullets ploughed through their wooden wall. They drew rings around the bullet holes with a pencil and labelled them, 'Easter Eggs, Sagan, 1944.'

A couple of minute after that, a guard got an American sergeant standing innocently in the doorway of his hut in the next compound. The bullet went in his mouth and he died instantly. It was not exactly unprecedented for a guard to kill one of the boys, but it was an unfortunate time for another killing. Some of that nice insulation we had wrapped around our minds began to wear thin; the people who believed the forty-one were still alive grew fewer and fewer.

At dusk one day Eichacher pinned a piece of paper on the notice board. Someone passing looked at it casually and gave a shout. 'Here are the names!' And in seconds there was a crowd around the board. For the benefit of those at the back a man yelled for silence and slowly read them out. There were little gasps and curses behind as people heard their friends named.

Someone said, 'That isn't forty-one! It's forty-seven.'

A dozen people checked his count. He was right. Forty-seven!

It was a terrible list. Roger Bushell was on it. That wasn't unexpected. The ever-courteous Tim Walenn was on it. So were Gordon Brettell, Henri Picard, Birkland, Casey, Willy Williams, Al Hake, Chaz Hall, Tom Kirby-Green, Johnny Stower, Valenta and Humphries, who had been caught with Royle. Denys Street was on it, too. He was the son of the British Permanent Under-Secretary For Air. The Germans certainly hadn't been discriminating.

Faced with the names we got back that stunned horror. Some of them were only kids, a year or two out of school. People stood about talking it over almost in whispers. Some still wouldn't believe it wasn't a bluff. Germany had been the first nation, in 1929, to sign the Geneva Convention, which lays it down that escape attempts from prison camps are quite legitimate and are not to be punished harshly.

A couple of days later another list was pinned to the board. It was a short one, just including the names of three more who had been shot – Tobolski, Cookie Long, and Danny Krol. It brought the names up to the round figure of fifty. It was noted that, with the exception of two Czechs, every non-Briton who had escaped had been reported shot.

A few days later a group of prisoners who had been badly wounded when they were shot down were taken out of the compound for repatriation to England. Massey was among them. About two hours before they left the compound the Germans called for all the kit of the fifty and took it all away.

It must have been rather senseless bluff. They knew the repatriates would tell everything they knew of the shootings when they got home, and presumably the Germans thought that the demand for the kit of the fifty would indicate that they had not, after all, been shot but removed to another camp.

None of it seemed to make sense. We'd been worrying ourselves sick over it for weeks when the few escapees who had returned came out of the cooler and back into the compound. We pumped them for news, and they, dazed by our news, wouldn't believe the others were dead. Some of them had seen them taken from the cells at Goerlitz, presumably for another interrogation. They were perfectly all right then. It must be a bluff.

There didn't seem to be any common factor in the shootings. Why shoot some and send others back? Al Hake had had badly frostbitten feet and was in no condition to try to escape again. Yet he'd been shot. And no one was wounded. So they certainly hadn't been shot trying to escape again. We began to think once more it must be a bluff.

And then the Germans brought back the kit of the fifty that they had taken on the morning the repatriates left. A couple of days after that, they brought in some of the personal belongings of the missing fifty – photographs, and things like that. Some of them were bloodstained.

A fortnight later it was all put beyond doubt. The Kommandant informed the new SBO, Group Captain Wilson, that there had been delivered to him the urns carrying the ashes of the fifty. No need to ask why they had been cremated. It destroys the evidence of the manner of death.

Engraved on each urn was the locality where death had occurred. Four were engraved 'Danzig,' and just four of the escapees had been making for Danzig. Four were marked 'Hirschberg,' two more with the name of a town near the French border. There were several from Leignitz and a lot from Breslau. Still we couldn't find any common factor in the shootings. The only clue was the round number of fifty. It was pretty clear they'd just taken fifty and shot them as an example. God knows that was logical enough under Hitler.

There was only one bright point in the whole affair. Bit by bit we pieced together information brought in by the tame guards and eventually established the fact that the rather staggering figure of 5,000,000 Germans had spent some of their time looking for the prisoners, and many thousands of them were on the job full time for weeks. That meant that the break was some sort of success, if one could overlook the heavy cost.

The Kommandant got us some stone and let a working party go to a near-by cemetery to build a vault for the urns. There was already a row of graves in that cemetery where other victims from the camp had been buried.

Fifty were dead. Fifteen were back with us. We wondered what had become of the other eleven.

CHAPTER XXI

I n June a letter came in the prisoners' mail signed with two prearranged fictitious names. Rocky Rockland and Jens Muller had made it back to England, via Sweden.

They had got to Kustrin, near Frankfurt on Oder, the morning after the break and changed trains there. By evening they were in Stettin. Everything went smoothly. They met some Swedish sailors whose ship was about to sail for home, and the sailors took them on board and hid them. The Germans checked the ship before it sailed but did not find the stowaways. At dawn the next day they landed in Sweden, and a few days later the RAF flew them back to England. It was the perfect escape.

Weeks later another letter arrived signed with another fictitious name. Bob Van Der Stok had made it too.

Van Der Stok, Number 18 out of the tunnel, had travelled alone, wearing a dark-blue Australian Air Force greatcoat, Dutch naval trousers and a beret. As he came out of the woods by the station, a German soldier stopped him and asked him curtly who he was and where he thought he was going. Before the shaken Van Der Stok could answer, he went on, 'Don't you know there's an air raid on? You should be in a shelter.'

'I know,' Van Der Stok apologised, 'but I am a Dutch worker and do not know where the shelter is.'

'Well, you'd better come with me,' the soldier said. 'You'll be all right. The police won't touch you because I'm an armed guard from the prison camp back there.'

Van Der Stok went with him, feeling most peculiar, praying he wouldn't be recognised. The guard took him right into the station booking hall and left him with an amiable smile. He bought his ticket to Breslau, looked around and recognised several prisoners from the camp standing around. He thought it would be safer to get into conversation with a German and began talking to a girl standing near by. She shook him considerably by telling him she was a censor from the camp and on duty at the station watching for officers trying to escape.

After a while she called a German military policeman and asked him to question two men of whom she was suspicious. She pointed to Kirby-Green and Kidder. The policeman crossed to them, and they started talking fast in Spanish and waving their hands. After a while the policeman came back to the girl and said she needn't worry. They were only Spanish workers. Van Der Stok was sweating.

He was thankful the train to Breslau was so full that he could only just squeeze himself in. It meant the security police couldn't walk through it checking papers. By 4 a.m. he was in Breslau and, producing his papers at the booking office, bought a ticket all the way through to Holland. On the station he counted ten other escapees. There was no trouble going to Dresden where he changed trains, and at Halle he changed again to a through train for Holland. The journey took thirteen hours, and every four hours the Gestapo walked through checking the papers of every passenger. The funny thing was that the Germans, including the soldiers, had much more trouble than Van Der Stok. One poor little gefreiter who had one stamp missing from his pass was handed over to the military police.

At the Dutch border the Gestapo peered very closely at his papers but again he was completely unsuspected. He got off at Utrecht and found some old friends who sheltered him. It was just thirty-six hours after he had left the tunnel.

He waited six weeks in Holland till the Dutch underground fathered him to the south of Holland and smuggled him into Belgium across the Maas in a skiff. On the other side they gave him a bicycle and he pedalled to Brussels, to a Dutch family, and lived with them another six weeks before the underground could get him on a train for Paris, travelling now as a Flemish employee of a big Belgian firm. It was just before the invasion and during an 'alert' they stopped outside a station on the way. Just as well. A formation of American Fortresses pattern-bombed it and wiped it out.

He had been told to make for Toulouse, and at St Lazare Station in Paris, where he bought his ticket, they told him he must get it stamped at German control in the station.

He took it to the German who said, 'You must have a special permit to go to Toulouse before I can stamp this.'

'I've got a permit,' Van Der Stok said. 'Otherwise how could I have got my ticket?'

'Oh,' said the German, 'of course,' and stamped it.

In Toulouse Van Der Stok found a group of guides who were taking refugees across the Pyrenees – for a price. He sold his watch for 10,000 francs, handed the money over, and was taken to a farm high up in the mountains. Three days later he walked to the rendezvous on a hill and down the road saw a German barrier with sentries and machine guns. Standing watching, he saw the car with his guide and three other men race toward the post, and as it got near, the men in the car opened up with Sten guns and shot their way through, killing all the sentries. A moment later they drove into machine-gun fire from another German post down the road, and the car stopped and burst into flames. No one got out.

At the farm there were now twenty-seven of them stranded – two Dutchmen, two American pilots, two Canadians and twenty-one German Jews. That night Van Der Stok made contact with a band of Maquis on a near-by hill. They provided another guide. The Maquis did not trust the refugees. On the way to the frontier the refugees walked in single file, four Maquis just behind them with Sten guns.

The Maquis stopped after a while and pointed to a saddle back in the mountains.

'Beyond that,' they said, 'is Spain. Good luck,' and left them.

A few days later, Van Der Stok was in Madrid. The British Consul sent him on to Gibraltar, and he was flown back to England. It was just four months since he had crawled out of the tunnel.

So eight were still missing. It wasn't till after the war we found out what had happened to them. Plunkett and the two Czechs, Tonder and Dvorack, were sweating it out in Czech concentration camps. The Gestapo had arrested all of Tonder's relatives. Van Wyeermisch was held in another concentration camp. The Gestapo shot his father in Belgium.

Wings Day and Tobolski had been taken to the police chief in Stettin. He was an affable man and told them they had been caught through a young Frenchman in the labour camp where they had sheltered. The young Frenchman had got 1,000 marks for betraying them.

'That's a bloody dirty trick,' said Wings, disgusted. 'I'd like to wring his neck.'

'Don't worry about that,' said the police chief, who was a very practical man. 'When we've no more use for him, we'll tip off his friends about him. They'll wring his neck for you.'

Day and Tobolski were taken by train to Berlin, and there, on Stettiner Bahnhof, Tobolski was taken away and Wings didn't see him again.

They took Day to Kriminalpolizei headquarters and escorted him into an office where a thin-lipped, white-haired man covered in braid and badges (it was General Nebe) said to him, 'You've been giving us a lot of trouble.'

'It's my duty to escape,' Wings said.

'Well, we're sending you where you won't give any more trouble.'

Wings thought it was a polite way of telling him that he was to be shot, and did not feel very comfortable when he was taken out and put in a car. They drove for an hour and pulled up outside a high stone wall that encircled Sachsenhausen Concentration Camp north of Berlin. Day was pushed into a small compound close inside the wall, and there he found the Dodger, Dowse, and James. In the same compound were some Irish soldiers (always fighting), some Russian generals, Italian orderlies, and a British commando, Major Jack Churchill.

There were no ferrets in the compound. They had never been needed. No one had ever escaped from Sachsenhausen, except horizontally in a wooden box. Two weeks later, the five Britons started tunnelling, without telling any of the others, because they were not sure they could trust them and there would have been an enormous row if the tunnel had been found.

They cut a trap under Dowse's bed and worked in the dark all the time as in the first tunnel at Dulag. No such luxuries as fat lamps at Sachsenhausen. The soil was firm, unlike the sandy stuff at Sagan, so they didn't have to shore it, which was just as well because there was nothing to shore it with. There were also, as far as they knew, no microphones buried around the wire, so they were able to make it shallow, running about six feet deep.

Appell was at 6 a.m., and one man went below immediately afterward and dug. The others dispersed the sand under the hut. The tunnel wouldn't have lasted a week at Sagan, but at Sachsenhausen, free of ferrets, they kept at it for four months until in August it was nearly a hundred feet long and they calculated they were outside the compound wire. Their security had been perfect. The other people in the little compound still didn't dream that the tunnel existed.

Then Day came across a sheet from a weeks-old German newspaper in the latrine, and his blood literally seemed to run cold as he read a story at the top of the page, a report of the fifty from Sagan being shot trying to escape again or avoid recapture.

The five of them held a grim little meeting in Dowse's room. It was not a long meeting, and the vote was to take a chance and carry on. Having taken the tunnel so far, they couldn't bear the thought of not using it. It was rather a courageous vote.

They waited for a suitable time, and early in September there was a moonless night with the added cover of a drizzle of rain. About 11 p.m. they surfaced outside the wire, helped each other over the nine-foot outer wall, and dispersed into the darkness.

Wings Day, the old campaigner, still had a little of his money left from the Sagan break. He had sewed it into his coat, and the Gestapo had not found it. One of the Irish soldiers in the compound had given him the address of some people in a town south of Berlin who might help him.

Day and Dowse were travelling together, and in the darkness they asked a man the way to the nearest railway station. Only then did they notice he was in police uniform. Suspiciously he asked them who they were, and they ran off into the darkness. At dawn they found the railway station and caught the first train to Berlin, changed trains there, and reached the town they were aiming for. That night they sheltered in the cellar of a bombed house, but someone must have seen them going in because some people surrounded it and then men came in with revolvers and the police arrived.

They spent a couple of nights handcuffed in a Berlin Gestapo jail waiting for the firing squad and thought the time had come when they were taken out and put in a car. For an hour they drove out of Berlin expecting all the time to stop, be taken out and shot, and they were considerably surprised when they pulled up at Sachsenhausen again. There each was chained to the concrete floor of a dungeon in solitary confinement. They spent nearly five months in unspeakable conditions. Churchill and James had been caught also and were in cells near them.

The Dodger had an extraordinary time. He had gone off on his own from Sachsenhausen, aiming for Luebeck, and jumped into a coal truck of a goods train trundling roughly in that direction. At dawn he jumped out of the coal truck miles from the danger area of Sachsenhausen and slept all day in a thicket by the banks of a stream. At night he found a near-by siding and was going to try 'jumping the rattler' again when he was caught in the beam of a watchman's torch. Not waiting to answer the challenge, he vanished into the darkness and went back to his hide-out.

All the next day he walked northwest in pouring rain and just outside a village met two friendly French slave labourers who sheltered him in a barn for a week, bringing him food every day. On the seventh day they said an untrustworthy Pole had seen him and he must move. They took him to a near-by café used by slave labourers, where an old, stone-deaf German served them with gallons of beer, and they talked openly in front of him. The Frenchmen hid him in another barn, and he was seen by a Russian whom the Frenchmen didn't trust, so they took him out the next day and put him for the night in a rabbit hutch. Again an unreliable Russian came across him so the Frenchmen took him to a hayloft, and there he spent a week, bedded down in clover hay listening to the pigs underneath. Once or twice he saw the German farmer walking by with his shotgun under his arm. The Frenchmen brought him food every day, and the German farmer must have seen them.

On the seventh morning the Dodger awoke to find the farmer

210 | PAUL BRICKHILL

looking at him from behind the hollow end of a pistol. The local policeman came around shortly after. He had been a Luxemburger, and when he got the Dodger by himself he apologised for having to hold him. He had to arrest him, he said, or be shot himself, but made up for it as far as he could by feeding him on hot oatcakes made specially by his wife. He brought out the *German Police Gazette*, and in it the Dodger saw a picture of himself, an unlovely and villainous one taken over four years earlier when he had first been captured.

It was the adjutant of Sachsenhausen himself who arrived by car with guards and handcuffs to take him back. In a cell along the corridor from Day and the others, they chained him to the floor, and the months passed in wretchedness. The five men heard nothing of the war except for scraps the guards told them about the 'wonderfully successful' German offensive in the Ardennes. They made it sound as though the war might go on forever.

CHAPTER XXII

On 3 February, they came to the Dodger's cell, took the chain off his ankles, and led him outside. A young German officer helped him into a car, climbed in after him, and off they drove to Berlin. What followed had the air of a dream. The young officer took him into a shop and bought him a complete outfit of civilian clothes: suit, shirts, socks, shoes, hat – the lot. Then he took him to a flat, introduced him to the SS major, his wife and child who occupied it, and showed him into a delightfully furnished bedroom.

'This will be your room,' said the young officer, and to the man they had chained in a dungeon, none of it was real.

'Tell me,' the Dodger asked the young officer, 'what is all this about?'

'You will find out in due course,' said the officer. 'Now change into your new clothes. You will feel much more comfortable.'

'Look here. I'm an officer,' the Dodger said. 'Will you, as an officer, give me your word I can wear these things without compromising myself.'

'Yes,' said the German decisively. 'I do.'

A few hours later a thickset man in civilian clothes arrived and greeted the Dodger warmly. Dr Thost had been London correspondent for the *Voelkischer Beobachter* in 1938–1939. Now he was a fairly high official in the German Foreign Office. He put the Dodger in a car and drove him off to the Adlon Hotel, Berlin's finest.

'Will you please tell me what this is all about?' asked the Dodger, blinking unbelievably at a sparkling chandelier in the foyer, one of the few parts of the hotel not bomb-damaged.

'You will know soon,' Thost promised. He took him up to a private room and introduced him to a large, fleshy man with a booming voice and an expansive, enveloping smile.

'This is Dr Schmidt,' said Thost. 'Dr Schmidt is Herr Hitler's interpreter.'

'Have a drink, my dear fellow,' boomed Dr Schmidt, spilling over with bonhomie. He handed the Dodger a glass.

The Dodger looked at it.

'Scotch whisky,' boomed Schmidt. 'Not much of it left, I'm afraid.'

The Dodger looked cautiously at Dr Schmidt – the same kind of look that is in a small boy's eyes when he gazes first, suspiciously, upon Santa Claus, not knowing what to expect.

'You are going home, my dear sir,' said Dr Schmidt, as if the news made him happy. 'No doubt you will be seeing your kinsman Mr Churchill when you arrive.' And then, confidentially and solemnly, 'I want you to remember three things. One . . . no unconditional surrender. Two . . . ethnographical boundaries, and three . . . the balance of power in Europe. For Britain's safety, it must be maintained.' He nodded vaguely toward the east where the Russians were preparing their assault on Berlin. 'You know what I mean.'

And the Dodger at last understood.

Thost took him to lunch in a small restaurant the next day and in the afternoon drove him to Dresden. They gave the Dodger his own room in a hotel there. He was taken to meet the chief of police, and at lunch the chief spoke graciously about the traditional bond between the British and the Germans. The Dodger met a lot more pleasant people who all thought the same. You wouldn't have thought they'd chain a dog in a dungeon, or even, for that matter, shoot fifty British bunny rabbits.

Thost took the Dodger (grinning grimly to himself) to the circus, and they were watching the lady on the tightrope when the sirens went and the first of the three great air raids on Dresden started. In an hour the centre of the city was a sheet of flame. Thost and the Dodger got out of the danger area, and Thost escorted him to an administration headquarters outside the city where an SS General greeted him warmly.

'Major Dodge,' said the General. 'I am so glad to see you are safe. I have been on the phone to Herr Himmler and you are going home.'

At the headquarters he met Frau Von Kleist, wife of the field marshal who had been relieved of his post. The Dodger was able to get a few words with her alone.

'Why don't you people put up the white flag?' he asked.

'That's what my husband thinks too,' she said. 'But we can't. We're not allowed to.'

Back in Dresden they found their hotel in ruins. Thost took him on a bus to Weimar, where they were bombed again but spent several days in the town. The Dodger toyed with the idea of escaping again but couldn't quite see what good it would do. On the other hand, staying with Thost, observing the country and the people, and getting back with Schmidt's message might be of some conceivable benefit.

At last they struck off southeast through Regensburg to Bayreuth, and there someone overhead them talking in English in an *estaminet*. Thost and the Dodger knew nothing about it until the police arrived, handcuffed them, and marched them off as spies. Thost, the high official, was livid with rage and almost speechless for a while until he got his voice back, and then the air was quivering with his protests, which the police stolidly ignored. They were thrown into a cell and spent two days waiting for execution. At night they could hear the American guns, and the Dodger, so patient since 1940, felt only bitterness. With freedom just by his fingertips it seemed so unfair that death should come like this from the little officials, when the German Foreign Office itself was bowing to him as a mediator.

Thost was sweating with fright and fury, and that was not without humour, but the most sardonic touch was the manner of their release. The local Gestapo freed them after a message had penetrated to Berlin and the answer had come back clearing the 'spies.'

Thost and the Dodger went on to Munich, stayed a day or two in a little hotel in the mountains to the south, and on 25 April reached the Swiss border at Lake Constance. That night the Dodger left Thost and walked up to the Swiss police at St Marguerita. In a couple of days he was lunching in Berne with army intelligence officers, and within a week the RAF landed him in England.

It was two days before VE Day that the Dodger dined with Churchill and the American Ambassador, John Winant, and told them of his adventures. When he got to the part about Schmidt and no unconditional surrender, Churchill took the cigar out of his mouth and grinned from ear to ear.

Chained to the dungeon floor at Sachsenhausen, Wings Day had passed the time by learning by heart a Hitler speech on a piece of latrine newspaper. In February, he and Dowse, James, and Jack Churchill were unchained and taken by train to Flossenberg Concentration Camp in the Harz Mountains. They heard the volleys of the execution squads there and saw the bodies of the victims being carried past. It was not a comforting sight, and they waited rather tensely for their own turn but no one came for them. After a fortnight they heard the approaching American guns, and just as release was beginning to seem possible the Germans took them out, loaded them into trucks, and drove them to the notorious Dachau, where they were locked in the hut that had been the camp brothel. Again they heard the rifles of the execution squads, and again they waited for their own turn.

They heard the American guns again, and just as it seemed once more that release might be on the way, they were taken to a camp up in the hills near Innsbruck. The strain of alternate hope and dread was tearing their nerves to pieces.

After a fortnight the Germans took them across the Brenner Pass to an Italian village. By now they were deep in Hitler's 'Southern Redoubt,' and with them were about fifty more important prisoners. It was uncomfortably clear that they were being held as hostages. Among them were Blum, Pastor, Niemoeller, Schuschnigg, Schacht, the Dutch Minister of War, Greek generals, Italian generals, a nephew of Molotov, a son-in-law of the King of Italy, and a sprinkling of princelings.

Wings got away from the party, met an Austrian called Toni, and got him to drive him in his car to Bolzano. He contacted the Italian Resistance and continued on by car and foot toward the Allied Lines. He joined in the fighting in one town and took over the Gestapo headquarters in another. He commandeered another car, drove full tilt through the German lines, and with a bursting feeling of exhilaration reached a forward American patrol. It was his ninth escape since being shot down in 1939, and at last he had made it. It was one day before the Italian Front Armistice.

It was from Wings Day that the Allies learned about the colony of important prisoners up by the border. The Americans sent a column pelting up to the border and rescued them just in time. The Germans had had orders to shoot them.

And north compound?

About the time of the Hitler bomb plot in July, 1944, 'George' was creeping out under the theatre toward the wire. 'George' was 'Harry's' successor, and Crump and Canton had cut a trap for it under a seat in the twelfth row of the theatre. They were dispersing the sand under the floor, and a re-formed 'X' organisation' was very active, though there was no definite policy, just yet, on mass escapes. We wanted to get 'George' finished first, and then see what the situation was.

A few weeks later the contacts picked up a few hints from Pieber and one or two others that if Germany fell – and nothing was surer – the camp might be wiped out. After the shooting of the fifty that seemed logical enough. We had no illusions as to the popularity of the Allied Air Forces. Wilson, the SBO, formed the Klim Klub. 'Klim' was the name of a milk powder in the food parcels, but the Klim Klub was the camp self-defence unit. Everyone was in it – the whole compound population being split up into sections, platoons, and companies. There were secret lectures and training, and a special commando company was to have the honour of having their heads blown off first as shock troops. I don't suppose there was much we could have done, but if the regrettable business of impromptu demise had to be faced, it was better to be doing something about it rather than be sitting on one's bottom waiting for it.

Over in the kommandantur, a German stenographer, disgusted at the shooting of the fifty, sent in a message by a tame guard that she had heard through her work that all prisoners who escaped henceforth were to be shot. A bony-faced Scot called McCulloch wanted to try it anyway, but 'X' wouldn't let him. He argued and argued until, rubbing their chins dubiously, they agreed to let him try.

He got out hiding under a pile of empty tins in one of the garbage wagons but was back in the cooler a couple of hours later, still alive. Some good-tempered Wehrmacht soldiers had nabbed him down the road and brought him straight back to the camp. It didn't prove anything one way or the other. It was a question of what would have happened if the Gestapo had got hold of him.

By the time the snow came and finished escapes for the winter, 'George' had reached just beyond the wire. It was kept there as a bolt-hole in case the rough-stuff started.

In the middle of January, the Russians started their winter offensive and the Ostfront came sweeping toward Sagan like a whirlwind. We were praying they would overrun the camp. They did, but we weren't there any more. The Germans marched us out on 26 January into a foot of snow and force-marched us more than sixty miles for days and nights to Spemberg, where they loaded us into cattle trucks. It was a fairly grim trip. We'd been on half-issue of food parcels for some months, and they gave us only one meal (barley soup) on the way.

There was one laugh on that march. Glemnitz was back with us for the march. He'd always guessed we had a radio and came tramping along the column of men and boomed affably, 'Well, I suppose you've brought your radio with you. Who's carrying it? Who's got it, eh . . . you?' (pointing to one man) . . . 'you?' (pointing to another) . . . 'you?' (to a third).

And one or two of us who knew where the radio was felt there was still something to laugh at in life.

Pieber, that kind and prudent man, had parts of it in his attaché case in his car.

We were two days in the cattle trucks. There was just room to sit, but not to move, and after thirty-six hours they *did* give us each a cup of foul water drained off the engine. They let us out of the trucks near Bremen, and we marched to an old condemned camp and waited seven hours outside in the rain to be searched before we entered. A lot of the men collapsed at that point. About seventy-five were already missing – about half left at various places through illness and the rest just 'missing,' maybe escaped, maybe shot. Of the rest of us, 70 per cent were sick, and everyone had lost more weight, up to thirty pounds. We really hadn't had that much to spare, and most of us were looking a little bony.

The Allies crossed the Rhine and came surging up toward us, but again the rosy dreams of liberation didn't come off. They marched us out again, heading north. I've got to hand it to the Germans. They were really reluctant to let us go. This trip, though, was a picnic by comparison with the last one. A few people were shot by trigger-happy guards and a few more killed by strafing aircraft, but the weather was good and we traded Red Cross coffee for eggs and bread and stole bushels and bushels of potatoes.

We didn't know it at the time (just as well) but the guards had orders to execute all of us if we didn't reach the Elbe by a certain day. We didn't reach the Elbe by that day but at this late stage the guards were getting rather prudent about mass murders so they decided to overlook the order.

We were sheltering in barns up near Lübeck when we heard the barrage as the British First Army crossed the Elbe. Two days later, on 2 May, we heard firing down the road and two tanks rumbled through the trees from the south. We didn't know whether they were Germans or British, and you could practically see the nerves sticking out of everyone's skin and vibrating like piano wire. The hatch of the front tank opened, and two Tommies stuck their heads out. We ran up to them screaming at the top of our voices.

AFTERMATH

'It was cold-blooded butchery and we are resolved that the four criminals shall be tracked down.'

Anthony Eden,
House of Commons, May, 1944.

In August, 1945, Wing Commander Bowes, of the RAF Special Investigation Branch, flew to Germany to find out what had happened to the missing fifty. There was no final proof they had been murdered, though there didn't seem much doubt about it. Bowes was to find out if they had, in fact, been murdered, track down the people responsible, and arrest them.

He was a good choice for the job, an ex-Scotland Yard detective with no frills about him, a square red face and a reputation for dogged toughness. Back in Victoria's day, they'd have called him one of the Bulldog Breed. He didn't have much to go on – the stories of the people who had come back from Goerlitz, the bare German announcements of the deaths, and the urns of ashes engraved with the places of cremation. He naturally suspected the Gestapo, but there was no real evidence to pin on them.

In Hamburg he formed six interrogation teams of four men each, and they toured the length and breadth of Western-occupied Germany questioning captured Germans, now held in scores of thousands in the camps where they had imprisoned us. They couldn't get into the Russian Zone, or Poland – the Russians wouldn't let them in – and that was the big snag. Sagan lay now across the new Polish border that had moved forward to embrace German Silesia. So did Breslau. Goerlitz lay half in the new Poland and half in the Russian Zone. In those forbidden cities lay the keys to the mystery.

Day after day, week after week, and month after month, the interrogators went from camp to camp in the British, American, and French zones, questioning and questioning. One by one, Germans of the Wehrmacht, the Luftwaffe, the Kriegsmarine, the SS, the Gestapo, and all the other police forces were marched in front of them. A man might question 250 of them in a day but every time, day after day, with the same result – nothing known.

They concentrated particularly on the areas named on the urns and leafed doggedly through reams and reams of records. They questioned altogether 250,000 Germans. No result. Not the vestige of a clue. The murderers, whoever they were, had covered their tracks and the mystery seemed impenetrable . . .

Until, in March, 1946, a message came from Prague. The Czechs were holding a Gestapo man named Kiowski who they thought knew something about Kirby-Green and Kidder. Bowes flew to Prague, taking with him another ex-Scotland Yard detective, Flight Lieutenant Lyon, who spoke German.

The Czechs were holding Kiowski in Pangratz Prison, which the Gestapo had used during the war. A Czech officer showed Bowes over it.

'This is the efficient part,' he said as they came to a long corridor with thirty cell doors on one side and a single door on the other.

'No accused man who went through this single door ever came out again,' said the Czech. Behind the door was a courtroom and across the back of the room stretched a thick curtain. He pulled the curtain aside and showed them where the execution gangs waited for the victims of the court. This was sudden death. There was a rail across it, like the rails in butcher shops, and a row of nooses was hanging down from it. As men were sentenced, they strung them up and slid the nooses along the rail through another curtain into a room full of cheap coffins.

In a corner of the execution chamber, there was a guillotine.

'They used to lie them face-up on this,' said the Czech.

Bowes found Kiowski in a cell by himself, a dry-lipped, nervous little man with black hair. The Czechs had proof of ten murders against him. Kiowski admitted he *did* know a little about Kirby-Green and Kidder. It was the first break in the entire case. He had been stationed at Zlin, said Kiowski, on the German-Czech border, on 28 March, 1944, when two suspects were caught trying to cross the frontier into Czechoslovakia. Their names, he found out later, were Kirby-Green and Kidder. The local Gestapo chief, Hans Ziegler, interrogated them, and later that night a Gestapo agent called Knuppelberg arrived from area Gestapo headquarters at Brno with orders about the two prisoners.

Kiowski said he was duty driver that night, and about 2 a.m. in the morning Ziegler called him and another driver named Schwarzer to drive the two prisoners back to Sagan. Knuppelberg sat in the back of his car with the handcuffed Kidder, and a local Gestapo man called Zacharias sat in the other car with Kirby-Green, also handcuffed.

About forty miles along the road, some ten miles before Moravska Ostrava, Knuppelberg stopped the cars and they let the two prisoners get out to relieve themselves, removing the handcuffs. Kiowski said that as they got to the side of the road, both Kirby-Green and Kidder made a sudden dash into the darkness. Sitting in the car, he heard shots from Zacharias and Knuppelberg, and both fleeing prisoners fell dead.

Bowes was certain Kiowski was lying. He had always expected that when he found the murderers they would say that the prisoners had been killed trying to escape. He and Lyon straddled themselves on two chairs, rested their arms on the backs, and settled down to cross-question Kiowski. They kept at it for six straight hours till they were all hoarse and sweating, Kiowski still sticking to his story.

And then they caught him in a flat lie. Hours earlier, Kiowski had said his orders were to drive straight to Sagan without stopping. And then later, in answer to what seemed an innocent question, Kiowski described how he had fuelled the cars before they drove off and told how much petrol he had put in. It was only enough to get them to Moravska Ostrava (where there was a crematorium) and back to Zlin. Sagan lay another 140 miles further on. Bowes put his red face close to Kiowski and shouted the lie back at him, and Kiowski fainted.

They brought him around by pouring slivovitch down his throat, and then Kiowski told the truth.

Before they set out from Zlin, he said, he had asked Zacharias what was going to happen to the two prisoners, and Zacharias had pointed with his thumb downward. About ten miles from Moravska Ostrava, as he had said before, they had stopped the cars and let the two prisoners out to urinate. As they stood by the side of the road, Zacharias stood behind Kidder and Knuppelberg behind Kirby-Green, both with drawn pistols. Knuppelberg looked at Zacharias across the few feet of darkness and raised his arm, the prearranged signal. Both lifted their pistols and fired simultaneously, and then Zacharias fired a second shot to make sure. Kirby-Green and Kidder slid to the ground without a sound. Death was instantaneous. Knuppelberg drove on to Moravska Ostrava and got an ambulance to take the bodies to the crematorium.

The Czechs wouldn't let Bowes take Kiowski. They had too much on him themselves, and later they executed him.

Bowes and Lyon went to Zlin to start the search for the others, and there they found that Ziegler had committed suicide when Germany collapsed. In the local jail, however, they found Frau Zacharias. They learned a lot about Zacharias from her. Hell hath no fury like a woman scorned. He was not, it seems, either a good man or a good husband. There was the case of the Czech typist to whom Zacharias had paid some attention, and when she began to get a little difficult he murdered her. And after that there was the little girl of seventeen, a displaced person and suspected spy. Zacharias took her out into the woods and later he sent a Russian slave labourer to bury the body.

'He is in Bremen now,' said Frau Zacharias, and gave Bowes the address. Bowes sent a man flying to Bremen, and at the address the wife had given, he arrested Zacharias, a big, blond-haired man with thin lips and nostrils; a very tough character as he proved within twenty-four hours by escaping from American custody.

Bowes was seething. They searched half of Germany, but there was no trace of Zacharias till on the seventeenth day they intercepted a letter card addressed to a relative which said, 'Uncle Erich is well and is leaving shortly on a trip.'

Zacharias' Christian names were Herman, August, Erich. The letter

England (Bowes knew that well enough). An alarmed Ribbentrop had demanded of Himmler that the shootings be adequately covered.

Schauschutz said that Gestapo headquarters in Berlin sent for Knuppelberg, and there in Gestapo chief Mueller's Berlin office Knuppelberg saw a man called Scharpwinkel, who was Gestapo chief at Breslau, and Gestapo men from Karlsruhe, Munich, Strasbourg, Saarbrücken, Danzig, and Kiel. As Schauschutz spoke, the case was breaking wide open.

Mueller, said Schauschutz, roughly rebuked the Gestapo representatives present. Their reports of the shootings of the escaped Air Force prisoners were all unimaginatively the same. Without exception, they said the prisoners tried to escape while being allowed to urinate beside the road on the way back to Sagan. They were to go and prepare fresh reports, said Mueller, putting more variety and convincing detail into them. Schauschutz said that Knuppelberg came back to Brno and made out a new fake report, which was sent to Berlin.

Bowes sent his teams to the cities mentioned by Schauschutz and applied to Warsaw for a permit to go to Breslau himself.

On four of the urns no town name had been engraved but in the Kiel Crematorium record book one of Bowes' men found an entry showing that, on 29 March, 1944, four people had been cremated there. The column where the names should have been showed four blanks. Otto Fahl, the old crematorium attendant, said he vaguely remembered the four. They were men. He understood that they had come from Flensburg, on the Danish border.

In Flensburg, Bowes found some of the old local Gestapo in British custody, and they told him that the four had been escaped airmen who had been collected from them by men from Kiel Gestapo, led by a Major Post.

Bowes tracked down Post and arrested him in a garage at Celle. He was a dark, strong-looking, arrogant man and said he knew nothing of four such men. Bowes and his teams picked up more of Kiel Gestapo – Kaehler, Oskar Schmidt, Franz Schmidt, Jackobs and others. Franz Schmidt was the first to crack, and he told the story.

Jimmy Catanach, the Australian, Christensen, a New Zealander, and two Norwegians, Espelid and Fugelsang, had been arrested at gunpoint right on the Danish border and thrown into jail. Fritz Schmidt, chief of Kiel Gestapo, received a secret order from Mueller in Berlin that the four were to be shot. He called Post and several more reliable executioners and told them what they had to do. Then he shook hands with each man to bind him to secrecy under his Gestapo oath.

Post and the others drove to Flensburg, and Post put Catanach in his car. The other three travelled in the second car. Post drew a couple of miles ahead of the others and stopped by a field near Rotenhahn. He led Catanach behind the hedge and shot him in the back. Catanach died instantly. A couple of minutes later the other car drove up. The other three prisoners were pushed into the field. One of them saw Catanach's body and let out a shout, and the three of them scattered, running, but were shot down before they had gone ten paces.

Bowes' men gave Schmidt paper and a pen and sent him to his cell to write out his confession. When they went back they found he had taken his singlet off, stood on a chair, tied the end of his singlet to the cell ventilator, twisted the arm-holes around his neck and stepped off the chair. He was hanging, quite dead. He *had* written something on the paper they had given him – a note addressed to his daughter. It said, 'Hitler was right,' and told her not to forget her Nazi teachings.

The other Kiel prisoners talked freely and gladly about Post, telling Bowes that he was an insatiable sadist. One of them told how Post had built a slave-labour camp outside Kiel and suggested that a certain one of the huts should be pulled down. The British put German workmen on to pulling it down, and under the foundations they found 160 corpses of Post's victims.

Bowes finally got around through Warsaw to Breslau, Goerlitz, Hirschberg, and Sagan but from the Russians and the Poles met only obstructionism and was not able to see a single one of the local Gestapo whom they had in jails. A Polish officer trailed him wherever he went, and Bowes finally sat down next to his shadow in a café and bought him drinks till he was glassy-eyed, in which condition the Pole freely told Bowes he was regarded as a spy.

Curiously enough, a report came through from Moscow that Scharpwinkel was being held there. Captain Cornish of the British Army flew there, and the Russians took him to see Scharpwinkel, a dark, ruthless man whom the Russians persuaded to speak. Though Scharpwinkel himself was economical with the truth, the details he gave implicated Wielen, and Wielen was tracked down in Western Germany. Wielen implicated Scharpwinkel, and bit by bit the truth came out.

Scharpwinkel had gone with Lux and his murder gang to Goerlitz on 30 March, 1944, and there they had interrogated some of the prisoners. After lunch they put six of them in a truck – Cross, Mike Casey, Wiley, Leigh, Pohé, and Al Hake – and drove off toward Sagan. Five miles past Halbau, Scharpwinkel ordered the truck to pull up, and Lux and his gunmen prodded the prisoners into the roadway. They escorted them about a hundred yards into the wood and there Scharpwinkel told them they were to be executed.

('I was surprised,' Scharpwinkel said reflectively in Moscow, 'that they took it so calmly.')

They were lined up, and Lux gave the order to fire. By the second salvo they were all dead. Lux told Scharpwinkel that the following day they would go to Hirschberg.

The next day Lux and his men took ten more from Goerlitz – Humphries, McGill, Swain, Hall, Pat Langford, Evans, Valenta, Kolanowski, Stewart, and Birkland. The urns containing the ashes of these men showed they were cremated at Liegnitz. Either that day or the day after, Lux also took his men to Hirschberg, where they took Kiewnarski, Pawluk, Wernham, and Skanziklas and shot them.

On 6 April, Lux took another six from Goerlitz – Grisman, Gunn, J. F. Williams, Milford, Street, and McGarr. They were cremated at Breslau. But it was not till 13 April that Lux took Cookie Long from Goerlitz. His urn shows that he was cremated at Breslau.

That brought Lux's murder total to twenty-seven, a figure to which Tobolski can probably be added, and also, perhaps, Danny Krol, who was caught with Dowse at Oels, in the Breslau area. He was last seen alive there, and his urn is marked 'Breslau.'

Gradually, through patient research into regional Gestapos, Bowes brought to light the details of most of the other shootings.

Willy Williams (Squadron Leader J. E. A. Williams), Johnny Bull, Kierath, and Mondschein were caught trying to cross the Czech border near Reichenberg, and after interrogation and several days in the cells they were taken away from Reichenberg at four o'clock in the morning of 29 March, and not seen again. They were cremated that same day at

Bruex. They certainly weren't killed trying to escape again. Baatz, the local Gestapo chief, had signed the order for their cremation the previous day. Stower also vanished from Reichenberg Jail.

Kriminalpolizei took Gouws and Stevens off a train south of Munich and, on the evening of 28 March, three Gestapo men were ordered to shoot them and pledged to secrecy by handshake. They drove the two prisoners out of Munich in a car, stopped in open country, and told them they could get out to relieve themselves. As they stood by the side of the road, a Gestapo agent called Schneider shot both with a machine pistol. They were cremated at Munich. A year later, when the American Army was approaching Munich, Weil, one of the shooting party, went to the crematorium and tried to rub their names out of the record book with a penknife.

Cochran was caught near Karlsruhe, and on 31 March, he was taken out in a car toward Natzweiler and shot from behind in the woods by a Gestapo agent called Preiss. Tony Hayter was not caught for nearly two weeks and then police picked him up at Strasbourg on the French border. On 6 April, two Strasbourg Gestapo men drove him out on the autobahn toward Breslau and shot him, as the others had done, by the side of the road.

Bushell and Scheidhauer had caught their train all right from Sagan. (Van Der Stok saw Bushell buying train tickets in Breslau station.) A day or two later they reached Saarbrücken and were waiting on the platform for a train down to Alsace when two security policemen questioned them. They showed their papers, which were almost perfect. Roger had some of the original passes. Scheidhauer spoke natural French, of course, and Roger spoke good French and faultless Bernese German. They had their stories word-perfect – they were Frenchmen who'd been working in Germany and were going home on leave. They answered perfectly questions about their homes and families, and at last the police seemed satisfied and handed the passes back.

As they were walking away one of them pulled an old trick. He swung around and shot a sudden question at Scheidhauer, and Scheidhauer, who had been speaking English in the compound for two years, involuntarily answered in English. The police had their pistols out in a second and took them away to Lerchesflur Prison.

During the next few days they were interrogated by the Kriminal-polizei, and as the alternative seemed to lie in being regarded as spies, they finally admitted they had escaped from Stalag Luft III. On the evening of 28 March, Dr Spann, Gestapo chief in Saarbrücken, received a top secret teleprint order from General Mueller that the two prisoners were to be shot. Spann sent his triggerman, Emil Schulz, to collect them from the prison. Schulz handcuffed them behind their backs, and a Gestapo driver called Breithaupt drove him, Spann, and the two prisoners out along the autobahn toward Kaiserslautern.

A few miles out, Spann ordered the car to stop, and they took the handcuffs off the prisoners and told them they could get out and relieve themselves. By the side of the road, Spann and Schulz each fired two shots. Scheidhauer fell straight forward on his face and did not move. Bushell crumpled slowly onto his right side. They were cremated at Saarbruecken.

Schulz and Breithaupt were not popular in Saarbrücken. Bowes found some of their old colleagues in prison camps there, and they told him everything they knew, including the probable whereabouts of the two. A couple of days later, Schulz was arrested at his home in the French Zone, and about the same time they found Breithaupt hiding in a hut in a wood in the American Zone. Retribution had already caught up with Spann. In the closing days of the war he had been killed in an air raid on Linz.

Spann wasn't the only one beyond human justice. Fittingly enough General Nebe, who had selected the fifty victims and given their names to the Gestapo, had had his own name handed to the Gestapo. He had been imprudent enough to become implicated in the Hitler bomb plot of July, and his old friend, General Mueller, with whom he and Kaltenbrunner had lunch every day, hanged him.

Mueller did not grieve long. He died in the fighting when the Russians took Berlin. Kaltenbrunner died at Nuremberg with other top Nazis.

Lux died in the fighting in Breslau, and so did most of his murder gang. The rest vanished.

The Russians did not hand Scharpwinkel over. They reported that he had died in Moscow after an illness. (Bowes will bet a pound to a penny that the brilliant and ruthless Scharpwinkel is still in an official uniform either in Russia or the Russian Zone of Germany, training men in the job he knows so well for new masters.)

Bowes now knew what had happened in varying detail to forty-six of the fifty, and in custody he had eighteen men for trial. There were several more smaller fry he wanted in addition to those who had died, but they had scattered throughout Germany and covered their tracks.

The trial of the eighteen started on 1 July, 1947, before No. 1 War Crimes Court in the old-fashioned grey courtroom of the Kurio Haus in Hamburg. The military judges, red-tabbed in khaki and in RAF blue, sat in a row before a table on a raised dais at the head of the room, a major-general, an air commodore, three colonels, and two wing commanders. In the middle of them, to guide them on law, sat the wigged and black-gowned Advocate-General, C. L. Stirling, CBE, KC, a tall spare man with pince-nez and a crisp, incisive voice.

On the other side of the room, the accused sat in two rows on benches in the large dock, and in front of them sat their black-gowned German counsel.

For fifty days – one for each murdered man – the damning evidence mounted against them, and on the fiftieth day the court convicted them all.

Grizzled, sixty-four-year-old Wielen was found guilty of taking part in the high-level conspiracy to murder the fifty and sentenced to life imprisonment.

Schulz and Breithaupt were convicted of murdering Bushell and Scheidhauer and sentenced to death.

Alfred Schimmel was convicted of the murder of Tony Hayter and sentenced to death.

Josef Gmeiner, Walter Herberg, Otto Preiss, and Heinrich Boschert were found guilty of the murder of Cochran. Death sentence.

Johannes Post and Hans Kahler were sentenced to death for the murder of Catanach, Christensen, Fugelsang, and Espelid; Arthur Denkman, their driver, got ten years for being an accessory.

Oskar Schmidt and Walter Jackobs were sentenced to death for the murders of Christensen, Espelid, and Fugelsang. Their driver, Wilhelm Struve, was sentenced to ten years for being an accessory.

Emil Weil, Eduard Geith, and Johan Schneider were found guilty of the murders of Gouws and Stevens and sentenced to death.

Zacharias was sentenced to death for the murders of Kidder and Kirby-Green.

Post was arrogant and sneering to the last. He must have realised that there could only be one way out for him. Most of the others became very subdued. Jackobs embraced religion.

Boschert's death sentence was later commuted to life imprisonment, but the other fourteen condemned men were hanged in Hamelin Jail, near Hamburg, on 26 February, 1948.

Four of the murdered airmen were still unavenged – Tim Walenn, Henri Picard, Gordon Brettell, and Romas Marcinkus. Bowes had traced them to Danzig, where they had been aiming. Police had taken them off a train near Schneidemuehl and lodged them for a day in a near-by prison camp. A British sergeant-major in that camp had reported after the war that they had a plot to escape again, and as they were about to put it into execution, the Gestapo arrived and took them away.

That, Bowes assumed, would be Danzig Gestapo. He had sixty of the former Danzig and district Gestapo held behind barbed wire at Esteveger, near Danzig, and he cross-questioned them repeatedly but could not get a lead. Danzig Gestapo chief, Dr Venediger, would be certain to know, but Venediger had vanished. And then one day in July, 1948, one of the prisoners called Achterberg asked to see him.

'I feel that a lot of quite innocent men are being held here,' Achterberg said. 'The man you want is called Burchhardt, and I think I can tell you where you might find him. His wife lives just north of Hamburg,' and Achterberg mentioned an address in a little town.

He and the others told Bowes a lot about their old colleague Burchhardt, and none of it was very nice. Burchhardt, they said, was Danzig's most reliable executioner because he took such a pride and pleasure in his work. He had a record of many murders in the name of duty. His favourite method, according to his comrades, was to take his victims to his own room and flog them to death with a rhinoceros hide whip. They said he was such a huge, gorilla-like man that he could almost take a man's head off with his whip. Bowes wouldn't believe it at first, but so many of Burchhardt's old colleagues repeated the story so sincerely that he came to believe them.

'Be careful of Burchhardt,' one of them said. 'He will probably shoot first.'

A party of armed men went to the address Achterberg had given and found Burchhardt's wife there, but no Burchhardt. They *did* find, though, that Burchhardt had made the same mistake as Zacharias.

'He's run away with his mistress,' said the abandoned frau with fury. 'I can tell you where you'll find him – in a town called Kempten in the American Zone. He calls himself Brandt now and is working as a carpenter. You'll probably find him with the woman, Toni Schatz.'

They drove all day and reached Kempten, near the Swiss border, about midnight, and at one o'clock in the morning they raided Toni Schatz' flat. Fraulein Schatz was a shapely blonde who welcomed them with shrill fury in a short slip that barely camouflaged what it did not hide. At first she said she'd never heard of Brandt, or Burchhardt, but when they threatened to confront her with Frau Burchhardt herself she broke down and gave them the address of a flat not far away.

Leaving a guard with Toni so she could not give a warning, Bowes posted twenty men around the entrances to the flats where the girl said Burchhardt was. He roused the janitor and got the master key, and at 3 a.m. Bowes and Lyon softly let themselves in the door of a flat where the janitor said Herr Brandt lived.

The flat was in darkness, and they felt their way into the bedroom. When they were quietly in position standing with drawn pistols over a dark form asleep in the bed, Bowes flicked on the light. Burchhardt was awake in a second and jumped halfway up the wall with shock at seeing them. They found a loaded gun under his pillow. He was so huge they could not fit the handcuffs over his wrists.

'I hope,' said Burchhardt, the unorthodox executioner, 'that I'm going to get fair play.'

Checking Burchhardt's story with the evidence of the Danzig Gestapo men held at Esteveger (they were talking freely now), Bowes found what had happened to the last four recaptured airmen. Burchhardt and a murder team had driven them to a wood outside Trampken about twelve miles from Danzig, and among the trees, seventy yards away from the road, they machine-gunned them and the four died instantly.

About the same time, Bowes caught up with Erwin Wieczorek, who had been with Lux's gang in Goerlitz, and Richard Haensel, Kriminalpolizei chief in Goerlitz. On 11 October, 1948, these two and Burchhardt faced the War Crimes Court, again sitting in the grey, panelled courtroom of the Kurio Haus in Hamburg.

The trial lasted twenty days and Wieczorek was found guilty of being concerned in the murders of Cross, Casey, Leigh, Wiley, Pohé, and Hake and sentenced to death.

Haensel was acquitted on the grounds that it was not proved that he had taken a real part in the murder conspiracy.

Burchhardt was convicted of the murders of Walenn, Picard, Brettell, and Marcinkus, and sentenced to death.

Wieczorek and Burchhardt did not hang. Wieczorek's conviction was not confirmed by the British occupation authorities. He claimed that he had not been present when the men had been shot in the woods but had stayed behind tinkering with the engine of one of the cars parked on the autobahn. He was freed.

The death sentence on that trusty executioner Burchhardt was commuted to imprisonment for life. The authorities considered it was a little too long since the four murders (four years) to exact the full penalty. Life imprisonment is twenty-one years. Some say there will be an amnesty long before that, and I expect they are probably right.

THE WHITE RABBIT

Bruce Marshall

CONTENTS

To the memory of the other brave

AUTHOR'S FOREWORD

I have always thought that Wing Commander Yeo-Thomas's story ought to be given to the public, and I was glad when John Pudney persuaded him to allow it to be told, and flattered when Tommy asked me to do the telling. As a chronicler I have, however, only two quali-fications: those of having been in 1943 and 1944 a reprehensibly chairborne Intelligence officer to 'RF' Section and of having lived in France for twenty years.

In order to tell the story tidily and without digression I have often been obliged to allow characters to disappear without stating their fate. It may, therefore, interest the reader if I say that Peulevé is now in England and Hessel in Paris; that the nine others who escaped with Yeo-Thomas from the death convoy are all alive; that Pister, Kraut-wurst, Schobert and Wolff were, largely on evidence given by Yeo-Thomas at the Buchenwald trials, condemned to death by the Allies and hanged; that Möller is now working on a farm in Germany; and that Hubble's chess set, also of the cast, is now in the possession of his family.

In order to avoid confusion only one name has been used for each agent, either his real name or his alias, according to convenience.

Although the opinions expressed in this book are not necessarily Yeo-Thomas's they are not those of one who has never been in action.

I have to thank Mr W. Somerset Maugham and William Heine-mann Ltd. for permission to quote from *Ashenden*, William Collins, Sons & Co. Ltd. for permission to quote from Mr Arthur Bryant's *The*

Age of Elegance, and Eyre & Spottiswoode Ltd for permission to quote from Mr Geoffrey Cotterell's *Strait and Narrow*.

Finally, my thanks are also due to Yeo-Thomas for the very considerable trouble which he has taken to set out his story for me.

Bruce Marshall

'. . . il ne faut dire dès maintenant que personne, dans les rangs britanniques, ne fit plus pour nous aider que Yeo-Thomas.'

COLONEL PASSY
10 DUKE STREET, LONDRES.

CHAPTER I

No arms and the man

'Fact', says Somerset Maugham in his preface to *Ashenden*, 'is a poor story-teller. It starts a story at haphazard, generally long before the beginning, rambles on inconsequently and tails off, leaving loose ends hanging about, without a conclusion.' His contention is generally true. In the case of *The White Rabbit*, however, which, like *Ashenden*, is the story of a British Agent, I shall hope to prove that there are occasionally exceptions to the rule.

At the beginning of the 1939–1945 war those who joined the colours most readily were the veterans of 1914–1918, who had sworn that they would have to be fetched if their country ever called upon them again. I don't know if Forest Frederick Edward Yeo-Thomas was among those who made this boast because I was not acquainted with him in the mean years, although his turbulent nature inclines me to believe that he may have shouted rebellion like the rest. At any rate, there was no question of the policeman being sent for him on 3 September 1939, and not only because he was then already thirty-eight years old.

Born of a family which had lived in France since 1855, Yeo-Thomas was a director of Molyneux, the famous Parisian dressmaker. I suppose that dressmakers get as bored with the sight of beautiful mannequins as sales girls in confectioners' shops are said to become tired of the taste of chocolates, although I should hesitate to ascribe both immunities to excessive consumption. Certainly it was not of mannequins that Tommy was thinking as he entered his office in the rue Royale on the morning of Monday, 4 September 1939, and probably he didn't think of them even as they gave him their usual morning greeting. '*Bonjour, Monsieur Thomas*,' said the beautiful young women with the gravity of those whose profession is to serve the frivolous. Tommy returned their salutations and tried to settle down to work, because in war as in peace the variable and the changeable thing which Virgil called woman has to go on having variable and changeable clothes.

'Dresses are going to be slightly longer this year, Monsieur Thomas,' I like to think of a young woman in a black silk dress with a bottle-green sash saying to him. Perhaps the lovely Russian Countess Grabbe said something like this. If she didn't she ought to have, to give that twist to fact to make it as entertaining as fiction. But whether or not she said something significantly meaningless, when Tommy told her that he was going to enlist she gave him a small brown canvas sachet to wear round his neck for safety. And although Yeo-Thomas was not stupid enough to believe that his lack of faith in the Holy Ghost entitled him to believe in the sacramental potency of black cats, white heather, frothblowers' cuff links and the great Umkulukulu, he wore this charm all through the war in order to please the donor.

'Rhetoric has ruined religion,' Thornton Wilder once wrote with permissible alliteration and considerable accuracy. It may also be said to have almost annihilated patriotism, for among statesmen only Mr Churchill takes the trouble to mint new phrases which inspire rather than tire. But in 1939 Mr Churchill wasn't speaking very often and the politicians who were kept trotting out trite and dusty words about 'glory' and 'supreme sacrifice', and of this high-falutin' balderdash the French talked even more than the British. Tommy must have heard the big-mouthed belchings in two languages. It is to his credit that he managed to be patriotic in spite of them.

For it was burning patriotism which prompted Yeo-Thomas to exchange his comfortable job with Molyneux for the rough and tumble of life in the ranks. And burning patriotism was harder to find in 1939 than in 1914, because old soldiers had learned by experience, and their sons by hearsay, to distrust promises of fidelity made by politicians and principal boys in pantomimes. Perhaps it was because he didn't 'only England know' that Tommy, born in England, and educated for the most part in France, was patriotic. Or perhaps it was because he was a very honest decent pagan who paradoxically admired that approximation to Christian thought and action of which the British are almost certainly the world's most noteworthy practitioners. Or perhaps it may have been because he had two countries to love instead of one and liked doing something difficult.

Whatever the reason, Yeo-Thomas, like a great many other hard-boiled and disillusioned men, unhesitatingly chose to risk his life in defence of a morality which politicians by their practice, intellectuals by their scepticism and clergymen by their badly aimed predications, had done their best to destroy. It was, subconsciously perhaps, the conviction that cruelty, and not girls showing their knees in church, was the unforgivable sin which led Tommy immediately to volunteer to fight against the first swarm of barbarians which uncontrolled progress had raised up to threaten Europe.

It is not unlikely that his decision was strengthened by the fact that he was temperamentally ungovernable. Born in London, on 17 June, 1901, he had been educated at three schools in France and one in England, from two of which he had been expelled for unruly behaviour. Although under age he had served with the Allied armies in the latter part of the 1914–1918 war and, not satisfied with this introit to arms, had fought for the Poles against the Russians during 1919 and 1920. He was captured by the Bolsheviks at Zitomir and sentenced to death, but managed to escape the night before he was due to be shot. Since then he had worked in Paris, first as an apprentice mechanic with Rolls-Royce and later as an accountant with a firm of travel agents. After working with three banks he was engaged as a temporary audit clerk by an international firm of accountants. In 1932 he entered the firm of Molyneux.

But if Yeo-Thomas was ready for the Army, the Army was not ready for him, in spite of Lord Halifax's statement, broadcast earlier in the year from the Lord Mayor's Banquet, that all steps had been taken to resist aggression against Poland from whatever direction it might come. The Military Attaché at the British Embassy in Paris told Tommy that no further volunteers were being accepted for the moment, as the Army had more recruits than it required. This rejection was tempered by the information that if Yeo-Thomas were willing to travel to England at his own expense there was always the possibility that he might be accepted after a wait of several months. An attempt to join the French Foreign Legion also failed, because the authorities had instructions not to enlist Britons.

In desperation Yeo-Thomas accepted an invitation to place his services and car (without payment) at the disposal of the Air Attaché. A fortnight later this altruism was rewarded by permission to join the RAF. A man whose method of arguing with bank managers was to lay them out on the floor of the bank naturally wanted to fight; but Tommy's request to be employed as an air gunner was refused on account of his age. In spite of his protest that he did not wish an office or a base line job he was enlisted as an AC2 interpreter and, as no uniforms were available, was given a light blue armlet with the letters IC embroidered on it in green. After a few days he was promoted corporal.

Tommy's phoney war was like everybody else's: a mixture of enforced indolence and being pushed around *au ralenti*. He met the average sensual men, cads and potential saints who are to be found in all assemblies of human beings, but whose less pleasant attributes are accentuated when they are separated from their womenfolk. He reacted to the cads, and especially to those more highly placed than himself, with an uncompromising vehemence unlikely to accelerate his promotion. To a squadron leader who, referring to a pilot officer, asked him to 'send that sod out there in', Tommy replied that he would comply with the order when it was properly expressed. I don't know how he answered the monocled pipsqueak flying officer who said to him classily: 'Of course, you're not an officer and you can't expect the same respect as I can,' but I can imagine that Tommy's round, ruddy face was full of resentment and that his pale blue eyes held an insubordinate gleam. This same officer, when he learned that Yeo-Thomas was in the dressmaking business before the war, exclaimed: 'My God, what is the RAF coming to!' Tommy subsequently became interpreter to the Forward Air Ammunition Park at Nogent l'Abbesse. By this time he had been promoted to acting sergeant (unpaid).

Towards the end of the year he was ordered to report to HQ Fighter Command at Stanmore in England, but when he arrived there he found that the authorities had no knowledge of him. As there were no spare sleeping quarters available he was given seven days' leave, which he spent in hotels in the West End of London, where he was received with suspicion because he was wearing a sergeant's uniform. It was during this period that Yeo-Thomas first discovered the discrepancy between public acclaim of the defenders of the realm and private practice towards them. In his own words 'our gallant soldiers for whom nothing could be too good were expected to pay for their room in advance when they had only a haversack for luggage'. This baseness of innkeepers and potboys and of civilians generally ought not to have astonished anyone with sufficient history to remember the aftermaths of Waterloo and of the 1914–1918 war.

In the end they found room for Yeo-Thomas at Stanmore, with the Bomber Liaison Section in the filter room. Having been in the Army myself, I don't know what they do in filter rooms, but I find it easy to believe that Tommy's perfect knowledge of French was as wasted there as the fluent Arabic of the soldier who was sent to Iceland. Once again an application to become an air gunner was refused.

But what is important about Tommy's stay at Stanmore is that it was here that he first met Barbara, who was then a young WAAF of twenty-four. I don't know quite what to say about Barbara except that she was, and still is, slim and beautiful. Except in fiction, when one can transmute one's own early miseries into imaginary characters' happiness, it is impossible to write about other people's love affairs. Tommy refers to her, not very originally, as having been his 'inspiration'. Now that romance has mellowed into domesticity I have heard him tell her that she was other things as well, but such frankness is common to couples who have the daily irrelevancies of holes in socks and gas bills to cope with. What I do know about Barbara can be said in a single sentence: she is one of the few exceedingly pretty women I have known who are also sweet and humble and charitable. It was one of Barbara's friends who nicknamed Tommy 'the white rabbit'.

On 6 April, 1940, Yeo-Thomas returned to France, in time to assist at the disaster which ought to have surprised nobody who was familiar with the internecine quarrels of contemporary French politicians.

As soon as the attack began the rot set in, and Yeo-Thomas saw a great deal of it. Stationed with a Bomber Liaison Section at Le Bourget, he tried to forget the moaning of a defeatist French aircraftman in his pity for the refugees streaming down the roads. The bombing of the aerodrome on 3 June again aroused his desire to fight. But there was to be no fighting in France for Yeo-Thomas, or, indeed, for many others for a long time. On 11 June, when all lines of communication had been broken, the OC of the Section, Flight Lieutenant James, and Tommy reported to the Air Attaché's office for instructions and found that the whole British Embassy staff had left. They decided to fall back to Tours.

Yeo-Thomas, who had been sleeping at his father's flat, went to Passy to pack his things. The sky above the city was covered with a huge black cloud of smoke which came swirling down into the streets and darkened them. This smoke came from the burning oil factories at Port Jerome near Rouen, and even the summer sun was powerless to pierce it. Like a gigantic pall it lay over the whole town, seeming to symbolise the extinction of hope.

There were few people on the pavements, and those who were looked sullen and cast angry looks at Tommy in his RAF uniform. '*Tiens, un Anglais,*' one of them said. '*Je croyais qu'ils avaient tous foutu le camp depuis longtemps.*' '*Aussitôt que les Anglais entendent parler de la guerre ils font dans leur culotte,*' was his friend's attempt to explain the French reverses. Although resenting the reproach, Yeo-Thomas realised its partial justice. The British, owing to the folly of their own politicians, had sent too few troops and too few planes. Tommy was bitter, feeling that he had two sets of buffoons to be ashamed of.

Because he loved Paris and was afraid that he might never see it again, Yeo-Thomas walked slowly through the familiar streets. The Champs-Elysées were deserted, invisible almost in the fog of rolling smoke. He walked slowly along the Avenue Kléber, took a last look at the Trocadéro and the Eiffel Tower, and dropped into a small café at the corner of the rue Franklin for a drink. He was the only customer. He drank in silence because the patron was too numbed and shattered to talk. After dining in an empty restaurant he went home and wrote a farewell note to his father, who was in the country.

Next day the small unit left Paris in three cars. Miserable and angry, Tommy was further distressed by the terrible scene. The roads were jammed with refugees. There were limousines filled with the glossy rich. There were young women riding in hearses. Lorries, buses, carts and wagons crept slowly away from the city in a never-ending stream. The cyclists moved as quickly as the cars and the pedestrians moved as quickly as the cyclists. Children pushed babies in perambulators or barrows. Old men and women shuffled along with tears in their eyes and fear or fury on their faces. There were soldiers too in the crowd, soldiers who had thrown away their arms and officers hurrying from the battle. Every now and then German aeroplanes flew overhead and dived to bomb the rag-taggle procession, and the wretches rushed in terror to the ditches.

The section carried on with its duties for a few days at Tours, until the rapid German advance compelled them to retreat to Limoges. The announcement of Pétain's request for an armistice forced them to move on from there by night to Bordeaux, and in the darkness they lost a car with two of their men in it. In Bordeaux they caught a glimpse of that grand old man General Gouraud, Military Governor of Paris, erect and dignified even in defeat. For Yeo-Thomas this was the last sight of the honour of France.

At Bordeaux they were ordered to drive with all speed to Pointe-de-Grave, about sixty miles distant, whence two cargo-boats were on the point of sailing with the last British troops. Flight Lieutenant James and Yeo-Thomas sent the others on ahead while they remained behind to have a last look round for the two missing men. Failing to find them, they warned the local military authorities to keep a look-out for them and themselves set out for Pointe-de-Grave. On their way they ran out of petrol and had to threaten the driver of a chance-encountered tanker in order to obtain a couple of gallons.

There were about forty assorted military personnel still to be ferried out to the cargo-boats when they reached the harbour. While they were waiting their turn Tommy made a brief pilgrimage to the monument on the Pointe which commemorates the landing of the American troops in 1917. Here, at a stall, he bought a postcard which he sent to a lifelong school-teacher friend, Mademoiselle José Dupuis. 'Dear José,' he wrote, 'I know how you're feeling at present, but don't get discouraged. We will return and liberate France.' This postcard reached its destination.

Gazing at the sun shining on the bright blue sea, he was saddened again by the mockery of the fine weather. The irony of flight on such a day from a country he loved was almost unbearable. For a moment he was tempted to stay behind and help the French to prepare for the invasion which he was sure would take place when Britain had had time to build up her strength. But he knew that if he did so he would have no means of communicating with England and that he would be branded as a deserter. So quite untheatrically the obstinate, cantankerous, insubordinate but utterly loyal little Briton swore his oath; as soon as he reached England he would offer to come back to France and raise volunteers to help the British on the happy day on which they should land again. Then he went back to the harbour and lined up with the other airmen and the soldiers and the FANYs.

It took them three days to reach Milford Haven. When they arrived a highly polished RAF warrant officer crusader was waiting to greet them. 'Make it slippy, you f–ing lot of slovenly bastards,' he barked at them.

It was a happy homecoming.

CHAPTER II

Marking Eternity

Carrying out his resolution to return to France was not as easy as Yeo-Thomas had imagined it would be as he stood in front of the American monument at Pointe-de-Grave, and it took a long time; so perhaps the title of this short chapter is not too far-fetched.

After a brief but happy reunion with Barbara he was posted to the Personnel Dispatch Centre at Uxbridge, where he was given the job of conducting parties of airmen to the Burroughs Wellcome Institute near Euston Station for inoculation against yellow fever. His talents were not as wasted as might be imagined, for he used this unpromising task to develop the ingenuity which was later to stand him in good stead when he became an agent. It was difficult to get a pass out of the camp, but no questions were asked when, two or three times a week, Tommy showed the guard an OHMS envelope addressed to 'The Medical Officer, Burroughs Wellcome Institute, London'. He procured two similar envelopes, stuffed them full of blank paper, addressed one to the Medical Officer at the Burroughs Wellcome Institute and the other to 'The Commanding Officer, No. 1 PDC, Uxbridge'. He was thus able, without a pass, to get in and out of Uxbridge as often as he liked.

At Odiham in Hampshire, where the Free French Air Force officers and men were being trained, he served as an interpreter, and in October was recommended for a commission. His fellow candidates, in his own words, were 'wingless wonders determined, if chosen, to do all they could to save the Administration Branch'. When his turn to be interviewed came, Yeo-Thomas, with shining buttons and neatly pressed uniform, marched smartly in and saluted the selection board. Critically, coldly, searchingly, superciliously, the beribboned inquisitors stared at him.

'You are Sergeant Yeo-Thomas?' an air commodore with a face as wrinkled as a walnut asked him.

'Yes, Sir.'

'How long have you been in the Air Force?'

'Since 27 September 1939, Sir.'

'Where did you live before the war?'

'In France, Sir.'

'Why did you live in France?'

'Because my father and my mother and my family lived in France, Sir.'

'Why did they live there?'

'Because my grandfather and my great-grandfather lived there, Sir.'

'Why did *they* live in France?'

'Because they had business interests there, Sir.'

'Where were you educated?'

'At the Collège de Dieppe and the Lycée Condorcet, Sir.'

'Collège de Dieppe? Never heard of it. What sort of college was it?'

'It is a college belonging to the Académie de Caen, Sir.'

'What was the Lycée Condorcet?'

'A Lycée belonging to the Université de Paris, Sir.'

'What is that equivalent to?'

'I imagine, Sir, that it is approximately the same as Oxford or Cambridge, Sir.'

'You speak French fluently then?'

'Yes, Sir.'

'*Ays-ke parlay-voo fronsay?*' a squadron leader asked.

'*Oui, mon commandant.*'

'His French is good, Sir,' the squadron leader said.

'What have you been doing since your incorporation in the RAF?' the air commodore asked.

'A bit of everything, Sir.'

'In other words, you don't know much about anything?'

'So far I have managed to do everything that has been asked of me, Sir,' Yeo-Thomas replied, restraining his anger because of his respect for Group Captain Flower, who had recommended him for a commission.

Military psychology was then in its infancy and Yeo-Thomas was not asked what colour of dress Queen Elizabeth had worn at her wedding or at what age he had left off wetting his bed. Perhaps because of this omission his candidature was accepted. But the Medical Board, although it passed him A1-4B, disappointed him by the decision that he was too old for flying duties and must remain chairborne. Still anxious not to let down Group Captain Flower by expressing his natural tendency towards revolt. Pilot Officer F. F. E. Yeo-Thomas reported to Baginton, near Coventry, for duty as an intelligence officer with 308 Polish Fighter Squadron.

It was not until 3 February 1942, and then only after threatening the Air Ministry to have the matter of his mis-employment brought up in Parliament, that the right man found his way into the right place, in the 'RF' Section of Special Operations Executive.

CHAPTER III

The old firm, or explosions arranged

Prior to the 1914-1918 war Christian nations had required only armies and navies to protect them from the dastardly deeds of other Christian nations. (This is not a sneer at religion, but at our manner of practising it.) By the end of that war, however, science had so far outstripped morality as to make an Air Force an essential item in a nation's armoury; and in 1940 a fourth and not very easily classified form of warfare had been added: subversive activities or hitting the enemy behind his lines, but not necessarily below the belt.

The British organisation for prodding the Germans in unexpected places had its headquarters, unsuitably perhaps from a security point of view, in Baker Street, where the ghost of Sherlock Holmes driving past in a phantom hansom with Watson, might notice the variegated uniforms disappearing into the main entrance and murmur deductions in the doltish doctor's ear. Outside the door of Norgeby House a black *plaque* with INTER-SERVICES RESEARCH BUREAU engraved upon it in gold letters attempted to explain to a possibly curious public the number of Naval, Army and Air Force officers, British, American and French, constantly entering and leaving the building. Michael House, on the upper floors of which the high brass sat, pitched between heaven and Marks and Spencer, was slightly more discreet, because the admirals, the generals and the air commodores entered from a lane at the back. Into both buildings, morning and evening, there also poured a stream of pretty secretaries. Some of them, to judge by their literacy, might have been employed as a cover. There the pleasantry ends: in Special Operations Executive, known to its members as the Old Firm, even the sedentary were much too busy to have any time for dalliance.

For the purpose of SOE was deadly serious, and men's lives depended upon its efficiency. The organisation operated under the direct control of the Ministry of Economic Warfare, with tentacles reaching out to the Admiralty, the War Office, the Air Ministry, the Foreign Office and the algebraic MIs. Its activities, as Yeo-Thomas says, were 'multiple, secret and complicated', and their purpose to harass by all means possible the enemy in his own country and in those which he had occupied. This was achieved, for the most part, by the infiltration of agents who alone, or with other agents recruited locally, disrupted the enemy's communications by blowing up railway tracks or hindered his war production by destroying pylons, electricity generating plants and machinery in factories. This form of warfare was both more accurate and benign than aerial bombardment. An agent insinuated into a factory could sabotage effectively and without loss of human life a piece of essential machinery which a squadron of bombers would be lucky to hit by chance. *Pace* Air Chief Marshal Harris, cruelty at a remove is, as the late George Bernard Shaw pointed out, still cruelty, even if the flight lieutenant who lets the phosphorus bomb drop doesn't see the baby catch fire.

For practical purposes and to maintain secrecy, SOE was divided up into a number of water-tight compartments. Yeo-Thomas was sent to work in the Western Europe Directorate, commanded by Lieutenant-Colonel Keswick. Under this Directorate there were two French Sections, 'F.' Section and 'RF' Section. 'F.' Section, commanded by Major (afterwards Colonel) Maurice Buckmaster, was a purely British-operated section employing agents, French or French-speaking British, recruited by the British and not connected officially with any of the French Resistance Movements. 'RF' Section, commanded when Tommy joined it by Captain Piquet-Wicks, was a British-staffed section which worked in close liaison with General de Gaulle's Bureau Central de Renseignements et d'Action; it arranged the supply and parachuting of arms and equipment to the French Resistance Movements and the transport to and from France of agents recruited and employed by the Free French.

Colonel Passy, the head of the French BCRA, deplores, in his *20 Duke Street, Londres*, the existence of 'F.' Section, and, in conversation, Yeo-Thomas does not always refer to it cordially. The attitude of both is comprehensible. Passy, a loyal and very courageous Frenchman, did not like to see the British meddling in what he considered to be a purely French province; he forgot that if it had not been for Britain's example there would almost certainly have been no large-scale French Resistance Movements to encourage and arm. Yeo-Thomas, impulsive by nature but certainly understanding the French much better than many of his masters, was perhaps actuated by healthy rivalry; experience has shown that the competitive spirit, if carried only slightly too far, can make an Argyll and Sutherland Highlander hate a Cameronian in the same brigade much more thoroughly than the German whose misdeeds he only reads about in the newspapers.

There were, however, many good reasons for the existence of 'F.' Section. The British wanted to be sure of having at their sole disposal and under their sole control on 'D' day a number of small groups in French territory on whom they could rely to destroy military installations. The fact that these groups were small and had no communication with one another or with the larger French Resistance Movements increased their security, never a very strong quality of the French. There was also the uncertain French internal political situation to be taken into consideration and the prima-donna-ish vapours of de Gaulle, who would temporarily cut off all dealings with the British when he imagined that he had been snubbed by Churchill. In any case, the value of the work done by 'F.' Section has been widely proved, and one of its heroic agents, Odette Sansom, has made its excellence known to the public.

This, however, is a polemic upon which I would not insist, and I mention it only because others have done so.

'RF' Section, in those days, 'lived out' at No. 1 Dorset Square, in a house in which, suitably enough according to the Section's critics in Baker Street, they had succeeded as tenants the directorate of the Bertram Mills Circus. It was here that Yeo-Thomas, running through reams of mostly supererogatory courier from the field, had to learn to

separate the essential from the useless and the possibly informative
from the certainly nonsensical. It was here that he memorised the
symbols of his colleagues so that he was able to act immediately when
AD/E ordered him to contact D/R about the communication which
MA2 had received from L/IF.

Yeo-Thomas had by now been promoted to flight lieutenant to
enable him to cope with his new responsibilities.

In between reading superfluous intelligence about German divisions
on the Eastern Front which had been issued with women's knickers
and brassières in mistake for Balaclava helmets, he had to equip and
prepare the section's current operations. His work soon brought him
in contact with his colleagues of the French BCRA, with some of
whom he was to work later in the field. He came to know and like the
cool, steely-eyed and efficient Commandant (later Colonel) Passy and
his hard-working second-in-command Capitaine Manuel. He made
friends with their assistants and agents, with Pichard, a slim young
man with wavy chestnut hair, and with Ayral, and with other agents
with whom he was afterwards to be intimately associated in the field.

1942 was a building-up period for the Free French and 'RF' Section,
and the BCRA worked without respite. In spite of the protests of their
commanding officers the best men available were selected from the
French troops to be trained as agents. When they had been screened by
the BCRA and MI they were sent to schools specializing in the
functions for which they had been chosen. Radio operators and
saboteurs and men to train agents recruited in France had to be
instructed. Others had to be taught the difficult art of finding new
landing and parachuting grounds in France and organising reception
committees to man them. These last were picked with special care, as
many of them would ultimately be required to supervise all air
operations in a large area.

By the autumn the section had grown to such importance that a
lieutenant-colonel was appointed to command it. Colonel J. R. H.
Hutchison was a dapper little cavalry officer with a passion for tabbing
documents with pink slips inscribed with the order: 'PLEASE
SPEAK'. Under his instructions French was exclusively spoken at
No. 1 Dorset Square and, as not all the staff was bilingual, liberties
were taken with the language of Racine. An agent was once referred to

as '*un vrai fil vivant*', and such literal translations as '*chanson de cygne*' and '*moi, mon vieux, si j'étais dans vos souliers*' enlivened the rooms where Bertram Mills had once contracted their clowns. 'Hutch', as he was inevitably called, was an enthusiastic and courageous soldier: in 1944, when he was more than fifty years old, he was dropped into France, where he valiantly conducted himself as a 'Jedburgh'.

Yeo-Thomas was now in charge of Planning, and Johnson had been recalled from Inchmery to supervise Operations. But, although he no longer needed to waste time reading administrative irrelevancies about Polish and Czechoslovak officers being required to pay for the maintenance of their trusses, Tommy was not happy in his job. Perhaps the memory of a signal received from France in July helped to unsettle him: ALLEZ VOUS ENVAHIR AVANT LE QUINZE AOUT? REPONDEZ OUI OU NON. He felt guilty briefing men for dangerous missions when he himself had never been in the field, and he remembered the vow which he had made at the American Monument at Pointe-de-Grave. He made repeated requests to be sent to France, but all were refused on the grounds that his presence at Headquarters was essential. At last, however, it was agreed that if a mission important enough to require his special knowledge could be found he would be sent to France. Yeo-Thomas quickly found himself this mission.

At that time the Navy was short of small craft for coastal operations. Tommy remembered that Captain Molyneux, his peacetime employer, owned a fast motor-yacht which was moored in Monte Carlo harbour. Thinking that the vessel might interest the Navy, he proposed that he should be entrusted with the mission of seizing her and making a dash for Gibraltar. This suggestion was finally approved and Yeo-Thomas was authorised to approach Captain Molyneux, who agreed to hand over his yacht without compensation. An agent called Charvet, recently sent to unoccupied France, was to provide a crew of three. Four hundred and fifty gallons of petrol, fifty of oil, food and two light machine-guns would be provided by felucca operation. Yeo-Thomas himself would be infiltrated in by the felucca or by parachute or Lysander operation. For this operation he was given the not very opaque name of 'Sea-horse'.

To Tommy's disappointment the whole situation in the Mediterra-

Wing Commander Yeo-Thomas, G.C., M.C. and Bar, Légion d'Honneur, Croix de Guerre, Polish Gold Cross of Merit. Portrait taken eight hours before he parachuted into France for the second time in September, 1943

Pierre Brossolette

Actual message written (on page torn out of a fellow-prisoner's diary, with the lead out of a pencil) by Tommy while wearing handcuffs and travelling in a lorry. This message was thrown out into a street in the outskirts of Paris. Tommy saw two bicyclists pick the message up and it eventually arrived on Barbara's desk in London

ARMEE DE L'AIR

Fiche N° : 3 (1, 2 ou 3)

Centre de Démobilisation du Bataillon de l'Air 3 de Marignane

FICHE DE DÉMOBILISATION

CORPS : _____ GRADE : Caporal

SPÉCIALITÉ : Téléphoniste _____

NOM : THIERRY _____ PRÉNOMS : François Yves _____

DATE : 17 Juin 1904 et lieu de naissance : Arras (P.d.C.)

NATIONALITÉ (1) Française de naissance - naturalisé - ne justifiant d'aucune nationalité tort 3
de la loi de recrutement)

SITUATION DE FAMILLE (1) : célibataire, marié, veuf, divorcé — enfants

PROFESSION (exercée avant les hostilités) : Employé dans une agence de Tourisme

ADRESSE (avant les hostilités) : 22 rue de Nanterre à Asnières (Seine)

ADRESSE où se retire l'intéressé : { provisoire : 22 rue de Nanterre à Asnières
{ définitive : _____

BUREAU DE RECRUTEMENT : Dieppe _____ N° Mle de recrutement : _____

ou, à défaut, localité dans laquelle a été passé le Conseil de Révision : _____

DERNIÈRE UNITÉ D'AFFECTATION : Service de recueil des avions - Le Bourget

BATAILLON DE L'AIR (ou Unité) rejoint au { Service de recueil Date : 4 septembre 1939
moment du dernier appel sous les drapeaux : { d'avions le Bourget

AFFECTÉ SPÉCIAL au titre de l'établissement : _____

(1) Rayer les mentions inutiles   A Marignane , le 25 juillet 1940

Le Commandant
du Centre du Démobilisation :

Empreinte des deux pouces	Signature de l'intéressé

The certificate of demobilisation, bearing the false identity of
François Thierry, manufactured in London during the war

The identity card, also manufactured in London, for François Yves Tirelli, another of the identities assumed by Wing Commander Yeo-Thomas nean suddenly changed and the project was abandoned. He was, however, allowed to hold himself in readiness for another mission and on 29 November, 1942, set off for the parachute school at Wilmslow.

CHAPTER IV

Tommy would a-jumping go . . .

W hen Yeo-Thomas returned to Dorset Square he found that the situation in France had become critical. The Free French agents working for the BCRA were in constant and grave danger. They were tracked and harassed not only by the Gestapo but also by the Vichy Police, the Group Mobile and Darnand's Milice. The weakness of the various Resistance Movements was accentuated by the fact that, largely because of their political differences, they were all working independently. In order to increase their efficiency it was necessary both to finance and to co-ordinate them. And if they were to aid the Allies when they invaded France, the paramilitary organisations of all groups must be welded into a unified Secret Army, working under a single Commander with an efficient staff. In particular, the activities of the Communist Party must be ascertained and their leaders persuaded to allow their combat units to join the united paramilitary branches.

It was therefore decided to send Colonel Passy and Commandant Brossolette to France to effect the co-ordination of the Resistance Movements in the Occupied Zone.

Passy, the head of the BCRA, who had taken his *nom de guerre* from the métro station, was then thirty years old. Fearless, cultivated and intelligent, his real name was André Dewavrin. He had been educated in Paris at the Collège Stanislas, the Lycée Louis le Grand and the Ecole Polytechnique. In 1938 he had been assistant professor of fortifications at St Cyr and in 1940 had fought in Norway. He had left France to join General de Gaulle on 18 June, 1940. At the end of the war he was to hold the British DSO and MC as well as French and Norwegian decorations.

Pierre Brossolette, still under forty, was small and thin. He had thick black hair with a bright white lock in front. Passy says of him: '*Brossolette fut, sans conteste, l'homme qui, parmi tous ceux que j'ai été amené à rencontrer dans ma vie, fit sur moi la plus forte impression.*'[1] Educated at the Ecole Normale, where he had taken his degree in history, he had, before the war, been a regular contributor to the Socialist daily *Le Populaire*. The Popular Front Government had appointed him an official foreign news commentator on the national radio, from which post he had been dismissed in 1938 because of his violently expressed disapproval of the Munich Agreement. After the Armistice in 1940, refusing to write for the collaborationist Press, he had purchased a small bookshop in the rue de la Pompe near the Lycée Janson de Sailly, whose pupils were his principal customers. He had arrived in England in April, 1942, and had already been on a mission in France.

Passy felt, rightly or wrongly, that British agents making use of Frenchmen living in France often left them under the impression that they were working for de Gaulle, whereas in reality they were working only for the British. Suspecting, too, that British agents had caused trouble by contacting groups already linked with the BCRA, he wanted to find out the truth for himself. This he proposed to do during his mission of co-ordination. But in order to avoid his report being regarded as biased he requested that a British officer should be sent with Brossolette and himself to make an independent report, both on this subject and on the co-ordination of the Resistance Movements. Because of his knowledge of France and of his perfect command of the language Yeo-Thomas was chosen. Security was increased by his retaining the code name of Seahorse. He was sent immediately to Beaulieu, where he learned the difficult art of sending messages in cypher.

1 'Brossolette was, without doubt, the man who, amongst all those I have met in my life, made the greatest impression on me.'

On his return to London, Yeo-Thomas was given false papers in the name of François Thierry, whose story he had to learn by heart and make his own. He had been born on 17 June, 1901, at Arras, and was a bachelor. Before the war he had lived at 41 rue St Ferdinand, Paris, and had worked as a clerk. During the war he had served with the 34 Bataillon de l'Air and had been demobilised at Marignane on 27 August, 1940. He lived now at 9 rue Richepanse, Paris, and had taken up his previous employment as a clerk. To support this story he was provided with a Carte d'Identité issued by the Paris Préfecture de Police on 16 April, 1941, a Feuille de Démobilisation issued in Marseilles on 2 September, 1940, and a Permis de Conduire issued in Paris on 12 June, 1934. He was also furnished with a current French ration card issued in the name of Thierry.

Finally, Yeo-Thomas received his orders, which read:

SEAHORSE OPERATION ORDER

1. Seahorse to investigate with Colonel Passy . . . the potentiality of Resistance groups in the 'Zone Occupée'.

This investigation will comprise:

(*a*) A thorough examination of the set-up, especially with regard to its effectiveness.
(*b*) An inquiry into the nature of existing groups and their relation to the present central staff, known as Etat-major Zone Occupée.
(*c*) The consideration, in conjunction with the Forces Françaises Combattantes staff officers, of the means for establishing a system of joint control, firstly in France and secondly in relation to a future inter-allied command.

2. An especially important function, from the point of view of SOE, is to decide, as near as possible, the real capacity of individual organisations to furnish men and equipment, and carry out precise tasks or directives emanating from London but issued by local commanders.

On the basis of the above an approximate estimate of the requirements of these groups in the way of equipment, communications, arms and explosives will be furnished.

3. Special attention should be paid to the Communistic Organisation, known paramilitarily as FANA, in order to ascertain:

(*a*) whether it is seriously willing to fall in with the FFC plans for a local general staff, or, if not, whether use could be made of the organisation on the basis of liaison rather than direct control;
(*b*) whether we may be able to implement the progress and action, especially on the side of training and ability.

Rather a tall order, don't you think?

CHAPTER V

The seahorse is amphibious

In those days operations took place between the end of the first quarter and the beginning of the last quarter of the moon, preferably when the moon was at its fullest. Yeo-Thomas calculated that he would be leaving between the 17 and the 28 of February. As the day approached he was surprised that he did not feel frightened. Instead he found himself thinking of José Dupuis, the school-teacher friend to whom he had sent a postcard on leaving Pointe-de-Grave. Sure that she at least was loyal and hoping that she listened into the French news from London, he sent her a message by the BBC '*De Tommy à José. Nous reboirons bientôt du bon vin de Chignin.*'[1] During holidays before the war he had drunk this wine with her in the village near Chambéry after which it was named, and he was confident that she would understand the message if she heard it.

Meanwhile plans had been slightly changed. Brossolette had already left for the field and Passy and Yeo-Thomas were to follow him.

On the morning of 24 February Tommy was warned that the operation would take place that night. He had a farewell lunch with Barbara, who by now was a civilian working for the BCRA. At three o'clock he left Dorset Square for 10 Duke Street, where he picked up Passy. They were driven through the cold misty countryside to Tempsford in the Midlands, where they arrived about five o'clock.

1 'From Tommy to José. We'll soon drink again good Chignin wine.'

After a cup of piping hot tea they went through all their kit under the vigilant eyes of an accompanying officer. The clothing which they were going to wear in France was examined for tell-tale English labels and the pockets turned out to make sure that they did not contain any forgotten bus tickets or British-stamped envelopes. No objection was made to the Countess Grabbe's sachet which Yeo-Thomas still wore round his neck. When they had changed from their uniforms into their civilian suits they put in the now secure pockets their false French identity papers, their money, their benzedrine tablets and other appurtenances. In case of sudden need Yeo-Thomas placed his cyanide tablet in his waistcoat pocket while Passy concealed his inside a small signet ring with a swivel top. They were dined by the CO, who produced a bottle of excellent burgundy.

The two agents then put on their strip-tease suits, rubber helmets and spine pads. An outer thigh pocket carried their revolvers and other special pockets their compasses and knives. To their already cumbersome gear they attached their parachutes. With all their armour on they were driven out to the waiting Halifax bomber whose shape loomed up eerily through the mist. The accompanying officer wished them luck by saying '*merde*'. They climbed clumsily into the aircraft, because the hole was not very large and their parachutes made ingress difficult.

Inside there was not much room for them to sit because of the packages piled up all around. Each package was protected with sponge rubber and heavy canvas and had its parachute attached. The packages, inside one of which were Passy's and Tommy's suitcases, contained arms, wireless transmitting sets and explosives.

The despatcher, a sergeant, busied himself upon last-minute jobs. The engines started up, the aeroplane vibrated and began to move slowly forward. Because there were no windows or openings, Yeo-Thomas could not see out, but he could feel that they were taxying up to the end of the runway, where the aircraft would turn into the wind. The aircraft stood still. The engines broke out into a roar and then quietened down again. The pilot opened the throttle, and the great Halifax began to move forward once more, gradually going quicker and quicker. Soon a light, thin feeling beneath his legs told Yeo-Thomas that they were airborne.

In those days there were two nights in the world, one which we believed to be the right kind and the other the wrong kind. It was from the right kind of night to the wrong kind of night that Yeo-Thomas was going, so that the wrong kind of night might again become the right kind of night. A thought similar to this occurred to him as he sat there among the packages unable to talk to Passy because of the noise of the engines. He was wondering what it would feel like to be surrounded by Germans, to walk in familiar places and to know that all around him were enemies, the constant perception of whose presence might lend an appearance of rectitude to their purposes.

About half an hour later they were over the French coast. Soon the bursts of flak could be heard above the drone of the engines. The pilot took avoiding action, mounting, diving, swerving. Suddenly there was silence, the machine side-slipped wildly, and for a second Yeo-Thomas thought that they were going to have to bale out. Abruptly, however, the engines roared into life again and the aircraft went steadily on. Shortly afterwards they began to circle and Tommy knew that the pilot must be looking for the pinpoint and the lights of the reception committee. But although they kept there, there was still no sign from the despatcher, and at last the circling stopped and the sergeant came forward and shouted in Tommy's ear:

'Low cloud over your pinpoint. Pilot can't find it. We're going home.'

Yeo-Thomas passed the message on to Passy. Angry at the anticlimax, they sat in silence. They passed through searchlights and more flak as they re-crossed the French coast, but both of them were too dejected to feel afraid. At 4.30 a.m. they were back in Tempsford, so short a distance separated the wrong from the right sort of night. Tired out, they went to bed and next morning, on instructions from Headquarters, returned to London.

On Friday, 26 February, they made another attempt. The aircraft took off shortly after midnight in the pale light of the waning moon. Apart from a little flak over the French coast, the flight was uneventful. At about 3 a.m. the despatcher came to tell them that they were over the pinpoint, which was near Lyons-la-Forêt in Normandy. He opened the hatch, round which he had already arranged the packages, ready to be pushed out after the agents had jumped. Passy and Yeo-Thomas climbed over and hooked up the static lines which would pull open their parachutes as they fell through the hole. (In operations over France the drops were too low to permit the use of self-opening parachutes.)

Passy, who was to jump first, got into position with his back to the engine and his legs dangling through the hole. Tommy sat opposite him, ready to swing in as soon as he had jumped. Below him he could see the lighted torches of the reception committee, twinkling like an incandescent necklace. The red lamp went on. Seeing his companion stiffen, Yeo-Thomas edged nearer the hole. The despatcher's arm went up, the lamp turned to green and Passy disappeared. Surprised at his own fearlessness, Tommy swung his legs into the hole and gave a push. He felt the rush of air in the slip-stream and then the slight jerk of his parachute opening out as he started to float down.

Slightly to the right and underneath him he could see the monster flower of Passy's parachute shining in the moonlight. The air was crisp and cold. The light of the torches came rushing up to meet him. He touched the ground, rolled over, undid his harness, stood up and drew in his breath. He had fulfilled the vow which he had made in 1940 in front of the American memorial at Pointe-de-Grave. He had returned to France. Seahorse had arrived.

A man came rushing up to him and vigorously shook his hand.

'*C'est vous, Shelley?*'

'*Oui,*' Yeo-Thomas replied, a little puzzled by the vocative but realizing that it was more prudent to agree than to ask for or attempt explanations. (He discovered later that this name, which was to become famous throughout the whole of French Resistance, was a second code name about which no one had told him.)

By now the packages were coming down, braked by their pretty balloons of puffed-up parachute. When they had landed Passy and Yeo-Thomas helped the reception committee to carry them to a small wood a few hundred yards away, where they were concealed in a pit specially dug to receive them. Then they took off their strip-teases and handed their flasks of rum round to their almost frozen hosts.

'*Allons, mes enfants, au travail?*' the leader of the reception committee said.

This leader was Jacot, one of the original members of the Resistance

Movement known as the Confrérie de Notre Dame, and he spoke with the authority gained by experience. The members of the reception committee were to remain behind to bury the packages. Passy and Yeo-Thomas, accompanied by a guide, would proceed on bicycles to the safe house fifteen kilometres away where they were awaited. Curfew, however, was at midnight and they had no right to be out after this hour. As there was always the danger of running into a German patrol on the road a story had been concocted in case of mishap. They were to say that they had been at a wedding party at which they had stayed too long through being slightly drunk and were out after curfew because they had to be back at work in Rouen the next morning. In order to lend plausibility to this explanation it was essential they should carry nothing compromising on their persons or in their suitcases.

Accordingly Passy and Yeo-Thomas handed over their pistols. They said that there was nothing compromising in their cases, which, groping in the darkness, they removed from the package which had contained them.

'On no account must you make any noise,' the guide said. 'If I make a sign you are to dive into the nearest ditch or bush.'

There were carriers on the bicycles for their bags. That on Tommy's was fitted with an extensible elastic fixture which went round the case and clipped back on to the carrier. The bicycle itself had been made for a man of over six foot and, as Yeo-Thomas was only five foot eight, he had to climb on to a pile of stones in order to mount.

The guide, putting a finger to his lips, moved off. Passy followed and Yeo-Thomas came last. They had gone only a hundred yards when Tommy's case fell off with a resounding crash. Alarmed, the guide looked round, put his finger to his lips again and hissed for silence.

Yeo-Thomas got off his bicycle. But when he attempted to fasten his case on again he found that the elastic of the strap had perished and was beyond repair. The only thing he could do was to lay the suitcase across the handle-bars with one end against his chest and the bottom on the top part of the frame. Then he had to find another pile of stones in order to mount again. Lurching over the ruts, he found it almost impossible to balance the case and at the same time reach down with his too short legs to the distant pedals. At the first big bump the case banged against the bell on the handlebars and made it tinkle. The guide looked round again angrily. Yeo-Thomas dismounted once more and tied his handkerchief round the bell while his companions waited impatiently. Then he had to find a mound in order to be able to mount again. Almost immediately the leader thought he heard a suspicious noise and he signed to them to dive for cover. This happened several times. After each alert Yeo-Thomas had to hunt for another pile of stones or a mound.

By the time they reached the outskirts of Lyons-la-Forêt Tommy's chest was sore, his fingers half-crushed and his legs aching. The guide signalled to them to dismount and hide in the shadow of a wall while he went forward on foot and reconnoitred. After a little he returned and motioned them on. Once again Yeo-Thomas had to climb on to his uncomfortable machine, but this time the ride was short. Soon the leader stopped in front of a small door which opened immediately. They pushed their bicycles through it and leaned them against a wall. Their guide led them into a brightly lighted room, in the centre of which was a huge table covered with food.

Their hostess was a young and attractive woman called Madame Vinet. She was the wife of the local chemist, who was a member of the reception committee. The rich meal of Bayonne ham and galantine with truffles surprised Yeo-Thomas, accustomed to the dreary rations of Great Britain. There was also a delicious cider to drink and to end up with a glass of old calvados. It was only afterwards that Tommy learned that the Vinets, although living sparingly themselves, had spent their savings on the black market in order to give their helpers from England what they considered to be a fitting welcome. When the members of the reception committee turned up and handed the two agents the revolvers which they had taken the risk of carrying on their persons, Yeo-Thomas was moved almost to tears. Solemnly they all stood up and drank a toast to victory. He discovered, however, when Passy and he went up to their room, that their own journey through the night had not been devoid of serious danger: in the darkness Passy had taken by mistake and carried on his bicycle a case containing a wireless transmitter, hand grenades and explosives.

Next morning, when Passy's suitcase had been retrieved, they and Jacot set out by bus for Rouen. The bus, belonging to the local hotel

and driven by producer gas, was a rickety affair, with worn seats and
broken springs. Their fellow passengers, mostly peasants on their way
to town to sell their produce on the black market, did not talk much,
perhaps because they were afraid that the three strangers on the bus
might be German agents. Smelling of onions, sweat, garlic and stale
wine, they sat, meanly purposeful, like characters in a short story by
Guy de Maupassant. In silence too, Yeo-Thomas gazed out at the
Normandy countryside which he had known since boyhood and
which he had not seen for so long.

Their first rendezvous was with Brossolette in Paris. To help pass the
two hours which they had to wait in Rouen before their train left, Jacot
took them to a café. On their way Yeo-Thomas had his first sight of the
occupying troops: on the pavements where Madame Bovary's best
dress had billowed in the breeze in beautiful syntax strutted the SS in
black uniforms with skull and crossbones; on the cobbles over which
the curtained cab had clattered tore the tyres of tremendous Teutonic
trucks. The high peaked caps and shining riding-boots of the officers
brought such fury to Tommy's expression that Jacot had to warn him:
'*Faites attention, Shelley. S'ils vous voient les regarder comme ça, vous
vous ferez arrêter.*'[1]

In the café the customers were badly dressed, dowdy and depressed.
The drinks were ersatz: Campari tasted like Cinzano and Cinzano like
Noilly Prat. Later, on a walk round the town, Jacot told them of
further changes: there was no longer any milk in France and to ask for
a *café crème* might indicate suspicious unfamiliarity with contemporary conditions; there were meatless days and days when even substitute
alcoholic drinks were not served except in black-market restaurants.
He explained to them how to use their ration and tobacco cards.

The Paris train was crowded with the same sort of wooden-faced
people they had seen on the bus, so familiar with tragedy that they
were bored by it. The two agents and Jacot travelled first-class, avoiding the compartments marked '*Nur für Wehrmachts-angehörige*'.[2]
Their journey was uneventful.

They arrived at the Gare St Lazare at 8 p.m. The station was blacked-

1 'Look out, Shelley. If they see you looking at them like that you'll be arrested.'
2 'Reserved for Wehrmacht.'

out. Passengers were scurrying through the darkness to catch the forlorn suburban trains. Groups of Feldgendarmerie moved menacingly up and down in the obscurity.

There were also German soldiers in the métro, entering by the exit stairs and pushing out of the way the civilians whom they met. Their discipline, however, was good: even in the first-class compartments, in which all military travelled free, other ranks saluted officers. At Villiers, where Jacot and the two agents changed, there were more troops on the platform of that already dismal junction. By the time they came out under the cold bright stars at the Porte Dauphine Tommy was beginning to be able to look at the enemy without glaring.

Brossolette was waiting for them in the rue de la Faisanderie, in a flat which belonged to another school-teacher, Madame Claire Davinroy. Her apartment was considered as specially safe, as the rest of the building was occupied by members of the Gestapo, who would be unlikely to expect such temerity on the part of the subversive. Brossolette, to avoid recognition, had dyed his white streak of hair.

After dinner it was decided, as an additional precaution, to split forces and to organise other safe houses to which they could move if the need arose. Yeo-Thomas, who arranged to meet Passy and Brossolette at the Porte Maillot next morning at eleven, was taken to a nearby flat belonging to Roland Farjon, son of the ex-vice-President of the Senate. Monsieur and Madame Farjon welcomed him warmly and invited him to stay as long as he liked. But as they had young children and were already running great risks to help the Resistance, Tommy declined and, thanking them, said that he would seek another lodging next day.

In the morning he breakfasted with his hosts in an ice-cold room on ersatz coffee without milk, grey-brown bread and approximate jam. This meagre table of the rich made him realise how much greater must be the privations of the poor. As he left to take his first walk in occupied Paris, Yeo-Thomas was more than ever conscious of the urgency of the work he had undertaken.

It was as yet only 8.30 a.m. and the sky was grey, but with a promise of sunshine later. As he walked along the rue de la Pompe towards the Trocadéro, he made rules for himself: he must get used to working surrounded by the enemy, he must study the habits of the police, watch out for new regulations and merge himself as much as possible with the French population.

The silence of the streets struck him at once. There was almost no motor traffic except for German staff cars or lorries. An occasional French car snorted along, belching flames from its cylindrical produ-cer-gas containers. Instead of taxi-cabs there were vélo-taxis. These consisted of one- or two-seater wooden or wicker trailers fitted behind cycles or tandems on which the husky drivers pedalled. There were also numerous bicycles, with number plates. Then he noticed the Jews with yellow stars sewn on to their clothes. They and most of the other people on the pavements looked shabby and unhappy and cold. Almost everybody was wearing wooden-soled shoes. Paris seemed even sadder than the last time he had seen it, with the black smoke swirling down in oily coils from the sky.

In the rue de Passy there were long queues of miserable shivering women outside apparently empty food shops. Yeo-Thomas walked into a bistro on the Place and ordered a coffee. It was served of course without milk and to sweeten it there was liquid saccharine in a bottle. The usual assertive know-alls were lined up along the counter, but instead of running France at a few million removes they were talking about food. A man with a small yellow pool in his eye had managed to acquire ten pounds of potatoes. A man with a face like a petulant Clemenceau had received half-a-pound of butter. There was no talk of the Germans. For the mean muttering men the disaster had already receded into history. Disgusted, Yeo-Thomas paid and went out.

When he reached the end of the street he turned down towards the métro station from which he could look down at his father's flat. It was more than two years since he had last heard from the old man and he gazed at the familiar windows with affection. Then he turned and walked up the rue Franklin towards the Trocadéro. Rounding the bend, he was startled to see a cordon of French and German police drawn up across the street. His first inclination was to turn and walk back in the opposite direction, but he knew that he could not do this without arousing suspicion. Mastering his fear, he pulled out his false identity card and approached the police.

The police were working in pairs, one French and one German.

When his turn came Yeo-Thomas showed his card. He trembled inwardly as both policemen glanced at his photograph and read through his description. He did his best to look unconcerned while they examined him closely. Was there, after all, something wrong with his card? Had SOE slipped up? Then the German policeman said '*Gut*'. He was handed back his card and allowed to walk on.

Confident now that his identity card was a first-class forgery, Yeo-Thomas moved on, but not too quickly, in case the police might still be watching him. A pale sun was beginning to pierce the sky. In spite of the swastikas flying from requisitioned buildings the city still looked beautiful. Tommy's heart grew bold and happy. He was back in Paris, not yet in uniform it was true, but that would come. His content vanished when, approaching the Avenue Victor Hugo, he ran into a second police barrage.

The short distance between the two barrages seemed significant. Had the Gestapo already got wind of his arrival or were they after some other agent? To his consternation he saw three or four men being pushed into a waiting Black Maria. Fearful but again feigning indifference, he approached the policemen. Once again he was allowed to pass.

Good agents always arrived punctually at their rendezvous, as hanging about attracted attention. Yeo-Thomas reached the Porte Maillot at eleven o'clock exactly and so did Passy and Brossolette. They went at once to 102 Avenue des Ternes, where relations of Brossolette's, the Peyronnets, lived. Madame Peyronnet, whose flat was to become a regular meeting-place for the agents, at once found a safe house for Passy in the nearby rue Marcel Renaud and for Yeo-Thomas at Neuilly in the rue Casimir Pinel. The rue Marcel Renaud opened on to the busy rue Demours, in which their comings and goings would be unlikely to be noticed, and the flat, on the ground floor and giving on to a courtyard itself backing on to that of an adjacent building, would be easy to escape from if the police arrived suddenly. Tommy's safe house was in a luxury flat belonging to the blonde and attractive French cinema star Jeanne Helbling. This flat was on the first floor and it too overlooked a courtyard, escape from which would be easy. Brossolette was to remain with Claire in the rue de la Faisanderie. Apart from these three flats they gradually located a number of subsidiary apartments to which they could retreat if any of their present safe houses became 'blown'.

Work was begun immediately. While Passy busied himself with intelligence matters, Yeo-Thomas got in touch with agents already sent to the field to organise parachuting and landing operations and the storage of weapons and explosives. These agents were Schmidt, Ayral, Fassin, Pichard and Deshayes. Brossolette established contact with the various Resistance Groups with whom their mission chiefly lay.

In order to accomplish their operational orders, it was decided to:

1. Ascertain the strength, the geographical distribution and the nature of each Resistance Group in the Occupied Zone.
2. Explain to the leaders of each Group and obtain their acceptance of the principles of organisation to which they would be required to conform upon incorporation in the Secret Army.
3. Separate in each Group Intelligence from Action and the Military side from the Civil side.
4. Prepare the Co-ordination of the paramilitary bodies, after having organised them on sound bases with proper General Staffs.

This was an immense task. There were many Groups in France of whose existence and location they were ignorant; all had to be included if their co-ordination was to be effective. They had to distinguish between Resistance Groups proper and purely intellectual associations. Prior to their departure for the field it had been assumed that names like *Voix du Nord, Le Cerle* and *La Ligue* represented Resistance Organisations. It was found that they did not. *Voix du Nord* was a clandestine publication expressing the opinions and aspirations of not very active resisters, while the last two movements were of purely political or masonic origin. A common denominator had to be found before the values and merits of the real Resistance Groups, embryonic as yet, could be assessed. After a process of elimination the following five important Groups emerged:

1. Organisation Civile et Militaire.
2. Ceux de la Libération.

3. Ceux de la Résistance.
4. Libération.
5. Front National.

Their first meeting was with Colonel Touny, the leader of the Organisation Civile et Militaire. An ex-regular cavalry officer, he was a tall, powerfully built man in his middle fifties. He was assisted by a Commandant Berthelot and Roland Farjon, who had sheltered Yeo-Thomas on his first night in Paris. Both Touny and Farjon were later arrested and died.

The Organisation Civile et Militaire was found to be the most complete and highly organised of all the Groups and to possess the best security. With members at all levels in the Société Nationale des Chemins de Fer, the Postes, Télégraphes et Téléphones and other public services, it would be able seriously to harass the Germans on 'D' day. Although non-political in structure, the views of its followers inclined towards the right. From its highly organised paramilitary branch, strong in the north and the centre, it was hoped to recruit high-grade cadres and troops for the Secret Army. The effective membership of this Group was estimated at 40,000.

Shortly afterwards, Passy, Brossolette and Yeo-Thomas made their first contact with the Communist Party in the person of a young man called 'Joseph'. Oval-faced, clever and courageous, Joseph was a representative of the Communist Intelligence branch, known by the code letters FANA. Although they all got on well together, their first meeting did not resolve many problems. When it was suggested that a WT link should be established between FANA and London, Joseph replied that the party's communications were already overwhelmed with transmissions. As there were then no communications between FANA and London, the supposition could only be that there were plenty between FANA and Moscow. When Joseph complained that the Communists were not receiving any arms from the Allies, Yeo-Thomas proposed that they should first send men to London to be trained in their use. Joseph promised to do so but the men were never sent. The non-political Yeo-Thomas anticipated Mr Ernest Bevin by at least three years in arriving at the conclusion that the Russians wished to keep their adherents as far removed as possible from contact with those who subscribed to other ideologies. Another meeting, destined to be more successful, was arranged for a later date.

On 7 March they met M. Lecompte-Boynet, the professor-like Chief of Ceux de la Résistance. This was an almost solely para-military organisation, particularly strong in Paris and with branches in the Champagne, Vendée and Cotentin areas. Its members, recruited from all classes, were opposed to political intrusions, seeking, if not a new heaven, at least a new earth. Although at present only about a thousand strong, their cadres and their troops were good and ready for action. Their Intelligence had already done valuable work for MI6. M. Lecompte-Boynet agreed immediately to obey the instructions of the Inter-Allied-Staff. He calculated that he would have at his disposal on 'D' day between 25,000 and 30,000 troops.

Their next meeting was with the leader of Ceux de la Libération, M. Coquoin, who was accompanied by his assistant Médéric. This was a solid Group, again mainly paramilitary and anti-political. Chiefly concentrated in and around Paris, it had offshoots in the Nièvre, Cher, Allier and Brittany. On its staff was the Managing Director of the 'Transports Routiers', an organisation which controlled all road transport in France. In this way the Group obtained valuable information about the transport of German troops, which was carried out largely in commandeered vehicles. Of these the Germans had, as a precaution against invasion, already concentrated stocks in motor transport parks which would be sabotaged by members of the Group when the time came. The Group had also trustworthy agents among the Police, the Fire Brigade and the Garde Mobile, who could be counted upon to take charge of operations on 'D' day. These promises were all kept. The potential of this Group was estimated at 35,000 men.

M. Coquoin readily accepted the instructions which Passy and the others gave him. But Colonel Schimpf, the chief of the para-military organisation whom they met later in a flat on the Avenue de l'Opéra, was a die-hard of the 1914–1918 war and took more convincing. He favoured a more dramatic use of the Secret Army and was all for blood with plenty of thunder. Eventually he reluctantly agreed to obey what at heart he considered very boy-scout orders, but he did not live long enough to implement his word: within eight months he was arrested and died later in Buchenwald. Coquoin was killed at the end of 1943 and the jovial, effervescent and impetuous Médéric was betrayed in 1944 and swallowed his cyanide tablet.

Contact with its baldish chief, M. Périgny, showed that Libération was mainly occupied with intelligence work, the greater part of which was carried out by the subsidiary *Vois du Nord* under the direction of M. Van Wolput. As in the case of its parent, Libération of the Unoccupied Zone, founded by M. Emmanuel Astier de la Vigerie, its paramilitary organisation, only recently started, was almost negligible; indeed, the commanding officer himself was unaware of the number, quality or location of his troops. With Libération were also incorporated the Confédération Générale du Travail, the Confédération Française de Travailleurs Chrétiens and the Comité d'Action Socialiste; the last-named and the Communist Party were the only two survivors of the pre-1940 political parade.

It was Joseph who introduced the three agents to Ginsburger, also a Communist. Ginsburger in turn invited them to attend a meeting of the 'Comité Directeur' of Front National. On 18 March, Passy, Brossolette and Yeo-Thomas sat, at a pre-arranged hour, on a bench near the bandstand in the Luxembourg Gardens; there they were met by a bearded and secretive agent-de-liaison. After they had been made to double several times on their tracks they were led to the Luxembourg Station, where they caught a train for Sceaux. On their arrival at Sceaux, after more tortuous perambulations, they were conducted to a small villa where they found the Directorate awaiting them. The members were Ginsburger, Professor Joliot Curie, Max André, Chanoine Chevrot, Lenten preacher at Notre Dame and Curé of St François Xavier, and a religious known as Father Philippe. If the lion wasn't exactly lying down with the lamb, the weaned child seemed to have put his hand in the cockatrice's den.

Ginsburger presided at the meeting. His opening speech was a foretaste of discourses which were later to become familiar: the Franc-Tireurs et Partisans, the paramilitary organisation of the Communist Party, were the most powerful Group in the Resistance; therefore all the other Groups should unite under the control of the Front National.

For, as Yeo-Thomas was later to point out in a very able report, the

Front National was, in effect, the Communist Party. The apparently anodyne umbrella name had been chosen for the same purpose of concealment as inspired Hitler to include the adjective 'Socialist' in the official title of his oligarchy. The Communists knew that, with their record of trouble-making in 1936 and of disloyalty in 1939, they could not hope to unite under their own fiery label the bourgeois and Catholics. Their tactic was simple, and their reasoning not altogether invalid. Unity was strength, and as their Group was the strongest in the Resistance, it was the duty of the lesser Groups to amalgamate with theirs. Under the name of 'Front National', governed by an obviously representative directorate, they would federate the smaller Groups and bring them without their knowledge under the control of the Communist Executive, whose true identity could be withheld from the curious under the plea of wartime security.

That the Franc-Tireurs et Partisans formed the strongest and most effective Resistance Group could not be denied. Already their shock troops numbered between 25,000 and 30,000. They claimed to carry out roughly 250 attacks and to kill between 500 and 600 Germans every month. These acts had resulted in reprisals, and losses among the rank and file of the Group had been heavy. Such casualties were, however, compensated several times over by the numerous recruits subsequently enrolled. But there was a factor which the Communist leaders did not assess correctly: many of these recruits were not Communists and, as Yeo-Thomas pointed out in his report, 'joined the movement because they were unaware of the existence of any other and because they wanted to hit back at the Germans'.

This swelling of the ranks had lessened the security of the Group. Careless talk had enabled the Gestapo and the Vichy Police to penetrate the organisation. To counteract this the Franc-Tireurs et Partisans had been split up into small hermetically sealed cells. As a result the Group had become unwieldy and the communication of orders a lengthy and laborious process. Possessing many leaders of tiny units, the Movement was almost entirely lacking in cadres.

The eventual strength of the Franc-Tireurs et Partisans was estimated at 100,000 men.

In France, as in most countries, the Communist Party derived the greater part of its membership from discontented workers in the industrial centres: its rank and file were to be found in the lower levels of the metallurgical industries, the French National Railways, the Post Office and other administrations. But although most of them had adhered to the Party since before the war, it was not until after the invasion of Russia by Germany that they were given resistance directives by their leaders. It was clear, therefore, that the Franc-Tireurs et Partisans were directly subordinate to Moscow. Moscow, however, did not contribute any funds and, in order to obtain material assistance, the leaders had to place their troops officially at the disposal of General de Gaulle. Yeo-Thomas summed up the situation thus in his report: 'From my contacts with them I imagine that the rank and file are really patriots and only interested in a free France, whereas the heads have other ideas in mind and are planning well ahead, in fact, so far ahead as the period which will follow the "Gouvernement Provisoire".' Subsequent events were to prove him right. The avowed aim of the Communist Party was the mass uprising of Frenchmen on 'D' day; their real purpose was the expansion of the Party to such a size that it would dominate all others after liberation. Meanwhile BBC newscasters continued to jeer at Frenchmen who feared the 'Communist bogey'.

At this meeting of the Directorate of the Front National the Communists present, while professing political impartiality, tried to impress upon the three agents that the Communist Party was the only pre-war political party still in existence and that its members had always resisted actively. They maintained that it was they who had unified resistance and represented its opinion. In that case, Passy and Brossolette asked, why were none of the other four Resistance Groups represented on their Committee? The plain question was put to the Directorate: were they or were they not going to participate on the same terms as the others in the co-ordination of the Resistance Movements? A reply was promised for a later date.

The first steps had now been taken to the formation of a unified Secret Army. As efficiency rather than numbers was desired, it was intended at first to limit its ranks to 20,000 well-trained troops. This Army would be commanded by a common General Staff known as the 'Etat-major de la Zone Occupée'. Each individual Resistance Group would, through its chief, be required to accept formally the following conditions:

1. That the officers composing the EMZO would be appointed regardless of their groups of origin.
2. That such officers would be appointed on the grounds of their personal merit and not on the basis of proportional representation.
3. That all directives would come from Great Britain in accordance with the plans laid down by the Inter-Allied General Staff.
4. That all troops belonging to the Secret Army would no matter what their origin, obey the orders of those set in authority above them (*sic*).

No effective Secret Army could, however, be mustered until steps had been taken to counteract 'La Relève' or the Compulsory Labour Service. Under order of the occupying authority all Frenchmen between the ages of 19 and 32 had been registered and were being sent to Germany, to work in factories or in the Organisation Todt. Some had even been sent to the Russian front. Although many Frenchmen had avoided registration or had taken refuge underground, combined German and French police forces were combing town and countryside for deserters. In Paris there were continual round-ups in the streets, and men whose papers showed that they were between 19 and 32 years of age were put in lorries and shipped to Germany immediately. Every week 20,000 men were taken from Paris in this way. If, as was stated to be the case, the age limit was to be raised to 42 and then to 55, all hopes of a Secret Army would vanish.

On 14 March, 1943, Yeo-Thomas reported this fact and his fears to London, and suggested a solution. Men must be encouraged by propaganda to evade this conscription. They could, however, do so only in one of two ways: either by leaving the country or by living clandestinely. As for the majority the first alternative was impracticable, there remained chiefly the second. But to live clandestinely the outlaw required both money and forged ration cards with which to obtain food. Both must be provided by the Allies if the potential members of the Secret Army were to be given the means of avoiding deportation to Germany. And the money, he insisted, must be 'on a generous scale and not in driblets'. It was thus that what was later known as the 'Maquis' had its origin.

During their negotiations with the leaders of the Resistance Movements, Passy and the others kept in touch with London. Telegrams for transmission had to be taken to the agent-de-liaison, who, in turn, handed them on to the WT operator. This was a dangerous task for all concerned. The messages, printed in code on thin paper, were carried in an article which could be easily destroyed in case of necessity, such as packet of cigarette papers or a matchbox. But it was the WT operators who ran the greatest risks, as the Gestapo sent special direction-finding vans round the streets and country roads to pick up their transmissions. Consequently the operators had to vary their emplacements; and, transporting their sets in suitcases, they were always liable to be stopped by the German police and required to open their valises.

While Yeo-Thomas went about his business in Paris he took special precautions against being followed. Shadowing, he discovered, was generally carried out by teams of which one member would pass on to another the description of the suspect. In order to vary his appearance he purchased several hats of different shapes and colours and scarves of various patterns and changed both hats and scarves several times a day. He also learned that a sleuth is trained to recognise his prey by his walk. Sometimes, therefore, he wore shoes with steel tips, sometimes shoes without tips and occasionally he put under the heel of one foot a wedge of cardboard, thus completely changing his gait.

The morale of the population, although undernourished, poorly clad and suffering from lack of heating, he found good on the whole. While the rich could resort to the black market, where a meal cost 800 francs and a pair of shoes 450, ordinary men and women, earning from 1,800 to 2,500 francs a month, suffered terrible privations. In spite of their misery few were active collaborators. The mass avoided all contact with the Germans, looking the other way when they passed through the street. The old political parties and 'les cons illustres' of Third Republican Governments had been discredited. All patriots were Gaullists. General Giraud had few followers.

He visited José Dupuis, his school-teacher friend, in her flat at 39 rue de la Félicité. Alternately laughing and sobbing, she told him that she had received the postcard which he had sent from the Pointe-de-Grave and heard his BBC message. She was still teaching at her girls' school in the *premier arrondissement* and her thirty pupils were all patriots. She begged him to give her something active to do even though it were dangerous. Yeo-Thomas engaged her at once, to help him to build up a small circuit of his own by means of which he could keep in touch with his contacts. Eventually she became his second-in-command. The risks which she ultimately ran were considerable, as she was easily recognisable, being five foot ten.

Yeo-Thomas had still plenty of work to do; there were the final details of the amalgamation of the various Resistance Movements to settle, and the Groups in the provinces had to be visited. Pending the arrival in Paris of Moulin and General Delestraint, who had been delegated by de Gaulle to command the unified Resistance, Passy set off to inspect the Somme, the Nord and the Pas de Calais. Yeo-Thomas, accompanied by Pichard, went to visit the Organisation Civile et Militaire on the Nièvre, the Cher and the Allier.

Train journeys were always dangerous on account of the frequent check-ups made by the German and French police. Yeo-Thomas and Pichard travelled first-class for the same reason that they always wore good clothes and smart hats: an appearance of prosperity suggested profitable collaboration with the Germans and rendered them less liable to interrogation. Their journey however was not to be without risk. Just as their train was about to leave Paris a Frenchman whom Yeo-Thomas had known in pre-war days entered their compartment. He was, Tommy remembered, both pro-German and anti-British. Deciding not to go and stand in the corridor in case his abrupt retreat might arouse suspicion, Yeo-Thomas buried his face in his newspaper. Eventually, laying down the paper, he turned to look out of the window. As he raised his head he saw the man look at him and give a start. Gazing out of the window he could feel that the man was still staring at him. He turned again and their eyes met. Yeo-Thomas gave no sign of recognition and began to talk to Pichard. The man leaned forward and touched him on the knee.

'*Monsieur, votre visage m'est familier,*' he said. 'Haven't I met you before the war?'

Yeo-Thomas looked him full in the face.

'*Je pense que vous faites erreur, Monsieur,*' he said. 'Perhaps I look like somebody you know or maybe you've seen me somewhere else, but I'm sure I've never seen you before.'

His bluff succeeded. The Frenchman agreed that he must be mistaken, although he maintained that Tommy's resemblance to an acquaintance of his was startling. After that they talked about the curious and constant recurrence of 'doubles'. Yeo-Thomas was glad when the train reached Nevers.

After lunch in the house of a family which Pichard used as a letter-box they met Courvoisier, an ex-regular NCO of the Zouaves who was the local Resistance leader. A dynamic, bull-necked man, he had as his assistants the Secretary of the Préfecture and the Director of the local-waterworks. Yeo-Thomas spent three days in the area, visiting the reception committees and the resistants.

The Group numbered 2,000 and had well-organised Intelligence, Supply and Operational branches. Among their members they in-cluded the 350 local gendarmes and their Commandant. These policemen protected the reception committees during operations; as they were able to move about the countryside without arousing com-ment they also carried messages, transmitted orders and reported on German troop movements. Invited by the Commandant to meet the senior NCOs and introduced as 'le Capitaine Shelley de la Royal Air Force', Yeo-Thomas gave them a short lecture. Because of the harm already wrought to Resistance by the Giraud affair he emphasised the necessity of recognizing de Gaulle as the only leader of the French. The men were visibly heartened at hearing such an opinion expressed by a British officer.

Later, after visiting M. Jeanneney, ex-President of the Senate and pre-war second personage of France, Yeo-Thomas returned to Paris and reported the result of his mission. The austere Passy, the learned and militant Socialist Brossolette and the jovial, humorous and Conservative Yeo-Thomas had now become intimate friends. Shared danger and a common purpose sought for other ends than personal profit bind bonds more lasting than those which derive from the pitiful commercial pursuits of peace. A house that is founded on shared dividends accruing from the sale of zip fasteners shall not so surely stand.

On 23 March, 1943, they learned that their efforts to unite the paramilitary organisations of the various Resistance Movements had been successful. Colonel Passy's conditions had been accepted by all the Groups. On 26 March there met in Jeanne Helbling's flat in Neuilly the following leaders: Colonel Touny of the Organisation Civile et Militaire; Lecompte-Boynet of Ceux de la Résistance; Coquoin of Ceux de la Libération; Périgny of Libération; and Ginsburger of the Front National. All were accompanied by their assistants and, in the presence of Passy, Brossolette and Yeo-Thomas they signed an agreement which had already been approved by their directing committees.

> Réunis le 26 Mars 1943 en zone occupée les chefs ou représentants mandatés, ci-dessous, de la zone occupée:
> 'OCM.';
> 'Libération', organe de résistance, notamment du Comité d'Action Socialiste, de la Confédération Générale du Travail et de la Confédération Française de Travailleurs Chrétiens;
> 'Front National';
> 'Ceux de la Résistance';
> 'Ceux de la Libération'
> renouvellent collectivement l'assurance, individuellement donnée déjà par chacun de ces groupements, de leur entière confiance dans le Général de Gaulle et le Comité National pour réaliser l'union de tous les français de la Métropole et de l'Empire, pour libérer la France et redonner la parole au peuple français.
> Avec le Général de Gaulle et le Comité National Français ils sont résolus:
>
> > à poursuivre la lutte contre l'ennemi par tous les moyens et particulière-ment les armes à la main; à abattre toutes les dictatures, celles de Vichy comme celles de Berlin et de Rome, et de quelque masque qu'elles se parent; à rétablir les libertés républicaines en rompant, par une profonde rénovation politique et administrative, avec les faiblesses du régime passé aussi bien qu'avec l'arbitraire de Vichy; à promouvoir des réformes économiques et sociales décisives.

The style was perhaps a little bit pompous, and employed many words to say what perhaps could best have been said in a few; that all the French Resistance Movements backed General de Gaulle.

The sincerity of those who signed was proved by each Group agreeing to:

1. Contribute officers and men to the Etat-major de la Zone Occupée and the Secret Army.
2. To obey instructions transmitted by the EMZO as received by it from the Inter-Allied General Staff in London, passing through General de Gaulle.
3. To furnish a true and accurate estimate of their cadres and troops.
4. To pool their possibilities under the control of General de Gaulle, acting in accordance with the Inter-Allied General Staff.

Agreement was also reached on the future employment of the Secret Army. Its members would not be used as regular troops, at least not until after liberation. Quality rather than numbers must be the aim; a few well-trained and tactically placed men would be of more value than unarmed hordes. On 'D' day picked troops from the Secret Army would be supplied with priority targets; troops not so employed would act as guerillas, attacking isolated detachments of the enemy, but would not attempt to deal with armoured formations or large organised units.

But before a truly effective Secret Army could be brought into being its men must be armed. The leaders of the various Groups pointed out that at present their men had almost no arms at all and that their WT communications were practically non-existent. The necessary equipment, they insisted, must be supplied by London. At the same time help must be given to potential recruits to enable them to avoid deportation in the labour drafts to Germany.

There was also the scarcely less important question of medical supplies: drugs, antiseptics and surgical instruments would be required in large quantities. Professor Pasteur Valéry-Radot, a descendant of the famous bacteriologist whose name he bore, had worked on this problem and had prepared a list of his requirements. The three agents undertook that these would be parachuted before 'D' day.

On 12 April Moulin and General Delestraint, whom de Gaulle had delegated to command united Resistance, arrived in Paris from the

Unoccupied Zone, where they, too, had been co-ordinating the various Movements.

Jean Moulin, a small dark man with laughing eyes, had been Prefect of Chartres at the time of the Armistice. There, unlike some of his colleagues elsewhere, he had been dignified and courageous in his attitude towards the invaders. Refusing to sign a declaration that the rotting corpses found lying in and around the town had been the victims of *French* atrocities, he had been imprisoned by the Germans and tortured. Rather than yield he had cut his throat with a razor. This attempt to destroy his life had been discovered before it had succeeded and he had been taken to hospital, where he recovered. On his discharge he had been dismissed by Vichy and accorded military honours by the Kommandantur because of his bravery. In September, 1941, he had landed in England. If Moulin had survived he would almost certainly have been the first post-war Prime Minister of France.

Delestraint was a regular officer of the French army who had made a big impression on the British. Although forceful and fearless, Yeo-Thomas considered him unsuited to clandestine warfare; later, when arrested and questioned, he was to pull out of his pocket two sets of identity papers.

Another meeting was called, at which Moulin and Delestraint were introduced to the Resistance leaders, to whom they expounded their plan for the construction of the EMZO and the Secret Army. Moulin, who rather overshadowed Delestraint, began by increasing the basic figure for troops from 20,000 to 50,000 men. But to achieve this strength, he insisted, every Movement would have to contribute its best men. Furthermore, behind these 50,000 there would have to be held a reserve of 100,000 men. In the meantime the 50,000 men would be organised into compact units and trained like a regular army. And being trained like a regular army, Moulin was careful to point out, meant other things besides being taught the art of killing: it meant learning discipline, how to salute officers and how to stand to attention – in other words, the much-derided and not yet exploded spit and polish.

Naturally the leader of the Communist Franc-Tireurs et Partisans objected. He drew attention to the fact that the immediate transfer of his shock troops to the Secret Army would mean the cessation of their present activities. The more acts of sabotage his men committed, he maintained, the better trained and the more aggressive they became. There was also the propaganda value of such acts to be considered. He was reluctant, under such conditions, to divert any portion of his troops to the Secret Army. While he was still willing to place his men at the disposal of General de Gaulle on 'D' day, he could not curtail their activities in the meanwhile. The meeting broke up without a solution to his objection having been found, although Moulin seemed to meet him half-way by agreeing to ask the Inter-Allied General Staff for a list of interim sabotage targets, against some of which Communist troops would be employed.

The leaders of the other Movements all agreed to concentrate on building up a Secret Army for 'D' day. All leaders were unanimous in insisting that the invasion should take place before the end of the year.

During his last few days in Paris, Yeo-Thomas established contacts for the future visit which he was sure he would have to make. With Passy and Brossolette he met the leaders of the French Trades Unions. Saillant, who had replaced Jouhaux as president of the Confédération Générale du Travail, and Tessier, president of the Confédération Française de Travailleurs Chrétiens, were both opposed to a revival of the old political feuds after liberation. At the time, no doubt, their feeling was sincere; in spite of what St John says, the only time that it is really easy to love our neighbour seems to be when he is helping us to hate another neighbour.

Tommy also went to visit his father in his flat at 3, rue des Eaux. As instructed by José Dupuis, he rang the bell five times. His father showed no astonishment when he opened the door. 'Entrez, Monsieur,' he said, as though his son were a stranger. Then, when he was sure that there was nobody to overhear him, he asked: 'What the bloody hell have you been doing for the last two years? You ought to have been here long ago.' He did not speak of his own imprisonment in Fresnes: he was, he said, doing a little resistance work on his own account. Both father and son were too wise to ask each other for details. After giving the old man some tea, cigarettes, coffee, sugar and money and promising to come and see him again as soon as he could, Yeo-Thomas left as discreetly as he had arrived.

On 14 April word was sent from London to the three agents that they would be picked up on the night of the 16th by a Lysander, from a field near Lyons-la-Forêt. They set out at once from the Gare St Lazare, taking with them an American pilot called Ryan who had been shot down from a flying fortress and sheltered by a friend of Professor Pasteur Valéry-Radot. Ryan had a fractured shoulder, which had been reset by the Professor, and could speak no French. He was told that if anybody spoke to him on the train his reply must be limited to an evangelical '*oui*' or '*non*'.

They travelled in two groups to Pont de l'Arche: Passy, Brossolette and another agent in one compartment, and Yeo-Thomas, Ryan and Dutertre of the Lyons-la-Forêt reception committee in another. During the journey nobody attempted to speak to Ryan, who pretended to be reading a French newspaper. In the buffet at Pont de l'Arche, fumbling for, and at first failing to find, his wallet, Yeo-Thomas committed his only indiscretion. 'Where the hell's my money?' he said in English. Fortunately there were a lot of people talking noisily in the buffet and his remark was not overheard.

From Pont de l'Arche they took a small local train to Fleury-sur-Andelle, whence they made another uncomfortable journey by bicycle to Lyons-la-Forêt. They reached the village after dark. Passy and Brossolette were again sheltered by the Vinets and Yeo-Thomas and Ryan in a neighbouring farmhouse. All next day they remained indoors. Ryan, unaccustomed to clandestine life, kept talking loudly in his unmistakable American accent and on more than one occasion had to be silenced by the farmer's wife.

At 10.30 p.m. Yeo-Thomas and Ryan climbed into a van drawn up in the farmyard and hid behind sacks of potatoes. Dutertre sat in front with the driver. After an hour's bumpy journey the van stopped and they got out. They found themselves on a deserted country road beside a road-mender's hut, into which Tommy's suitcase was pushed. Beside the road a field shimmered like a lake in the moonlight. The stars twinkled brightly in the sky. They hurried across the magic field and lay down in a copse, where they were presently joined by Passy, Brossolette, Vinet and Jacot.

Yeo-Thomas says that he was both happy and frightened while he lay waiting for the Lysander to arrive. He was happy to have accomplished so much and frightened lest a last-minute accident should ruin everything. So much depended upon so little. The district was heavily patrolled. The Lysanders might not turn up. The Germans might hear the hum of the approaching aircraft. Helpless in the huge indifference of the night, the three most-sought-after men in France lay fearful in the copse.

Soon, however, there was a buzzing sound in the air. Dutertre, Jacot and Vinet rose and ran on to the field, where torches had been fixed to three sticks arranged in the form of an L. Jacot flashed the recognition sign and the Lysander replied. The aircraft circled, landed, came down the longer branch of the L against the wind, turned along the shorter and came to a standstill with the wind behind it. A second Lysander hovered overhead.

In less than three minutes Passy, Brossolette, Yeo-Thomas, Ryan and their suitcases were in the gunners' cockpit and the Lysander was airborne again. An hour later they landed at Tangmere, back once more in the right sort of night.

Next evening the BBC French service sent out for the first time the message: *'Le petit lapin blanc est rentré au clapier'*. The little white rabbit had returned to his hutch.

CHAPTER VI

With Hutch in the hutch

The message was true in a double sense, for Colonel Hutchison was still commanding 'RF' Section. The section had grown and was to grow more: Captain Alex Murray had come from Costa Rica; Captain Thackthwaite, later to be awarded the OBE for his work in the field, enlivened the drudgery inseparable even from clandestine organisation by reciting undenominational clerihews. Flight Lieutenant Whitehead, shortly to win the MC for bravery, was to join from Tommy's former Polish squadron. The moon period was on, operations were in full swing and supplies had already been sent to some of the reception committees which Yeo-Thomas had visited.

It is possible that Yeo-Thomas's unceasing insistence upon the necessity of priority for the needs of French Resistance may have exasperated some of his superiors who had neither his knowledge nor love of France. Without losing any time he sent in a detailed report of the results of his mission. All day long he bombarded brigadiers, colonels and air commodores with written memoranda and spoken words emphasizing the importance of creating an effective Secret Army in France. He shot off his mouth at conferences, he counselled strategists and intimidated politicos, and always his arguments were the same. An invasion of the Continent could not be carried out expeditiously without the aid of a Secret Army already established on French soil. A Secret Army could not be found already established on French soil unless explosives and arms and money were sent to France.

Therefore explosives and arms and money must be sent to France. A Secret Army could not be mustered unless able-bodied young Frenchmen were helped to evade the Compulsory Labour Service. Therefore able-bodied young Frenchmen must be helped to evade the Compulsory Labour Service. General de Gaulle was the acknowledged leader of all patriotic Frenchmen. Therefore all those who supported General Giraud were knaves, buccaneers and fools. The French were afraid that the British and the Americans would amputate a part of their colonial empire after the war. Therefore the British and the Americans must immediately and publicly state that they had no intention of amputating a part of the French colonial empire after the war. It was impossible for WT operators in the field, tapping out their messages with one ear cocked for the rumble of a German DF van, to do otherwise than send mutilated messages. Therefore WT operators in the field must be excused for sending out mutilated messages. To Yeo-Thomas it was all as simple and logical as 'Socrates is a man; therefore Socrates is mortal', and if he repeated his arguments a little too often for some people's liking it was perhaps because he suspected that some of his superiors shared only Socrates's mortality.

On 20 May General de Gaulle asked to see him. Ushered into an immense room, Yeo-Thomas saw the immense General seated at an immense desk. He saluted. De Gaulle rose, held out his hand and said formally, as though he had learned the little speech by heart:

'*Je vous félicite de votre mission. Le Colonel Passy m'a fait votre éloge. Je vous remercie de ce que vous avez fait pour la France. Quelles sont vos impressions?*'[1]

Naturally Yeo-Thomas took advantage of this invitation to attempt to convert the General himself to Gaullism. When he had finished, the General said gloomily from the depths of his belly:

'*Moi je n'y suis pour rien, mais il me semble qu'en dépit de tout ce que disent les gens il y a en France quelque chose qui s'appelle la Gaullisme.*'[2]

It was said of General de Gaulle that he was temperamental and intransigent; both accusations were probably true. He was however

1 'I congratulate you on your mission. Colonel Passy has been singing your praises. I thank you for what you have done for France. What are your impressions?'
2 'I, myself, have nothing to do with it, but it seems to me that in spite of all people say there's something in France called Gaullism.'

first and foremost a patriot: entirely without personal ambition, his one idea was to serve France, and he didn't mind how much he offended red-tabbed Wykehamists in the process. The fact that his famous speech of 18 June, 1940, was at the time more courageous than prophetic only emphasises his nobility. It is now the fashion to accuse him of fascism. If a belief in the necessity of discipline is fascist then General de Gaulle is a fascist; but in that case so also is Mr Aneurin Bevan. At any rate the General knew how to recompense a British officer who had helped France: on 29 May he sent Yeo-Thomas the Croix de Guerre with palm.

There is a rule that no British officer can wear a foreign decoration without the sanction of high authority. When Yeo-Thomas applied for permission to wear the Croix de Guerre, the Air Ministry refused, on the ground that, in its opinion, General de Gaulle lacked the right to grant such a decoration. Embarrassed, because his French friends were already inquiring why he was not wearing the ribbon, Yeo-Thomas pointed out that he had seen in an illustrated paper a photograph of General de Gaulle bestowing the Croix de Guerre upon naval officers and asked why the Air Ministry refused to the General a power credited to him by the Admiralty. Eventually, upon the insistence of Colonel Hutchison, permission to wear the decoration was granted.

While on leave in Somerset he learned that he had also been awarded the Military Cross. He went and bought the white-and-purple ribbon, which Barbara sewed on his tunic. On his return to London his friends of the BCRA gave a dinner in his honour to celebrate the granting of the British decoration.

Next day the officer representing the Air Ministry at SOE sent for Yeo-Thomas. 'There's been a mistake,' he said. 'You were recommended for the MC all right, but for some reason the Air Ministry has refused to sanction it. I'm afraid you'll have to take down that ribbon.' This time even Hutch's high-power 'phoning was of no avail, and it was not until nearly a year later that the award was approved.

Once again Tommy was in an awkward situation. He had to visit the French almost daily, and if he appeared without his MC ribbon it would, in view of the previous blocking of his Croix de Guerre, make him look ridiculous and be bad for British prestige. In the end he had to resort to the tactics of deceit which he had learned in the field. He kept at the office a spare tunic with an MC ribbon sewn on it; this tunic he wore when visiting the French. On all other occasions he wore a tunic without this ribbon, and if while wearing it he met the French he explained that he had not yet had time to decorate appropriately all his uniforms. To such subterfuges do bureaucrats reduce the brave.

Meanwhile Moulin reported that good progress was being made with the Secret Army. General Delestraint had got matters well in hand. The Occupied Zone had been divided up into six districts each with its Regional Military Officer and Air Operations Officer ('Bureau des Opérations Aériennes'). The so-called Unoccupied Zone had been similarly divided and staffed. Each Zone was commanded by a senior officer, in charge of both military and air operations and directly responsible to General Delestraint.

Then suddenly disaster overtook them. On 9 June Delestraint was arrested by the Gestapo; on 20 June, Moulin, Larat and other important officers were also arrested. In less than a fortnight the Secret Army had lost its two top men and many of its most competent leaders. Every effort had to be made to rescue those who had been arrested and to enable the seriously damaged circuits to carry on. Fortunately only a few weeks previously two new men had been sent out, 'Z' to take charge of the Occupied Zone Secretariat and Bingen that of the Unoccupied Zone; it was decided that they should also administer the Secret Army until suitable replacements for Moulin and Delestraint had been found.

By August it was clear that, in spite of optimistic reports received from 'Z' and Bingen, things were going from bad to worse. Although parachuting and the landing operations were proceeding smoothly and co-ordinates of new grounds were being regularly received, little or no information was being received from the paramilitary side. The Regional Military Officers complained that they were receiving no help from the various Resistance Movements. Abandoning a plot for the capture by Médéric and himself of Admiral Doenitz, Yeo-Thomas accepted gladly when it was suggested that he should accompany Brossolette to the field on another mission of inspection. Centralisation of authority had proved dangerous and must be replaced by a more horizontal hierarchy.

This time Yeo-Thomas was given the cover name of Tirelli. A fresh set of false papers had to be prepared and another personal history memorised.

The code name for his new mission was Marie Claire; this was the name of a pre-war French woman's weekly which informed correspondents upon the propriety of such acts as a young wife walking about the bedroom in the presence of her husband with the tops of her stockings hanging down. The questions asked of Yeo-Thomas were slightly less domestic:

OPERATIONAL INSTRUCTIONS MARIE CLAIRE

1. Marie Claire will proceed as a member of a joint SOE/BCRA mission and will act as such. He will be responsible to his own HQ, and will report to them on return.
2. He will inquire into and report upon the state of the Resistance Movements in the Occupied Zone; their degree of training, their strength, their morale, the state and distribution of their armament, and in general their effectiveness for the activities envisaged.
3. He will report upon the personalities in charge of the various component parts of the organisation, and will make recommendations as to other personalities to fill vacant or weak places in the organisation.
4. He will impress upon the Resistance Groups the importance of sending to Britain the returns of strengths which have been asked for.
5. He will discover the time-lag necessary between the receipt of instructions by the HQ of any region and their receipt by local groups.
6. He will discover the degree of mobility of sub-units and the time taken for their movement.
7. He will endeavour to discover how far the plans already sent to the field have been permeated to the lower ranks and to assess how far they have been compromised.

Once again it was a tall order.

CHAPTER VII

Mission Marie Claire

This time it was to be a Pullman operation: there was to be no parachuting. Yeo-Thomas and Brossolette, who had just returned from Algiers, were to be landed like a couple of company directors by Lysander near Angoulême.

They took off from Tangmere at 11.30 p.m. on 18 September and once again, huddled in the cockpit, they were afraid that their journey was going to be abortive. It was cloudy and foggy over the Channel and the sea was invisible. Then the flash of German anti-aircraft fire lit up the clouds and made them look like monster pink powder-puffs. The excitement, however, was brief. The Lysander rocked, shot up, swerved, twisted and turned and then went steadily on.

Soon the pilot told them on the 'inter-com' that they were over Poitiers. About 1.25 a.m., flying low, they caught sight of the three lights of their reception committee. When the regulation signals had been exchanged the aircraft began to circle. Below them lay the landing ground, bordered on either side by a stream shining with inconsequent loveliness in the moonlight. As soon as the aircraft came to a standstill Yeo-Thomas and Brossolette threw out the packages and then climbed out themselves. A leading French Communist called Mercier climbed in, and within five minutes of landing the Lysander was airborne again.

Almost immediately a second Lysander appeared and landed. Two more agents got out after they had thrown out more packages.

The packages created a problem for the members of the reception committee, who had not been expecting so many and had only one car at their disposal. The agents, after sorting out their own suitcases, had to wait behind bushes and were guarded by two men with Sten guns, while the packages were driven to a ruined and unoccupied house fifteen miles away and concealed there.

About 3 a.m. the car returned. The car was a front-wheel drive Citröen, into which nine passengers had to be crammed. Once again they had to run the risk of being caught out after curfew, which was at midnight, and as they were in a car they could not quickly take cover. They resolved that if they met a German patrol they would fight their way through it. The possibility of such an encounter was considerable, as they had forty miles to go.

Three-quarters of an hour after they had started their near rear tyre burst while they were driving through a village, and they all had to get out. Changing the wheel was, in spite of their precautions, a noisy operation and it was necessary to keep a sharp look out. The two men with Sten guns guarded the car, one in front and one behind. Brossolette and Yeo-Thomas hid in the shadow of a big farm door and the other two agents on the opposite side of the street. Those who were changing the wheel worked speedily, but in the silence of the night the noise seemed deafening. They had to fear not only the arrival of a German patrol but also discovery by unfriendly villagers. Anxious and impatient, Yeo-Thomas suddenly saw pink lines of light from one of the shutters in a house opposite. The shutters opened slowly and a man's head appeared. Yeo-Thomas stepped out of the shadow and pointed his Colt threateningly. The shutters slammed shut at once and the light went out. Yeo-Thomas could only hope that if the man were a collaborator there was no telephone in the house.

Even when the wheel had been changed and the jack removed their troubles weren't over. The spare tyre turned out to be soft and a frantic search failed to reveal a pump among the tools. There was nothing to do but to climb into the car again and hope that the tyre would hold out under their heavy weight. They chose the lesser danger of driving quickly because they were afraid of being stranded far from their destination. The tyre had a slow puncture and as the miles went reeling past the bumps became heavier and heavier. By the time they reached the safe house they were riding almost on the rim of the wheel.

The safe house was a long low building with a flattish roof, called in that part of the country a 'mas'. While they were eating the copious meal which had been prepared for them the agents learned that this was their hosts' first Lysander operation. The members of the reception committee were thrilled by their success. They complained, however, that so far not nearly enough arms had been parachuted to them.

Next morning Brossolette and Yeo-Thomas breakfasted on specially-baked white bread and a mixture of young wine and brandy called 'Pinaud des Charentes'. At lunch they had to give an account of the insufficiently publicised British war effort and explain why the Americans had tried to replace de Gaulle by Giraud. A few months later the 'mas' was successfully attacked by a strong German detachment and of their eleven hosts only two survived: one had thirteen bullet wounds in his body and the other six through his stomach and an arm blown off.

At four o'clock in the afternoon Lepointu, the survivor who lost his arm, drove Brossolette and Yeo-Thomas to Châteauneuf. From there they caught a train to Angoulême, where, because of the curfew, they had to wait hours in a rainy night under a leaking roof on a platform for the Paris train, which left at half-past one in the morning. There were no seats in the train and they had to stand all the way. They arrived at the Gare d'Austerlitz at seven o'clock and telephoned at once to Madame Peyronnet, using a previously arranged convention.

Established once more at 102 Avenue des Ternes, their first concern was to get into contact with 'Z' and with Pichard, now Senior Air Operations Officer for the Occupied Zone. In each case this was done by means of a letter-box, which was the name given to a person willing to receive messages, verbal or written, and pass them on from one agent to another. Often, to increase security, two intermediary agents-de-liaison were used: one, who knew only the sender, carried the message to the letter-box; and the other, who knew only the recipient, collected it. Before his return to England at the end of his previous mission Brossolette had already fixed up such a letter-box for 'Z'; and at the same time Yeo-Thomas had made arrangements with Madame

Bosc, proprietress of a small restaurant in the rue Richepanse, to act as a letter-box for himself.

As soon as they had arranged these appointments with 'Z' and Pichard, Brossolette and Yeo-Thomas got down to the job of strengthening their circuits, which had been weakened by the recent wave of arrests. José Dupuis was asked to find two capable agents-de-liaison and two more safe houses. Madame Peyronnet's daughter, Poucette, aged sixteen, was engaged to carry messages on her bicycle. She in turn recruited a Danish physical culture teacher, Suni Sandöe, a fearless stocky woman with Scandinavian blue eyes, who placed not only her services but her flat at 11 rue Claude Chahu at their disposal. Madame Denise Martin, the wife of a solicitor, and her sister Nicole Bauer also volunteered to help them. Nicole Bauer, nicknamed Maud, became another cyclist messenger and she in turn brought in the plump little Jacqueline Devaux and her flat in the rue Leverrier. An attractive Canadian, Diana Provost, married to a Frenchman, allowed her flat in the rue du Colonel Moll to be used as a meeting place. All these women risked, in the event of discovery, torture and death.

The new flats were especially welcome for, with the Gestapo hot on the tracks of Resistance, it was necessary to possess a wide choice of retreats in case of emergency. Arms, food, clothes and money were concealed in those safe houses so that it was easy immediately and permanently to leave a threatened dwelling-place for one that was secure.

The Gestapo had a habit of waiting in blown flats for the arrival of unwarned agents, and for this reason Brossolette and Yeo-Thomas arranged to meet as many contacts as possible outside in the street. In this way they could make sure that they were not being followed and could also watch their approaching contact to ascertain that there was nobody who looked like a sleuth on his trail. If an agent were sure that he was not being followed he would carry a scarf or a newspaper in his hand; if he had reason to suspect that he was, the scarf would be round his neck or the newspaper in his pocket, and in that event the two agents would pass without speaking. At all such meetings the two people concerned approached the rendezvous from opposite direc-tions. In case, because of some unforeseen contingency such as an air-raid alarm, he missed an appointment, each agent arranged to pass a certain part of the city at a certain hour every day; the points and the times varied according to the day of the week and they were staggered, so that the time and point for Monday of one week became the time and point for Tuesday of the next.

Because they were so familiar with the details of the cover stories they had used on their previous mission, Brossolette and Yeo-Thomas continued to use their old false names. Thus Tommy, while able to become Tirelli at a moment's notice, remained Thierry. In his dealings with the French Resistance Movement, he maintained his former name of Shelley; this name had now become famous throughout the French underground and, in spite of the risks attached to its continued use, he judged, without conceit, that it would prejudice paramilitary morale if he were to abandon it. For Brossolette Tommy was 'Cheval', and for Tommy Brossolette was 'Polydor'. These private names were the symbols of their unspoken affection for each other.

At 9.15 on the morning after their arrival in Paris they started out on foot to a flat in the rue de la Pompe where 'Z' had given them a rendezvous. On their way they passed the bookshop which Brossolette had owned at the beginning of the war. 'Z' received them in a magnificent drawing-room with double doors with glass panels and chandeliers dripping crystal icicles. They sat on Louis XV chairs while 'Z' explained to them that he had chosen this palace of brittle splendours because it was only a hundred yards distant from the Secretariat situated in the same street.

This lack of elementary security alarmed Brossolette and Yeo-Thomas. 'Z', a brave man who had been seriously wounded by flak in his first attempt to parachute into France, ridiculed their protests. It was at once clear that 'Z', accustomed since the arrest of Moulin and Delestraint to exercise with Bingen supreme authority over the Resistance Movements, resented their mission as a reflection upon his competence.

Continued conversation showed that the situation was out of hand: little had been done to implement the decisions of the Allied General Staff; careless security, due to over-confidence, was jeopardizing the whole structure of Resistance; and Bingen, head of the Secretariat of the Unoccupied Zone, seemed to be spending most of his time in the Occupied, where in fact he was at present.

Arrangements were made to meet 'Z' and Bingen at the same flat next day, and a meeting was requested with Colonel Morinaud, recently sent out to supervise the Regional Military Officers. Arrangements were also made for regular contact through an agent-de-liaison. Brossolette and Yeo-Thomas particularly insisted that all messages should be verbal and in no case should a communication be committed to paper. 'Z's agent-de-liaison was to come to 102 Avenue des Ternes every evening at five o'clock punctually. If anything were wrong a pot containing a plant would be placed outside one of the windows of the flat, in which case the agent would not enter the house. Such possible lack of contact was provided for by agreement to meet every morning at ten o'clock in the rue de Sèze: 'Z' would enter the street from the Boulevard de la Madeleine and Brossolette and Yeo-Thomas from the rue Tronchet.

On Thursday, 23 September, they again met 'Z'. Bingen was also present and, when questioned about the organisation in the Unoccupied Zone, was vague. Neither 'Z' nor Bingen was able to reply to questions about paramilitary matters. Brossolette and Yeo-Thomas left the rue de la Pompe filled with foreboding.

That same evening the agent-de-liaison failed to keep his appointment at five o'clock. At ten o'clock there was a ring at the door which Madame Peyronnet answered. Their caller was the agent-de-liaison, accompanied by the concierge. The go-between, stopped by the concierge and asked where he was going, had replied that he was going to visit a Monsieur Shelley who lived with the Peyronnets on the third floor. Afraid that the intruder might be a burglar, the good lady had insisted on accompanying him. This placed Brossolette and Yeo-Thomas in an awkward position, as they had already given their names to the concierge as MM Boutet and Thierry, bombed out of their homes in Nantes. Luckily the woman was devoted to the Peyronnets and did not ask any questions. When she had gone the agent-de-liaison handed Yeo-Thomas an envelope addressed to 'M. Shelley' and containing a typewritten list of appointments with names and places set out in detail. Yeo-Thomas told the go-between to inform 'Z' that Brossolette and himself would call upon him in the rue de la Pompe at ten o'clock next morning.

At 9 a.m. on Friday, 24 September, Brossolette and Yeo-Thomas met Pichard, whose report confirmed their fears about the insecurity of the Secretariat. Pichard complained that he was getting no assistance from 'Z', that his funds were always delivered to him late and that 'Z' was fostering antagonism between the Air Operations Officers (Bureau des Opérations Aériennes) and the Resistance Movements. Before taking action against 'Z', however, Brossolette and Yeo-Thomas decided to obtain confirmation of those statements from other agents. Pichard also stated that he feared for the safety of Morinaud, who had lately missed several appointments.

One hour later they again saw 'Z' and Bingen, to whom they protested violently about the breach of elementary security committed by their agent-de-liaison on the previous evening. While promising that in future all their communications would be verbal, 'Z' and Bingen maintained that Brossolette and Yeo-Thomas overrated the dangers of clandestine activity. Angered by the insinuation that they were scared, Brossolette and Yeo-Thomas pointed out that two of the men employed by 'Z' and Bingen – Alain, who was Georges Bidault's WT operator, and Nard – were insecure because they had been blown, and requested that they be returned to London in accordance with instructions already given. This 'Z' refused to do on the grounds that the two men in question were too valuable to lose. Neither he nor Bingen appeared to be perturbed by the fact that Morinaud had not been seen for several days. After requesting an interview with the Regional Military Officers and the Air Operations Officers, Brossolette and Yeo-Thomas left. In the street they passed Nard, who, contrary to all regulations, gave them, a sign of recognition.

Fortunately they had their own means of getting in touch with the Resistance Leaders. Interviewed that day, Coquoin (Ceux de la Libération), Lecompte-Boynet (Ceux de la Résistance), Colonel Lacroix (Organisation Civile et Militaire), Joseph (Franc-Tireurs et Partisans), Colonel Aymon (Libération) confirmed their worst fears. The only progress achieved since their previous visit had been the nomination of regional movement heads. Sub-regional and district set-ups were still in the same chaos as in April. Regional Military Officers had no contacts and local leaders often refused to receive their visits. The conflict between the Air Operations Officers and the Movements was rapidly becoming an open breach. Instead of a united

General Staff innumerable committees met irregularly and bewildered the few who listened to them by their piddling and pettifogging pronouncements. It was superabundantly clear that 'Z' and Bingen possessed neither the authority nor the competence to replace Moulin and Delestraint.

Broken-hearted, Brossolette and Yeo-Thomas returned to 102 Avenue des Ternes. At five o'clock the agent-de-liaison again failed to turn up. At ten o'clock he still hadn't put in an appearance. Alarmed by the memory of the go-between's previous *gaffe*, they decided that it would be safer to leave the flat at once: Brossolette went to stay with Claire in the rue de la Faisanderie and Yeo-Thomas moved to Jacqueline Devaux's flat in the rue Leverrier.

Next day Maud was sent to find out if the Peyronnets' flat was still safe. At 6 p.m. she met Yeo-Thomas at the Etoile and told him that the agent-de-liaison had been arrested the previous evening carrying a piece of paper on which was written: 'Mme P, 3 étage, 102 Avenue des Ternes'. Surprisingly, however, the go-between had stalled for time before pretending that he was engaged in black-market transactions; he had told the Gestapo that he had been going to the flat, which he had never visited before, in search of a potential customer. Because of this delay the Gestapo had not raided Madame Peyronnet's flat until six o'clock that morning. Fortunately the concierge had been loyal and the Peyronnets, although severely interrogated, had been able to convince their inquisitors that they were in no way connected with subversive activities but had been attempting to procure black-market supplies for friends. A search of the flat had revealed no trace of Brossolette's and Yeo-Thomas's occupation. 102 Avenue des Ternes could, however, no longer be used as a safe house, as the Germans would be certain to watch it for some time.

On Sunday, 26 September, the news was very much worse: 'Z' and Bingen informed them that the Secretariat had been raided the day before and all the previous four months' courier and incoming and outgoing telegrams, kept in the office contrary to regulations, seized. Lists *en clair* of prominent Resistance supporters, among whose names figured those of M. Jeanneney and M. Farjon, had also been removed by the Gestapo. Nard and other important officers had been arrested. 'Z' himself had been arrested but subsequently released, and Alain had

had a narrow escape. In spite of the magnitude of the calamity 'Z' and Bingen appeared unconcerned.

A few days later they learned that Colonel Morinaud had indeed been arrested and had swallowed his cyanide tablet rather than run the risk of weakening under torture. This severe blow had decapitated the Regional Military Officers in the Occupied Zone.

The hunt was on in earnest now and to bamboozle pursuers of their own persons Brossolette and Yeo-Thomas again changed residences: Brossolette went to stay with the Danish physical culture teacher Suni Sandöe, and Yeo-Thomas returned to Jeanne Helbling's flat in Neuilly, where he became M. Tirelli.

It was fortunate that they decided to take matters into their own hands because the WT operator to whom Yeo-Thomas had entrusted his signal of 26 September had to go into hiding before he could transmit it; and the message did not arrive in London till 14 October. Demoting on their own authority 'Z' and Bingen, Yeo-Thomas and Brossolette took command and attempted to stop the rot. They called a meeting of Air Operations and Military Officers to settle the differences between the Bureau des Opérations Aériennes and the Resistance Movements. This was successfully held on 6 October, under the chairmanship of Colonel Mangin, the son of the famous general and now Senior Military Officer in the Occupied Zone. From him Brossolette and Yeo-Thomas learned that the Gestapo possessed a full list of the names, including naturally their own, of all agents sent out during the September moon period.

There were at that time 32,000 Gestapo agents concentrated in Paris on the drive against Resistance. Even such a threat failed to impress the nonchalant 'Z' and Bingen. Both they and the new go-between with which Yeo-Thomas had provided them continued to turn up late for rendezvous or to miss them altogether. In the end the inevitable happened and the agent-de-liaison was arrested on account of his own carelessness.

Arrests continued to be made in ever-increasing numbers. The two agents had to take special precautions against being followed. Bingen arrived one day at a rendezvous with no fewer than three men trailing him: Brossolette and Yeo-Thomas drew them after themselves and lost them by each jumping into a different vélo-taxi on the Place St

Augustin. Another sleuth Yeo-Thomas shook off in the métro by getting out at a station and jumping back into the train just before it left; yet another he drew down into the basement of the Printemps departmental store and dodged out of the employees' entrance while the shadow was blocked by a group of shoppers.

There was still much to be done: proper contacts had to be provided between the Regional Military Officers and the Resistance Movements; the morale of both Air Operations Officers and the Military Officers, seriously weakened by dissensions and arrests, had to be strengthened; security had to be tightened up by decentralisation; and the organisations in the provinces had to be visited and compelled to obey the directives received from London.

To carry out even the preliminary arrangements for such a scheme meant making and keeping appointments at a time when rendezvous were particularly dangerous. The courageous José, Maud, Denise, Jacqueline and Claire were used to maintain contacts with the many agents whom Brossolette and Yeo-Thomas were then directing. And even they were not enough. Through José Dupuis they recruited three young men recommended by a patriotic priest: Horace, a slim boy of twenty, who became Yeo-Thomas's personal agent-de-liaison; Josseaume, aged 25, who, as 'Agenor', was to perform a similar service for José; and another youngster of 24 who was to be Brossolette's go-between.

While waiting for 'Z' to secure the presence of the Regional Military Officers at a meeting of the Comité Militaire, Yeo-Thomas decided that in view of the heat of the chase it would be prudent to procure a third false identity. Through M. Coquoin of Ceux de la Libération he met the Commissaire de Police of the 17th Arrondissement, who provided him with a genuine identity card and a birth certificate in the name of Gaonach. The advantage of the new card over his two others was that its authenticity could be proved, as it was registered at the Préfecture de Police. But even the owner of a valid identity card must be able to prove that he lived somewhere; and so, through the agency of M. Huret of Molyneux, Yeo-Thomas rented in the name of Gaonach a flat at 33 rue de la Tourelle near the Porte de St Cloud. It was a spacious and well-furnished apartment, with several means of exit: situated on the first floor, it had a servants' staircase and the windows of a back bedroom gave on to the roof of a shed from which it would be easy to jump into the street behind. As the tenant of the neighbouring flat was a German colonel, personal assistant to General von Stulpnagel, Military Governor of Paris, it was a little like a tart trying to acquire an appearance of respectability by living next door to the Archbishop of Canterbury. When he had stored ammunition, revolvers, grenades and food in this new retreat, Yeo-Thomas explained to the concierge that he would not be taking up residence immediately as he was an engineer by profession and travelled a great deal. He also prepared her for the visit of his friend M. Boutet, a bombed-out refugee from Nantes.

He was soon to be glad of his acquisition, for proofs of the Gestapo's vigilance increased. One morning, opening the shutters of his bedroom in Jeanne Helbling's flat in Neuilly, he noticed somebody peeping through a discreetly drawn curtain in a window of the house opposite. The next morning the watcher was still at his post and a man in a greenish beige raincoat was loitering industriously at the corner of the street. Much as he disliked leaving Jeanne Helbling alone when danger was threatening, Tommy had no option but to step out of the house immediately by the back door. At dinner that evening in Les Mousquetaires in the Avenue Malakoff his hostess told him that the man with the raincoat had remained at the corner of the street most of the morning and then had vanished. There had been no signs of any other watchers since.

Brossolette, too, felt that it was safer to keep on moving, and changed from Suni Sandöe's flat in the rue Claude Chahu to Claire Davinroy's flat in the rue de la Faisanderie. He stayed there a couple of days and then Yeo-Thomas and he, feeling that the net was drawing closer and anxious not to get their friends into trouble, moved to the new flat in the rue de la Tourelle. A few days later Claire failed to keep an evening appointment with Yeo-Thomas at the Etoile. Disturbed, because Claire was always punctual, Yeo-Thomas went and telephoned her flat from a small café to which it would not matter if the call were traced. 'Bonsoir, chère amie,' he said. An obviously disguised woman's voice replied: 'Bonsoir, chéri. Viens tout de suite. Je t'attends.' 'Oui,' Tommy answered and hung up. It was clear that Claire had been arrested and that the Gestapo was waiting in her flat to trap any of her friends who might call upon her.

Brossolette, who had known Claire since childhood, was deeply distressed when he heard the news. Through a friend of his, Madame Marcelle Virolle, they soon obtained the details. An agent, whose code name was Gulliver, had recently been arrested. From the concierge of the house in which he lived the Gestapo had learned that his flat had been obtained for him by a Madame Claire Davinroy who lived in the rue de la Faisanderie. At six o'clock they had raided Claire's flat: in addition to 125,000 francs stored there by Yeo-Thomas, incriminating documents had been found on her desk and she had been arrested. All that day a Gestapo man in plain clothes had walked her little white dog up and down the street in the hope that it would show pleasure if any of her friends approached.

The danger didn't end with their escape from it at poor Claire's expense. As a result of Gulliver's arrest almost his whole circuit was rounded up; and one night the documents at the 'Centrale', where signals were encoded and decoded, were seized. Confident that all the guilty were already in prison, the Gestapo left the papers unguarded overnight, intending to collect them the next day. One of the circuit's agents-de-liaison, however, a woman called Berthe, had not been caught: learning of the raid, she removed the documents, with the complicity of the concierge, hid them in a safe house in the rue Jasmin and informed Brossolette and Yeo-Thomas that she had done so. When Pericles, Gulliver's assistant and Marcelle Virolle's brother, returned from London, they told him what had happened and forced him to go into hiding, as they had heard that the Gestapo was searching for him and possessed his description. Pericles then informed them that among the papers now concealed in the rue Jasmin were details of the as yet unused German V1 emplacements, and Yeo-Thomas said that he would go and get them. Having obtained the key of the flat from Berthe, he discovered that the house was already being watched by the Gestapo. He consulted the telephone directory and ascertained that a doctor lived at the same address. Accompanied by two of Pericles' friends he went to the house after dark, intending to tell anyone who tried to stop him that he was ill and going for medical advice. Luckily, however, there was nobody watching the house when they arrived and they were able to transfer the two suitcases containing the documents to another safe house in the same street. There they destroyed the unimportant papers and transported by métro those dealing with the new secret weapon to Pericles in his flat on the Boulevard Montparnasse.

This, of course, was only a sideshow; their real business was to put French Resistance on a sound footing again. At last, after a month of dangers, depressions and excitements, a meeting of the Comité Militaire was held on 27 October. Colonel Touny (Organisation Civile et Militaire) presided; also present were 'Z', M. Coquoin (Ceux de la Libération), Colonel Aymon (Libération), Joseph (Franc-Tireurs et Partisans) accompanied by another delegate to represent the umbrella Front National, and Maître Arighi (Ceux de la Résistance). Colonel Morinaud having been arrested, there was nobody except Bouloche, Paris Regional Military Officer, to represent the Regional Military Officers. Pichard, chief Air Operations Officer, had been brought in to voice the complaints of the Bureau des Opérations Aériennes.

It was a stormy meeting. Both 'Z' and Colonel Touny protested against the new decentralisation decree that Regional Military Officers should in future receive their orders direct from London. They claimed that the Comité Militaire was the proper channel for the reception and downwards transmission of such orders. Bouloche maintained that it was his duty to communicate all directives immediately to his subordinates. Coquoin and, rather surprisingly, Joseph agreed, as also did Pierre Kaan, the spectacled and professorial-looking secretary of the Comité. Yeo-Thomas clinched the argument by pointing out that if Colonel Morinaud had been the only man to know London's directives all Resistance in the Occupied Zone would have come to a standstill when he was arrested. In future, he ruled, the Comité Militaire, while it would be kept informed of all that transpired, would not be empowered to pass orders to lower echelons. He also insisted that, in order to prevent a recurrence of the strife which Brossolette and he had just settled, clearly stated details of the functions of the Air Operations Officers should be sent to all regional leaders and departmental heads.

Heartened by Joseph's support, Yeo-Thomas tried to persuade him to go to England for training; Joseph was keen to go but did not think that the Party would allow him. In this conjecture he was right. Joseph, Yeo-Thomas found, always tried to carry out London's instructions, but the complicated construction of the Communist organisation made co-operation difficult. Because of the slowness of communications imposed upon the Franc-Tireurs et Partisans by their horizontal hierarchy the greater number of the parachute operations arranged for them failed. Apart from Joseph, almost all their leaders were arrogant and, asserting that most of the victims of the Gestapo were Communists, claimed for their Movement the title 'Le Parti des Fusillés'. While there could be no doubt of their heroism, their martyrology was certainly swelled by the fact that the Germans always described all their opponents as 'Communists'.

Forced to keep on the move, Brossolette and Yeo-Thomas found a new safe house in the Latin Quarter, in the rue de Rennes; and almost immediately they had to vacate it because of their suspicions of Horace, Yeo-Thomas's new agent-de-liaison, who knew the address and brought messages there. Tommy had noticed that Horace was often late for appointments and made flimsy excuses. To test the boy he sent him on an errand to a house outside Paris which he knew to be empty and of which he also gave Horace the telephone number. Reporting in the evening, Horace said that he had been to the house and, having found nobody there, had made inquiries and arranged to return the next day. Unable to describe the house when asked to do so, he finally admitted that he had never visited it but had telephoned instead and got no reply. Suspecting him of treachery, Yeo-Thomas was going to kill the boy, but, on the intercession of José Dupuis, dismissed him with a warning.

For they could afford to run no unnecessary risks: the Gestapo had their descriptions and the Abwehr counter-espionage was on their tracks. Other agents were being arrested within an hour of having spoken with them. To ensure comparative safety Yeo-Thomas was driven to meet some of his contacts in hospitals, a trick he learned from Joseph. He would pass the contact without recognition at the intersection of two streets, turn and follow him at a distance of fifty yards to the hospital, enter the visitors' gate and talk with him in the grounds. Punctuality at such meetings was of course, essential, a point not realised by 'Z', who still continued to give trouble and would arrange rendezvous in dangerous places like the Gare St Lazare.

The morale of Resistance, Yeo-Thomas learned from those he met, was low and from a cause which he at the moment was powerless to remove. Although the Air Operations Officers had now built up a network of 600 grounds, although every month 150 reception committees stood by, possibly only five operations would be attempted in a moon period. As a result of this paltry parachuting the Secret Army was not being equipped and, for want of explosives, important targets were not being sabotaged.

The reason, of course, for the lack of air operations was that the RAF did not think that they could spare the planes. Yeo-Thomas accuses his masters of a lack of imagination. The load of one Halifax bomber dropped to a reception committee and handled by the right men could, he claims, have done more damage to the German war machine than the loads of 250 bombers dropped in a raid. Repeated air bombardment had failed seriously to hinder the work of a ball-bearing factory at Annecy; three saboteurs, with explosives and the complicity of one or two of the workers, so damaged the machinery that the factory never produced another ball bearing during the rest of the occupation.

The story of the 'Barrage de Gigny' even more properly illustrates his contention. At the time of the Allied invasion of Italy the Germans used the Saône to transport submarines in sections, motor torpedo-boats, artillery, tanks and ammunition, thus keeping the railways free for troop movements. Many heavy and accurate air raids would have been required to arrest this traffic; with floating mines dropped in containers and assembled afterwards a small group of Resistance men blew up the locks at Gigny and blocked this waterway for many months.

The harm done to Resistance morale by this lack of supplies was perhaps greater than that not done to the Germans. The saboteurs knew that the scientific department of SOE was producing time bombs with magnets which could be clamped on to the hulls of ships, explosive coal which could be introduced into German stocks and altimeter switches which, when inserted into aircraft, blew off the tail when the plane reached a certain height. They knew also that the reason they were not receiving sufficient quantities of such instruments was because all available British bombers were being concentrated on massive and often unsuccessful raids. The amount of arms that was being dropped in a month could equip only a hundred men of the Secret Army. It was small wonder that Brossolette and Yeo-Thomas found it difficult to convince Resistance leaders that their efforts were being appreciated in London.

This scarcity of arms was serious because lately the potential of the Secret Army had been increased by a new factor: the Maquis, to which all who desired to avoid compulsory labour in Germany were forced to resort. Of this vast and new body Brault was the national chief. Known to Resistance as 'Jerôme', he flitted about the country like a will-o'-the-wisp, organising all Maquis which were not specifically Communist.

Brossolette and Yeo-Thomas met Jerôme at a safe house in the Avenue Rapp. What he told them convinced Yeo-Thomas more than ever that here was the material for an effective fighting force. But once again he learned that the men lacked arms, equipment, clothing and cash. In order that he might accurately compute their wants he arranged to meet Jerôme at Cahors on 2 November and accompany him on his inspection of the groups in that area.

But before he left Paris he had another narrow escape. Arriving early for a mid-day meeting with an agent in a flat on the Boulevard Péreire, he had time to investigate the district before keeping his appointment. A couple of blocks from the safe house he saw a Citroën with German police marks drawn up in a side street. From his seat at the wheel the driver, who was in the car, could observe the house to which Tommy was going. Passing in front of the café which formed the ground floor, Yeo-Thomas entered the house, climbed the stairs and listened at the door of the flat in which he had his rendezvous. Suspicious because of the silence, he returned to the street and crossed the railway. At ten minutes to twelve he came back and, as the car was still in the side street, went into the café and ordered a drink. At twelve o'clock exactly the car drew up in front of the house and four men in civilian clothes got out. Almost immediately the concierge was bundled into the car, which drove off again, leaving behind three men who disappeared into the house. Paying for his drink, Yeo-Thomas left the café and, on his way to cross the railway, passed the car as it came towards him to take up its former position in the side street. It was obvious that the flat had been blown and that the three men who entered the house were waiting in the flat to arrest him when he kept his appointment. Shocked by this very close shave and by the thought of what his arrested contact must then be suffering, he began to think that it was a good thing that he was leaving Paris for a short time.

On 2 November he took care to see that he was not trailed when he went to catch the train. Nor did he take any chances when he arrived at Cahors in the small hours of the next morning: instead of leaving the platform by the official exit he dropped on to the track, walked in the shadow of a stationary goods train and got out of the station without giving up his ticket. His precaution was probably wise: Jerôme, who was waiting for him in the darkness with a car, informed him that Sicherheitsdienst officials had been waiting at the exit from the platform and closely scrutinizing all arrivals.

Over a meal Jerôme told him more about the Maquis: his groups in the Occupied Zone contained 6,000 men, he said, and those in the Unoccupied Zone 12,000. And, because quality was more important than quantity, *ne devenait pas maquisard qui voulait*: before being admitted to the Maquis proper, candidates spent from four to six weeks in holding camps, where they were screened and tested.

That day, accompanied by Jerôme, Yeo-Thomas inspected two camps in the Département of the Lot. The first was reached shortly after dawn. At the approach to the camp their car was met by the officer in charge, a wiry young man wearing a leather cap, a corduroy jacket and breeches and carrying a Sten gun. Stopping in a rutty lane, they got out and made their way across rough ground, through bushes, trees and rocks. Twice challenged by outposts, they arrived on a high plateau to find twenty-five variously clad and accoutred men standing to attention while the tricolour, with the revolutionary Croix de Lorraine superimposed upon its now conformist red, white and blue, was hoisted slowly into the cold morning air. The orders for this moving little ceremony were rapped out in military style and executed with promptitude and precision.

The thirty men in the camp were disciplined, well fed and happy. Divided into groups of five, each commanded by an NCO ('Sixaines'), all the armament they possessed between them consisted of one Sten gun with a hundred rounds, three French rifles with five rounds each and ten revolvers with ten rounds each: there were no grenades at all.

The available arms were used by all in turn for instructional purposes, drill, weapon-stripping and field-craft exercises by night. Lack of ammunition prevented target practice. The 'Q' side was well handled and accurate accounts were kept. Food was purchased from sympathisers in the surrounding villages. Although small *coups de main* were permitted against collaborators, looting was forbidden and severely punished. All were eager, but complained of their puny armoury.

In the afternoon they visited a similar group of thirty men whose sole armament consisted of one rifle and ten rounds of ammunition. Many of the men in this group were ex-soldiers of the Infanterie Coloniale and were wearing their old uniforms. Such were particularly chagrined by the knowledge that if they were attacked they could defend themselves only by flight to another district.

Returning to Cahors, Jerôme and Yeo-Thomas caught the night train to Lyons. As Jerôme had pressing business elsewhere, he delegated to a friend the duty of driving Tommy in a motor van to a country shop near Poncin in the Département of the Ain, where he was introduced to two members of the neighbouring Maquis as 'le commandant anglais Shelley'. This Maquis was also, he found, situated in an almost inaccessible position among trees and boulders. It could be approached only by two narrow, steep and slippery paths, both guarded by outposts in telephonic communication with the head-quarters hut. The camp consisted of sixty men living in five huts, camouflaged so as to be invisible from the air. An ex-regular army officer was in command. The armaments, although inadequate, were more ample than those of the camps in the Lot: ten Sten guns with a hundred rounds each, twenty rifles with twenty-five rounds each and a few grenades. There was also a resident doctor with medical supplies. Recently the men of this camp had successfully raided the larder of the Vichy quartermaster-general's stores at Bourg and felt strong enough to resist reprisals threatened by the police of the Groupe Mobile de Réserve. In combination with some 400 men in a neighbouring Maquis they were planning an operation against the armaments factory at Le Creusot.

Yeo-Thomas left this camp more than ever convinced that these mobile, spartan and well-trained bodies of men could, properly armed, render valuable assistance to the Allies on 'D' day. Already the news of the presence of a British officer had gone round the district, and on the way into Bourg the driver of the van told him that the members of other neighbouring Maquis had requested the honour of his visit. Tommy had, however, more pressing work to do in Paris, and on his arrival at Bourg at half-past eight he went straight to the station.

As the train for Paris did not leave till half-past eleven he had three hours to wait on the draughty platform: he judged it imprudent to go to a restaurant in the town because there was a strong Gestapo detachment in Bourg. Tired and sleepy, he sat on a crate and leaned against the wall. Soon there were so many people on the platform that it seemed impossible that each of them could have a personal destiny. Apart from some boys from a Vichy Youth camp, most of them were middle-aged men and women with hard-hating, mean, acquisitive looks on their shiny, brainless faces. Alert only in their misinterpretation of the world, purposeful in their essential purposelessness, clutching their umbrellas and their black-market purchases, they looked like figures on a canvas by Breughel: all God's children without wings. The warmth from their crowded bodies began to ooze in a damp mist along the platform and the smell of their stale sweat and dirty feet soon made it seem like summer.

At half-past ten it was announced that saboteurs had wrecked the line and that the Paris train had been withdrawn, but still the people continued to wait. Perturbed by the delay and cut off from his friends of the Maquis, Yeo-Thomas went to make inquiries of the station-master, to whom he justified his anxiety by saying that his wife was dying in Paris. The station-master told him that if the repair gang finished their work on the line promptly there might be an early morning train which would get him into Lyons in time to catch the nine-o'clock train to Paris. Promising not to arouse possibly vain hopes by communicating this information to the other travellers, Yeo-Thomas went and dozed standing up in the waiting-room, as his crate had already been annexed.

Hours later, but while it was still dark, an obsolete and rusty engine pulled alongside the platform a clattering assortment of archaic carriages. Each carriage was painted a different shade of green, which made the train look like a badly-darned stocking. The seats were all wooden and most of the windows were broken. Too cold to sleep,

Yeo-Thomas curled up in a corner after taking a swig of Mirabelle from his flask. At half-past six the train started with a jerk. The engine puffed, grunted, wheezed, whistled and roared; the carriages bumped as though rolling on square wheels; slowly, lumpily they trundled through the empty early morning world towards Lyons, which they reached at half-past eight.

At Lyons, after swallowing two cups of acorn coffee, Tommy bought a first-class ticket for Paris: in this way he could travel in any class dictated by convenience and the requirements of safety. Aware that his description had been circulated to the Lyons Gestapo, whose particularly pitiless chief had already been pointed out to him by Jerôme, he kept a sharp look-out. Although there were two German Feldgendarmes standing near the ticket inspector, he approached them without great apprehension, knowing that their stupidity had earned them the nickname 'têtes de veau primées'. The two policemen barely gave him a glance. Reassured he made his way along the dismal, dingy platform. After all, he argued, even if he had been trailed from Paris to Cahors and thence to Lyons, the motor van in which he had travelled the previous day had not been followed and the Gestapo could not know where he was.

It was perhaps this confidence coupled with the weariness resulting from three sleepless nights which prompted his next act of temerity. Except for the first-class compartment reserved and labelled 'Nur für Wehrmachtsangehörige', the train was packed, and he was unable to find a seat. In the reserved first-class carriage only one compartment was occupied, by a somnolent German general and one of his staff. Too tired to contemplate standing, Tommy climbed into the neighbouring carriage, passed through the narrow connecting passage into the reserved carriage and entered an empty compartment. Closing the door and pulling down the blinds, he stretched himself out on the seat and fell fast asleep.

Twenty minutes later, when the train was running through the lovely green countryside, he awoke to find a German railway policeman standing over him and shaking his shoulder. Tall and fair, with close-cropped hair and a long pointed nose, the policeman wore a black uniform with silver piping on the tunic and the usual eagle and swastika on his sleeve.

'*Afez fous la bermission de foyager dans la foiture réservée bour la Wehrmacht?*'[1] he asked in heavy, cold-in-the-head German French.

'It's the first I've heard of it being the carriage reserved for the German army,' Yeo-Thomas said.

'*Fous n'afez bas foo la blaque qui est dehors sur le côté de la foiture?*'[2] the policeman asked severely.

Yeo-Thomas looked at him with feigned surprise succeeded by apparently dawning comprehension.

'No, Monsieur, and now I'm beginning to understand how I didn't see the notice. You see, I got into a carriage and worked my way here along the corridors. I'm sorry, but that's how it happened.'

'*Montrez-moi fos biéces d'identité.*'[3]

Tommy was travelling under the name of Gaonach, and carried his identity card behind a celluloid window in a special wallet; facing it, and behind another celluloid window, was a photograph of a naked girl, specially placed there to distract the inquisitive.

'You see, Monsieur,' he said, handing the policeman the case, 'I am an engineer and I work for the German Todt Organization.'

But the policeman was no longer interested in M. Gaonach, Ingénieur. Breathing steamily, the whites of his eyes swelling out to the size and appearance of shelled eggs, he stood gazing glassily at the bare beauty.

'You see, I am an engineer and I work for the Todt Organization,' Yeo-Thomas repeated.

'*Oui, j'ai foo,*'[4] the policeman said, still goggling clammily at the wrong photograph.

'I've been inspecting some work for the Todt Organization around Lyons,' Yeo-Thomas went on. 'I was sent specially from Paris, but I've been held up everywhere by this infernal sabotage. I tell you, Monsieur, I'd like to get my hands on those bad Frenchmen who don't seem to realise that Germany is their best friend.'

It was laid on a bit thickly, perhaps, but the policeman had been too wrapped up in the photograph to notice.

1 'Have you permission to travel in the carriage reserved for the Wehrmacht?'
2 'You didn't see the notice on the outside of the carriage?'
3 'Show your identity papers.'
4 'Yes, I've seen.'

'That is a very nice case indeed,' he said, reluctantly returning the wallet.

'As I say, I'm very tired,' Yeo-Thomas said. 'For three nights I haven't slept.' He handed the policeman a cigarette and lighted it for him. 'I tell you, Monsieur, I'd like to get my hands on those rascals of saboteurs.'

The policeman, still with a reminiscent look in his eye, agreed that it was a pity that so many Frenchmen should be misguided; then he came back to the matter in hand, but this time his tone was friendly.

'*Fous ne boufez bas rester ici,*'[1] he said. 'If the General saw you I'd get a reprimand. But wait here for a few minutes while I see what I can do for you.'

Before long the policeman was back again. He told Tommy that a few carriages further up the train he had found a man travelling first-class with a second-class ticket and had turfed him out; he had ordered the other occupants of the compartment to see that nobody took the vacant seat, as he was going to bring along a loyal Frenchman who worked for the Todt Organization.

'*C'est barceque fous êtes un ami de l'Allemagne que j'ai fait cela bour fous,*'[2] he said.

'*Monsieur, vous savez que je suis de coeur avec vous,*'[3] Yeo-Thomas said.

Although his new travelling companions didn't welcome the friend of Germany the policeman had declared him to be, Tommy was too tired to care and fell asleep immediately. He lunched in the restaurant car at the same table as three young Frenchmen who told him that as the line had been sabotaged between Dijon and Lyons the train was making a detour. They also said that he might be surprised to learn that arms and explosives were constantly being parachuted into France. Yeo-Thomas replied that he did not believe them, as it was impossible for such operations to take place under the watchful eyes of the Germans. He was surprised to discover that his companions had a

1 'You can't stay here.'
2 'It is because you are a friend of Germany that I am doing this for you.'
3 'Sir, you know that I am with you entirely.'

very good idea how these droppings were carried out. After lunch he went back to his compartment and dozed while his fellow passengers continued to regard him with disapproval.

Late in the afternoon, returning to the restaurant car for tea, he was informed by the attendant that there was no more room. Protesting that he was hungry and thirsty, Yeo-Thomas tipped the man and asked him to take another look. The attendant walked away down the car, turned and beckoned to Tommy, indicating the only vacant seat. Approaching, Yeo-Thomas was horrified to see that the man opposite whom he was to sit was the ill-famed chief of the Lyons Gestapo, who had already been pointed out to him by Jerôme. He knew that the official had heard of him and suspected that he might even have seen his photograph. But to retreat, especially after having insisted on being found a seat, would have aroused suspicion, and he had no option but to sit down at the same table as this highly dangerous person. Pretending to be gazing out of the window, he covertly observed his new neighbour: a duelling scar ran down one side of his hard, clean-shaven face; through gold-rimmed spectacles two steely blue eyes were quite openly fixed upon himself with icy hostility. Yeo-Thomas says that he felt 'as though a gimlet were being screwed into his head'. He was glad when the waiter brought the bread, ersatz jam and tea so that he could avoid the man's gaze by looking down at his plate. Then, to his dismay, the Gestapo chief began to talk to him in a slow, precise French.

'*Vous venez de loin, Monsieur?*'

'I've come from Lyons, Monsieur,' Yeo-Thomas answered, terrified. Was the man suspicious? he wondered. Had he identified Shelley? Or, recognizing a familiar face, was he trying to place him? He knew that it would be no use telling such a perspicacious official any lies about M. Gaonach, Ingénieur, working for the Todt Organization; nor would the photograph of the naked girl be likely to beguile so seasoned an inquisitor. At that moment the train passed some overturned carriages and trucks, clearly visible from the window. 'Seems to have been a bit of trouble here,' Tommy said, seeking safety in an obviously dangerous topic.

'These unfortunate events are always happening.' The tone was cold, the eyes colder.

'I am surprised, Monsieur, that the German army has not yet found an effective means of dealing with such acts.'

'Sabotage is like the black market,' the Gestapo man said. 'It has so many heads that we cannot strike them all off at once. But rest assured that the German Army will master both these evils in the end.'

They continued to talk together. When they had paid their bills Yeo-Thomas forced himself to wait until the Gestapo official had risen and left the table with a curt '*Auf Wiedersehen*'. Following him closely, Tommy discovered that he was travelling in the same carriage as himself.

Still afraid that the German might have identified him, he spent the next two hours standing up in the corridor, determined to leap out on to the track if a move were made to arrest him. To allay suspicion he returned to the restaurant car for dinner, although he was careful not to choose the same service as the Gestapo official. When the train reached the Gare de Lyon at half-past eleven he got out on the wrong side of the carriage, left the station unobserved and took a vélo-taxi to the rue de Chevreuse. From there he walked to the rue Leverrier, where he spent the night in Jacqueline Devaux's flat.

Next morning he met Brossolette, who informed him that there had been more arrests during his absence. Pichart had had a number of narrow escapes; and Marcelle Virolle and Pichard's sister had become so compromised that they would require to be exfiltrated to England. For the next few days Yeo-Thomas took up the old round of meeting contacts and shaking off sleuths. At night he forgot his peril by listening to such programmes as Itma, in which some deliberately complicated intellectuals found the unfriendly fog of the neo-impressionists. But it did for the soldier in 1939–1945 what Bruce Bairnsfather did for his father in 1914–1918. Among the BBC messages there was also a *tendresse* from Barbara, sent '*du moineau au lapin*', 'from the sparrow to the rabbit'.

Among those recently arrested had been poor Roland Farjeon, leader of the Organisation Civile et Militaire in the north of France. About to visit this region and replace the lost chief by Deshayes and another agent called Piquier, Yeo-Thomas learned with surprise that he had been called back to London.

Both Brossolette and Yeo-Thomas were depressed by this news.

During the eight weeks that they had been together they had succeeded in tightening up French Resistance: they had settled the differences between the Regional Military Officers and the Air Operations Officers and acquired great influence over both; they had inspired and earned the respect of the various Resistance Leaders. This was not astonishing: Brossolette was a very distinguished, able and courageous man; and Yeo-Thomas's prestige as a British officer was enhanced by his bravery and by his love and understanding of France. Their presence was sufficient to assure the heads of Resistance that the difficulties and needs of their Groups were known and would be passed on to Headquarters. They decided, therefore, that one of them must always remain in France: as soon as Yeo-Thomas had made his report in London he would return and relieve Brossolette.

On 10 November word came through that Tommy would be picked up by Lysander in the neighbourhood of Arras. With a heavy heart he said good-bye to Brossolette and went to the Gare du Nord carrying two suitcases: in one were his clothes and in the other, under a layer of packets of cigarettes and slabs of chocolate, the documents dealing with the new German secret weapon which had been salvaged from the Gulliver disaster. Marcelle Virolle and Pichard's sister, who were to be exfiltrated by the same operation, accompanied him; all three travelled in separate compartments and the journey was without incident. At Arras they met outside the station and went in search of the corset shop in the rue Saint Auber where they would be put in touch with the local Resistance authorities: upon Tommy's asking for an outsize brassière he was to be invited to pass into the back-shop, where he would hand over one half of a bisected hundred-franc note of which the tradeswoman already held the other. Unfortunately, he went first to the wrong shop, from which the lady in charge, anxious to do good business by selling a super *soutien-gorge*, allowed him to escape with difficulty. However, the next shop he tried proved to be the right one and from there they were passed on to a perfumery, owned by a Madame Fraser, a Frenchwoman who had married a Scot. After having dined with this cheerful and intrepid lady, Yeo-Thomas passed the night with a gentlemen's outfitter called M. Doutreme-puich who, understandably, preferred to do business under the name of 'Marcel'.

Next morning Deshayes, who was in charge of the air operations in the district, arrived to say that a message had come over the BBC postponing the Lysander pick-up on account of bad weather. Accordingly Yeo-Thomas filled in the time by visiting, in the company of Deshayes's ruddy-faced assistant Thierry,[1] the local Resistance groups. At Amiens he found the men divided up into units of five, each headed by an NCO, with no lateral communications with other sixaines and receiving all communications vertically from their leader. (In spite of this security measure forty-eight men of this group were arrested the day after his visit.) He also inspected other groups around Lille and noted their requirements.

On 12 November he learned that the pick-up might be transferred to Tours. There was also more disturbing news: an agent-de-liaison came to inform him that a number of arrests had taken place in Paris and that among those rounded up had been a contact with whom Brossolette had an appointment for the next day. Unable to ascertain whether Brossolette had been warned or not, Yeo-Thomas decided to go to Paris and make sure: in view of the possibility of the Lysander operation being transferred to Tours he had to take his luggage with him.

On arriving at the station he remembered that on the inward journey from Arras to Paris the baggage of all passengers was ordinarily searched by the military authorities: he could not afford to take such a risk carrying a suitcaseful of documents relating to Vergeltungswaffen (V1s and V2s) and their emplacements. Then, just as he was about to turn tail, he caught sight of two German Luftwaffe officers walking along the platform towards the train following them was an orderly pushing a barrow stacked with a mountain of valises and trunks. Tagging along on the outskirts, Yeo-Thomas watched the orderly load the officers' luggage into the carriage and saw, as he had expected, that there was no room in the compartment for so much baggage: a great deal of it had to be piled up at the end of the corridor, where the orderly, who was accompanying his masters, mounted guard over it. Yeo-Thomas got into the same carriage and sat down on his own suitcases in the corridor beside the German soldier. As

1 Not to be confused with Yeo-Thomas's cover named

soon as the train started he lighted a cigarette and then, as though by afterthought, offered one to the orderly, who accepted.

'*Danke schön,*' said the orderly.

Tommy gave him a light.

'You are very kind,' the orderly said in bad French.

'It is always agreeable to share with someone pleasant,' Yeo-Thomas said.

The chief tragedy of the 1914–1918 war consisted, as a cynic not inaccurately remarked, in the number of people who weren't killed in it; and, when you look round the lounge of any fashionable hotel, you'll see that that goes for the 1939–1945 war as well. The smooth, deceitful men who have misinterpreted history and made the muddles are rarely required to go down into the arena and throw and receive the javelins. Because Yeo-Thomas was no more responsible for the pre-war ineptitudes of democracy than the Bavarian orderly for the threats and thefts of National Socialism they were soon conversing amiably. Although Tommy's kindliness was inspired by a very practical purpose it was difficult for him not to like the ordinary, stupid, bewildered, guiltless, decent little German soldier when he pulled out photographs of his fair-haired children and of his humble, badly dressed, pudding-faced wife, who certainly didn't know the difference between oligarchy and parliamentarianism.

'I've got children too,' Tommy said.

'War is bad for children,' the orderly said. '*Auch fü Soldate.* For soldiers too, war is bad.'

'War is bad for everybody,' Yeo-Thomas said.

'*Ganz richtig,*' the orderly said. 'You are right.'

Tommy took out his flask of Mirabelle.

'We must drink to the health of our families,' he said, raising the flask to his lips. When he had pretended to take a deep draught, he wiped the top of the flask with his sleeve and handed it to the soldier.

The orderly took a good pull. He accepted another cigarette. For a little they puffed away together in silence. Then Yeo-Thomas rose, ostentatiously opened the suitcase containing the secret documents, took out a slab of chocolate and handed it to the soldier.

'*Für Kinder,*' he said in his best German. 'For your children.'

Chocolate was scarce in Germany, even for the troops, and the

German was overwhelmed. Putting his arms round Tommy's shoulders he gazed at him tenderly with eyes full of tears which were not entirely Mirabelle.

'*Vielen Danke*,' he said. 'Milla mercis. I think that you are a good man.'

'On the contrary, I am a bad man,' Tommy said. 'Listen, I am in trouble.'

'Good men as well as bad men can be in trouble.' The German's broken French made him seem more than ever like an overgrown child, symbolic of humanity's frightful uncomprehending misery; but Yeo-Thomas had to go on lying to him if he was to achieve his very necessary purpose.

'You see, it is difficult for a Frenchman to make a living these days,' he said. 'To provide for my wife and children, I am forced to do things which I do not like: black market, in other words. In this suitcase here I have cigarettes and chocolates which I am taking to sell in Paris. I don't like doing this sort of thing, but, as I say, I've got responsibilities. And if the police and the customs search my case the goods will be confiscated. And what's even worse I'll be arrested and my family will starve.' Out came the flask again; and, after taking another fake swig, he handed it to the German, who emptied it. 'You do see that I am in difficulties, don't you?' He gave the German another cigarette and then a whole packet.

'*Vielleicht ist es nicht so schwer*,' the orderly said with a large alcoholic grin. Lifting up a couple of his officers' valises he signed to Yeo-Thomas to slip the suitcase from which the chocolate had been extracted in beneath them. 'Now I do not think that the police will say much to you.'

And when the police and the customs authorities arrived a few minutes later they did not have much to say to Yeo-Thomas, although they went through all his pockets and examined his papers carefully: his second suitcase, containing only his clothes, was found to be in order. As he had foreseen, the German officers' luggage was not examined.

The rest of the journey he passed in happy companionship with the now befuddled orderly. When they reached the Gare du Nord the soldier returned the suitcase containing the documents to Yeo-

Thomas, who helped him to unload the officers' baggage. To avoid too close scrutiny by the Gestapo men, who, like the hotel porters in the old Caledonian Railway advertisements, met all arrivals, Tommy accompanied the orderly to the exit, where the two friends parted after loud expressions of mutual goodwill.

Taking a vélo-taxi to the rue Claude Chahu, Yeo-Thomas found that his journey had not been in vain: Brossolette was in Suni Sandöe's flat, and, unaware of the arrest of his contact, would probably have stepped into a Gestapo trap the next day. They talked for a little together and, listening-in to the BBC, Tommy learned from a cryptic message that his operation had been retransferred to the Arras area. Having again promised to come out and relieve Brossolette in two months' time, Tommy left before curfew and went to spend the night in Jeanne Helbling's flat in Neuilly.

The following morning he arranged for José Dupuis to help another circuit during his absence and for Maud to act as Brossolette's agent-de-liaison. At one o'clock he left again for Arras and was seen off by Jeanne Helbling. During the journey he looked out of the train window with sadistic pleasure at the evidences of successful sabotage: four ammunition trains had been derailed during the previous few days and the tracks were littered with damaged carriages and trucks, overturned guns, light tanks and lorries. Beneath the leaden November purgatorial sky gangs of German soldiers and French civilians were clearing up the wreckage.

Arriving in Arras in the late afternoon he again saw Thierry, who gave him a list of the pressing needs of the local groups: among the grisly paraphernalia paradoxically required for the preparation of peace were automatics for sector officers, silent pistols, daggers, grenades, rifles and ammunition; benzedrine tablets, woollens, wind-jackets, torches, batteries, food and money were also wanted. A chance meeting with Piquier, Regional Military Officer for the north of France, confirmed the urgency of giving Resistance the tools without which it could not accomplish its task. Once again Yeo-Thomas realised that it was essential that the authorities in London should satisfy the requirements of the heroic men who were risking most painful forms of death in order to liberate their country.

The rest of the time he spent with Madame Fraser and M.

Doutremepuich waiting to learn the date of his exfiltration. As before, he was nervous, aware of the danger and consequences of a last-minute slip. His fears were increased when Deshayes informed him that the whole area was cordoned off and that German patrols, especially interested in the contents of suitcases, searched all whom they met on the roads after dark. M. Bisiaux, the local undertaker, had, however, found a rather macabre solution to the problem: Marcelle Virolle, Mademoiselle Pichard and Yeo-Thomas were to be driven to the landing ground shut up inside a motor hearse; apparently it was normal to transport a corpse at night for a funeral the next day.

On Monday, 15 November, a telegram was received to say that the operation would take place that night at a ground called Charente, some twenty miles distant. Tommy's luggage, which now included the presents of a Rolls razor from Madame Fraser and a black tie to wear when he should return to France in RAF uniform from M. Doutremepuich, was sent to be stored in the hearse. In the evening the operation was, according to custom, confirmed by two BBC messages. About eight o'clock, after a drink of champagne, the two girls left for the hearse, which had been parked in a dark back street; Yeo-Thomas followed a little later, with his Colt in readiness in his shoulder holster. A sharp wind blew through the narrow cobbled alleys: the weather was bitterly cold, the sky was overcast and the moon did not shine through the clouds. It began to look doubtful that the operation could succeed in such conditions.

Inside the hearse Yeo-Thomas was handed a Sten gun and a couple of grenades. Then the back was shut and they were in darkness. As the girls' teeth were soon chattering with cold Tommy gave them some brandy from his flask. Unlike a coffin the three passengers could not be clamped down and as soon as the hearse began to move they were thrown from side to side. The bumpy road jolted the Sten gun against Yeo-Thomas's thighs and bruised them. Boxed up in blackness they lurched uncomfortably across a timeless and invisible world. Then terror struck them all as the hearse stopped abruptly and they heard the heavy tread of Feld-gendarmerie patrol-men's feet. There was the sound of throaty German questions, of quick Gallic replies, of more questions. Then there was silence. Gripping his Sten gun, Tommy watched the blackness where the door was, prepared to shoot should the soldiers attempt to search the hearse. The big boots trudged away and the hearse moved on again.

A little later there was another stop, but this time the questions were asked in a muffled voice and the man who had asked them jumped up in the cab beside the driver. They were now under the protection of Resistance men who were patrolling the road for the last five miles. Soon the hearse stopped again, the back was thrown open and, cramped and stiff, the two girls and Tommy climbed down into a farmyard. Entering the house they were greeted by the farmer's wife, who had prepared for them a meal of vegetable soup, steak, fried potatoes, cheese and fruit, with wine, coffee and brandy. Half a dozen sturdy armed peasants watched them with interest while they ate: realizing that this was the first time that these men had seen a British agent, Yeo-Thomas spoke to each man individually and at length and thanked him for the risks he was running on their behalf.

The operation about to be undertaken was even more hazardous than Tommy had imagined. In a private conversation Alex, the hatchet-faced leader, explained to him that the Germans in the district were particularly vigilant. Twenty armed men had, therefore, been placed round the farm in such a way that nobody could come within 500 yards of it without being observed. Ten of those men would withdraw and cover Yeo-Thomas and the girls when they left for the airfield. Around the landing ground itself there were ten more men concealed in bushes and another six men were patrolling the approaches. If the passengers were caught it would be only after Alex and his helpers had been killed. Alex went on to apologise for the French defeat in 1940 and promised that Resistance members would do their utmost to be worthy of their liberation. He ended on a formal sentence of respect: '*Mon Commandant, c'est un grand honneur pour nous tous d'assurer la protection d'un officier anglais, surtout d'un anglais si grand ami de notre pays.*'[1] To show his gratitude for this touching little speech Yeo-Thomas gave Alex his platinum cuff links as a souvenir.

---

1 'Commandant, it is a great honour for us to be able to protect an English officer, especially an Englishman who is such a good friend of our country.'

But too much remained to be done to spend the rest of the night in protestations of fidelity. Deshayes came in and said that he had checked the direction of the wind and driven into the ground the stakes marking the places for the men to stand with lighted torches. The peasants filed out carrying their rifles at the trail. About midnight Alex and Deshayes led Tommy and the girls to the airfield.

It was pitch black outside and icy cold. The earth was frozen and crunched under their steps. They passed through a gate and, as they were traversing a field, a man with a Sten gun at the ready emerged from a hedge, spoke a few words with Alex and stepped back into the shadow. They passed through another gate, crossed a ditch and, after being silently challenged several more times, reached the landing ground.

While Alex went to inspect his men Yeo-Thomas and the girls waited in the darkness. The sky was still cloudy and the moon was not shining. The cold wind swirled around them, numbing their feet and their hands and making a moaning, whistling noise in the eerie silence of the night. Five miles away at most were German troops. Might they not be much nearer, creeping on their bellies through the black fields? But even in his discomfort and anxiety Tommy was able to realise the much more terrible dangers to which their helpers were exposed: even if he and the girls got away, Alex, Deshayes, the farmer and his wife and the others might still be tortured and shot if any trace of the operation were discovered. Once again he determined to do all that he could to help such brave people.

Imperceptibly almost the sky began to clear; the moon shone through the clouds, lighting them and making them look like a silver shawl. As the earth detached itself from the sky the landing ground became visible and Yeo-Thomas was able to distinguish their luggage heaped up in readiness for loading into the plane. As the light increased a faint buzzing was heard, and soon the Lysander could be seen above them, gleaming like a moth caught in the headlamps of a car. The recognition signals were flashed; the torches were lighted; the aircraft circled and came to a standstill within twelve yards of where Tommy and the two girls lay; the cockpit door was thrown open; two men got out and their luggage was thrown out after them; the customary champagne and perfume were passed in to the pilot; within four minutes the three passengers and their luggage had been picked up and the aircraft was climbing up into the sky again.

It was uncomfortable in the cockpit, with three passengers and fourteen packages or suitcases crammed into a space designed to hold one man and his machine-gun. With a girl on each knee, Yeo-Thomas was unable to reach up and close the cover of the cockpit, which had been inadvertently left open, nor were the girls able to do so. As usual, they ran into flak over the French coast, but they encountered no German fighters; the passage was rough and both girls were sick, but in little more than an hour they were back in England, where Major Johnson was waiting to welcome them at the aerodrome.

Next day Yeo-Thomas was ordered to report at the Air Ministry in Horseferry Road, to give an account of his experiences. Dressed once more in his uniform, he was shown into a room in which an Air Commodore with a square brick-red unspiritual face sat behind a large desk. Tommy stood to attention and saluted this highly paid officer, who eyed him critically and with disapproval.

'You are improperly dressed,' the Air Commodore said.

Conscious that he had polished highly both his shoes and buttons, Yeo-Thomas glanced down to see if one of the latter was undone.

'I'm sorry, Sir, but I can't see what is wrong.'

'Don't you read your Air Ministry Orders?'

'When I can; yes, Sir.'

'In that case you ought to know that you should no longer be wearing those VRs[1] on your lapels; it was in AMOs last month.'

Familiar as he was with the stupidity of officers promoted from their peacetime obscurity to conduct a war they didn't understand, Yeo-Thomas was flabbergasted. Did the braided oaf really imagine that while a man was facing torture and death he had the opportunity of keeping himself informed of the permutations of badges and phylacteries? Too angry to realise what a good story he had to tell to his friends, he answered coldly:

'Last month, Sir, I was in Occupied France and did not receive AMOs.'

---

1 Brass letters standing for Volunteer Reserve, and till then worn by all non-regular Air Force officers.

But the Air Commodore was dyed in the wool.

'Don't let it happen again,' he said gruffly.

And that wasn't all: a few days later Tommy found in the letter-box of his flat a typewritten envelope placed there by an anonymous neighbour critical of his apparently exclusively administrative war service; the envelope contained a white feather and a sheet of paper on which was printed in capitals: COWARD.

Unlike the unimaginative Air Commodore's rebuke, this insult was at least a tribute to his security.

CHAPTER VIII

The Gospel according to St Thomas

The hutch now contained a lot of new rabbits: the staff of 'RF' section had been increased; Lieutenant-Colonel L. H. Dismore was in command and there were no more pink slips ordering immediate conference. One thing, however, was still the same: the award of Tommy's MC had not yet been confirmed and he was once more forced to adopt his two-tunic technique. Offered a DSO for his second mission, Yeo-Thomas angrily refused; all that he wanted was his MC, and that only so as not to appear a fool before the French. The lean, efficient, good-humoured and deservedly popular Dizzy tried to kill two birds with one stone by recommending him for a bar to his contested MC.

Fresh from his nerve-racking experiences in the field, Yeo-Thomas became outspokenly critical of complacency at home. While he admired the energy of the many who wholeheartedly devoted themselves to the performance of necessary routine, he suspected that there were a few whose main ambition was to pump themselves up into full colonels and group captains. Others he considered doctrinaire xenophobes, fearful of arming underground foreign allies because the procedure had never been outlined in the military manuals. Perhaps because of his interview with the imbecilic Air Commodore he was especially disapproving of the Air Ministry. Night after night, he pointed out, Frenchmen were risking their lives to wait for arms and supplies which were seldom or never dropped to them; and they could

328 | BRUCE MARSHALL

not understand how Great Britain, with all her publicised air power, could not do more to satisfy their requirements. Co-ordinates of landing grounds were necessary and these had been given, but it was unreasonable of the authorities to exact measured surveys from those who were continually exposed to the vigilance of the enemy. For the Lysander pilots and for the majority of those engaged on parachuting operations he had the greatest admiration; he was, however, impatient with those who circled round pinpoints and returned home, *re infecta*, with the excuse that the torches marking out the ground had not been bright enough. In a lecture given to both RAF and USAAF crews he emphasised the dangers and the difficulties faced by reception committees:

'. . . When you go on operations you run the normal flying risks while you are over England. When you are over the Channel or enemy territory you run additional risks but only for a restricted number of hours. If you are shot down and captured you become a prisoner of war. If you get back to base you find a hot meal awaiting you and a comfortable bed in which you can immediately go to sleep. Unless there is an air raid you will not be disturbed and you will have nothing more to worry about until you go on your next operation. You have warm clothing and comparatively comfortable quarters. You get your pay, you get leave and, if you do a good job, you get a gong or promotion.

'Now look at things on the other side of the Channel. The man in the reception committee often has to travel many miles on foot or on bicycle in order to reach the landing ground. There is a curfew in France and he has to get to and from the ground without attracting attention, or he will be arrested. During the moon period he has to do this night after night, and often he has to wait many hours in vain for an operation which may have been cancelled at the last moment. He can never catch up on the sleep he misses because during the day he has to earn his living, working as a farm labourer, a mechanic or a clerk. And when he is working he lives under the hourly threat of a visit from the Gestapo. He gets no pay for his resistance work, no promotion, no gongs. If he is caught he is not treated as a prisoner of war but as a spy, and is tortured and shot. And not only will there be no pension for his dependants but he has to face the fact that his wife and children may also be tortured and shot . . .

'When you do not find the reception committee waiting for you you think that they have been careless; you do not stop to wonder why they are not there. You fail to understand that a sudden change in the German Order of Battle may make a ground which was safe one day impossible to use the next. While you fly fuming back to your base it does not strike you that the whole reception committee may have been arrested. You complain about the weak lights. Don't you understand that it is difficult to secure batteries in occupied territory? Do you realise that those obtainable are mostly of inferior quality? Do you know that a man may have to bicycle twenty or thirty kilometres in order to obtain one battery?'

To Tommy it was all such elementary pot-hook stuff that even an air commodore ought to have been able to understand it. To a congregation of vice-admirals, brigadiers and air vice-marshals he gave a detailed account of the situation in France. For the space of three hours he cried out aloud: 'Great is de Gaulle of the French.' With all the eloquence he possessed he pleaded the cause of the Resistance Movements, stressing their need for arms and equipment. He gave proof of the results which could be achieved with adequate supplies. 'Our present puny efforts are as likely to succeed as a man trying to fill a swimming-pool with a fountain-pen filler,' he thundered at the pews of wayward brass. Jutting out his chin, he besought the RAF to divert from bombing more than sixteen aircraft to serve the reception committees. If they withheld the necessary assistance they would be responsible for the loss of thousands of lives when invasion took place. The sermon failed and he was told that the bombing plan was far more important; it was like trying to convert a bench of bishops.

It is to his credit that it was almost exclusively with his superiors that he quarrelled. On only one occasion, when he was interviewing candidates for the 'Jedburghs', did he lose his temper with a sub-ordinate; Jedburghs were teams of Allied officers who were to be dropped behind the German lines just prior to 'D' day to take command of Maquis and Secret Army groups, and the qualifications required were high. An Army lieutenant, with dirty buttons and a greasy service cap, entered the room without knocking.

'G'morning,' he said, strolling up to the desk and failing to salute.

330 | BRUCE MARSHALL

'Mr X, you will please go outside and come in properly.'

Puzzled, the sloppy soldier retired and came in again, this time after knocking.

'G'morning,' he said, still without saluting.

'Mr X, GO OUTSIDE THAT DOOR AND COME IN PROPERLY.'

The product of football pools, free thought and progress went out, knocked, came in again and saluted slackly and wearily. Yeo-Thomas roared at him:

'You are the most outrageous thing I have ever seen in officer's uniform. Go outside and come in smartly or you will regret ever having come here.'

Lieutenant X did as he was told and put a hint of zeal into the performance.

'You realise that we are looking for officers with a good knowledge of French?'

'Yes, Sir.'

'Do you qualify?'

'I think so, Sir.'

'*Parlez-vous français?*'

'*Ung peutee.*'

Lieutenant X, it was clear, had volunteered merely in order to obtain a free railway voucher to London.

'Mr X, you are a disgrace to your uniform: your tunic looks like a sack; your buttons are filthy. We are looking for real officers and I reject you. See that you leave my presence smartly and properly. Dismiss!'

The anecdote is interesting for two reasons: it disproves the legend, current in the Army, that the RAF is a breezy egalitarian free-for-all where aircraftmen borrow the group captain's staff car to take the air vice-marshal's girl friend out to dinner and send in the bill to the air commodore afterwards; and it shows the value that Yeo-Thomas, an irregular soldier, placed on parade-ground formality. A strip was torn off Lieutenant X, not because Yeo-Thomas himself was always respectful when he insulted his superiors, but because the 'brown job' lacked what Arthur Bryant calls so neatly 'the spirit of proud subordination which makes an army'. Jedburghs, who if captured were

THE WHITE RABBIT | 331

liable to be treated as spies and tortured and shot, required to be courageous; therefore, they required to be disciplined. Such at least was Tommy's argument. Of the eight officers he interviewed that day he chose only two, one of whom he tried to dissuade because of the man's family obligations: Captain Hay, who was to die in action, and Captain Desmond Hubble, whom he was to meet again in Buchenwald.

Meanwhile in France the situation was deteriorating, and the weather wasn't making things easier. Networks of trained agents were being wiped out by the Gestapo and their French collaborators. M. Bollaert, who had been sent out to replace Jean Moulin, as General de Gaulle's personal representative, was having difficulty in exercising his authority; and both he and Brossolette were in such constant danger that it was decided to exfiltrate them immediately. Of two Lysanders sent to pick them and others up one had to turn back because of bad weather and the other was shot down in flames over the French coast. The house in which Bollaert and Brossolette had been sheltering while waiting for the operation to take place was raided within an hour of their leaving it. Heavy fogs made another operation temporarily impossible: on one night alone nine aircraft crashed. And when at last the fog over France lifted, England was still blanketed. Unable because of security regulations to refer to the weather in a signal to the field, Yeo-Thomas tried to explain to Brossolette in a message sent over the BBC the reasons for the delay: '*Du Cheval à Polydor: nous mangeons toujours de la purée de pois, mais nous aurons du dessert.*'[1] As the French always refer to English fog as 'mashed peas', Brossolette understood and replied that he would try to return by a sea operation organised by another branch of the service. Tommy signalled back that exfiltration by sea was much too dangerous at that time of the year and counselled patience and discretion till the next moon period, when another Lysander would be sent. '*Le Cheval n'oublie jamais ses amis,*'[2] he assured Brossolette by the BBC.

But the January moon period proved as unsatisfactory as the

1 'From Cheval to Polydor. We are still eating mashed peas, but there's a sweet in the menu.'
2 'Cheval never forgets his friends.'

December: the lost aircraft were not replaced, some of those remaining developed engine trouble and only three Lysander operations took place, in the south of France, where it was impossible to pick up Bollaert and Brossolette. His friend was still in danger and he had been unable to help him; and men and women who had pinned their faith on the Allies were being badly let down. With meagre means at their disposal the Secret Army and the Maquis would be wiped out long before they could attain their potential. Yeo-Thomas was so discouraged that he made up his mind that once Brossolette was safely back in England, he would send in his resignation.

It was in this rebellious mood that he took the train to Oxford to see Major-General Sir E. D. Swinton, whom he knew well and to whom he told his troubles, railing at the Air Ministry for refusing to provide sufficient aircraft. The General heard him patiently and, probably because he was familiar with Tommy's impulsive character, very sensibly pointed out to him that a squadron leader was not in a position to know the whole pattern of the war and that his superiors might have reasons for their policy which he ignored. But Yeo-Thomas stuck to his guns: he wasn't talking from hypothesis or hearsay; he had been and seen and learned, and he *knew* that those in authority were underestimating the value which a properly equipped French Resistance would represent on 'D' day.

'There is only one man who can decide on such an important point, and that is the Prime Minister,' General Swinton said. 'Would you dare to face him if a meeting could be arranged?'

Yeo-Thomas most certainly would.

The General took Tommy at his word: a letter was sent to Mr Churchill, to be handed to the Prime Minister personally by Mr Brendan Bracken.

On 1 February, 1944, Yeo-Thomas was summoned to No. 10 Downing Street to meet the Prime Minister at 3 p.m. Introduced by Major Desmond Morton into the long room where Cabinet meetings took place, Yeo-Thomas found Mr Churchill seated alone at the middle of a long table facing the windows. The Prime Minister had his chair tilted back, one knee pressed against the table, and was, not surprisingly, smoking a cigar. Nervous but determined not to show it, Yeo-Thomas came to a halt and stood smartly to attention in front of the man whom he most admired in the whole world. Mr Churchill looked at him critically.

'I'm a busy man and I have no time to waste,' he said. 'But when I get a letter from Ole Luke Oie I know it is about something of interest. He says you know France better than any other Englishman. I doubt it. What have you got to say? I can give you five minutes.'

It must have been rather like pleading against time for mercy with God the Father. Tommy knew that he had the proper arguments, but he was terrified that in his haste he might omit the most convincing. He started in right away on the Secret Army and the Maquis. He spoke of their appalling lack of arms and equipment. He spoke of the need for aircraft to drop supplies. He told the Prime Minister about the brave men and women risking torture and death, carrying messages through the crowded, police-ridden streets of Paris and waiting for agents in the darkness in the windy wilderness of central France. Panting, breathless, he threw a potted version of the whole sad story at Mr Churchill and hoped that his hero would understand. His hero did.

'Sit down,' Mr Churchill said and, when Tommy had sat down: 'What is the organisation of the Maquis like?'

Yeo-Thomas told him in detail, not forgetting to mention the group with one rifle between thirty men.

'They will need clothing besides arms?'

'Yes, Sir.'

'What sort of clothing do they need?'

'Thick woollen socks, underwear, gloves, wind jackets, strong heavy boots.'

'How many of each?'

'That, Sir, depends upon the number of aircraft at our disposal for dropping supplies.'

'How many aircraft are required to step up your operations effectively?'

'At least a hundred, Sir; more if possible.'

'I shall see that you get a hundred to start with.'

Yeo-Thomas dotted his 'i's and crossed his 't's.

'Thank you, Sir; but it is necessary for the hundred aircraft to be serviceable and to do at least two-hundred and fifty sorties in every moon period.'

'I shall see to that. If the hundred aircraft do not do the requisite number of sorties you will have to be given more machines.'

Sure now that he was making headway, Yeo-Thomas started off again. He told the Prime Minister all he knew about the situation in France. He told him about the sabotage and the fearful martyrdom endured by ordinary humdrum folks. Perhaps in his excitement he repeated himself, for Mr Churchill interrupted him again.

'Have you written reports about these things?'

'Yes, Sir.'

The Prime Minister turned to Major Morton.

'Why have they not been passed to me, Morton?'

'I don't know, Sir; I shall find out.'

'Yes, and see that I have them immediately.'

Mr Churchill turned back to Yeo-Thomas. Unerringly picking out the essentials, he asked a number of questions which Tommy described as 'dead on'. 'What a mind, what versatility!' he says. The Prime Minister, of course, was a man very much after Tommy's own heart; and I rather think that Yeo-Thomas must have pleased Mr Churchill, who looked at him with the hint of a smile and said:

'You have chosen an unorthodox way of doing things and you have short-circuited official channels; it might mean trouble for you, but I shall see that no such thing happens.'

There and then the Prime Minister dictated notes on what Yeo-Thomas had told him and an order to the Air Ministry to put a hundred aircraft at the disposal of 'RF' section. He had just finished when M. Astier de la Vigerie, whom Yeo-Thomas had already met several times, entered.

'Squadron Leader Yeo-Thomas has been pleading on behalf of France, Monsieur de la Vigerie, and I have been listening,' Mr Churchill said. 'I am going to increase substantially the number of aircraft doing parachuting operations to the Resistance, and greater supplies and more armament are going to be sent.'

Yeo-Thomas went out of No. 10 Downing Street walking on air; he had spent fifty-five minutes with the Prime Minister, that great man to whom he rightly attributed the preservation of Western civilisation. Something of this vicarious glory must still have been shining from him when he got back to Norgeby House, where 'RF' section was now installed, for he was immediately visited by some very senior officers, who prudently congratulated him upon his initiative.

The wand which Mr Churchill had waved was a powerful one: within forty-eight hours 'RF' section had at its disposal twenty-two Halifaxes, twelve Liberators, thirty-six Stirlings, six Albemarles and a number of small aircraft for pick-up operations; other planes were to operate from North Africa. 'RF' section went hard at it, sending telegrams to the field to reception committees and ascertaining the requirements of the various regions.

The only fly in the ointment was that they had not yet been able to bring back Bollaert and Brossolette. And it was impossible to get in touch with them because, in spite of Tommy's categorical warning, they had decided to come home by sea and were now in hiding somewhere near the coast. Then the inevitable happened, and it fell to poor Major Johnson to tell Yeo-Thomas of their arrest.

'Tommy, old man, this is going to shake you,' he said and then he told him.

Yeo-Thomas was stunned. Bollaert he had known, but Brossolette he had loved as men can love only those with whom they have shared discomfort and extreme danger. The whole man was physically present to him as he stood there in Johnson's office. The thick eyebrow, the piercing dark brown eyes which could gleam with kindness or glare with anger, the black hair parted in the middle and brushed straight back from the high forehead, the long, thin fingers, the strong hands, the hooked nose, the expressive, sensitive mouth, he loved them because he had been able to give them companionship in their essential loneliness in the world, and because their loneliness had companioned his when he was facing the hatred of cruel men. And Brossolette's friendly voice he heard too, as he had last heard it in Sun Sandoe's flat when he had gone to warn him of his contact's arrest: *'Alors, Cheval, qu'est-ce qu'il y a! Je vous croyais à Arras et sur le point de partir.'*[1]

'Any details?' he asked when he had recovered his self-control. 'What happened? Was he betrayed?'

There were no details as yet, Johnson said. All that they knew was

1 'Well, Cheval, what's the matter? I thought you were in Arras and just about to leave.'

336 | BRUCE MARSHALL

that Bollaert and Brossolette had been arrested in Brittany while attempting to get away by boat.

Dismore, Johnson, Thackthwaite, that nice DSO. Fife and Forfar Yeoman Murray-Prain, the bubbling little Kay More, the lanky energetic Clarke, Alex Murray, Whitehead and the sweet and sensible Barbara all did their best to comfort him. But it was no good. Even when he learned that Brossolette had not been identified and was in Rennes prison under his false name of Boutet it was still no good. For Tommy knew that in prison Brossolette would not be able to procure any hair dye and that sooner or later the tell-tale white streak would begin to show; and when that happened the Gestapo, who knew all about the white lock, would identify Brossolette and begin to torture him. Ashamed of his own safety in England, he felt that he had betrayed his friend when he had left him alone in France, and it was in vain that Dismore reminded him that he had been ordered to return home. I don't think that Tommy very often reads the Bible, but there is a lament in the Old Testament which expresses his grief: 'O Absalom, my son, my son. Would God that I had died for thee, O Absalom, my son.'

There was, he knew at once, only one thing that he could do: he must return to France and rescue Brossolette before the white streak of hair had time to show. And quite apart from that particular purpose there seemed to be every justification for his going: with the capture of Bollaert and Brossolette French Resistance had again been decapitated and demoralisation might once more set in, as it had after the arrest of Moulin and Delestraint; he knew all the heads of the Resistance Movements and all the cogs in the complicated machine of under-ground intrigue; he had acquired great authority over Regional Military Officers and the Air Operations Officers. Without excessively flattering himself he was sure that there was nobody else who could so adequately replace Bollaert and Brossolette. 'D' day was approaching, and when it broke his presence in the field might prove of great use to the Allies.

But the arguments with which he convinced himself did not so readily convince his superiors. His superiors knew what he knew and chose to pretend that he didn't know: that the Gestapo was informed of his activities and possessed his description and that there was every likelihood of his being captured. This they told him; they refrained from pointing out that it would be disastrous if anybody so well informed as himself about Resistance and staff planning were to break down under torture and talk. But Tommy guessed what his chiefs were thinking and he soon found a way of overcoming both their spoken and their unspoken objections.

He realised that his masters were right to entertain those fears; the bravest of men could not be certain that he would not talk under torture, especially if the executioner were subtle enough to suggest as he gave another twist to the thumbscrew that the war was not being fought about the Holy Ghost after all, but about exports and imports.

With the Gestapo constantly on the alert it was impossible to guarantee that he would not be arrested; talking could be avoided with certainty only if torture could be avoided; and torture might be avoided if, in the event of capture, he were able to pass himself off as a member of the crew of a British aircraft who had been compelled to bale out over enemy-occupied territory and who could consequently claim treatment as a prisoner of war. His cover story, of course, would require to be unshakable because the Gestapo, with its customary thoroughness, possessed the Air Force List containing the names of all those engaged on operational flying. Accordingly, through the agency of Wing Commander Redding, liaison officer between SOE and the Air Ministry, he got in touch with Squadron Leader Dodkin, whose name was on the operational list, but who had been grounded and would not be required to fly again. Tommy spent several hours with Squadron Leader Dodkin, whose life story he learned and whose serial number he suggested that he should assume. In the end his chiefs accepted the manœuvre and identity discs were struck for him in Dodkin's name.

Once more he had to learn new codes and conventions. He had also to provide himself with additional aliases and memorise their particulars, because the Dodkin cover could be used only in the event of arrest. He sent a BBC message to José Dupuis, 'de Tommy à Hélène . . .' to advise her of his return. Realising the very real danger into which he was going, he made a will, without telling Barbara. But Barbara guessed his forebodings because she shared them; she tried to reassure him by not reassuring him, and her own anxieties she bore alone. Not much has been said in this book about the gay, gentle and lovely Barbara, although her silent courage gives her a special part in the story: Tommy says that without her sympathy and love he could not have endured.

Although it was usual for the BCRA to have a French representative on missions chiefly concerning themselves, because of the exceptional circumstances they agreed to Tommy going alone as a bipartite delegate of Britain and France. '*Mais cette mission ne peut constituer en aucune façon un précédent,*' Commandant Manuel wrote to Dismore. '*Je ne suis d'accord qu'en raison de la personnalité d'Asymptote.*'[1] For Asymptote was the not very Dick Barton code name which Yeo-Thomas had been given for his third mission, and of which the titanic terms of reference were as follows:

OPERATIONAL INSTRUCTIONS FOR ASYMPTOTE

1. Asymptote will be responsible to his HQ and will make a full report on his return. This will not preclude him from sending an interim report during his mission.

2. He will inquire into and report upon the state of the Resistance Movements in the Occupied Zone, their degree of training, strength, morale and preparedness. He will see how far the distribution of arms has progressed and whether this distribution has been and is being made with due regard to the order of priority of plans as sent to the field with the Regional Military Officers.

3. He will see whether the general tightening up of security which he recommended during his last mission has been implemented.

4. He will contact the Regional Military Officers and ascertain whether they are getting adequate support and assistance from the Regional Movement Heads. If, in his estimation, this is not the case, he will approach them or their chiefs and exert all his efforts towards increasing and improving relations with a view to ensuring the maximum co-operation at all levels.

5. He will contact the Air Operations Officers and take similar steps to those in (4) above. In addition he will endeavour to ascertain the quantities and employment of stores already delivered to the field.

1 'But this mission must not be regarded in any way as a precedent. I give my consent only because of Asymptote's personality.'

6. He will endeavour to discover how far the plans already sent to the field have been set on foot and whether the teams selected to execute them are properly briefed and trained.

7. He will investigate current sabotage activities with a view to ascertaining whether instructions from HQ are reaching the proper people and are being followed. He will be provided with the list of targets of first priority and will check up in the field on the efforts being made to attack them. He will endeavour in every way to increase all sabotage activities on the lines directed by HQ.

8. He will contact such officers of the Maquis organisations as are nominated to him by Jerôme and will, as far as is practicable, inquire into the strength, armament, resources and morale of Maquis groups not covered by the Missions Cantinier, Xavier, Union and Citronelle (if then in the field).

9. It will be for Asymptote to decide, according to the situation which he finds in the field and his estimate of his own personal security, or of his contacts, which, if any, of the foregoing tasks should be deleted from this programme.

10. He will investigate any matters not specifically mentioned in this *Ordre de Mission* which he judges to be of importance to the prosecution of the war, and make comments and/or recommendations in consequence.

I doubt if he noticed that clause No. 9 constituted a let-out from the task which he had persuaded his chiefs to impose upon him, or that clause No. 10 almost cancelled the let-out. It was of Brossolette, lonely in a cell in Rennes, that he was thinking when he left for Tempsford on the night of 24 February, 1944. Brossolette was a man of courage and of vision and his own familiar friend. Brossolette would never have failed him, and he would not fail Brossolette. He must rescue Brossolette before his true identity was revealed by the white hair on his head beginning to show.

CHAPTER IX

Mission Asymptote

Once again he was travelling third-class, and he was to parachute. Because of the necessity for rescuing Brossolette before his identity was discovered, Tommy had elected to jump in the dark rather than wait for the next moon period. He was accompanied by a saboteur whose code name was Trieur and whose first trip this was.

They were to be dropped near Clermont-Ferrand, about 250 miles south of Paris, and had a long way to fly. There was the usual flak over the French coast, but the rest of the journey passed without incident.

The procedure was the same as on his first mission with Passy and Brossolette: when they were nearly over the pinpoint the despatcher hooked up their static lines and opened up the hole. Trieur looked nervous and Yeo-Thomas, who was to jump first, tried to cheer him up by giving him the thumbs-up sign as he swung his legs into the trap. Below it was inky black, and it was some time before Tommy could see the twinkling lights of the reception committee. Then he felt the despatcher's hand on his shoulders, the red light went on, the aircraft made a wide turn and ran in over the ground; the green light went on, he pushed himself out through the hole, whirled round in the slipstream, floated and, because of the lack of moonlight, began to count. Dropped from a height of 500 feet he had been told that he would touch the ground when he had reached twenty; instead his head hit it with a bang at thirteen and he was knocked unconscious for two or three minutes. He was still dizzy and shaken when he unfastened his parachute; getting up with difficulty, he found that he had sprained his left ankle.

His discomfiture was increased when the aircraft made its second run overhead and he had to dodge its dropped containers as they came hurtling down. He was helped to cover by the Air Operations Officer Evêque, whom he had already met in London. Trieur had landed safe and sound in the next field. Fortunately, the farmhouse where they were to spend the night was only half a mile distant, and Yeo-Thomas was able to hobble there painfully.

Next morning, although his ankle was still swollen, he determined to leave for Paris that afternoon: not until he was there could he get in touch with Abeille and Archer, who were in charge of the Brittany region, and with whom he hoped to be able to arrange a means of helping Bollaert and Brossolette. The farmer drove him and Trieur over rutty tracks covered with ice and put them in a bus which took them at a breakneck speed over even more slippery roads to Clermont-Ferrand. There they met and dined with Alain Bernay, the Regional Military Officer. Because of his hurry to get to Paris, Yeo-Thomas refused Bernay's invitation to remain with him for a few days and visit the local groups, and Trieur and he caught the half-past eleven train to the capital.

It is a favourite device of unoriginal film producers to translate to the chant of revolving railway train wheels the not particularly profound problems of their puppets: 'CAN I BE A BUSINESS GAL AND STILL BE A GOOD WIFE TO AL?' By the rules of such facile onomatopoeia Tommy ought to have heard the train wheels singing: 'BROSSOLETTE, BROSSOLETTE, BROSSOLETTE'. He heard nothing of the sort, nor did he require to: indeed, he sought relief from thinking about Brossolette in tipping off to the as yet untried Trieur some of the dodges which the saboteur would have to employ if he were to remain for long undetected in Paris.

As soon as he arrived in Paris he handed Trieur over to Maud, who passed the saboteur on to Jacqueline Devaux, who found him a flat. From Maud Tommy learned that Bollaert and Brossolette were still in Rennes prison, and that the latter was still believed to be a M. Pierre Boutet. Maud had established contact with some of the German officials and, by bribing the guards and passing herself off to them as Boutet's mistress, had managed to send him food, wine and clothing in which were hidden messages to which Boutet had replied when sending out his linen to the laundry; by this means she had ascertained that Bollaert and Brossolette were relatively unmolested and that the latter's lock of white hair had not yet begun to show.

His first night in Paris Tommy spent with the Peyronnets, whose flat in the Avenue des Ternes was again considered to be comparatively safe.

The next day, while waiting to contact Abeille and Archer, he got in touch, through the ever-faithful José Dupuis, with Pichard and with Clouet des Pesruches, who, under the slightly less Boulevard St Germain pseudonym of Galilée, was Air Operations Officer for the Touraine. From them he was able to obtain a clear idea of the situation in the Paris, Seine et Marne, Tours and eastern France areas. Partly because the recently stepped up parachutings had not yet been going on long enough for their impact to be felt throughout the country, the morale of Resistance was low. There were four main reasons for this: the weariness of constantly waiting and constantly disappointed reception committees; lack of arms; a growing belief that the Allies had no real intention of ever invading the Continent; and the increased vigilance of the Gestapo, now aided more and more by Darnand's Militia and the Lafont Organisation. It was the old story, with a few new drop scenes, and Tommy told his new version of the other old story to contradict it: parachuting operations were being formidably increased; Jerôme was now in London demonstrating the great potentiality of the Maquis; and the invasion *would* take place.

Not wishing too greatly to inconvenience the Peyronnets, whose flat had already been watched by the Gestapo, Tommy spent his second night in Paris in Jeanne Helbling's flat in the rue Casimir Pinel in Neuilly. Through his hostess he was able to contact Abeille and Archer. Abeille, who before the war had been a Prefect, immediately placed the whole of the Brittany organisation at Tommy's disposal for the rescue of Bollaert and Brossolette. But before determining upon a given course of action Yeo-Thomas decided to go to Rennes and conduct a preliminary investigation on the spot.

He left for Rennes on 1 March, taking Maud with him. With a local lawyer, who was a member of the Resistance, he discussed the possibility of getting Brossolette transferred on a trumped-up charge from Rennes prison to another prison in the south of France where he would be forgotten about by the Rennes authorities and whence they could ultimately secure his release on the basis of wrongful arrest. In the end they abandoned this plan, which failed to take into account Bollaert and which would be a lengthy process involving the suborning of at least two Gestapo officers and the manufacture of an imaginary but convincing misdeed. Because of the danger of Boutet's real identity being discovered, time was the essence of the problem which could, therefore, be solved only by force.

He then went to reconnoitre the prison and its precincts. Almost opposite the main entrance there was a grocer's shop, whose owner was a member of one of the Resistance groups and who numbered among his customers most of the French and some of the German prison officials. From the grocer Yeo-Thomas learned that the greater part of the prison had been handed over to the Germans and only a few cells left free for the French; the main entrance was heavily guarded; all the gates were closed and at each gate was posted a sentry with a light machine gun which could be trained on every avenue of approach; a direct telephone line connected the guard-room of the prison with that of an SS barracks not more than 600 yards distant. Tommy made a careful reconnaissance, found where the telephone line ran and where it could most easily be cut.

He saw at once that a frontal attack would be foredoomed to failure, but he soon hit upon a plan which he thought would stand a chance of success. When the telephone wire connecting the two guard-rooms had been cut, ten men from the local Resistance groups would keep watch from points of vantage situated in houses opposite the prison and would cover all approaches to the main gate. Three other men, of whom one would speak German perfectly and the other two fluently, would present themselves in German uniform with Sicherheitsdienst badges to the sentry at the main entrance; to him they would show forged instructions, supposedly emanating from the Paris or the Rennes Gestapo Headquarters and ordering the prison authorities to free Bollaert and Brossolette for transfer. Once in the guard-room, where it was the custom for those in charge to verify such documents by telephoning to the Headquarters from which they purported to have been issued, the three disguised men would overpower the guards, who, when not on sentry duty, so the grocer had said, always removed their belts and hung their weapons on the wall. The man who spoke perfect German would then return to the sentry at the main entrance, tell him that all was in order and ask him to open the gate so that a car, which would be waiting outside, could be brought into the yard in order that the prisoners might be picked up without attracting the attention of passers-by; the driver would back in and stop the car in such a position as to prevent the sentry from closing the gates again. Meanwhile the two other men would proceed into the prison proper, taking with them the corporal of the guard, whom they would threaten to shoot immediately if he did not obey their orders. Bollaert and Brossolette would be brought out of their cells, put in the car and driven to a second car which would be waiting round the corner from the grocer's shop. While the second car took them to a safe hiding-place in the centre of the town, the first car would continue south, leaving an obvious trail behind it.

The plan seemed a good one, but it could not be put into action immediately: three German-speaking Resistance members, two cars and petrol had to be found; and, owing to a recent lack of parachuting operations in Brittany, Sten guns, pistols, hand grenades and ammunition would have to be brought to Rennes from a remote region.

Full of energy and confidence, Yeo-Thomas returned to Paris and put the preparations in train. In the meantime he carried on with his official work: he held conferences with Sapeur and Commandant Palaud, who were responsible for the paramilitary organisation of Paris, with 'Z' and with the leaders of Front National, Franc-Tireurs et Partisans, Ceux de la Libération, Ceux de la Résistance, and Organisation Civile et Militaire. Because of the repeated hold-ups by German police in the métro, and because vélo-taxis were rare, he had to do a great deal of walking: seven or eight contacts a day in places as widely separated as the Porte Maillot, the Boulevard St Michel, the Trocadéro, the Porte de St Cloud, the Parc Monceau and the Place de la Nation laid a considerable strain on his as yet imperfectly healed left ankle. He had also to take the usual precautions against being followed and to make sure that his contacts were not being trailed when he met them. For the Gestapo was more than ever alert: Pichard and Clouet des Pesruches were being hotly chased and José Dupuis had become so blown that she had had to be sent into the country for a month's rest. In view of this constant danger, Tommy kept changing residences; but whereever he passed the night there was also a radio, and once a week a cryptic message came over the BBC to assure him that Barbara had not been a casualty in the little blitz to which London was then being subjected.

He was staying in Suni Sandöe's flat in the rue Claude Chahu when he was informed that all was now in readiness for the attempt to rescue Bollaert and Brossolette from Rennes prison. Deciding to go to Rennes on the night of 21 March, and anxious to assure himself before he left that the air operations in the Touraine were running satisfactorily, he made an appointment for that morning with Antonin, a new agent-de-liaison lent to him by Pichard; Antonin was to bring him any messages he might have received from a girl called Brigitte, who was Clouet des Pesruches' go-between, and to be prepared to pass on to Brigitte any instructions which Yeo-Thomas had for Clouet des Pesruches. The appointment had been fixed for eleven o'clock at the Passy métro station, situated, unlike most others, on a bridge above ground; Antonin was to walk down the steps on the left and Tommy was to come up them on the right; they were to cross in front of the newspaper kiosk next to the ticket office and to feign surprise when they met.

At eleven o'clock precisely Yeo-Thomas passed the kiosk, but Antonin was not there. Ordinarily Yeo-Thomas would not have broken his security rule of never waiting for an unpunctual contact, but it was imperative that instructions should be passed to Clouet des Pesruches at once, in case he was detained in Rennes longer than he anticipated. He therefore went down the steps on the other side of the station and came up again, using the same steps as before. Having ascended the first flight and still seeing no sign of Antonin coming towards him, he hesitated as to whether to pay a surprise visit to his father, whose flat was only 100 yards distant. Deciding to put duty before pleasure, he continued up the steps, meeting a crowd of people coming down from the train which had just arrived and feeling fairly safe in the other crowd which was climbing the steps towards the station. As he drew level with the last flight leading up to the ticket office five men in civilian clothes pounced on him, handcuffed him and began scientifically to search his pockets. Just then Antonin, escorted by another two Gestapo men in civilian clothes, passed by on the other side of the steps, looked at Tommy and was led away.

'*Wir haben Shelley,*'[1] Tommy's captors shouted with glee.

1 'We've got Shelley.'

CHAPTER X

He was not wonderful by mistake

s soon as Yeo-Thomas had been handcuffed, two of the Gestapo
men set about pushing back the excited crowd: they forbade
access to the station and threatened to shoot anybody attempting to approach their prisoner. For a few minutes Tommy,
tightly gripped by his captors, stood in a small arena of steps, hemmed
in by a throng twenty yards above him and twenty yards below him,
and reading on the spectators' faces fear or pity or the shamefaced
loathing with which men contemplate misfortunes which they try to
believe can never happen to themselves. This tableau, however, was of
brief duration: he was quickly hustled up the steps, through the crowd,
and propelled into a Citroën with a uniformed driver which had been
waiting at the corner of the Boulevard Delessert. He was made to sit in
the back with two policemen on either side of him. As soon as the car
started these two men began to take it in turn to punch him in the
face. 'Shelley,' they cried, '*Wir haben Shelley. Englischer Offizier. Terrorist.
Schweinehund. Scheisskerl.*'

This horrible little litany of imprecation continued until they
reached the Gestapo Headquarters in the rue des Saussaies, and so
did the cruel blows. Tommy's head felt twice its normal size and the
blood from his lacerated face was pouring down over his shirt and suit.
He says that he was surprised to find himself 'thinking in a completely
impersonal manner just as though it were another person being beaten
up, and it was a very extraordinary feeling'. It must have been. What

was even more extraordinary was that during this painful passage to prison he was able to wonder whether the attempt to rescue Bollaert and Brossolette would still be made and to think out what he was going to say when he was interrogated.

It was clear that the Dodkin story would no longer serve in its entirety: the fact that the Gestapo men had greeted him as Shelley seemed to indicate that Antonin had talked. (He learned later that the agent-de-liaison had been arrested while carrying in his pocket, contrary to all regulations, a piece of paper marked: SHELLEY PASSY 11.) It was obvious, therefore, that the Germans would know that the otherwise unimpeachable identity papers in the name of Gaonach which he was carrying were false. The Gestapo knew and had long known that Shelley was a British officer, but they did *not* know the name of the British officer. If they discovered his real identity and failed by normal methods to make him speak they would certainly arrest his father and torture the old man in his presence. Dodkin then he would have to be, and not a baled-out Dodkin: the absence of the identity discs stamped with this name and hidden beneath the floorboards of Suni Sandöe's flat would perhaps add to rather than detract from the credibility of the tale, as a British officer would be unlikely to carry such compromising property on his person while actually engaged in the field. All this he thought out while his face was being battered in the car.

When they reached their destination he was yanked violently out of the car and, with a pistol pointed at his back, was propelled into the lift. His abrupt arrival in an office on the third floor astonished the three men sitting there. '*Wir haben Shelley*,' the leading policeman shouted as Tommy was pushed into the room. At this the three men rose from their chairs and began to punch him and kick him, knocking him against desks and cupboards and walls. They stopped only when he had been beaten into semi-insensibility. Then they locked the door, stripped him naked and made him stand on a telephone directory. Enraged by the discovery of his tear-gas pen and the revolver in a special holster strapped to his thigh they started in on him again. '*Schweinehund, Scheisskerl*,' the thugs shouted as they slapped his face and kicked him in his bare groin with their heavy boots. They tore from his neck the small brown canvas sachet which the Countess

Grabbe had given him at the beginning of the war and laid it on a desk beside the other objects which they had removed from his pockets: among these were his identity papers, the keys of four of his apartments of which he had been intending to return three to the owners before he left for Rennes, and two monocles which he had worn to disguise himself. The discovery of the last particularly infuriated his tormentors, for they flung them on the floor and trampled on them. The spectacle was so ridiculous that Tommy laughed aloud in spite of his pain: thin earned him another beating up.

This new battering was scientifically administered to him as he stood heels together, arms handcuffed behind his back, naked on the telephone directory: as a blow made him sway sideways, a punch on the jaw, the nose or the ear or a kick in the stomach restored his equilibrium. 'I don't know how long I was kept in this position,' Yeo-Thomas says. 'To me it seemed hours, but in all probability it was only an hour and a half.' Although so dazed that the room was swimming before his eyes, he was still able to think fairly clearly. Two desires were in his mind: to avoid betraying his friends and to escape from his agony. He could do both if only he could get at the signet ring containing the poison tablet which the thugs had omitted to remove from his left hand. Sooner or later, he felt, they would be bound to unhandcuff him, and then he could slide open the top of the ring, swallow the tablet and put himself beyond treachery and pain.

He was still standing on the telephone directory when a tall, broad-shouldered man with cold steel-grey eyes and a cruel mouth entered the room. Tommy's tormentors stood sharply to attention, extended their arms in the Nazi salute and said '*Heil Hitler!*'

'*Heil Hitler!*' said the newcomer, returning the salute and stopping in front of Yeo-Thomas, who even on his perch was a head shorter. Looking down at the prisoner, the tall man spat in his face and gave him a crashing slap on the cheek which sent him careering against the wall. Unable to use his hands Tommy collapsed on the floor, where the tall man kicked him every time he tried to get up. Tommy let his body go limp to minimise the effect of the kicks. '*Schweinehund, salaud, terroriste,*' the brute cried in bilingual rage, as he bent down, pulled Yeo-Thomas to his feet and flung him into a chair.

Very deliberately the new thug drew up another chair and sat down in front of Tommy, staring at him with his expressionless icy eyes. Tommy describes the man's eyes as being like 'twin daggers, trying to pierce his brain'. Knowing that the man's purpose was to make him lower his own eyes Yeo-Thomas looked him full in the face. Once again the heavy fist crashed on to his lips and nose, drawing streams of blood. '*Tu as compris, ordure?*' the man asked in correct but guttural French. 'Now you know where you stand, you bloody swine.' Tommy did not answer.

At a word of command from the new thug two of the other men pounced on Yeo-Thomas and dragged him out of the chair: one stood in front of him with his arms on his shoulders and the other, going behind him, began to unfasten his handcuffs. The moment he had been waiting for seemed to have arrived. But just as his handcuffs were removed the big man noticed the ring. '*Dummkopf,*' he roared at the assistant, himself grabbed Tommy's hand, removed the ring and slipped it into his pocket. Yeo-Thomas was ordered to put on his clothes again. He dressed slowly and painfully, angry and frightened because he had been prevented from escaping from the very much more unpleasant attentions which he knew were in store for him.

As he dressed he made quick calculations: he had been arrested at five minutes past eleven; it must now be about three o'clock. Maud, with whom he had had an appointment at one o'clock, would now be aware that something was wrong. When he also failed to turn up at the Avenue Victor Hugo for his emergency rendezvous at six o'clock she would know for certain that he had been arrested. Within twelve hours all his letter-boxes would have been closed down, his meeting places changed and his contacts warned not to keep their appointments. In the meantime, to protect his network, he must, as was the rule for captured agents, hold out for at least forty-eight hours: to do this meant postponing unbearable pain by telling the Gestapo plausible lies and setting them hunting on a false scent.

As soon as he was dressed the big man made a sign to his companions and sat down behind a desk. Tommy was dragged from the chair into which he had deliberately slumped, propelled to the desk and dumped down again in the chair which had been brought up behind him. On the desk were laid out the objects which had been removed from his pockets and from his person: from them his gold fountain pen, his wrist-watch and banknotes of high denomination were already missing; but his pistol was still there, with the barrel pointing towards him and nearer to him than to his inquisitor. Intending to shoot the big man and then himself, he lifted his manacled hands and laid them on the edge of the desk. Nobody seemed to notice this gesture.

'*Vous avez joué et vous avez perdu*,' the big man began. 'You've had your flutter and you've lost. But nothing will happen to you if you're reasonable and listen to sense. But if you don't . . .'

Tommy did not answer; it was always a few seconds gained.

'Well, are you going to talk?'

Once again he did not answer.

'*Ordure*,' the big man shouted as one of his assistants slapped Yeo-Thomas across his puffed and bleeding face. 'Are you going to speak. Yes or no?'

Again Yeo-Thomas did not reply.

The big man sprang up and crashed his fist on to Tommy's mouth. '*Salaud, crapule, saboteur, espion, tu parleras!* I'll make you speak all right.' With the help of his two assistants he started hitting the prisoner again. They did not desist until, his mouth full of blood, his eyes so swollen that he could scarcely see, Yeo-Thomas crumpled up under their onslaught. The big man went back behind his desk and rang a bell.

Pretending not to have completely recovered consciousness, Tommy leaned forward in his chair and slowly slid his hand across the desk towards the pistol: but the big man saw the gesture, laughed, picked up the pistol and put it in a drawer.

'So you thought you'd use it, *cochon*?' was all that he said.

A young, fair, good-looking German with blue eyes and a pink complexion answered the bell. The big man, ordering him to go out and bring back a typewriter, called him 'Ernst', and the young man called the big man 'Rudi'. Tommy made a mental note of the names. When Ernest had fetched a typewriter he sat down at a corner of the desk, inserted a form, a carbon and a blank sheet into the machine and waited in silence.

'Name?' Rudi rapped at Yeo-Thomas.

'Shelley.' That at least it was no good denying.

'Fool. Your real name.'

'Kenneth Dodkin.' This answer seemed to be accepted, for Rudi went on to ask:

'Your serial number?'

'47,685.'

'Rank?'

'Squadron Leader.'

'Branch of the Service?'

'Royal Air Force.'

'Address?'

'I am not required to reply to that question.'

'You will reply all the same.'

'I shall not.' If he was to convince the Gestapo that he was indeed Kenneth Dodkin it seemed to him essential that he should not protest too much by giving them even false information on points about which they were not entitled to ask questions.

Rudi got up, walked round the desk, and using both his hands, began to slap Tommy's face from one side to the other, cutting the already bruised cheeks with his heavy signet ring. His ears crushed, dizzy with pain, Yeo-Thomas swayed in his chair: the two assistants propped him up so that Rudi could go on hitting him.

At last Rudi stopped and sat down behind the desk again.

'Listen,' he said, suddenly changing to a friendly tone. 'It's no good being obstinate. You've had your flutter and you've lost.' Tommy wondered to how many others Rudi had used this phrase which seemed to come so readily to his lips. 'We know all about you, but we'll treat you as an officer if only you'll be sensible. You're a prisoner; you've done your duty; nobody can say a thing against you. Now I'm going to ask you a few questions; all you've got to do is to answer and it'll be all finished with. I say, what about a cigarette?' He took a cigarette from a gold case, stuck it between Tommy's bruised lips, lit it with a gold lighter. 'That's better, isn't it?' he said as he watched Yeo-Thomas take a couple of puffs. 'You see, we're not such brutes after all. If you're reasonable you've got nothing to fear. And when you've answered we'll give you some food and something nice to drink.'

Tommy did not reply, nor did he make any sign; he went on puffing at his cigarette. Ernst sat expectantly at his typewriter.

'I may as well tell you that it's no use telling us any lies,' Rudi went on. 'Your agent-de-liaison has made a clean breast of everything. We know all you've been doing here since the beginning of the year. We know that you know all about the arms dumps. You've only got to tell us where they are and we'll leave you alone'.

Behind his sore face Yeo-Thomas almost smiled. Rudi had been too clever; if Rudi had been as well informed as he pretended to be he would have known that his prisoner had not been in France at the beginning of the year; and Antonin, who had been working for Tommy only for a week, could not have given him much information. Rudi was bluffing; to gain time Yeo-Thomas decided to bluff too.

'Then he's talked?' he asked.

'Naturally.'

Tommy pretended to be shocked and distressed.

'So you know about my appointments?'

'Of course. You see it's no use your making a martyr of yourself. You've had your flutter and you've lost.'

'Did he tell you I had an appointment for this afternoon?'

'We know everything, I tell you.'

'In that case it won't do much good my talking, will it?'

This unexpected piece of logic made Rudi's face harder again.

'This is no time for joking,' he said. 'We know that you have an appointment this afternoon. All I want to know is with whom and where.'

'What time is it now?' Tommy asked.

'Half-past four.'

'In that case it's too late because my appointment is for a quarter to five.'

'Where?'

'At the Porte Maillot.'

'Whereabouts exactly?'

'In front of the *ceinture* railway station.'

'With whom?'

'With a woman who's bringing me a message.'

Rudi picked up the telephone and ordered a car to stand by immediately. One of the guards was sent to fetch another two thugs in civilian clothes, to whom instructions were given by Rudi in

German too rapid for Yeo-Thomas to understand. '*Heil Hitler!*' said the thugs and ran from the room; removing Tommy's revolver from the drawer and pocketing it, Rudi prepared to follow them.

'What's this woman like?' Rudi asked.

Yeo-Thomas gave him a fantastic description of an imaginary woman who, he said, would be carrying a bouquet of flowers in one hand and a newspaper in the other.

'If you're lying you'll pay for it,' Rudi shouted as he rushed after the other two men.

Yeo-Thomas knew only too well that he would soon pay dearly for having sent Rudi on a wild-goose chase; but he had gained time, and so far he had not talked. Although his whole head was aching he tried to think out how when Rudi came back again he might gain still more time. His two guards watched him stolidly out of their square, unimaginative, unpitying faces. Ernst moved from his typewriter to Rudi's chair and began examining the property which had been removed from Tommy's person.

'Whose telephone number is this?' Ernst suddenly asked, peering closely at a banknote.

'What telephone number? I don't understand.'

'The telephone number you've written on this banknote.'

'I've written no telephone number on any banknote.'

'Liar!'

'I am not a liar.'

'Yes you are; look at this.' Ernst came over and showed him a ten-franc note on which a telephone number had been scrawled in pencil.

'I didn't write it,' Yeo-Thomas said. 'It must have been there when I got the note.'

This was true, but Ernst didn't believe him and showed his scepticism by punching him heavily in the face.

'Now will you tell me whose number this is?'

'I don't know, I tell you.'

'Well, we shall soon find out.' Picking up the telephone, Ernst gave an order, of which the only part Tommy understood was the repetition in German of the numbers on the ten-franc note. 'You'd have done much better to tell me straight away, *salaud*,' Ernst said, as he laid down the receiver.

Within a few minutes the telephone rang. Ernst listened eagerly. '*Danke,*' he said, asked for an internal number and gave elaborate instructions. 'I now know the name of your friend and his address; you'll be seeing him soon,' he told Tommy. 'The German police are very powerful, you know, and you're very foolish to try to pull the wool over our eyes.' After some insulting epithets he continued his examination of the objects on the desk. 'What's inside this?' he asked, holding up the little brown canvas sachet.

'I haven't the faintest idea.'

'Liar, *pourriture, Scheisskerl.*' With a string of filthy words Ernst unconsciously proved Talleyrand's contention that swearing is the means by which the inarticulate give themselves the impression of eloquence. 'It's no good your coming the innocent with us: we're not bloody fools.'

Taking out a penknife, Ernst slit open the sachet; inside was a small slip of paper, folded in two and covered with small Russian characters. It was the first time Yeo-Thomas had seen this document, which Ernst examined with a scowl.

'Ha, ha,' Ernst said. 'So you work for the Russians, do you? It's your code, isn't it, *Scheisskerl?*'

'I tell you I don't know what it is.'

'You're a liar.'

'I am not.'

'*Scheisskerl!*' Once again Ernst came round from behind the desk and began to beat up his victim. Tommy went limp; it was his only protection. Tiring at length of his sport, Ernst left off and went back to continue his examination of the objects on the desk.

Through the slits which were all he now had for eyes Tommy tried to examine his possessions too. There was only one, he thought, which was really dangerous: the bunch of keys, of which one belonged to the flat in the rue de la Tourelle, the address on his identity card. Of his use of this flat only two people knew: Brossolette, who was in prison, and Maud, who, when he failed to turn up for his six o'clock appointment, would give the place a wide berth. He must avoid answering any questions about the keys until after six o'clock, when, if the persistence of his tormentors became too painful, he would tell them which was the key of the flat in the rue de la Tourelle. The

Germans would then rush round to the flat, and, when they found nobody there, bait a trap which would immobilise a couple of their men for a few days. About the keys of the other flats he would have to lie continuously if their owners were not to get into serious trouble. He was still thinking all this out when Rudi burst into the room, livid with rage.

As Rudi had promised, Yeo-Thomas paid for having lied: battered again on his puffed and swollen face, he was knocked down on the floor, picked up and knocked down again. He ached all over; his head throbbed; all his teeth felt loose; his nose was squashed and his lips were split; his jacket and his shirt were soaked with blood. Eventually he was picked up for the last time and thrown back on to his chair; Rudi resumed his seat at the desk.

'You've made me lose my time, *salaud.*'

'I told you you'd be late,' Tommy said. 'She can't have waited. It's not my fault.'

'Liar.'

'It's not my fault if you won't believe me.'

Rudi glared at him; he glared ever more fiercely when Ernst had shown him the folded slip of paper.

'Russian? So you're a Communist as well?'

'It may be Russian; I don't know. But I am not a Communist.'

'You never know anything, do you, you dirty liar? But I'll show you. I'll have this paper examined by our experts. They'll decipher it all right and then you'll see how much you'll pay for your lying.' He telephoned, handed the slip of paper to a small, rat-faced man with gold-rimmed spectacles who came in answer to his summons, and then turned to Yeo-Thomas again. 'Where are the arms dumps you know of?'

'I know of none.'

'Are you going to talk: yes, or no?'

'I don't know anything, I tell you.'

'We'll see if you know nothing.' Rudi signed to the two guards, who grabbed Tommy's arms and jerked him to his feet. Taking from a drawer a long chain and an ox-gut whip with a flexible steel rod inside it, Rudi swished the latter threateningly in the air. Tommy was propelled out of the room, up steps and along a narrow passage lined on one side with small circular windows which looked like portholes; he guessed that he was being taken to a torture chamber.

He had a rough journey: every time he stumbled from weakness he was jerked up by the handcuffs, which bit deeply into his flesh. At the end of the passage a door opened and he was flung on to the tiled floor of a bathroom, through the open window of which blew in a freezing draught. He was dragged to his feet and two men pulled off his trousers and underpants; his hands were unmanacled while his jacket and shirt were torn off and then handcuffed again behind his back. While Rudi bent and twisted the chain tightly round his ankles Ernst opened the cold-water tap and filled the bath. At an order from Rudi one of the guards left the room and came back accompanied by a crowd of German girls in uniform, who crammed the doorway and laughed and mocked at Yeo-Thomas as he stood naked and shivering in the icy draught.

'Where are the arms dumps?' Rudi asked.

'I don't know.'

The ox-gut whip came slashing down on Tommy's chest, searing it and raising a weal; Yeo-Thomas gritted his teeth.

'So you're going to be pig-headed, are you?'

Aching in every joint, Tommy remained silent. He was forced to sit on the edge of the bath. Rudi bent down again, caught hold of the chain around his ankle and gave it a twist and a tug: drawn into the bath on to his feet, Yeo-Thomas stood in the freezing water, facing the grinning, jeering girls. One of the men scooped water up in the palm of his hand and splashed him with it.

'Where are the arms dumps?' Rudi asked again.

'I don't know.'

Rudi crashed his big fist into Tommy's jaw and, as he staggered, pushed him headlong into the bath, so that his face was under the water while his legs stuck up in the air. With his hands manacled behind his back Yeo-Thomas was helpless. Panicking, he tried to kick, but his legs were caught and held in a powerful grip. His eyes were open and he could see faces distorted by the water wavering above him. His mouth came open and he swallowed water. His lungs felt as though they were bursting. He made another attempt to kick himself out of the bath, but the vice-like grip still held him. He tried to lift himself up with his handcuffed arms and failed. Swallowing more water, he became limp; the strength went out of him and he began to lose consciousness; he was drowning and he knew it.

He came to feeling an agonizing pain in his chest. Water was gushing out of his mouth and there was a big wavering black shadow in front of his eyes. The shadow slowly dissolved into lighter filmy circles which shimmered like hot air on a summer's day. As the circles became faces Tommy realised that he was lying on the tiled floor of the bathroom and looking up into Rudi's sadistic eyes. The German girls were crowding round the door, chattering and laughing. Feeling half dead, weak and sick, he closed his eyes so as not to see them. He could breathe only in gasps and his heart, in his own phrase, 'was thumping like bellows in a forge'. He had been pulled out of the water just as he had been about to drown and given artificial respiration.

He was lifted to his feet.

'Where are the arms dumps?'

'. . . don't . . . know?'

Thrown brutally back into the bath, his head hit the edge. Once more the water engulfed him. Once more he tried in vain to kick and to push himself up with his handcuffed arms. Once more he swallowed water. Once more he felt himself drowning. His mouth opened and the water poured in. There were rushing noises in his ears.

As before he was hauled from the bath just as he was about to drown and was artificially revived. As his consciousness returned he saw the same shimmering visions which slowly took the form of Rudi, his assistants and the laughing girls. Again he was pulled to his feet, but this time he was so weak that he had to be held up. His ears were still buzzing when he heard a voice coming from far away:

'Where are the arms dumps?'

And he heard another voice, which he presumed to be his own, answering faintly:

'I . . . don't . . . know.'

He was thrown back into the bath several times. Kicking and swallowing water, oblivion succeeding consciousness and consciousness oblivion, he lost count of his torments and soon was unable to trace their sequence. As soon as he saw the distorted faces of Rudi and Ernst he lost sight of them again. The sound of the girls' laughter was absorbed by the pain in his lungs. He no longer had the strength or the desire to kick. He was brought round for the last time by a kick from a heavy boot and knew from the agony that he was still alive. He was lying on the bathroom floor, with walls, bath and faces swirling around his head. Abominably sick and with his stomach as large as a barrel, water came gushing out of his mouth on to his chest. He saw with surprise that the girls were no longer in the doorway. Numb with cold, he was dragged to his feet, on which he could no longer stand, as the chain had stopped the circulation. As he tottered he was struck heavily over the head with a rubber cosh and again collapsed.

When he had recovered from the sickening effects of this blow he was hustled, still naked and dripping with water, along passages and corridors lined with mocking laughing girls in uniform and female secretaries. Back in Rudi's office, the chain was removed from his feet and he was pushed into a chair while his underpants and trousers were slipped on. His handcuffs were loosened, but fastened again as soon as he had been thrust into his shirt and jacket. Once again Rudi sat at his desk facing him.

'Where are the arms dumps?'

'I don't know.'

'Haven't you had enough, *ordure?* Well, we'll see.'

At a sign from Rudi the two guards produced rubber coshes, with which they began to beat him. He was beaten on the head, arms, legs, body and testicles. He did not cry out. Still less did he speak.

'Where are the arms dumps?'

'I don't know.'

Each time that he said this the beating up started all over again. He saw flashes before his eyes; the furniture and Rudi's face began to float in circles. In the end he lost consciousness.

When he came to lying on the floor he pretended that he was still unconscious by keeping his eyes closed; this was not difficult because his eyelids were now so swollen that he could scarcely see out of them. He felt sore and bruised all over. He says to-day that he 'did not know that it was possible to have so many pains in so many places at the same time'.

It was then that the devil took him up into an high mountain and showed him the blessed cities of the plain in which men were not tortured: '*Haec omnia tibi dabo si cadens adoraveris me.*' His sufferings, he knew, would cease immediately if he talked. He rejected the temptation with surprisingly little effort. 'Do you really think, Master, that the Stoics or Epicureans were right in saying that a good man might be happy on the rack?' an undergraduate once asked Dr Jowett. 'Well, perhaps a very good man on a very bad rack,' the Master of Balliol answered. Yeo-Thomas would have been the last to describe himself as a very good man and even more certainly the last to deny that the rack upon which he was stretched was good; but he knew that he would have been even unhappier in the knowledge that he had betrayed his friends. 'They were wonderful, but sometimes it seemed as though they were wonderful by mistake,' Geoffrey Cotterell makes Tarrant think of certain RAF officers in *Strait and Narrow*; Yeo-Thomas was not wonderful by mistake.

When his tormentors saw that he had recovered consciousness he was picked up and dumped in his chair again. The handcuffs were cutting into his wrists and making them ache. He was beginning to feel hungry too, having had only a cup of coffee for breakfast and nothing since.

Rudi faced him with a malevolent grin, holding up the bunch of keys.

'What keys are these?'

'They are keys.' The question which he had feared had come. The keys had been found in his possession and he could not disown them. However, the lights in the room were already on and through the window he could see that it was dark outside: it must therefore be after six o'clock. Maud would know by now that he had been arrested and would take care not to go near the flat in the rue de la Tourelle. But in order to protect the owners of the flats to which the other three keys belonged he must not yield even harmless information easily.

'For what doors?'

'For no doors. The keys are cover. A man looks suspicious if he doesn't carry keys, so to be in the swim I had some made.'

'I warn you once again not to take me for a fool. I want to know what doors they open.'

'I tell you they open none.'

'Where did you sleep last night?'

'I don't remember.'

'In that case I shall force you to remember.'

Rudi rose from his seat and, with the key-ring hooked round one of his fingers, approached Yeo-Thomas; using the keys as a flail, he lashed his face with them until the blood began to flow.

'Now are you going to tell me, *salaud?*'

With his face pouring with blood, his eyes streaming and his nose feeling as though it were on fire, it was not difficult for Tommy to let his head fall on his chest as though he were in such agony he could not speak. He allowed Rudi to go on scourging his face with the keys for a little longer and then he deliberately flopped.

'There's only one that works,' he said at length. 'It's the big one.'

'Where does it work?'

'33 rue de la Tourelle, Porte de St Cloud.'

'Couldn't you have said so sooner, *ordure*' Making me waste my time like this. If you've been lying again you'll pay for it.'

After giving some instructions over the telephone Rudi took the keys and walked out of the room. Ernst was about to continue the interrogation when a man came in and whispered a few words in his ear.

'We've found your friend,' Ernst said to Yeo-Thomas.

'What friend?'

'Your telephone number friend.'

The door opened again and two burly Sicherheitsdienst men came in, dragging with them a limp and terrified wretch. The new prisoner was a weak-looking man with long hair. His face was swollen from the beating up which his guards had obviously already administered to him. When he caught sight of Tommy's battered, bleeding face he cringed and lowered his startled eyes. But on a sign from Ernst he was roughly pushed into a chair facing Yeo-Thomas and slapped by one of his guards until he looked at him.

Ernst glared at them both.

'A pleasant surprise for you both to meet like this, isn't it?' He turned to Yeo-Thomas. 'You see, it's no use your telling any more lies. You may as well talk now.'

'I've never seen this man before,' Tommy said. 'He's totally unknown to me.'

'You're a bloody liar. Don't think I didn't see you tremble when he was brought in.' Ernst threateningly addressed the new captive: 'Even if he's not going to talk I hope you'll be a little more intelligent. You've only got to be sensible and tell us all you know and we'll let you go. But I warn you that it won't be pleasant for you if you tell us any lies.'

The innocent man, caught up in a turmoil of which he had not the slightest understanding, cowered in his chair.

'But Monsieur, I swear to you that I don't know this gentleman,' he pleaded. 'I swear to you that I haven't had anything to do with the Resistance. I am a musician. I earn my living playing in a night club. I've a wife and two children. Why should I lie to you?'

'That's enough of the funny stuff, *crapule*. I'll make you talk all right. If you don't, my men here will put you through your paces. You've got exactly one minute to make up your mind.'

The miserable little man looked in bewilderment at his captors as he pleaded for mercy.

'Don't hurt me, please, Monsieur. I swear to you on the head of my wife that I don't know this gentleman.'

'So you're going on lying, are you?'

'I am not lying, Monsieur. I cannot say that I know this gentleman opposite me when I have never seen him before.'

The Sicherheitsdienst men got to work as soon as Ernst gave them the sign. One of them plunged his heavy fist into the little man's face, drawing blood from his nose and mouth and making his victim shriek. Then the other man joined in and together they beat up the unfortunate creature while he howled with pain and screamed protestations of innocence. Ernst looked on with a satisfied smirk on his cruel face.

The spectacle was too much for Tommy.

'Cowards!' he roared at them. 'I tell you the poor chap doesn't know me. You're hurting him for nothing. Can't you see he's in terrible pain? If a windy chap like him were guilty he'd tell you all he knew. Bloody fools and brutes.'

'You'll get another dose too for that,' Ernst shouted back.

The two guards beat Yeo-Thomas again with their coshes. When he fell off his chair they kicked him in the ribs with their boots. He fainted again.

When he came round he heard the musician whimpering. Before he could protest again he was picked up and dragged from the room and across the landing. A padlocked door on the same floor was opened and he was thrown into a cell about three feet wide, five feet long and ten feet high; on one side was an opening about a foot square with an iron bar across it. Jerked to his feet he was flung on to a chair, over the back of which his handcuffed hands were slipped. One of the guards gave him a parting blow on the jaw; then they both left, slamming and padlocking the door behind them. Not a ray of light came from the aperture which he had seen when the door had been open; he was in complete darkness.

For the first time since his arrest he was alone. He was all aches and pains. The clotted blood on his face was beginning to draw the skin. His head was buzzing and his nose felt as big as a pumpkin. His jaw hurt terribly and all his teeth were loose. His mouth was full of the salt taste of blood, his eyes burned and the handcuffs were cutting into his wrists. Worn out, he sagged on his chair and the handcuffs bit more deeply into his flesh. As he stiffened he heard a shriek of agony coming across the passage.

The shriek was followed by others more piercing: in the room opposite the Sicherheitsdienst men were beating up the little musician whose only crime had been to have given his telephone number to a friend who had inscribed it on a ten-franc note. The shrieks and groans grew louder and louder and soon were accompanied by even more terrible sounds: there was the thump of a human body being battered against walls; there was the crash of falling furniture; there were sickening thuds and flops. Yeo-Thomas began to roar blasphemies and dirty words at the top of his voice, hurling insults at the perpetrators of this brutal injustice. But the shrieks and groans of the victim were louder and drowned his fiery protests, and Tommy gave up. After half an hour the groans became weaker and weaker and finally there was an appalling silence.

Very tired, Tommy tried to sleep, but every time his head fell forward his handcuffs jabbed him back to agonizing wakefulness. He did not know the time, but guessed that it was already past midnight. His bladder, surcharged by the water he had swallowed in the bath, felt like bursting, but he could not get up nor could he use his hands. He began to shout; nobody came. Once he heard footsteps but they died away again. Once the padlock outside was rattled and somebody yelled: '*Englisches Schwein.*'

When at length he was taken back to the interrogation room Ernst was still sitting at the desk, and Rudi, who obviously considered that he had been sent on a second wild-goose chase, was standing menacingly beside him. In a corner a crumpled body lay huddled, shivering pathetically from time to time and emitting low, shuddering moans. It was clear that the torturers now realised they had been barking up the wrong tree; it was equally clear that they felt no remorse for having battered into insensibility and perhaps maimed for life an innocent man.

Rudi glared at Yeo-Thomas.

'You've made me lose my time again. You haven't been in that flat for months. Where did you sleep last night?'

'I don't know. I slept with a whore. I always do that: whores don't talk.'

'Liar! I'll get the truth out of you.'

At a sign from Rudi the two Sicherheitsdienst men went over and hoisted up the moaning, whimpering mass in the corner. Hanging limp and bleeding between the thugs' arms, his head wobbling from side to side, the miserable little man was dragged roughly out of the room. Yeo-Thomas never saw him again and does not know whether he was released or, in order to conceal the mistake which had been made, transported to Germany and liquidated in a concentration camp.

The pain in Tommy's bladder was now becoming unbearable.

'I need very badly to relieve my feelings,' he said.

'*Crapule!* Do it in your trousers like the dirty dog you are.'

A soldier came in and laid on the desk a tray on which were food and a bottle of wine. Rudi and Ernst, fortunately too tired to go on asking awkward questions about the other keys, sat down and began to eat and drink. They did not speak as they ate, although they kept glancing at their prisoner from time to time. Tommy sat watching them munch, forgetting his own hunger in his desire to urinate: his patriotism was now reduced to the pathetic loyalty of not wetting his trousers in the presence of the enemy. Every minute his bladder seemed to get larger and larger and his penis began to burn and ache. He pressed his legs together, knowing that he could not hold out much longer. At last Rudi and Ernst finished eating and ordered the guards to take him back to the tiny cell on the other side of the landing.

'Look here,' he said to the guards as they were about to lock him in, 'if you won't let me pee it'll all come flooding out under the door.'

The guards, after solemn consultation, led him to a lavatory and allowed him to pass water, cursing him for the time he took. Conducted back to the cell, he was thrust on to the chair as before, with his hands slipped over the back, and left in pitch blackness.

Congratulating himself on having won the very essential first victory of having given his contacts time to disperse themselves, Tommy tried to rest in order to gain strength for the trials which he knew still awaited him. Unable to sleep with his arms fastened behind the chair, he attempted to free them. But each movement he made was agony, and when he attempted to rise to his feet his legs and his shoulders were so stiff that all that happened was that the chair slid back until it reached the wall. Finally he fell forward, the chair tipped, his forehead struck the wall in front of him and his arms were free. With difficulty setting the chair upright again, he sat on it and, although more comfortable, found that he had less room than before, as his handcuffed arms now intervened between his body and the back of the chair. He then shuffled the chair into a corner of the cell and leaned his head against the wall. With pain racking him from head to foot and wanting desperately to blow his nose, he eventually dozed.

He was awakened by the noise of the bar outside being lifted and of the padlock being opened, and by a shout of *''Raus!'* Luckily the guards did not notice that he had freed his arms from the back of the chair. Yanked out of the cell, he was pushed back into the now familiar room where two new interrogators awaited him. Smaller than Rudi and Ernst, the new inquisitors were clean-shaven and bull-necked and had glistening, beady eyes. Both began firing questions at him at once, starting not where Rudi and Ernst had left off but, in the evident desire of trapping him in a contradiction, where they had begun. Tired and sleepy, it was fortunate that Yeo-Thomas knew his story by heart.

'Name?'

'Kenneth Dodkin.'

'Number?'

'47,865.'

'Rank?'

'Squadron Leader.'

'Branch of the Service?'

'Royal Air Force.'

'Address?'

'I am not required to reply to that question.'

'Where are the arms dumps?'

'I don't know.'

As previously, the interrogation was punctuated with punches, slaps and insults. He was knocked off his chair and kicked as he lay helpless on the floor. After about an hour he was taken back to the bathroom, undressed and the all-but-drowning process began again, this time without the horrible young women. He had now, however, elaborated a new technique: as soon as his head went under water he kicked vigorously and then, just as he felt himself about to lose consciousness, let himself go limp. As before, he swallowed a lot of water and under-went what he euphemistically terms discomfort, but the icy cold dispelled his torpor and he was brave enough to derive consolation from the thought that he was still gaining time. He was alternately half-drowned and artificially revived for about another hour until he deliberately collapsed and took his own time to recover. Dragged back to the interrogation room he was forced to sit and watch his tormentors eat their breakfast of hot coffee and croissants. Then he was beaten up again until he was almost insensible.

Nearly past caring what happened to him, he was left to recover from the blows. Day was beginning to break, and the screams of prisoners being tortured in other rooms showed that the Geheime Staatspolizei[1] had already opened shop. Tommy began to try to think up a means of escape.

But he was not left alone for long. Rudi and Ernst soon turned up again and started in as soon as they arrived:

'Where are the arms dumps?'

1 Gestapo.

'I don't know.'

Although the keys weren't mentioned again Rudi made his prisoner pay for having sent him on two useless errands and prevented him from exploiting his capture: his questions were accompanied by mighty beatings-up, and another visit was paid to the bathroom, where the half-drowning treatment was again vainly employed.

In the afternoon a new master and a new technique were tried. Put into a car and accompanied by two Sicherheitsdienst men, Yeo-Thomas was driven to No. 84 Avenue Foch, where an armed escort awaited him. He was led into a small office, where a small studious-looking man, whose spectacles increased his appearance of benignity, sat at a typewriter; beside him stood a giant of about six-foot-five, dressed in SS uniform with skull and crossbones on the collar. The giant, lifting Tommy almost with one hand, placed him on a chair in front of his new inquisitor, who for quite five minutes examined him with dispassionate, silent curiosity. Then, when he had filled his typewriter with foolscap and carbon, he leaned back in his swivel chair and joined his hands professorially on his chin.

'I am not like the others,' he said, speaking in the customary correct Gestapo French. 'I shall not hurt you. If you are sensible we shall be good friends. Come now, you will do yourself no good by obstinacy. You've had your flutter and you've lost. Now all you've got to do is to answer my questions.'

Yeo-Thomas did not answer; although the repetition of the flutter phrase amused him, he was very much on his guard.

'Your name?'
'Kenneth Dodkin.'
'Your number?'
'47,865.'
'Your rank?'
'Squadron Leader.'
'Your Branch of the Service?'
'Royal Air Force.'
'Your address?'
'I am not required to answer that question.'
'Where are the arms dumps?'
'I don't know.'

Unlike Rudi and Ernst and their second strings, the little man did not swear or threaten: he just typed down Tommy's answers.

'You know Cadillac?' ('Cadillac' was one of Bingen's code names.)

'Cadillac? I know nobody of that name. It's the trade name of an American car, isn't it?'

An ominous look came into the little man's eyes.

'It would be as well if you were to refrain from playing the fool. I happen to know that you know Cadillac.'

'You are making a mistake.'

The little man shook his head sorrowfully.

'My friend, you are going to force me to resort to methods I don't like very much.'

Yeo-Thomas did not answer; he found this detached manner of examination much more disturbing than Rudi's brutal onslaughts.

'Where is Cadillac?'

'I tell you I don't know Cadillac.'

'What a very great pity! You are forcing my hand, you know. Listen. We not only know who you are; we also know a great deal about you, much more than you imagine. So it's no use your telling us lies and making us lose our time. Although we're kind-hearted we don't like being treated like fools. All you've got to do is to answer our questions; we'll know when you are telling the truth.'

'I can't very well tell you that I know Cadillac when I don't know him.'

'And Pic? Do you know him?' (Pic was one of Pichard's code names.)

'Yes, I know Pic.' This time Tommy could not lie, knowing that Antonin, who had been Pichard's agent-de-liaison, had almost certainly admitted the connection between his normal master and himself.

'What does he look like?'

Almost as much to test his inquisitor's knowledge as to protect his friend, Yeo-Thomas gave a description of Pichard which was the contrary of reality: omitting to mention that Pichard had a mutilated hand, he made him short and plump instead of tall and thin and when asked the colour of the Air Operations Officer's hair, stated that he could not say because Pichard, who in fact was always bareheaded, never took off his hat. To his surprise his bluff succeeded.

'It's just as well you've told us the truth,' the little man said. 'You see, we arrested Pichard yesterday.'

Realizing that his interrogator had lied and did not know as much as he pretended, Tommy tried to stall for time by answering dilatorily the next very insidious questions and by feigning surprise at their nature. But suddenly the little man, employing the now famous Russian technique, asked him once again:

'Where is Cadillac?'

'I don't know Cadillac.'

'You're lying and I know it. You know Cadillac very well. What's more, you knew him in London. He's a Jew.'

'You know more than I do.'

'Dear me! I can see that my method doesn't suit you at all. Well, I have a friend who is not quite so gentle.' The little man picked up the telephone and spoke in German.

Presently a strongly-built bullet-headed man with small, piercing, pig-like eyes came in and, without a word, crashed his heavy fist into Tommy's face. The small inquisitor looked on with an expression of regret and commiseration.

Led out of the office by the giant, Yeo-Thomas was handed over to two Sicherheitsdienst men, who escorted him to a small room on the fourth floor, where they were immmediately joined by the bullet-headed man. The links on his handcuffs were attached to a hook on the end of a long double chain which hung from a pulley on the ceiling; the other end was pulled and, as his heels left the ground, the steel of the handcuffs was forced deeply into his wrists. Agony shot through his shoulders, a red film obscured his eyes and, unable to restrain himself, he groaned. As he fainted he heard the bullet-headed man laugh. In intermittent spells of consciousness he suffered pain worse than any he had so far endured. Not until it was dark did they loosen him, and at once he crumpled up on the floor.

When he came to he was in atrocious agony; the circulation in his arms had been stopped by his handcuffs, which had been tightened by the pull on them, and his shoulders had been dislocated. He felt that he had reached breaking point and was afraid that if they tortured him again he would speak and tell them all about the arms dumps and the Secret Army and the Maquis. He knew that his tormentors were fully aware of the extent of his knowledge and would recoil before no brutality in order to make him talk.

But there was to be no more torture for him that night: flat out after more than twenty-four hours' almost continuous interrogation and chastisement, he was half-carried to a small cell at the top of the building, from which he was almost at once removed to another room, in which sat the giant and a mean-looking NCO. Flopping on a settee, he asked desperately and was allowed to be taken to the water-closet, where, unbuttoned and watched by his guards, he was forced to sit with the door open and clean himself painfully with his manacled hands.

He had to spend the night chained by his arms and legs to the settee. Hungry and thirsty, he was refused food, but was eventually given a mug of water. The only time he managed to sleep was during the short period when his guards were snoring; otherwise as soon as he dozed off he was shaken awake by the mean-looking NCO, who roared at him: '*Nicht schlafen.*' He thought of Barbara and longed like a child for the comfort of her arms. He thought of Brossolette and wondered if he would still be rescued. (He did not know that Brossolette, whose identity had been discovered, was already dead: brought from Rennes to Paris for interrogation, Brossolette, who had previously discarded his poison tablet, had either been thrown out of a window by the Germans or had fallen from it while trying to escape, and, with his cranium fractured and his arms and legs broken, had died in the Hôpital de la Pitié).

When dawn came the giant went out and brought back bread and sausage and a steaming jug of hot coffee for himself and his companion. The sight and the smell of the warm food made Tommy feel hungry and cold and he asked hopefully for a drink: he was given another mug of water.

'*Ich bin kalt*,' he said, but the only answer he was vouchsafed was '*Englisches Schwein*' and he was left to freeze.

Nor was it only with cold that he was freezing; he was freezing also with fear. As the morning grew lighter he knew that the moment was fast approaching when he would again writhe under the torments of his captors. He was at the end of his tether; he felt that if they did anything too painful to him this time he was bound to break down and speak. He wished for death because it was only in death that he could be sure of not speaking. Terror tore through his bowels when his chains were undone and he was pulled to his feet. Behind his swollen lips this modern saint who did not admire sanctity prayed that the cup might pass from him. 'Ah, yes, for there are times when all pray,' his friend and hero Mr Churchill had said.

But his resolution returned as he thought of Barbara, of his friends who trusted in him, of Dismore, of Thackthwaite, of Johnson, of Whitehead, of Passy and of Brossolette. Brossolette would never have betrayed the cause and he would not be false to Brossolette. In another office on the fourth floor, with lacerated face, swollen eyelids, tousled hair, collarless and in crumpled clothes covered with coagulated blood, and with the giant seated behind him, he faced a new, sinister and menacing interrogator:

'Are you still going to be pig-headed? Or are you going to talk?'

'I have nothing to say.'

'I can see quite clearly that you are a liar. But we have methods of making even liars talk, methods you don't know yet.'

Yeo-Thomas made a quick calculation: already he had held out for almost forty-six hours; in another two hours he would have accomplished the statutory forty-eight, and then perhaps he could afford to let slip a few unimportant details. In the meantime he must still strive to gain time.

'You know Cadillac, I think. His real name is Bingen. He is a Jew.'

This unexpected knowledge relieved Tommy. In view of his rôle in the Resistance he could not deny knowing Bingen; if he had denied knowing him under his code name of Cadillac it had been in order to avoid being forced to admit that, while he was ignorant of his whereabouts, he could get into touch with him when he wanted.

'I didn't know he was called Cadillac,' he said.

The German seemed surprised.

'Do you mean to tell me that you didn't know that Cadillac and Bingen were one and the same person?'

'No. You see, everybody has several names and one can't be expected to know them all.'

'But you know where he is.'

'No.'

'Yes, you know quite well, and what's more you're going to tell us.'

'How can you expect me to tell you where he is when I don't know myself?'

But the new inquisitor seemed to know all the tricks of the trade.

'In that case you must have a permanent rendezvous with him. Where is that rendezvous?'

'I have no permanent rendezvous with him. In any case he must know by now that I have been arrested.' In spite of his pain, hunger and weariness he still had the energy to lie fluently: 'You see, I had an appointment with him yesterday. As I didn't turn up he will know what has happened. So even if I wanted to I couldn't find him.'

'Ha, ha! So you had an appointment with him yesterday? And you won't tell us, *Schweinehund?* That's another thing you've still got to pay for.' The interrogator suddenly abandoned his threats and spoke in honeyed tones. 'Listen. I am certain that you know where to find him. If you will tell us we'll be kind to you. Of that I give you my word as a German officer.'

'I can't tell you anything.'

'Come, come. Don't be obstinate. What would you say if I were to make a bargain with you? I think perhaps we could release you. We'll organise an escape. You see how simple it is? Nobody will ever know that you have talked.'

Battered, caked with blood, trembling in every limb, Yeo-Thomas looked the German full in the face out of his puffed eye-lids.

'I can't tell you where to find Bingen,' he said. 'And even if I could I wouldn't.'

His defiance made the inquisitor splutter with rage.

'You're the friend of a dirty Jew,' he shouted. 'I'm beginning to think that you must be a Jew yourself.'

'I am not a Jew and I don't know if Bingen is one, and in any case it's none of my business.'

The German came out with one of those seventeenth-hand boring but incendiary lies which contemporary demagogues serve up as political thought to literate barbarians:

'You English are not a pure race like we are. You're infected with Jewish blood and you'll lose the war because you're decadent. You're governed by Jews, you're owned by the Jews and you're the slaves of Jews.'

'Mr Churchill governs us and he is not a Jew.' Tommy held himself erect in his chair as he thought of the man who had been kind to him and who had helped him to help France.

'Our Führer is the superior of your Churchill, who is only the lackey of international Jewry.'

Realizing that he was gaining time by this absurd political argument, Tommy did his best to prolong it.

'Germany has lost the war,' he said. 'You couldn't invade Britain, but we shall invade France and you'll be beaten.'

The German rose to the bait; another stream of verbal reach-me-downs poured from him: the British Royal Family was tainted with Jewish blood; impoverished English peers had married the wealthy daughters of greasy Levantines and turned the House of Lords into a Sanhedrin; the House of Commons was a synagogue; Wall Street was a ghetto and Roosevelt a rabbi. It was to liberate the world from the slimy machinations of the yellow-livered yid that Hitler was fighting the war.

To this folly Yeo-Thomas made the mistake of answering with almost equal folly:

'And your Führer. He's not a German; he's only an Austrian house-painter gone wrong.'

The remark was stupid, not only because there was no reason why an Austrian house-painter should not have made a better politician than the suave incompetents brought up in the chancelleries, but also because it put an end to their comparatively polite conversation. The inquisitor again became persistent and threatening:

'Where are the arms dumps?'

Seated within three feet of a window, Tommy gathered all his strength for a desperate leap across an intervening table: provided that he got through the window quickly enough there was every chance, as the office was on the fourth floor, that he would kill himself or at least hurt himself so badly that he would not recover; and even if he didn't die the Germans would have to put him in hospital, where they might forget about him and leave him to be freed by the Allies when they arrived in about three months' time.

'Where are the arms dumps? You have suffered, I know, but I promise you that you shall suffer much more if you do not answer my question.'

He sprang and, taking his captors by surprise, jumped clean over the table. His head hit the glass pane and smashed it and his shoulders passed through. But the giant was too quick for him: seizing Tommy by the ankles, he pulled him back into the room and sat him back on his chair, to which he was now securely fastened by chains hurriedly brought by a soldier.

'So you are frightened, are you?' the interrogator said with a leer. 'Well, now's the time to speak. If you don't it'll be very unpleasant for you indeed. We'll use new methods and you'll suffer. Make up your mind and be quick about it because I can't afford to waste my time.'

Tommy did not answer: he knew that if he spoke it would be to beg for mercy. The faces of those whose lives depended upon his silence passed before his blurred vision in a long pleading procession. He could not keep what the militarists and muscular clergymen used to call a stiff upper lip because his upper lip was smashed, but he obstinately held to the only loyalty he knew: he said nothing and by doing so proved himself to be that rarity in a world of mean shifts and compromise: a man of integrity.

'Well, we shall see,' the interrogator said as he rose.

Accompanied by his inquisitor and an escort, Yeo-Thomas was driven back to the rue des Saussaies, where another glaring and cursing interrogator awaited him in a different room with a long table in it.

'Now you'll speak,' the thug roared at him. 'You're afraid. It's now or never.'

Desperately terrified, Tommy remained silent. He knew that he was protecting the unjust as well as the just and that brick-faced, martini-sozzling company directors sticking their snitches into black-market lobster would never appreciate his sacrifice. But there was Brossolette, with whom he had walked in the nearest thing he could find to the house of God as friends, and Brossolette would never have spoken. He would not speak either; and he didn't.

Five new thugs came in. Thrown on to the table, chains were fastened round his legs and attached to the desk in such a manner that his feet were spread out. Two men held down his arms; with rubber coshes the other three rained thudding blows on his face, legs and body, concentrating on his testicles. He screamed with agony. The thugs slammed away till he fainted.

When he came to he found himself lying on a couch with broken springs in an empty, bare room. Through the only window, barred and high up, he could see that it was already dark outside; it had been morning when they had started beating him up. He was sobbing and the tears were welling out through his inflated eyelids. His penis and his testicles felt as though they had been crushed. The excruciating pain in his lower abdomen made him want to vomit, but each time that he retched nothing came up and the strain sent deep stabbing pains slicing through his entrails. In spite of his nausea and agony he was hungry. His suffering soon sent him back into semi-conscious-ness, in which his sore body seemed to float away from him like a balloon.

He began to lose track of the sequence of events. He remembers being questioned, but recollects the questions only hazily:

'What is your name?'

'Kenneth Dodkin.'

'Your serial number?'

'47,685.'

'Where are the arms dumps?'

'I don't know.'

'Where have you been living for the past few weeks?'

'I have been sleeping with whores. With many whores in various places.'

This last was the dangerous question and he knew it, but his interrogators knew it too, and they came back to it again and again. One inquisitor, a fair, good-looking man of twenty-six or twenty-seven called Ernst[1] was, however, more subtle and less brutal than his colleagues:

'I know where you live. It's no use your trying to gain time.'

'If you know where I live why do you ask me?'

'Because we have several of your addresses and we want to arrest everybody whom we suspect of helping people like you.'

1 Not the same as the 'Ernst' mentioned previously.

'When you talk like that it's quite clear to me you don't know where I live.'

'I'll prove it to you that I do. All you've got to do is to show me on the map the district of Paris you live in.'

'That won't help you much.'

A map was brought and on it, with a temporarily freed hand, Yeo-Thomas drew a large circle taking in at least a quarter of Paris. To his surprise Ernst laughed.

'You think you're clever, don't you? But I'll show you that I'm even cleverer. You live at 11 rue Claude Chahu.'

'What makes you think that?'

'I don't think; I know. And, what's more, I know that you weren't the only person to use this address.'

Flabbergasted, Tommy did not reply.

'Had you firearms hidden in this house?'

'What on earth should I be wanting with firearms?' But it was of the identity discs stamped in the name of Kenneth Dodkin and hidden between the floorboards of Suni Sandöe's flat that Yeo-Thomas was thinking: if the Gestapo discovered these they might realise that such compromising possessions could have been brought by an agent to France only in order to conceal his true identity.

'What about that pistol you were carrying? That's a firearm, isn't it? Look here, if you tell me the names of the persons who sheltered you I promise you that no harm will come to them.'

Tommy did not answer.

'I give you my word of honour as a German officer.'

'I do not believe in the word of honour of a German officer.'

'You're wrong, and I'll show you. There's an English prisoner here who'll tell you that we keep our word.' A shortish man with a toothbrush moustache was brought in. 'This is the English officer. Ask him if German officers keep their word of honour.'

Yeo-Thomas turned to the newcomer.

'What is all this about?' he asked in English. 'Are you British?'

'Yes.'

'How do they treat you?'

'Not too badly.'

'Do they keep their word?'

'Yes,' the British officer replied with studied carelessness, giving Tommy a look which was almost a wink.

'So you see,' Ernst said when the British officer had been led out again. 'Now what about giving us that name? Not that it matters really. Our men are there already and they'll soon find out from the concierge.'

Tommy knew that whether the Gestapo men were or were not at 11 rue Claude Chahu they could soon force the concierge to tell them that a stranger called Gaonach had stayed from time to time in Suni Sandöe's flat on the ground floor. Whatever he did or did not say, Suni Sandöe was now blown. If she had already been arrested she would be beaten up until she admitted that she knew him and they would ultimately be confronted; there was, however, every chance that, warned by his failure to return for his suitcase in the evening of his planned departure for Rennes, she had gone into hiding. The only thing that he could now do to help her was to represent her as ignorant of the nature of his activities. This he did and Ernst said that he could now go back to the rue des Saussaies, from which, in his fuddled state, he did not recollect having been removed.

Rudi slapped him on the face when he got back and had him flung once more into the tiny cell opposite his office. Still handcuffed and sore, Tommy sat on the chair and waited until he was taken to be interrogated by a sallow-faced, dark-haired, black-jowled man with bad teeth, who asked him in a rough voice questions about sabotage. Yeo-Thomas sagged on his seat and ignored his questions. He was then conducted again to the bathroom, stripped and, as far as he can remember, half-drowned and artificially revived six times.

He did not know whether it was night or day when he was taken to his next interrogation, which was conducted on entirely different lines, by a man of about fifty and by a slim young man with hornrimmed glasses.

'They've been rather unkind to you, I see,' the young man said. 'It's unfortunate, but that's war for you. I expect you're rather hungry.'

Almost immediately a soldier carried in a tray on which was a jug of hot soup, a cup and a plate of sausage sandwiches.

'It's not much, but at four o'clock in the morning Maxim's is shut,' the young man said. He came round, undid Tommy's handcuffs and fastened his sore, stiff arms in front of his body, and with the handcuffs looser than before. 'I'm afraid I'll have to put them back again afterwards. And you mustn't say I've done this, because I'm not supposed to be humane.'

While the young man poured out the soup for him Yeo-Thomas saw his hands for the first time since he had been tortured on the chain: the handcuffs were rusty with blood, the flesh around his badly cut wrists was purple and his left arm was swollen up to the elbow. However, when he had eaten the sandwiches and drunk a cup of soup he was able to pour himself out a second cup. Then the older man stuck a cigarette in his mouth and lighted it for him. Warmed by the food, Tommy felt his strength returning. Knowing that this clemency was part of a technique, he waited warily for the first question.

He was shown a photograph of Clo, who had been Air Operations Officer for the Bordeaux area and whom he knew to be dead.

'Do you know who this is?'

'I think so.'

'I think that you know very well indeed who it is, but unfortunately he is dead.'

Tommy pretended to be surprised.

'I didn't know that; poor chap.'

Many more questions followed, but they were kindly and not too persistently put, and showed a vast superficial knowledge of Resistance plans and as vast an ignorance of the details. Yeo-Thomas was, therefore, able to appear co-operative by restricting the truth of his replies to what his interrogators already knew and by giving them false information about what they obviously didn't. He was shown a faulty chart of the BCRA apparently compiled from similar interrogations and purporting to give the names of all the component officers and their duties; pretending to be impressed by its accuracy, he increased the war establishment by giving the names of non-existent officers to whom he ascribed almost fantastic duties; this information was gravely inscribed on the chart and he was given two more cigarettes as a reward.

At noon he was collected by two guards from Rudi's section and on his way downstairs was horrified to meet Suni Sandöe, also under the escort of guards. Surprisingly he was allowed to say a few words to her and tried to convey to her that she must pretend to have been ignorant of his activities and deny having seen any arms in her flat. He learned later that, having neglected to go into hiding, she had been arrested in her flat in the rue Claude Chahu.

Later that day, which he was astonished to discover was only Friday, he was again interrogated by Rudi, who seemed very pleased with himself and was unexpectedly benign. When this interview ended at dusk he was made to enter a large room in which, seated on chairs evenly spaced but staggered so that no two were side by side, were assembled Commandant Palaud, second-in-command of the Paris area, Doyen, the younger brother of Commandant Manuel of the BCRA, Anne-Marie, Yvonne and Georges of Pichard's secretariat and circuit, Chaland, saboteur and executioner of traitors, and others. Palaud's face was puffed and swollen, his clothes were torn and his hands smeared with blood. Anne-Marie's hair was dripping with water and lay in wet strands down her pale face; and most of the others looked tired and worn. Yeo-Thomas now understood the reason for Rudi's good humour: the catch was certainly a good one.

Made to sit in the chair next to Palaud, but with his back towards him, Tommy turned to warn his old friend not to say that he knew him and was immediately slapped on the face by one of the three guards stationed behind the row of chairs. Determined to prevent the Gestapo from discovering contradictions between Palaud's story and his own, he began to hum the tune of *Madame la Marquise*. When he saw that the guards took no notice he hummed a little louder. Then he sang the words: '*Toot va très bien, Madame la Marquis-e*'. When he saw the guards were still paying no attention he substituted words of his own: '*Je ne connais pas Artilleur*. ('Artilleur' was Palaud's code name.) *Je ne l'ai jamais vu. Il m'est inconnu ainsi que Chaland. J'ai été pris mardi, et vous?*[1] Then he lapsed into humming again, and Palaud joined in, chanting in his turn information as to when he himself had been arrested and what he had and had not told his captors.

About two hours later, when it was dark, there were shouts of "*Raus! Los! Schnell!*". Accompanied by guards armed with sub-

---

1 'I don't know Artilleur. I've never seen him. I don't know Chaland either. I was caught on Tuesday. When were you caught?'

machine-guns, the prisoners were marched downstairs into a hallway, where Rudi and Ernst checked their names off on a list. 'Dodkin' seemed to be the first name on this list, for it was Tommy who was made to lead the way into the prison van waiting outside; inside the van he was propelled along a narrow passage lined with steel doors and locked into a dark cell with only a vent to give him air. Other doors slammed and they were off. As the van bumped off the pavement on to the causeway Tommy saw through the vent the toes of a pair of German jackboots, but it was with his mind rather than with his eyes that he was able to follow the beloved streets along which they bowled: the Avenue Marigny, the Champs Elysées, the Boulevard St Germain, the Boulevard Raspail were familiar decades in his rosary of the city, and they lingered in his thoughts even when the van was out in the country, lurching over the cobbles towards Fresnes.

CHAPTER XI

Fresnes

On their arrival in the courtyard of the famous prison they were greeted with the same brutal shouts of small men giving themselves the illusion of greatness: *"Raus! Schnell!"* Yeo-Thomas was helped to be quick: yanked from his cell, he was almost flung out among the others and found Chaland seated on the cobbles, so badly injured that he could not walk. It was a case of the halt having to help the halt, but, luckily, the halt were not also dumb: as they carried Chaland into the prison Tommy and Palaud told him that so far his name had not been mentioned in their interrogations, and Chaland informed them that theirs had not been mentioned in his and that the Germans had fortunately not discovered his identity as chief executioner of traitors. They agreed that they would try to keep together in prison and, if possible, occupy the same cell.

This, however, was not to be. After a preliminary roll call in the prison hall, the prisoners were marched down a subterranean passage, Tommy and Palaud again carrying Chaland. They were halted in a larger hall, around which gangways and galleries, lined with doors running right up to the roof, resounded with the heavy tread of sentries. Here a second roll call took place, to which Yeo-Thomas again answered in the name of Dodkin. At a shout of '*Troisième Division*', Palaud, who had spent the previous night in the prison, moved off down another subterranean passage: Chaland, unable to walk, could not follow, and Yeo-Thomas, who tagged on behind

Palaud hopefully, was fetched back with a blow from a rifle butt when his absence from the prisoners allocated to the *Deuxième Division* had been discovered.

Angry at having been kept waiting, an NCO in Wehrmacht uniform slapped him, spat several times in his face and kicked him all the way to a darkened cell, into which he sent him careering with a snarl and a parting kick; unable to mitigate his fall, with his hands manacled behind his back, Tommy's head hit a stone wall and he fell full length.

When he was able to stand on his unsteady legs he began, gingerly and in complete blackness, to explore his new dwelling-place: a few steps forward brought him to a wall, another few steps to the right to a corner, and another few steps again to the right to what felt like a flap table; skirting this table he came to a w.c. pan and finally bumped into an iron bed with a palliasse, upon which he sank exhausted.

He could, however, lie only on his right side, because of the position of his hands and the shooting pains in his left wrist. He dozed off, but almost immediately the screams of a prisoner being beaten up awoke him, and after that, as he had no blankets or overcoat, the cold kept him awake for the rest of the night.

In the dismal grey light of dawn he was able to make out the form and furniture of the cell: the sight of a tap over the w.c. pan and a mug on the flat table increased his thirst. But even with his back towards the table his handcuffed arms could not stretch far enough to reach the mug, and he had to give up without having tried the very much more difficult feat of simultaneously holding the mug under, and pressing the button on, the water tap. In misery he began to pace the cell: it was four paces wide and eight paces long.

Soon he heard a noise with which he was to become familiar: the sound of steel trucks on rails. The food trolleys were beginning their rounds. A little later a key grated in the lock and a man in rags, obviously a French prisoner employed as an orderly, stood holding out a steaming ladle.

'*Amène ta gamelle*. Bring your mug. And look slippy about it or the Fritz will start shouting.'

The Fritz started shouting almost before Yeo-Thomas had time to explain why he could not bring his mug.

'*Schnell, schnell, Schweinehund,*' he roared as he came rushing in from the corridor; but when he saw Tommy's plight he filled his mug for him and placed it on the edge of the table.

To drink the hot liquid, which turned out to be a very dubious ersatz coffee, Yeo-Thomas had to kneel on the floor and suck it up the side of the mug. More than once he had to use his head to prevent the mug capsizing and rolling off the table; the last few drops of coffee poured down his chin when the mug finally toppled over.

Another prisoner-orderly came and flung a dirty blanket on his bed and handed him two minute squares of toilet paper cut from a newspaper.

'You must clean up your own cell or Fritz will start creating,' he said.

'How do you expect me to clean up my cell when I can't even go to the water-closet?' Tommy was explaining to the orderly his very urgent need when the NCO who had bullied him the previous evening came in and slogged the orderly on the jaw. When Yeo-Thomas tried to illustrate his requirements by turning his back and waggling his hands he was cursed and given a kick which sent him sprawling to the floor, where he was given another kick for calling the NCO a coward.

Shortly after this visit he heard knocks on the other side of the wall and, although he guessed that a neighbour was trying to communicate with him, he was unable to reply because of the fetters on his hands. Then, from somewhere in the prison, a voice shouted gaily: '*Patrice vous dit bonjour à tous: courage et confiance!*'[1] Almost immediately another voice cried: '*Laurence dit bonjour à Patrice et à tous ses amis: on les aura!*'[2] More shouts followed. Antoine greeted Lecocq and Lecocq hailed Lucien. There was a storm of abuse from the German guards, who rushed about trying to quell the noise, but as they ran to where the shouting seemed to come from the cries broke out somewhere else. Encouraged by this demonstration, Yeo-Thomas went to the door of his cell and contributed to the rebellion by bawling at the top of his voice: 'JE VEUX ALLER AU CABINET! JE VEUX AU CABINET! JE VEUX ALLER AU CABINET!'[3]

---

1 'Patrice wishes everybody good morning. Don't lose heart.'
2 'Laurence wishes all her friends good morning. We'll get them yet.'
3 'I want to go to the closet! I want to go to the closet! I want to go to the closet!'

A German soldier came bursting in almost at once.

'*Ruhe, Schwein!*' he ordered.

Once again Tommy explained his need, but the soldier did not possess enough French to understand either the euphemisms of the Boulevard St Germain or the exactitude of Ménilmontant, and Tommy was obliged to give a pantomimic display on the pan of w.c.

'*Ach, scheissen?*'

'*Oui, mon vieux.*'

'*Ich werde den Unteroffizier holen.*'[1]

But the Unteroffizier when he came could not do much about it because he hadn't the keys to the handcuffs, for which he said he would have to telephone to the Tribunal.

'And,' he said, 'when a German soldier comes into your cell you must stand to attention.'

Tommy looked the man full in the face, noticing that he wore the Iron Cross and two campaign medals and that he had a kindly expression; but his reply to him was the same as it would have been to the NCO who had kicked him:

'A British officer stands to attention only in the presence of his superiors.'

The Unteroffizier, as he had half-expected, grinned.

'In that case stand well to the rear of the cell or you'll have trouble with my colleagues,' he said as he unbuttoned him and then handed him, in return for a pledge of secrecy, a sheaf of toilet paper of more than the exiguous regulation size.

Late that evening the professorial-looking interrogator from the Avenue Foch arrived and, fawned upon by the bullying NCO, removed Tommy's handcuffs and slipped them in his pocket.

'I'm afraid we'll have to put them on again when you go for interrogation,' he said. 'In the meantime that wrist of yours doesn't look very pretty and we'd better put some disinfectant on it.' He gave a sharp command to the orderly, of which Yeo-Thomas understood only the word '*Sanitäter*'.

The Sanitäter, a drunken little runt with a wild alcoholic gleam in his squinting eyes, turned out to be anything but sanitary. Spraying

1 'I'll fetch the Unteroffizier.'

spittle on a foul-smelling breath into his patient's face, he poured ether
on a piece of dirty cotton-wool with which he removed the pus from
the deep, long, wide cut on Tommy's wrist. 'It's a waste of time
treating swine that are going to die anyway,' he snarled. He then held a
bottle of iodine upside down over the wound and leered in expectation
of the protest which did not come. Smearing a black ointment on
another piece of dirty cotton-wool with even filthier hands, he bound
it with a crêpe paper bandage round the wrist and, after swallowing the
remains of the ether in the first bottle, staggered out of the cell with a
parting '*Schweinehund!*'

Yeo-Thomas slept better that night because his arms were now free
and he had a blanket. In the morning there was more knocking on the
wall of his cell, but as it was not Morse he could not interpret it.
Anxious to make contact with his fellow-prisoners and at the same
time to avoid communicating with black marketeers, delinquent collaborator and stool pigeons, he began to whistle loudly the tune of a
French Protestant hymn which he thought only the right sort of
wrongdoer would know: '*Jusqu'à la mort nous te serons fidèles.*'[1]

Almost immediately a voice shouted:

'*Je demande à savoir qui vient de siffler.*'[2]

'A newcomer,' Tommy shouted back. 'A British officer.'

'You're a Protestant, aren't you? What chapel do you belong to?'

'The Protestant chapel at Dieppe.'

'Careful. Here comes the Barker.'

The Barker was the bullying NCO, and he came roaring along the
passage, trying to find out who had been whistling. When he had gone
away Tommy's new friend began again:

'*Ecoute, Dieppois.* I'm going to call you Tartarin. My name is Lecocq.
When did you come here?'

'The day before yesterday.'

'You're the man with his hands handcuffed behind his back?'

'Yes.'

'Then you're in the cell next to me.'

He heard knocking on the side of the wall behind the lavatory pan,

1 'Well be true to Thee till death.'
2 'I want to know who's just been whistling.'

to which he tapped back. On further instructions he unscrewed the press button of his tap and listened: he heard a scraping noise and then the voice of Lecocq:

'You can communicate with me and the boys above this way, but you must be careful not to be caught. The guards are on the job the whole time and the Barker comes sneaking up to doors in carpet slippers. So you say you're a British officer?'

This was fun; this was glorious: he no longer felt lonely and abandoned; already he could see himself organizing a revolt among the prisoners.

'I'm a British officer serving on General de Gaulle's staff,' he said into the tap.

'I'm on de Gaulle's staff, too.'

'What circuit?'

'Pic's circuit.'

This sounded too good to be true and, fearful that Lecocq might turn out to be a stool pigeon, he asked for proof of his membership; but Lecocq showed that he knew that Pichard had a mutilated hand and was fully conversant with the history of the circuit.

'How long have you been here, men?' he asked.

'Three months, and it's not funny, especially when they take you for questioning.'

'How often does that happen?'

'Fairly often at the beginning, and after that it all depends.'

Tommy thought that he could guess upon what it all depended. But there was something even more important than finding out how much more he was likely to be beaten up, and that was to let his friends in Paris and London, and above all Barbara, know that he was still alive.

'Can you get a message through to the outside for me?' he asked.

'I think so.'

'Say that Shelley's well.'

'I rather think I know that name. Listen, Shelley: speak to me in the morning after breakfast and in the evening one hour after supper. Careful. Here comes the Barker.'

Convinced that the Barker had guessed from the remark about the handcuffs who had been shouting. Tommy was afraid when the NCO came swaggering into his cell. But the bully had come only to transfer

him to another floor, and apparently not because of the shouting but
because he was more amiable than usual. Korrel, however, the six-
foot-four guard to whom he was handed over and who marched him
up two flights of steel stairs and along a gangway to cell number 293,
was, to begin with, anything but benign; pushing Yeo-Thomas roughly
into his new abode he roared:

'Stand to attention. *Schweinehund!*'

'To hell with you; I am an officer.'

'Stand to attention, I tell you!'

'I am a British officer and I refuse.'

Korrel took Tommy in his powerful arms and shook him.

'Stand to attention!' he bawled.

'I tell you I'm a British officer.'

The NCO's rage vanished as inexplicably as it had begun; he was
suddenly simultaneously ingratiating and suspicious, in the manner of
Continental doorkeepers anxious to be promoted from the house of
the Lord into the tents of ungodliness.

'So you're a British officer, are you? You speak French well for a
British officer.'

'So do you,' said Tommy, not wanting to make an enemy of the
man now that his principles no longer seemed to be involved.

His flattery succeeded, and the man became friendly. Korrel told
him that he came from Mainz and had learned French when he had
been a prisoner during the 1914-1918 war.

'But the French were beasts to us,' he said. 'I'd much rather have
been taken by the British.'

'The French couldn't very well have been worse to you than the
Gestapo have been to me.'

'Those fellows aren't soldiers,' Korrel said.

'That's quite obvious. Soldiers like you and me would never behave
like that.'

Korrel was delighted at the compliment.

'It's easy to see you're an officer,' he said as he went out. 'Well, I'll be
seeing you.'

Glad that he had apparently established amicable relations with yet
another gaoler, Yeo-Thomas set about examining his new abode. The
cell was lighter and cleaner than the one he had just left, the palliasse

was thicker and the blanket not so dirty. One of the lower panes in the window had very little putty round it and, when he had scraped the putty with his fingernails, he was able to remove and replace the pane at will: with the pane out perhaps he would be able to shout a message to Lecocq, from whom he had been so abruptly and regrettably separated.

He paced the cell, thinking of Barbara and wondering if she were thinking of him. He had nobody to talk to, nothing to do, nothing to read; the solitude which lay in front of him was likely to end only in death, when they took him away, tied him to a post and shot him as a spy. So as not to think about these gloomy things be counted his steps as he paced the cell: four steps one way and eight the other. This small world could be conquered only by escaping from it.

Removing the pane of glass, he made a preliminary reconnaissance. Opposite was the massive Third Division building with rows of heavily barred windows and crowned by a gangway running round the roof. Below, a low construction connected the Third Division with the Second Division in which he still was, two floors above and about twenty-five windows to the left of his previous cell. On either side of this connecting passage was a series of pens enclosed by twelve-foot walls which stopped abort before they reached the roof propped over them like a canopy. Along the walls there was a gallery from which guards were watching the pens, in some of which prisoners were beating blankets. More guards were walking on the gangways and on the wide alley of meagre grass between the pens. Birds flying across the sky symbolised in beauty the liberty so hard to attain.

Replacing the glass, he sat down on the bed and tried to think. People had escaped from prison before, and what others had done he could do. As both Lecocq and the professorial-looking interrogator had hinted, he was almost certain to be taken back to Paris for questioning. He must study the habits of the guards on such occasions: perhaps during transfer or while arriving at or leaving the Avenue Foch or the rue des Saussaies what seemed out of the question here in Fresnes would not be impossible.

But to escape he must keep fit. He must do physical exercises every day. Whatever the temptation he must not get slack, lazy or careless. And somehow, without soap, tooth-paste, towel or change of linen he must keep clean. He began to inspect his body and his clothes with the same thoroughness as he had examined the layout of the prison, and the result was almost as discouraging: when, with difficulty because of the pain in his left arm, he had removed his gory jacket and trousers he found his shirt and underclothes too rusted with blood for him to wash them without soap in the w.c. pan; and his body was covered with cuts and bruises, and his testicles were swollen and discoloured. He dressed gloomily and, to cheer himself up, removed the pane of glass and looked out again at the sweet blue promise of the sky. The pens were now empty and there were no guards in sight.

He heard footsteps approaching and had just time to slip the glass into his pocket before the swivel cover on the outside of the door was lifted. Standing in front of the window and trying to look uncon-cerned, he saw an eye watching through the spy-hole; but even when the cover was lowered again he did not replace the pane of glass and allowed a little of the freedom of the outside world to go on pouring into his cell.

Suddenly, to his joy, he heard a voice shouting in English from the building opposite and another, more muffled, replying. He waited until the conversation had finished and then he bawled with all his might through the hole in the window:

'Who is that speaking English?'

'RAF Warrant Officer. Who are you?' the first voice asked at once.

'An RAF officer.'

'Where were you shot down?'

'I wasn't shot down; I came down on purpose.'

'What the hell do you mean?'

'I came down with an umbrella.'

'Cave.' There was a pause. 'Hello, RAF. What is your name? Over to you.'

'Call me Tommy. What is your name? Over to you.'

'Jim. Just where are you? Over to you.'

'Opposite you, I think. Second floor. There's a broken pane. Look for a bandaged arm.'

'Target sighted. Are you alone?'

'Yes. And you?'

'There's a Yank with me and there's an Aussie. I'll call you again later. Cheerio.'

Heartened by this exchange of messages and the ordinarily meaningless valediction, Yeo-Thomas began to pace his cell again, counting the boards on the floor instead of his steps. Between two planks he noticed a nail, which he picked up and pocketed as a weapon for his armoury. Then he read the inscriptions pencilled and scratched on the walls of the cell. Apart from crude pictorial manifestations of concupiscence and threats of death to Jews, fascists, clergymen and cabinet ministers, the pre-war tenants of the cell had not been communicative: Julot de la Bastille had merely noted that he had still forty days to do ('*Quarante au jus*'), and Totor de la Villette had restrained the expression of his antipathies to a run-of-the-bistro 'MORT AUX VACHES'.[1] Recent occupants had been more dignified in their legacies, and some of them had even chiselled out prayers on the plaster: surmounted by a cross between two tricolor flags was this particularly moving message inscribed by a man whose name Tommy has unfortunately forgotten:

'. . . CONDAMNE A MORT PAR LES BOCHES ET DEVANT ETRE FUSILLE DANS LES 24 HEURES, DIT COURAGE ET CONFIANCE A CEUX QUI LE SUIVRONT DANS CETTE CELLULE. NOUS VAINCRONS. VIVE LA FRANCE!'[2]

Humbly Yeo-Thomas scratched in a corner with the point of his newly-found nail his own contribution to this fresco of arrogance, lechery, pride and petition: a calendar on which the first date was 21 March, 1944.

Before he went to bed that night he had to reply to quite a number of greetings:

'*Lecocq demande des nouvelles de Tartarin.*'

'*Tartarin va bien, merci.*' This message was relayed by somebody opposite.

---

1 'Death to the swine.'

2 '. . . sentenced to death by the Boches and due to be shot within 24 hours bids those who follow him to be brave. We shall conquer. Long live France!'

'Tommy, Jim calling. Good night from Texas and me.'

'Good night, Jim and Texas. Good night, Aussie.'

'Good night, Tommy.'

'*Ruhe.*'

He had barely replaced the pane of glass when he heard the cover of the spy-hole move. Pretending to be absorbed, he did not look up. The cover dropped. He still did not move. The cover opened again, dropped again. When he had made the pane secure with a substitute putty obtained from his lunch slice of bread he tucked himself up in his blanket and went to sleep with the shadow of a shade of happiness in his slightly less lonely heart.

Next morning a knock at his door and a shout of '*Tribunal*' warned him to prepare for interrogation. He was marched by Korrel down into the main hall, where other prisoners were already waiting under the surveillance of a dozen guards armed with submachine-guns. The Barker called the roll, and as Tommy answered his name he was handcuffed. With the others he marched down the subterranean passage and was locked up alone in a compartment of the prison van.

The second Ernst, in uniform but without badges of rank, was waiting for him at the Avenue Foch. He was bland, genial and insidious. Remarking on the bandage on Tommy's swollen wrist, he undid the left cuff and fastened it to the chair. He then gave him a cigarette and lighted it for him.

'You've been telling us quite a few lies, Shelley, haven't you?' he began. 'There's not much use your denying it. After all, it's your duty to tell us lies, isn't it? But now I think that you can talk without feeling guilty. You see, we know everything now.'

'In that case why bother to ask me questions?'

'Routine, that's all.' The falsely smiling eyes never left Tommy's face. 'We want to know what arms dumps you visited in January.'

'I visited no arms dumps in January; in January I wasn't in France.'

'It's no use your lying, Shelley: we have proof.'

'That's quite impossible. Well, show me your proof.'

'You're surely not going to deny that you know Horace?' (Horace was the young man whom Yeo-Thomas had engaged as agent-de-liaison on the recommendation of José Dupuis and a priest and whom he had dismissed for unpunctuality and falsehood.)

'Of course I know Horace.' His suspicion that Horace, while working for him, had simultaneously been in the pay of the Gestapo seemed now to be confirmed. 'Do you mean to say that he told you that nonsense?'

'It's not nonsense. Horace is one of our best agents.'

'Horace is a traitor and a thief and a liar.'

'Then why did you keep him in your employ?'

'I didn't keep him in my employ after I had found out what he was. I ought to have killed him last year and I'd kill him now if I could get my hands on him.'

'I forbid you to insult him. He's a good Frenchman who serves his own country and Germany. It's through him I know what you've been doing this year and that you've been visiting arms dumps all over France. You saw Horace as well and you told him everything.'

'That's not true.'

'Be careful now. I can confront you with him and prove it.'

'Confront away. That's just what I should like you to do. And what's more I'll make a bet with you: I'll prove to you that Horace is a traitor, a thief and a liar. And I'll show you that he's unpunctual as well.' The vehemence of Tommy's anger ought to have convinced Ernst of his sincerity.

'I warn you. You'll be exposing yourself to terrible consequences.'

'I am not afraid of them. Do you hear me? I demand to be confronted with Horace.'

'Then your blood be on your own head. I shall arrange a confrontation for some morning next week at ten o'clock.'

'He'll be late and if he knows whom he's going to meet he won't turn up.'

'He will not know whom he is going to meet.'

'I bet you he'll still be late.'

Ernst passed to other questions, to which Yeo-Thomas replied within the limits of what he believed to be his interrogator's knowledge. Rudi, however, by whom he was questioned later the same day in the rue des Saussaies, came back at once to the starting point:

'Where are the arms dumps?'

'I don't know.'

And, as before, he beat up his victim, although, with unaccountable clemency, he did not throw him in the bath.

Next morning when he awoke Tommy was bitterly cold; stone walls might not a prison make, but they certainly kept out warmth. His arm too was hurting him badly. Depressed, he lay listening to the measured tread of the guards, telling time like a clock. Soon there was the quick patter of feet running from one cell to another and cries of 'Tribunal', 'Tribunal'. But to-day there was no warning for him, which he felt was just as well, because Rudi's bludgeoning of yesterday had made him feel frightened again. 'Am I letting down the Service of which I have the great honour to be a member?' he asked himself; the doubt was as pathetic as Jean-Marie Vianney's fear that God would send him to hell for having been a bad priest.

But the question strengthened his resolution: he would not give in. Warmed by the bitter coffee, he walked up and down his cell until the orderly came to present him with his meagre daily ration of toilet paper; one of the two small squares had been cut from the *Pariser Zeitung* of 22 March and provided him with the mental exercise of trying to reconstitute the ampulated sentences. When he had success-fully failed to divine them he set about cleaning his cell with a rusty and perforated dustpan and an almost hairless brush, but, because ersatz coffee, mangel-wurzel soup and magma bread were as unpro-ductive of crumbs as the mutilated newspaper article was barren of subject and predicate, his task was soon finished. For exercise he polished the wooden floor with the handle of the brush, deciding to shine two laths a day. Then he did physical exercises, limiting himself because of his sore arms to flexing his legs and trying to ignore the throbbing in his testicles.

But the relief he obtained from these occupations did not last for long. Hearing the key turn in the lock he retreated to the window, where he stood legs apart, determined not to come to attention for anybody. His visitor was a burly Wehrmacht Feldwebel with pig-like eyes, a long upper lip and a short nose: striding across the cell in heavy jackboots he stood in front of Tommy and glared at him. 'Pritish officer?' the Feldwebel said. 'Vee will kill you slowly.' He then smashed one of his fists on Tommy's nose and mouth, crashed the other on his chin, kicked him in the groin and laughed bestially. Dazed and bleeding Yeo-Thomas staggered against the wall. 'Thank you,' he said, but the irony was lost on the NCO, who laughed again as he went out.

He was back in the depths of despair again when a gay voice came from the building opposite:

'Good morning to Tommy from Texas and Jim. How are you?'

He rushed to the window and removed the pane.

'Good morning, Jim. I have just been beaten up by a bastard.' The complaint was made almost joyfully now that he was again talking to a friend. 'Jim, can you get a message back to Blighty for me?' The very sound of the old 1914 – 1918 name made the cliffs of Dover seem nearer, and near they had to seem if he wasn't going to lose heart at the thought that he might be taken out any moment and shot.

'Not from here. But when I get to a POW camp I'll be able to write.'

'All you've got to do is to send a postcard and say that you've seen Tommy and that he's well. I'll give you the name and address.'

Making sure that no guard was approaching and under the cover of the other messages that were then being shouted across the yard he spelled out in Able Baker Charlie Dog his own true name and number and Barbara's sweet name and address. His message was simple and telegraphic: 'I AM QUITE WELL KEEP CHIN UP I LOVE YOU TOMMY.' This short salute eventually reached 5 Queen Court, Guilford Street, London, and after the war Yeo-Thomas met Warrant-Officer Jim Gillman in England and thanked him for sending it.

Korrel was so delighted when he came in and found the cell looking clean and tidy that, after showing Tommy photographs of his wife and children and giving him a cigarette, he went out and brought back a cake of grey gritty soap and a tooth-brush with dubious bristles. Undressing, Tommy washed first his body and then his blood-soaked underclothes, using the wc flush as a basin; the operation wasn't very successful and his vest and pants still looked dirty when he laid them out on the table to dry.

About five o'clock the evening messages began:

'Good night to Tommy from Jim and Texas.'

'Good night to Tommy from Aussie.'

'*Lecocq demande des nouvelles de Tartarin.*'

But tonight there was also a new one:

'*Brigitte demande des nouvelles du grand poète.*'

Brigitte was Clouet des Pesruches' agent-de-liaison, to whom Tommy had been about to pass instructions through Antonin when he was arrested. Suspecting that the desire for news of the great poet might come from the Gestapo, he replied with a reference to a small Pluto which Brigitte had recently given him.

'*Pour Brigitte: j'ai perdu mon chien.*'

But the reply came without hesitation and so was obviously authentic:

'*Brigitte regrette beaucoup que le grand poète ait perdu son chien mais elle est heureuse d'avoir des nouvelles. Elle tâchera de les transmettre au dehors.*'[1]

It was thus that he gathered that Brigitte, like himself, had been arrested when she went to keep her rendezvous with Antonin on 21 March. This realisation depressed him in spite of her hint that she was still able to communicate with their friends outside.

After his third day his life in prison began to settle down into a routine. In the morning there was coffee. When he had finished doing his physical exercises and cleaning his cell the Feldwebel with the long upper lip came in to say 'Pritish officer, vee will kill you slowly,' punch him, kick him in the groin and laugh when he said 'Thank you'. Then there was the daily attempt to decipher the bowdlerised and fragmentary news on the toilet paper. For lunch there was mangel-wurzel soup with a slice of magma bread and for supper there was neither soup nor bread. And at all times there were messages from his good and loyal friends and families, Jim, Texas, Aussie, Lecocq and Brigitte.

This routine was, however, broken by frequent visits for interrogation to the Avenue Foch and the rue des Saussaies. Much as he disliked being beaten up by Rudi and his associates Tommy welcomed these journeys because they afforded him an opportunity of studying the route taken by the prison van and the habits of the guards. After four trips he had prepared his plan of escape.

The prison van was always followed at a distance of about ten yards by an open car in which were four Gestapo men armed with sub-machine-guns. In the van itself were two guards with Sten guns, of

[1] 'Brigitte is very sorry that the great poet has lost his dog, but is pleased to have news of him. She'll try to pass it on to those outside.'

whom one sat beside the driver and the other stood inside the rear door of the van watching the central passage. This central passage was always crowded with black marketeers and lesser delinquents for whom there was no room in the cubicles, reserved for terrorists and those under sentence of death. From conversations with those strap-hanging prisoners through the air vents in his cubicle Yeo-Thomas learned that when, as frequently happened, the guards were Italian, the guard at the door of the van, with the incorrigible laxity of the Latin, sat down on a small folding seat and propped his Sten gun against the opposite corner. By leaning heavily with his shoulder against the door when he was shut into his cubicle at the rue des Saussaies, Tommy thought that he could prevent the top lock from closing; with the aid of a friendly prisoner from outside he hoped to be able to open the lower catch, which was the common model found on railway carriage doors. Then, when at the end of Boulevard Raspail the van turned into the Avenue d'Orléans, he would leave his cell and, under cover of the prisoners standing in the passage, approach the back of the van and grab the Sten gun while the others overpowered the guard. Through the grille in the rear door he would fire the contents of the Sten gun into the windscreen of the following car: the men in it would either be killed or wounded or the vehicle itself would run off the road and pile up. Then, followed by the other prisoners, he would hop out of the car and, concealing his fettered hands under a scarf already obtained from an obliging woman prisoner, vanish in the confusion, making his way to the nearby rue d'Alésia; there, in an artist's studio, he had hidden away a set of false papers, money, a change of underclothes and a pistol. He could arrange later for a friend to come and remove his handcuffs.

He put this plan into execution one evening at the beginning of April when the prison van was late in leaving the rue des Saussaies and it was already dark. When the guard, who was an Italian, shoved him into his cubicle, Tommy pressed with his shoulder against the door and, as he had foreseen, prevented the top lock from closing. Speaking through the air vent to one of the prisoners standing in the passage, he told him that he was stifling and persuaded him to open the lower catch with a penknife, which, as the man was only a minor offender, had not been removed from his person. At the customary stop at the Cherche-Midi prison this prisoner got out, unaware, because Tommy had not yet moved, of the true purpose for which his help had been asked. When the van reached the junction of the Boulevard Raspail and the Avenue d'Orléans, Yeo-Thomas left his cell and, edging his way along through the standing prisoners, observed that the guard had indeed propped his Sten gun against the corner and was sitting on the folding seat with his eyes shut. Creeping up until he was within two feet of the guard, he saw through the grille of the door the car following behind. As they passed the Alésia métro station he acted: grabbing the Sten gun, he shouted to the prisoner next the guard: '*Prends le garde et tiens-le pendant que je liquide les gars de derrière.*'[1] Unfortunately the man was scared and refused to co-operate, and when Tommy raised his one good arm to slog the guard with the Sten gun another two prisoners prevented him. The struggle aroused the guard, who gave Yeo-Thomas a smashing blow on the jaw, disarmed him and led him, railing at the faint-hearted, back to the cubicle. For some hours after his return to Fresnes Tommy trembled in fear of terrible reprisals; but next morning when Korrel presented him with a tin basin he gathered that the Italian guard had been too frightened of being reprimanded for carelessness to report him.

It was not long before he made a second attempt. One evening the van was late in arriving to collect the prisoners at the rue des Saussaies, and Yeo-Thomas managed to hide behind a bale of straw while they were waiting in the hall. When the van arrived and the guards moved forward to herd the prisoners into it he was left outside the cordon. While the guards were counting their passengers he dodged round the van and, crouching, crossed the courtyard in the shadow of the building, dashed past the two sentries at the gate and out into the street. Intending to hide somewhere in the maze of surrounding alleys, he sprinted along the pavement and might have escaped had not a German soldier emerging from a doorway noticed his handcuffs and tripped him up. The guards from the van, who had noticed that they were a man short, came tearing along, picked him up and dragged him back to the van, where they beat him cruelly. He was given another

1 'Look after the guard and hold him while I bump off the chaps behind.'

beating when he got back to Fresnes and deprived of his scanty food every alternate day for a fortnight.

After that he was so carefully watched that his only hope was that his discoloured left arm would become so swollen that it would require to be amputated. Once he was in hospital he was sure that he would be able to organise a Gestapo-proof means of escape. But the interrogators at the rue des Saussaies, afraid lest their victim should die of blood-poisoning before they had made him speak, gave orders that his arm was to be more carefully attended to in his cell; and although the additional dressings were applied by the same filthy Sanitäter the cure succeeded and his arm slowly healed.

His circle of unseen friends in the prison increased. Besides Jim, Texas, Aussie and Brigitte there were now a badly beaten-up elderly man in the cell next door and Patrice and Laurence, his fiancée, who relayed messages to and from Lecocq. This exchange of messages was not as simple as it sounds because both parties had to calculate the time necessary for the approach of a guard and make sure that no spies were lurking in the courtyard. The use of names became dangerous, as the guards beat severely those whom they suspected of shouting or being shouted to, and a call sign, consisting of a masturbatory moan from one of the more revolting American dance songs, was substituted. In this way Tommy was able to instruct Brigitte how to corroborate in her replies to her inquisitors the answers he had already given to his.

In addition to the private messages there was the news bulletin to circulate. Every week-day as hundreds of cyclists passed alongside the prison walls on their way to work they shouted snatches from the Allied official communiqué and extracts from the BBC news. These were memorised by the prisoners in the cells at the end of each block of buildings and relayed diagonally across the courtyards. Because of his powerful voice Tommy became one of the chief relayers.

He used this powerful voice to broadcast rebellion as well. When the pathetic little calendar which he had scratched on the wall told him that it was the twenty-third of April he celebrated St George's day by singing 'God Save the King' at the top of his voice. The hymn was taken up by the whole prison, and as the subsequent cries of 'Vive l'Angleterre' died away, Tommy added his own personal defiance.

'*L'Allemagne a perdu la guerre,*' he bawled. '*Deutschland kaputt.*' On other occasions he organised the communal singing of the *Marseillaise* and *Madelon* and on others the simultaneous banging by the prisoners on the doors of their cells. To all these demonstrations the guards reacted violently, rushing along the corridors in a roaring and vain search for the offenders, who temporarily ceased singing or banging when they heard the crash of their feet.

One morning towards the end of April Ernst gave him a cigarette when he arrived at half-past nine at the Avenue Foch for interrogation.

'I shall be confronting you with your old friend Horace at ten o'clock,' Ernst said.

'I'm ready,' Tommy said. 'But if he turns up at all I'll bet he'll be late.'

'Once and for all I forbid you to talk like that. Horace doesn't know whom he's going to meet and you'll be proved a liar.'

Tommy smiled.

'On the contrary, it is I who shall prove to you that Horace is a liar. I shall also prove that he is unpunctual, a thief and a traitor.'

At ten minutes past ten there was still no sign of Horace.

'What did I tell you?' Tommy said.

At ten-thirty Horace was ushered in. At first he did not see Yeo-Thomas, who was seated to the side of the door through which he entered. After rebuking Horace for being late, Ernst made him sit beside him at the desk, facing Tommy.

'Do you recognise this gentleman?' Ernst asked.

Horace, looking hard at Tommy's bearded face and tangled, uncut hair, seemed genuinely puzzled.

'I don't think so,' he said. 'Let me think.'

'You're going to have a good deal of thinking to do before I'm through with you, you dirty traitor,' Tommy spat out.

Horace began to look uneasy.

'Why, of course, it's Shelley,' he said.

'So you recognise him now?' Ernst said.

'Yes, yes. But you see it's the first time I've seen him with a moustache and a beard.'

'Well, Shelley,' Ernst asked. 'And what have you got to say?'

'Nothing. As it is Horace who is doing the accusing it's up to him to say on what grounds.'

'All right. You've asked for it. He's going to put you in an awkward spot and it won't be much use your lying.'

Tommy's face took on the stubborn expression with which he was accustomed to confront bullying bank managers and ivory-from-the-navel-up air commodores.

'We'll see about the lying when the time comes,' he said.

Horace, now obviously frightened, fidgeted as he said to Ernst:

'It's Shelley all right, but as I've already told you all about him there's not much good my going over the whole story again.'

'On the contrary, I insist upon hearing it,' Yeo-Thomas said. 'You're a liar, a thief, a traitor and a miserable mercenary and I'll prove it.'

Ernst interrupted impatiently.

'I forbid you to talk like that. Come on, Horace. It's your turn now.'

With trembling hands Horace pulled out a small diary and nervously flicked over the pages. He began by saying that he had had a meeting with Yeo-Thomas on the evening of the 17 November, 1943.

'You're quite sure of the date?' Tommy asked at once. 'You're certain that it was the 17 November?'

'Of course,' Horace answered unhappily. 'It's all written down. And I see here that I spoke to the Herr about it the very next day.'

'I remember perfectly,' Ernst said. 'The date is exact. He told me and I made a note of it.'

Tommy said nothing. He let Horace stumble on and, still consulting his diary, speak of other meetings with himself alleged to have taken place in December, 1943, and January, 1944.

'How much do you pay this scoundrel?' he asked Ernst when Horace had finished.

'Fifteen thousand francs a month, but I don't see that it's any business of yours.'

Tommy smiled. It was quite clear now what Horace had been doing. Pretending that he was still employed by himself, Horace had invented a lot of meetings with the important Shelley, and, to conceal the falsity of this and the majority of his other information, had denounced a few agents of minor importance. In this way he must have, at the current rate of exchange, earned about £430 in five months.

'In that case he has swindled you out of seventy-five thousand francs,' Tommy said.

'Don't talk nonsense,' Ernst said. 'And take that silly grin off your face. This is no laughing matter. And for once you'll not be able to lie yourself out of it.'

'Please bear with me a little longer,' Tommy said. 'I have already proved to you that Horace is unpunctual. I shall now keep my word to you completely and prove to you that he is a liar, a thief and a traitor as well. Tell me. I presume you keep a record of all the BBC messages?'

'We do.'

'Then it may interest you to learn this. Every time I returned to England from France I sent this message: "*Le petit lapin blanc est rentré au clapier.*" This was done for three consecutive nights, beginning with the night immediately following my return. The first time I returned to England was on 16th April last year; therefore your records ought to show this message as having been sent on 17th, 18th and 19th April, 1943. The second time I returned to England was on 16th November, 1943, and that's why I say that it was quite impossible for me to have met Horace on the 17th. Once again your records ought to show that my message was sent on 17th, 18th and 19th November. Furthermore, as I was in England during the whole of December and January, Horace couldn't have had any contact with me during those months. I came back to France on 24th February of this year, landing in the early morning of the 25th. A few days before I left I sent the phrase "*De Tommy à Hélène*" to warn my friends of my arrival.'

Ernst immediately gave an order for the register to be brought to him. But any doubts which he may still have had must have been dispelled by Horace's green guilty face, spasmodically shaking jaw and trembling body. It was quite clear that Horace was terrified.

The register was brought in; it did not take Ernst long to confirm the truth of Tommy's statement.

'*Pourriture, infecte, crapule,*' he roared at the quaking Horace.

'I think that I have now done what I said I would,' Tommy said. 'I have proved Horace to be unpunctual, a liar, a thief and a traitor.'

Ernst stood up.

'I apologise for having preferred the word of a traitor to that of a British officer,' he said in a rather theatrical manner.

The catechizing of Horace which followed was also theatrical and cruel as well. Chained to a chair outside the room in which it took place, with one of Ernst's cigars stuck in his mouth and with two silent guards on either side of him, Tommy heard it all through the door. The story was one of those sordid treacheries which have become a commonplace of war since the essentially below-the-belt weapons of machine-guns and bombs have outmoded the comparative chivalry of the sabre. Caught stealing a few months previously in a German office, Horace had been allowed to go unpunished upon his promise to act as an indicator for the Gestapo. On the instructions of the Germans he went in the company of another young *agent provocateur* to St Mars, where the local curate was a well-known recruiting agent for the Maquis. Professing a desire to join a Resistance Group, they won the confidence of this brave priest, who had recommended them and the loyal Josseaume to his good friend José Dupuis when she had asked him to find her reliable go betweens for herself, Yeo-Thomas and Brossolette.

Horace, as was to be expected, did not face the punches and the kicks with heroism. He squealed and shrieked and cringed and begged for mercy.

'I told you about Josseaume and the only reason you didn't catch him was because you were too slow,' he pleaded. 'I told you about Madame Bosc, who was Shelley's letter-box.'

'Why did you lie to me about Shelley?' Ernst asked.

'I was frightened. Shelley had threatened to bump me off on the slightest provocation. Shelley's a hard nut. He'd bump me off now if he got the chance.'

Horace went on to reproach the Gestapo for not having arrested the curate of St Mars. Ernst said that the priest was much more valuable to them free than as a prisoner. Whereupon Horace begged to be allowed to prove his devotion to the German cause by going back to St Mars and obtaining from the abbé, who still trusted him, the names and hiding-places of the leading men in the Maquis. But there were depths to which even the Gestapo could not sink.

When the interrogation was over Yeo-Thomas was given his first decent meal since his arrest: a bowl of warm soup, bread, sausage and cheese, a bottle of red wine and another of Ernst's cigars to wind up with. And that evening Horace, handcuffed, accompanied him in the van on his journey back to Fresnes Although Tommy is not the sort to kick a man when he is down, for traitors he had no mercy. Through the air vents in the door of his cubicle he communicated to the others the nature of Horace's defection, and Horace, standing miserably among the black marketeers in the corridor, was reviled both by them and the locked-up terrorists. And that night, knowing that Horace would stoop to any treachery in order to curry favour with the guards, Tommy broadcast a warning message round the prison: '*Tartarin prévient tout le monde qu'un mouton est arrivé aujourd'hui à Fresnes. Il se nomme Horace. Il a vendu ses camarades à la Gestapo.*'[1] The cruel words must have chilled even Horace as he heard them, cowering in his cell. Horace had backed the wrong horse: after the war he was rearrested by the French and sentenced to hard labour for life.

Tommy's confounding of Horace must have earned him a new reputation for veracity, for at his now almost daily interrogations his inquisitors seemed to swallow every lie he told them. Their absorption in typing out those untruths for his signature was such that one day he managed to steal a pencil from under their noses. Because he was still constantly searched he removed the casing and kept only the lead, with which he inscribed his code name and dates of interrogations on the wall of the small cell in the rue des Saussaies in which he was so frequently locked. José Dupuis, moving heaven and earth to find and deliver him, discovered this austere little memento after the liberation of Paris. '*C'était si simple et si tragique,*' she says. '*Mes jambes tremblaient. J'aurais tant aimé être seule et pouvoir un peu pleurer.*'[2]

He now found it easier to ward off his interrogators than his constantly recurring fits of loneliness and depression. Korrel brought him a Bible, which he read from cover to cover, pacing his cell like a Trappist reciting his breviary. Some of his other diversions were less

1 'Tartarin warns everybody that a stool pigeon has arrived in Fresnes today. His name is Horace. He betrayed his friends to the Gestapo.'
2 'It was so simple and tragic. My legs almost gave way under me. If only I could have been alone and wept.'

monastic. On 1 May he looked out through his window and saw a formation of RAF fighter bombers flying across the sky towards the airfield at Orly. There was a noise of concentrated ack-ack as the aircraft dived to bomb. Removing the pane of glass, Yeo-Thomas began to broadcast a description of the event, hopping with excitement and yelling '*L'Allemagne est foutue!*' Immediately singing, cheering and banging of doors broke out all over the prison, and shouts of '*A bas Adolphe*,' '*A mort Hitler*' and '*Vivent les Alliés*' almost drowned the clatter of the boots as the guards rushed down the steel stairs for shelter and the noise of the exploding bombs.

But there were not air raids every day, and when his friends Jim, Texas and Aussie were transferred to a POW camp Tommy's depression deepened. Characteristically he sought to forget his own misery by trying to banish the very real despair of those who had been in Fresnes for much longer than himself, some of them for two or three years. He launched a series of slogans which, relayed by Laurence and by Brigitte, went reverberating through the prison with the threatening thunder of revolution: '*Tartarin salue tout le monde. Ayez du courage.*' '*Tartarin dit bien le bonjour à tous ses amis et leur annonce qu'Hitler commence déjà à faire pipi dans sa culotte.*'

Naturally the guards set about trying to discover the identity of this Tartarin who alleged that the Führer was piddling his trousers, and on 17 May the bullying Feldwebel unmasked him, reading the Bible in his cell: 'Vell, Tartarin; how are you, Tartarin? You are surprised, English swine, that I know that you are Tartarin? You think that you are clever, Tartarin. You cause a lot of trouble, Tartarin. Now vee will punish you, Tartarin.' But perhaps Tartarin's worst punishment was to learn that it was a newcomer to the next-door cell who had betrayed him, in return for a promise of increased rations.

His official chastisement, however, was anything but benign. After having been thoroughly beaten up, he was deprived of his socks and handkerchief and, barefooted in his shoes and clad only in his shirt, trousers and jacket (his underclothes, which he had just washed, were drying), was taken downstairs and thrown into a damp subterranean punishment cell.

Shut up in complete darkness, he felt his way round the dungeon. The floor was spongy and covered with fungus. The walls were clammy with moisture. Where the bed should have been there were only two iron clamps jutting out from the wall. There was no table. There was a w.c. pan but no tap.

Even when his eyes had become accustomed to the darkness he still could not see. The blackness was so black that he knew that it would be impossible for him to distinguish day from night. Cold and shivering, he leaned against the wall near the door, hoping against hope for an improbable delivery. In the silence he could hear the click-cluck of drops of water as they dripped with dreary rhythm from the invisible roof. Panicking at the thought that he might be left here to die, he began to walk up and down: the dungeon, like the cell he had just left, was eight paces long and four paces wide. When he began to feel sleepy he guessed that it must be night, and squatting on his heels he let his head fall between his knees. But it was so cold and damp that he could doze only fitfully. In misery he rose and began once more his restricted perambulation, varying his route as best he could. Crossing the cell diagonally instead of laterally, he unexpectedly stumbled on a broken chair, with a back leg missing. By propping it in a corner by the door he found that he could sit on it, but did not dare to take his ease for long in case a guard might come and confiscate this possibly un-intended mitigation of his discomfort.

It was only, he calculated, when he had been incarcerated for thirty-six hours that the Feldwebel with the campaign medals arrived to give him a mug of cold water: from this still kindly NCO he learned that the Commandant of the prison had sentenced him to three weeks' solitary confinement in the dungeon, with food once every three days.

The prospect was terrifying, and Yeo-Thomas decided that he must keep active if he were to avoid tuberculosis, pneumonia or lunacy. As soon as the Feldwebel had left he began violent physical exercises, marking time, jumping up and down and swinging his arms. When a hint of warmth had been restored to his frigid body he walked up and down the dungeon until he felt drowsy, but at first he was afraid to doze off for fear of becoming cold again. Eventually, after a sip of water, he gave in and, sitting on his rickety chair with his hands stuffed up his sleeves, fell asleep. When he awoke his body was frozen, his jacket was soaking, moisture from the wall was oozing down the back of his neck and his teeth were chattering. Long and vigorous exercise was required to accelerate his circulation. Then, so as not entirely to lose heart, he started on a campaign of annoyance.

He began by singing all the songs he knew, bawling them out at the top of his voice: the mahogany patriotism of *God Save the King* was succeeded by the now almost reactionary respectability of the *Marseillaise*, the wink to *Madelon* mingled with the curtsey to *Annie Laurie; Tipperary, The Yanks Are Coming, We'll Hang Out Our Washing on the Siegfried Line, Roll Out the Barrel, There'll Always be an England* were roared out in a tremendous thunder in which the old confidence lost its anachronism in the shining actuality of the new. From song he turned to brief, but loud insults in English and in French: 'To hell with Hitler', *'J'emmerde Adolphe'*, 'F— Germany' and *'L'Allemagne est foutue'*, punctuated by lusty kicks at the door of the cell at last drew a *'Ruhe'* from a nearby guard. 'Yew called me babee doll a year ago-oh'. The preposterous plaint of the 1916 flapper did the trick. The door was opened and, in a blaze of light, a guard stepped in and caught the singer a heavy blow with the butt of a rifle. Even so Tommy did not stop, perhaps because even a painful break in the monotony was a relief. As soon as the door closed he began again, dancing and hopping round his cell, singing and shouting until his throat was sore and he tired himself into sleep.

After three days they brought him some macaroni soup, which he had to drink out of the can, as he had no spoon. The soup warmed him, and, leaving some in the tin to be drunk later, he pranced gaily round the dungeon, bawling and singing even more loudly than before. Then, while he paused for breath, he heard voices talking above him in the darkness, in the blessed accents of Belleville:

'Il y a un Anglais au cachot. Il gueule comme un âne.'

'Il doit s'emmerder, le pauvre type.'

The second speaker was right. The Englishman that bellowed like a bull was so bored that he immediately propped his three-legged chair in a corner and climbed up in a risky attempt to reach the air vent in the ceiling down which he guessed that the sound of the voices must have come. Standing unsteadily on the back of the chair and fumbling over the ceiling until he got his fingers in the grille, he pulled himself up until his lips were level with the opening.

'It's the Englishman who bellows like a bull,' he said. 'What day of the month is it and what's the time?'

'It's the 20 May and it's ten o'clock,' the reply came.

'Ten o'clock in the morning or ten o'clock at night?'

'Ten o'clock at night.'

'Thanks. I can't hang on any longer, but I'll come up every day for the news.'

The chair toppled as his legs returned his weight to it and he fell sprawling on the floor. But he was happier when he went to sleep because now he would be able to count the days by the number of news bulletins he received from his new friends upstairs. He was awakened by rats scurrying over his face in search of the remains of his cold and soggy soup, but even then he did not finish it, knowing that it would be almost three days before he got another ration.

There were four men in the cell above, and he communicated with them regularly. In return for the consolation of the daily communiqué he tried to encourage them by promising that it would not be long before the Allies invaded and set them free. Then one day, when he was feeling too weak from lack of nourishment to be able to pull himself up to the air vent, a voice came shouting down to him:

'Our comrade Louis has just been taken away to be executed. *Vive la France!*'

With difficulty Tommy climbed on his chair and pulled himself up to the air vent.

'*Vive la France et bon courage!*' he said simply.

When he had been silent for a little he sang for poor Louis his own private requiem: it consisted of *God Save the King*, the *Marseillaise*, *Madelon* and *Auprès de ma Blonde*. I think that Louis would have liked it, and it's quite on the cards that God liked it too.

That night he had a dream. In his dream he saw a monster calendar whose leaves kept slowly flicking until they stopped at 5 June. It was prophetic. He was sure that that was the day on which the invasion would take place.

'*Dis donc, l'Anglais, et le fameux débarquement?*' one of the men upstairs asked next day through the air vent. 'If your invasion doesn't take place this year we'll all be dead.'

The man's doubts convinced him that the dream had been sent to him as an augury with which to hearten the despondent.

'The invasion will take place at the beginning of next week,' he said and, deciding that it would be imprudent too definitely to commit General Eisenhower, added: 'On Monday or on Tuesday.'

'How do you know?'

'Don't ask me. I know. That's all.'

He could hear the man discussing the news with his companions.

'The English officer says that the invasion will take place at the beginning of next week.'

'*Il se fout de nous.*'

'No, he's sure. Pass it on to the chaps next door.'

He knew that if the invasion did not take place as he had predicted he would have done great harm to the morale of his fellow prisoners. When on the evening of 5 June there was still no news of the invasion he sang more loudly than ever in order to buoy himself up. But he wasn't alone in his doubts; through the air vent came the question.

'Twenty-four hours to go. You're still sure?'

'Yes, I'm still sure.'

He dreamed that night, not of calendars, but of the sun shining on the green and golden fields of France. The contrast of his freezing cell when he awoke was terrible. Hopping and dancing to get warm, he heard a shout from the air vent:

'*Allo, le camarade anglais.* Your comrades have landed. *Vive la France!*'

In the depths of his dungeon he could hear the other prisoners singing the *Marseillaise*; to him it was like the heavenly choir. With tears pouring down his bearded, battered face, in his clammy rags he stood to attention and added his own paean of *God Save the King*. If it was anybody's victory it was his. If anybody had worked for French Resistance it was he. There was still every chance that he would be shot before he saw the full results of his labour, but he knew that the Germans would now feel the full weight of French Resistance, properly equipped at long last thanks to the help of Winston Churchill who had listened to him in his moments of despair. The hope that had come to him at the Pointe-de-Grave in 1940 had been fulfilled; Pierre Brossolette had not died in vain. In those moments he experienced the joy of

Péguy's chair-maker, who took care that the unseen straws should be as carefully plaited as the seen. He sang *Tipperary* as his *Te Deun* and then knelt and scratched with his nails on the damp walls of the cell another record of his witness which José Dupuis discovered also when she passed that way to look for him: S/L. K. DODKIN, RAF, 17–5–44; the date of his departure was added before he left the dungeon.

His friends in the cell above, who shared his jubilation, kept him informed of all that was happening in the prison and of how the guards were unable to quell the riot; he heard his prescience celebrated in a message shouted to the cell two storeys above his own:

'*Il avait raison, le camarade anglais. Maintenant il est heureux comme un poisson dans l'eau, mais il a froid et faim; si seulement on pouvait lui faire passer quelque chose.*'[1]

But the Englishman as happy as a fish in water was much too excited to be cold or hungry. For the next three days, in spite of Oberkommando der Wehrmacht reports that the Allies would be thrown back into the sea, he hopped and jumped and shouted and sang.

On 9 June his sentence was up. He was removed from the dungeon and, after a brief visit to his old cell to collect his soap, toothbrush, underclothes (still damp) and overcoat, he was transferred to cell number 30 on the ground floor. This cell was colder and less well lighted than that which he had previously inhabited. It was one of the cells ordinarily used for the beating up of prisoners, and the walls, floor, blanket and palliasse were stained with congealed blood.

His first visitor was his old enemy the Feldwebel, who struck him, knocked him to the ground and kicked him as he lay prone.

'Pritish officer, vee will kill you slowly.'

'Thank you. Thank you so very much.'

'Pritish officer, vy do you say "thank you"?'

'You would not understand, but in England we are always polite, even to our enemies.'

The Feldwebel glared and went out, but he never struck Yeo-Thomas again.

He was lonelier now than he had been on the second floor. Korrel

---

1 'Our English friend was right. Now he's as happy as a fish in water, but he's cold and hungry; if only we could give him something.'

no longer came to see him and, instead of a Bible, he had only the generally senseless snatches of news on his daily ration of toilet paper to read. To pass the time he counted the two hundred odd fleas he caught in his palliasse and killed each day and, imitating the psalmist, longed for the wings of a bird that he might fly away and be at rest. This desire became almost a conviction that, with the exercise of will power, he could transform himself into a sparrow and fly through the window, one of whose panes, inadequately secured with unhardened tar, he had quickly succeeded in removing. But a sparrow, he realised, might very well fall victim to a cat and so he decided that he had better change himself into a crow as soon as he had flown out of the window. A crow, however, might be shot by a farmer anxious to protect his crops and so, perhaps, he might as well change himself into a snail right away and see what he could do by slithering.

As he could not read toilet paper, count dead fleas and transmigrate his soul all day long he began shouting messages again, through the hole in the window out of which he hesitated to fly as a bird. This time he called himself 'Edouard' and to allay the suspicions of the guards he shouted 'Edouard demande des nouvelles de Tartarin.' Some hours later the reply came. 'For Edouard: Tartarin has been put in the dungeon. Since then we have had no news of him.'

One day the NCO with the Iron Cross came in with a newspaper in his hand.

'The war will soon be over,' he said. 'You'll be able to go home.' Although he knew that the invasion had been a success, Yeo-Thomas was surprised and excited by the news.

'So Hitler's going to throw up the sponge?' he asked.

'Of course not.' The NCO was shocked. 'It's the Allies who are beaten. The Führer is using the secret weapon. London is in flames, the Government has left for the north of England and the population has fled.' He unfolded the *Pariser Zeitung*, on which under tremendous headlines, there was a photograph of a V1 falling through clouds of smoke on a burning city. 'You see, it's true. London has been destroyed. The war will be over in a few days.'

Tommy's first thought was for Barbara. Had she perished among the flames? Then, although he could not read the headlines, he saw that the photograph was faked. The morning after his arrival in France in February he had read in the *Pariser Zeitung* that London had been half wiped out by a small tip-and-run raid which he, himself, had experienced two nights previously.

'Listen,' he said. 'When you and Korrel are prisoners of war I shan't forget you, as you two have always been decent to me.'

Nor did the German authorities appear to share the NCOs' confidence in the nearness of their victory. Aware that the Allies were approaching Paris, they prepared to evacuate compromising prisoners from Fresnes. On 10 July, Yeo-Thomas was medically examined and passed as fit for forced labour in Germany. The night of 16 July he spent in a larger cell with eleven other prisoners, among whom were the two brothers Simon who had helped him to plan Brossolette's escape from Rennes prison; from them he learned the sad news of Abeille's death. Apart from them and two others called Luquet and Deschamps most of the rest were black marketeers, thiefs and ponces. When one of these tried to steal food from the Simons, too weakened by torture to resist, Tommy laid him out with a punch in the solar plexus. He was getting his hand in.

CHAPTER XII

This side up . . .

The bullying Feldwebel seemed to be getting his hand in too, wishing for war but preparing for peace.

'Sorry, Sir,' he said to Yeo-Thomas next morning as he slipped a pair of handcuffs round his wrists.

A roll call was held in the big cell by the Feldwebel, in the presence of armed guards. As each prisoner answered his name he was required to file out. Tommy's was the last name to be called. 'After you, please, Sir,' the Feldwebel said, stepping respectfully aside. Tommy was dumbfounded: it sounded just like his favourite Itma.

Perhaps the Feldwebel knew more than Yeo-Thomas: perhaps he knew that Tommy was being transported to Germany only as a minor offender. But he could not have known how this had come about. While in Fresnes, and without being informed, Tommy had been sentenced to death, and his execution had been fixed for 18 May, the day when he had begun to bellow in the dungeon. José Dupuis had, however, with great difficulty succeeded in tracing him to Fresnes and, through an intermediary, had approached the Gestapo officer in charge of the case; in return for a bribe of four million francs cash specially parachuted by HM Government this official had agreed to lose Tommy's file. (Further negotiations to facilitate his escape had fallen through because the Gestapo officer in question had been killed while making an arrest.) This was possibly the reason why the Feldwebel was attempting to make unto himself friends of the mammon of the coming unrighteousness.

Yeo-Thomas, of course, at the time knew nothing of this, and when with the other prisoners he was made to climb into an uncovered lorry he began to watch anxiously for an opportunity to escape. But four armed guards sat on a bench at the back of the lorry, which travelled quickly, and all he could do was to drop to a group of cycling workmen a message to José Dupuis scribbled with his uncased lead on paper provided by one of his companions. In this message, which, like others, was ultimately delivered, he told her that, as the guards had informed him, he was being transferred to Compiègne, whence he would shortly leave for Germany.

The camp to which they were taken was an old Army barracks situated not at Compiègne itself, but at the neighbouring Le Royal Lieu. It consisted of about eight low one-storied buildings separated from one another by alleys and situated in a compound surrounded by Miradors. On the high covered platforms of each Mirador were a searchlight and a machine-gun manned by SS troopers.

Yeo-Thomas, Deschamps, Luquet and the brothers Simon managed to get into the same room in block 'B'. This room was a long dormitory lined with two tiers of a double row of bunks placed head to foot, and with a long table in the middle. Outside there were washing troughs, daytime latrines next the cookhouse and a library for the use of prisoners. Although the mattresses were infested with bugs and at night-time latrine buckets overflowed their nauseous and dysentery-charged contents on to the floor it was, in comparison with Fresnes, Claridges.

The daily routine of the camp began with a morning roll call. The inmates of each block lined up under the supervision of their block chief, a privileged prisoner, who counted them and reported to the German duty NCO in charge of the parade. Apart from such chores as cleaning out their dormitories and peeling potatoes, the prisoners were free until the evening, when another roll call was held. After seven o'clock they were confined to their blocks and forbidden as much as to put their heads out of a window. This discipline was enforced by two armed soldier thugs, each with a good score of would-be escapees to his credit, who paraded the camp with police dogs.

In spite of their leisure, escape during the day turned out to be as impracticable as escape during the night. As soon as the five friends approached the Miradors the SS men shouted and trained their machine-guns on them. They studied the habits of the working parties that left the camp, but found their category of prisoner had been forbidden such employment. They discovered a large sewer which ran behind one of the blocks and out of sight of the Miradors towards a corner of the barbed-wire enclosure; but on lifting the cover of the manhole they found that after a few yards the concrete passage became too narrow for them to crawl through it, and they had no tools with which to enlarge it.

A solo reconnaissance by Yeo-Thomas revealed that the enclosure in which they had been searched on their arrival in the camp was poorly guarded. If only he could hide somewhere near he thought he might be able to creep out under the barbed wire at night. But the hiding-place, he realised, would have to be especially secure, as a search would be made as soon as he was missed at evening roll call. A hut in the enclosure storing straw for palliasses seemed to afford just such a refuge. One day, assuring himself that he was unobserved, he made his way stealthily towards this hut, but just as he reached it a German NCO opened the door and came out. Fortunately the NCO was a notorious homosexualist and had his own reasons for concealing his visit to the straw, and all he said was: 'I know that it is your duty as an officer to try to escape. Perhaps you will have better luck next time.' Marching Yeo-Thomas back to the camp as though he were a work fatigue, the NCO dismissed him with a twinkle in his eye. From that time on, although he was not reported, Tommy was carefully watched.

He fell back on a variation of the plan which he had evolved to rescue Brossolette from Rennes. A wealthy French resistant in the camp called Roberty had managed by bribing two of the guards to get into touch with his friends outside. With him Tommy hatched a plot for German-speaking accomplices wearing German uniform to drive up in a car carrying a German military number and present the camp authorities with forged instructions for the transfer of Roberty and himself to the bearers.

But while the preliminary negotiations were taking place another group of 150 prisoners arrived to overflow the camp, and to relieve the congestion the immediate departure of a convoy to Germany was announced. In order to avoid this inconvenient departure Yeo-

Thomas arranged, with the connivance of the camp dentist, Marty, to be given an injection producing a high temperature. When the parade for medical inspection took place he was lying tossing with fever in his bunk, and, because the Germans feared any disease which might cause an epidemic in their homeland, he was not sent on the convoy. Unfortunately, the Simon brothers, Luquet and Deschamps were selected, and none of them returned.

Fearing another convoy, Yeo-Thomas prolonged his convalescence, reporting daily to the infirmary for pills which he never took. Then about a hundred priest prisoners arrived: Oblates of Mary Immaculate, they were deprived of their cassocks and forbidden to say Mass or to pray together. Almost immediately afterwards several hundred more prisoners were crammed into the already overcrowded camp. It was obvious that the next convoy would be a big one, and morale in the camp sank low. Depressed himself, Yeo-Thomas went about preaching his solemn, platitudinous but, coming from him, always effective little sermon of never-say-die: Britons had held out in 1940 and they had won through; therefore if Frenchmen held out in 1944 they too would win through. His sincerity was so evident that if there was an undistributed middle in his argument his congregation didn't notice it.

Through the agency of the Block Leader of Block 'B', a character called Michel, one of the prisoners who was a wealthy brothel owner had received food parcels from outside; and, as the only Briton in the camp, Yeo-Thomas was invited to a feast at which the wages of sin confounded the theologians by appearing as cold lobster, smoked salmon, sausages, hefty hams, chocolate, cigarettes, coffee, vintage wines, brandy and a case of champagne. Fuddled as he became with this hospitality, Tommy was, nevertheless, able to notice the excellent terms on which Michel was with the German guards, who kept dropping in and partaking of a portion of the pimp's bounty.

Anxious to have an alternative means of escape to that in preparation with Roberty, Yeo-Thomas asked Marty the dentist to approach Michel with the offer of a bribe. After much haggling and argument about procedure, it was ultimately arranged that for the sum of two million francs the Sonderführer of the camp would allow Tommy to escape: five hundred thousand francs were to be handed over as soon as the prisoner was through the barbed wire and the remaining fifteen hundred thousand when he was safely in hiding; to avoid all possibility of double-crossing, Tommy was to be allowed to arrange for the money to be sent directly to himself from his friends outside who, he was confident, would help him; and the Sonderführer was to accompany the escapee and surrender to the Allies under his protection.

While Tommy was trying to get into touch with José Dupuis a second convoy to Germany took place which another massive injection enabled him to avoid. Then, just as his plan to escape with Roberty was about to be carried out successfully, disaster overtook him.

On 8 August his name was called out on parade and he was informed that he was to leave at once for an unknown destination. Handcuffed by an NCO, he was marched between two armed guards to the gate of the camp and, after farewell gifts of food from his comrades had been confiscated by a corporal in charge of the sentries, pushed into a waiting Paris motor bus. There he was chained by an additional pair of handcuffs to one of the guards who sat on either side of him. Two more guards sat behind him and yet another two stood on the rear platform.

Discovery of the loss of his file had caused an investigation which had revealed that his classification had been altered. Consequently, from a one-star minor offender he had been promoted once more to his former three-star rank of *Nacht und Nebel, Rückkehr Ungewünscht* – dangerous terrorist, to be exterminated.

CHAPTER XIII

. . . murder with care

To make the threat quite plain a Gestapo official in civilian clothes accompanied them. When after a little the bus broke down this official stormed at the French driver, who seemed to be taking his time about getting it going again. Perhaps he suspected that the engine trouble was not accidental, as the area in which it had occurred was thickly tenanted by groups of armed partisans. At any rate he was running no risks. Transferring Yeo-Thomas, the guards and himself to a passing coach carrying armed German soldiers to Paris, he ordered the driver to take them to the Gare de l'Est. There, surrounded by his imposing escort, Tommy was marched along the platform to a waiting train, in a wagon of which were two special compartments with windows covered with grilles. When his handcuffs had been removed he was pushed into one of these compartments.

There were already eighteen other prisoners in this compartment, constructed to accommodate eight, but from which the seats had been removed. They were handcuffed together in nine Siamese pairs, and among them, as the Resistance world was small, Tommy was not surprised to find a French officer, Lieutenant Hessel, whom he had known in London and who spoke German. Another Frenchman was Robert Benoist, the pre-war world champion racing motorist. Among the British were Squadron Leader Southgate and two Canadians, Captain Pickersgill and Lieutenant McAlister. From Hessel Tommy learned that they were being deported to Germany.

His privilege of being the only unhandcuffed and separate prisoner did not last for long. A quarter of an hour later a six-foot-four, leather-faced Wehrmacht NCO in charge of the guard came along to inspect the new prisoner. Finding Yeo-Thomas unmanacled, he grabbed him with an enormous hand and, thrusting a Lüger automatic into the pit of his stomach, threatened to shoot him. Shaking with rage and still covering Tommy with the pistol, he ordered one of the guards to search him; the discovery of a small clasp knife acquired at Compiègne and concealed under the lining of the prisoner's waistcoat roused the ranting NCO to roaring but illogical fury. Confiscating the knife, he gave orders for Yeo-Thomas to be handcuffed to two other men, of whom one was a Belgian called Rechenmann. Rechenmann, although he had been searched before, was then unhandcuffed, made to strip and stand naked while his garments and his person were examined minutely. When this search was over and he had dressed again Rechenmann was handcuffed to another two prisoners, and Yeo-Thomas, whose misdemeanour had caused the trouble, was left handcuffed in comparative comfort to only one prisoner. There were now eight pairs in the compartment and one group of three.

When the train eventually started, Yeo-Thomas, as senior ranking officer, assumed command and, with the assistance of Squadron Leader Southgate and a French major called Frager, organised the group. As space was too restricted for all to sit on the floor at once, they arranged to take it in turns to rest and to stand up. The two days' food which the guards had given them was then split up equally. Selfishness, however, is not exclusively confined to civilians: when those fortunate enough to possess Red Cross parcels were asked to pool the contents two of them refused, and it was only under pressure that they finally consented to contribute a portion of their privilege. Yeo-Thomas was unfortunate enough to be handcuffed to one of these recalcitrants.

At first the guards refused to allow them to use the toilet, but in the end Hessel, appointed interpreter, persuaded the now more reasonable NCO to allow them to go in staggered groups, provided that they were accompanied by a guard and that the lavatory door remained open. In any case it was an awkward and embarrassing procedure, especially for the group of three. When his turn came Yeo-Thomas noticed on his way along the corridor a compartment without a grille in which were huddled a number of women prisoners; among them, although he did not know it at the time, was the renowned and indomitable Miss Violette Szabo.

The Resistance world turned out to be smaller than even Yeo-Thomas had imagined: as the occupants of the other compartment with a grille passed along the corridor on their way to the toilet he recognised in the sorry procession Captain Barrett, who had been a sergeant of his at the beginning of the war, and Captain Desmond Hubble, whom he himself had recruited for the Jedburghs and who had served under him in 'RF' Section. He managed to speak to them, impressing upon them that his name was now Kenneth Dodkin and no longer Forest Frederick Edward Yeo-Thomas.

The roster for sleeping that night was even more complicated to arrange than the shifts for resting. As only four men could lie on the floor simultaneously and as the three handcuffed together had to count as four, each group had only two hours of sleep and the last on the roster had to wait eight hours for its turn.

Those not sleeping had to stand and, while not dozing, occupied their time with discussing possibilities of escape, which were slender. There were two factions: those who wanted to make the attempt at any risk and those who preferred to play for safety. It was to one of the prudent that Yeo-Thomas was handcuffed, and with him he had acrimonious argument. The ratchet attachment on their handcuffs caused further disputes: when a prisoner moved without warning his twin, the handcuff on the latter's wrist tightened and caused him pain, and Yeo-Thomas, Major Frager and Robert Benoist spent half the night patching up the consequent quarrels. A Frenchman called Yves Loison helped to restore harmony by attempting, even although vainly, to unfasten his handcuffs with a hairpin which he had found in his pocket. The remarkable fortitude of the two Canadians, Pickersgill and McAlister, weaker than the rest because of a recent and heavy beating up from the Gestapo, also increased morale. To strengthen them Tommy gave the Canadians a cardboard box of malt syrup which was the only parting gift from his fellow prisoners at Compiègne that the sentry at the gate had allowed him to retain. They were both very grateful and Pickersgill put the box in his pocket.

Next morning they were again allowed to go to the toilet, but were not permitted to wash. As the August sun beat down upon the roof of the carriage the heat in the compartment became unbearable, but it was only after an eloquent appeal by Hessel that the guards allowed them a tumblerful of water each. Their discomfort increased when Pickersgill, searching for the syrup out of his pocket, found that he had crushed the carton in his sleep: when he withdrew his hand it was covered with a gooey, sticky mess which soon smothered not only his own clothes, but those of McAlister and his immediate neighbours as well. Trying to lick his hand clean Pickersgill succeeded only in smearing syrup all over his face, and all the time more syrup was oozing from his pocket. McAlister, attempting to help, spread the stickiness further. And when the guards refused Hessel's request that the two Canadians be allowed to go to the lavatory and clean themselves the surly members of the party became vituperative.

As the day drew on the heat became more intense, and the prisoners, refused more water by the guards, grew thirstier and thirstier. The train crawled along, with an occasional alarm when aeroplanes were heard above. In the middle of the afternoon the guards appeared nervous and the NCO kept looking anxiously out of the window in the corridor.

Suddenly there was the roar of fast aircraft flying low and the noise of 20 mm. cannon. British fighters were coming in to attack the train with that slap-happy administration of vengeance which so often punishes the just more heavily than the unjust. As the guards cowered in the corridor there was a thundering explosion and the train stopped. But the German NCO kept his head: rapping out an order to the guards to follow him after they had locked the prisoners in the carriage, he ran alongside the train carrying a light machine-gun. Standing next the grill, Tommy could see him mount the gun and start firing at the aircraft which were still circling round the train. Amid the roar of engines and the blast of cannon civilians rushed terrified across the fields. As he saw the shells bursting against the train Yeo-Thomas prayed that an incendiary might not hit their carriage, in which case they would all be burned to death. His fear seemed to communicate itself to his companions for he felt a painful wrench at his wrist as he was jerked forward by his twin on top of a mass of bodies seeking cover from the shells and the machine-gun bullets. They were all rather ashamed of their panic when, a few minutes later, Violet Szabo and another girl came crawling along the corridor to bring them water.

The raid was successful: either the engine or the track must have been damaged, for the train did not move on again when it was over. Eventually two motor trucks arrived to collect the prisoners, who were warned by the NCO that all of them would be shot out of hand if any single man or woman attempted to escape. The women were piled into one truck and the men into the other, and both were heavily guarded.

The men from both compartments were now together, and Tommy met for the first time new friends who were going to be his constant companions in distress: the British section now consisted of Yeo-Thomas, Squadron Leader Southgate, Captains Kane, Mayer, Wilkinson, Peulevé, Hubble, Barrett, Steele, Pickersgill; Lieutenants McAlister and McKenzie; and the French and Belgian section of Commandants Frager, Robert Benoist, Allard, Defendini, Detal, Leccia, Garel, Garry, Geelen, Rechenmann, Corbusier, Chaignot, Gerard, Loison, Mulsant, de Seguier, Vellaud, Culioli, Guillot, Evesque, Avallard, Rambaud, Hessel and two others. In all there were thirty-seven of them.

Their first stop was at Châlons-sur-Marne, at Gestapo Headquarters, where the Sicherheitsdienst officer accompanying them dropped off for instructions. While the guards were keeping the local population at a distance some of the prisoners managed to scribble messages to their friends which they let fall later on the road in the hope that sympathisers would find them and send them on. Then in the courtyard of another building they were allowed to wash at a fountain, a privilege especially appreciated by the two sticky Canadians. Here the men were able to exchange a few words with the women prisoners, whose fortitude was inspiring: although they had been insulted, beaten and tortured, these women had remained undefeated.

Late that night they were driven into Verdun. The town was blacked out and the streets rang with the tramp of jackboots and the harsh staccato singing of invisible German troops. 'The impression created in the dark,' Yeo-Thomas says, 'was one of brute strength and impersonal discipline.' For the underground fighters in the trucks this sound of organised troops symbolised the merciless strength of the enemy whom they had seldom met face to face, and whom they now only heard without seeing. For Yeo-Thomas, who had done more than any other Briton to organise French Resistance, the experience was especially galling: the Allied Armies were advancing across France and the partisans were now coming into open conflict with the Germans. Because he had not fought with the irregulars he had raised he felt that he had kept only half the oath which he had sworn at the Pointe-de-Grave and he was beginning to be afraid that he might not live to see the liberated France for which he had worked. Listening to the trudge of the heavy boots, he experienced the bitter pride of the poet who knows that he will get good reviews in *The Times Literary Supplement* when he is dead, but would have liked to spend just one night at the Waldorf-Astoria when he was alive.

They slept that night in the stables of Verdun barracks, six to eight men in each stall on the right of the centre alley and the women similarly apportioned in the stalls on the left. A long string was fixed along the alley to separate the men from the women and the Sicherheitsdienst officer ordered the guards to shoot anyone attempting to cross from one side to the other. Because of the dim lights, however, several of the men and some of the women were able to crawl near enough to the string to exchange stories and to warn one another what to say and what not to say when they were next interrogated. They did not know that there were to be no more interrogations for any of them and that they had all been condemned to death.

Next morning they were not only allowed to wash, but their handcuffs were also temporarily removed in order that they might clean themselves properly. Yeo-Thomas took advantage of this privilege, which they owed to the fact that they had a Wehrmacht and not an SS escort, to lose his grumbling partner and be handcuffed instead to Hubble, upon whose co-operation he knew he could count if an opportunity to escape presented itself. After a cup of ersatz coffee they were loaded into the trucks again.

It was a lovely day, with the sun shining in a cloudless blue sky. Liberty seemed both far and near: far when they looked at their guards and their manacles, and near when they beheld the green and gold leaves of the trees, with here and there a shine of silver in the refracted magic of the sun. Liberty seemed near too when, at long last, Loison managed to open his handcuffs, but for the present his success was kept a secret between himself, Yeo-Thomas, Southgate and Frager in case a careless word might warn the guards. And liberty seemed nearer still when they saw the expectancy on the faces of the inhabitants of the town and villages through which they passed, and the glares of hatred directed at their guards. Their hearts rose high when some of those men and women hesitatingly returned their greeting of the V sign, and they began to hope their trucks might be attacked by maquisards and themselves set free.

Soon, however, there were no more timorously friendly villagers, and no more villages. Instead, there were rows and rows of concrete blocks. With the sun beating down upon their heads and blistering them with heat and thirst they passed through the Maginot Line, that monument to the folly of those who, putting their confidence neither in the Lord nor in princes, omitted to extend their distrust to the sea. After that they crossed the Siegfried Line, upon which we had so signally failed to hang even our pocket handkerchief. There could be little hope now: they were in Germany, and in front of them loomed the dark grimy town of Saarbrücken.

Hope vanished finally as their truck slowed down at the approaches to barbed-wire enclosures, surrounded at intervals by machine-gun-manned Miradors. The truck turned in between two rows of wire, lurched through a heavily guarded gate and came to a stop in an open space surrounded by low wooden huts. In the middle of the space was a tank of water, filthy with dust from the black gritty soil.

A dozen or more SS men and NCOs with cruel, bestial faces stood waiting for the prisoners to alight when the flap at the back of the lorry was lowered. Yeo-Thomas and Hubble were the first to receive their attentions: as his feet touched the ground Tommy was given a stunning blow on the nose and, when he staggered, a kick in the back which sent him forward to get another smash on the jaw, followed by a kick in the stomach and several slaps on the face. When his eyes cleared and he regained his balance he saw two NCOs standing over him and laughing at him.

Still spitting blood, he had to line up with the others while the SS men passed along the ranks, punching, kicking and slapping the prisoners all over again. Hubble's uniform seemed specially to attract their spite, and he and Tommy were given a more thorough beating up then the rest. While this process, which lasted for half an hour, was going on the women prisoners were driven in in their truck and marched away under an escort of jackbooted SS female plug-uglies flourishing whips; Tommy never saw any of them again and does not know whether they survived.

After being listed in a register the men prisoners were then chained together in groups; in Yeo-Thomas's group there were five. The chains were in the shape of an X, in the centre of which was a ring fitted to a pair of handcuffs which were fixed round Hubble's ankles so as to force him to take short, shuffling steps. At the extremities of the chains were more handcuffs which were fastened to the ankles of the four others in the group. To prevent them from using their hands to keep their balance, the prisoners were no longer attached to one another in pairs by their wrists, but each man's hands were shackled separately. In these cumbersome fetters they were marched across the camp to the distant latrines and, as they tripped and stumbled, were kicked and beaten with truncheons, coshes and fists by the SS men. In the latrines, where fat slimy worms crawled among the overflowing faeces, they were forced to relieve themselves in these chained groups. After this painful, humiliating and awkward procedure they were marched back across the camp under the gaze of scared white faces crowding the dirty windows of the huts round the square. It is not surprising that their hearts were filled with anger and hatred.

For the moment, however, their tormentors had had their fun; the chains were removed from the prisoners' feet and they were again manacled together in pairs, except Yeo-Thomas, who was given a pair of handcuffs to himself. The thirty-seven of them were then locked in a small hut behind the camp kitchen. This hut was nine feet long, eight feet wide and approximately nine feet high and was lighted by one small window about a foot square situated some six feet from the ground. Narrow benches, about eight inches wide, ran along three of the walls. An old oil drum had been placed in a corner near the door to serve as a latrine bucket. With the August sum beating down on the tin roof the heat in this confined space was overpowering.

Once more they were faced with the problem of disposing themselves so that all could rest in turn, and once more the uncooperative grumbled. Yeo-Thomas, Southgate, Kane, Benoist, Frager and Hubble silenced them and worked out a plan. It was found that only twenty-three or twenty-four men could sit on the benches, and that most uncomfortably, while the rest who stood or squatted were even more uncomfortable, and when one moved all had to move. A more satisfactory variation of this pattern was finally adopted: eight men lay on the floor, four with their heads under the benches on one side of the hut and four with their heads under the benches on the opposite side; the twenty-four men sitting on the benches placed their feet on either side of the bodies of those lying on the floor; and the remaining five stood leaning against the door or against the wall on either side of the door. When one man wanted to go to the oil drum the man to whom he was handcuffed had, of course, to accompany him; Yeo-Thomas paid for the privilege of being handcuffed alone by being ninth man on the floor when his turn came and he slept under a bench with less air than he had sitting or standing up. All that evening and night they remained like this, hungry, thirsty and sweating, without food, without drink, in a foetid atmosphere progressively polluted by the stench coming from the oil drum.

In the morning they were ordered out with the customary shouts of "*Raus*', '*Schnell*', '*Los*', qualified by a vocative '*Schwein*' or two. Lined up outside their hut they were compelled to watch a distressing spectacle which was obviously of daily occurrence. Cringing and yelping under blows from coshes, sticks and rifle butts wielded by SS thugs, hundreds of haggard, gaunt, almost fleshless men in rags and with a hunted, helpless look in their eyes were advancing across the compound towards a narrow railed-off passage leading to the kitchen door. Each miserable man carried a small metal pannikin, and as he entered the gangway, broad enough to admit only a single file of prisoners, he was belaboured and bludgeoned by SS guards armed with truncheons who stood on either side and whose blows he could not avoid if he was to eat. As soon as a prisoner was given his ration he rushed back across the compound, gobbling his food as he went, so as to have finished before the guard posted at the door of his hut beat him and knocked the pannikin from his hand as he entered. None of the thirty-seven watching prisoners was maltreated by their guards, who laughed uproariously at the spectacle and kept running into the crowd to administer extra kicks and punches to the milling skeletons.

Sick and horrified and wondering what might be in store for themselves, the thirty-seven were marched to the latrines, where they emptied their oil drum. After that they were allowed to wash in the grimy water of the pool in the middle of the compound; this turned out to be merely a relative clemency because the water came up to within only four feet of the top of the tank on the sloping edges of which the prisoners could not get a grip, and each man had to slide down to the level of the water and, hanging by his handcuffs to his partner's wrists, wash himself as best he could. Occasionally the guards would push a prisoner down into the water and stand laughing while his companion struggled to pull him back.

Then they in their turn visited the kitchen and each was given a pannikin of boiled water with pieces of mangel-wurzel floating in it, a slice of bread which appeared to be made of dark flour and sand, and a tumbler of cold water. Instead of being lashed by the guards while they were eating their meal they were treated to a second spectacle. SS men with coshes and sticks lined up outside the doors of each hut on the square in the middle of which stood an NCO who shouted *"Raus, 'raus, los, schnell!'* As the prisoners came running out the guards slogged at them and beat them and when the wretches were ordered back to the huts they beat them again. As soon as the last prisoner had regained his hut the NCO shouted *"Raus"* again and the performance was repeated.

Although quite a few among the thirty-seven guessed that this demonstration had been staged as a warning to break their morale, more managed to believe that the fact that they themselves had been exempted from this brutality proved that they were on their way to an Oflag, where they would be treated with the consideration due to their rank. And as they sweltered once more in their tiny hut they argued and hoped and despaired. One school of thought maintained that for them this was only a transit camp through which they were passing to better things, and the other, the minority, that, although here indeed they had no lasting habitation, it was to very much worse things that they were passing.

It seemed at first that the majority was right: three days later they were paraded outside their hut and formally handed over by the Sicherheitsdienst officer who had accompanied them from Paris to a kindly-looking Feldgendarmerie officer and about a dozen comparatively unferocious Feldgendarmerie guards. They were then locked in pairs into the cubicles of proper prison vans into which the pathetic bundles of those who possessed them were also loaded. Hubble was especially pleased by this latter attention: in his bundle were two shirts, a pipe and a portable chess set which his mother had given him.

They were driven to the station in Saarbrücken which they could see had been badly bombed; but even the sight of the scared and underfed civilians who gaped at them as they were escorted along the platform failed to move Yeo-Thomas to pity.

The train in which they were to travel was a Germany-bound troop carrier and was already crammed with jubilant janizaries. Two trucks had, however, been rescued for the prisoners: one for their bundles and bags and for the guards when they were resting; and a goods wagon for themselves in which there was room for them to recline at ease. Immediately in front of this goods wagon was an anti-aircraft wagon armed with a 20 mm. Oerlikon-type gun manned by Luftwaffe soldiers. Only three guards were left to watch over the prisoners and when the train moved off a door on the side of the wagon was left open. The presumption seemed to be that handcuffed prisoners were helpless and could make no attempt to escape.

The presumption was wrong, or very nearly wrong. With the aid of a small piece of tin, recently acquired, Loison unfastened his handcuffs and those of his companions. Under cover of the noise of the train and keeping in small groups so as not to attract the attention of the guards, the prisoners discussed the possibility of escaping when night fell. The faint-hearted opposed the scheme, arguing that even if only a few attempted all would be shot summarily and that it would be foolish to exchange the almost certain comfort of an Oflag for so unpleasant a death. In the end the decision was left to Yeo-Thomas as senior officer and he naturally opted for escape. Roles were assigned to each man. As soon as it was dark the guards were to be strangled or killed with their own weapons. The prisoners would then jump out of the train in small groups of three or four and, taking care to keep out of the beams of the Oerlikon searchlight which would probably be sweeping the countryside, would, still in their small teams, make their way back to France. This plan had, however, to be abandoned when the dissidents informed Yeo-Thomas that they would warn the guards if he persisted in carrying it out. Forced to fasten their handcuffs again and await another opportunity, it was only fear of compromising the loyal which restrained Tommy and Robert Benoist from taking violent action against these men.

In any case the train stopped at a station before it was dark and the prisoners were transferred to another train. And at first it seemed that the uncooperative had been justified in their prudence: accompanied by all their guards and by the Feldgendarmerie officer the thirty-seven now sat in a real railway carriage with rows of unpartitioned seats in which they reclined at ease. The Feldgendarmerie officer who sat in one of the bays with Tommy, Hubble and a guard was so friendly that, after explaining the difference between the Intelligence Corps and the Intelligence Service, Hubble unpicked one of his Intelligence Corps flashes from his battle-dress and gave it to him as a souvenir. And when it turned out that the officer knew the vineyard owner, Julius Kayser, with whose family Hubble was distantly related, Yeo-Thomas was emboldened to ask if it was indeed to an Oflag that they were being transported.

No, said the Feldgendarmerie officer, they were not being taken to an Oflag, but to a very special kind of concentration camp where they would be treated as officers. There would be amusements, very little work, a band to cheer them with martial music and, who knew? perhaps a not too *farouche* girl friend or two. The name of this holiday camp was, so the Feldgendarmerie officer said, Buchenwald.

CHAPTER XIV

Buchenwald

About midnight their carriage was detached from the train and shunted along a side-line bordered by barbed-wire fences. On the platform of a station also surrounded by barbed wire an SS officer and SS guards were awaiting them. The Feldgendarmerie officer handed over to the SS officer a brief-case containing their documents and the latter took over command.

Under their new escort the prisoners were marched off through an unreal, pale, moonlit world. The ground crunched under their feet and occasionally there were weird howls from unseen dogs, but otherwise the night was silent and eerie. If the prisoners whispered among themselves the guards cursed them loudly and the night was silent again except for the gravelly sound made by their feet and the sinister moaning of the dogs. Faint lights appeared in the silver grey darkness and gradually grew brighter than the twinkling of the stars: they came from Miradors set up all round the camp in case any of the prisoners might be tempted to escape from the military bands or the girl friends.

The darkness of a square building with a tower was thrown up into the sky against the lesser darkness of the night, and the prisoners were halted in front of an iron gateway bathed in a pale mean light. Guttural words were exchanged between the NCO in charge of their escort and an unseen guard behind the ghostly gate. Then the gate was opened and they were marched into a large compound surrounded by low huts lying in darkness against a shimmering curtain of moonlight.

Here was awaiting them another escort, clad in what appeared to be a variant of the old Keystone comedy striped convict garb.

Handed over to these geometric gaolers, the prisoners were marched over rough ground past rows and rows of darkened huts sepulchral in their share of moon. Again the night was silent save for the occasional whine of a dog crying its antiphon of loneliness to the loneliness of the stars. The world was empty, empty, empty, but everywhere there was a feeling of hidden purgatorial hosts. In spite of the warmness of the summer night air Yeo-Thomas was chilled to the bone.

Light in this plain of macabre shadow came upon them with blinding suddenness, from electric bulbs hanging from the roof of a huge hall into which they were pushed by their warders, whose grotesque clothing they now saw clearly for the first time: clad in blue and white vertically striped suits and dark berets, these tough and expressionless officials wore black armbands on which was lettered in white 'LAGERSCHUTZE'; but, to make it quite plain that they, too, were men under authority, on their jackets and on their trousers were red triangles with numbers on white tapes sewn on below the triangles.

For the present, however, these Lagerschutze were the vicars of their vicious masters and exercising their portion of power. On an order from their leader, another expressionless ghoul with 'KAPO' on his armlet, the prisoners were led into a long room, made to lay their belongings on a long table and lie down on the cold tiled floor to sleep. No sooner had they done so than they were ordered to stand up again, undress and fold their clothing and pile it neatly on the table. When they had stood naked in line for about half an hour they were commanded to dress and lie down and sleep again. They had barely dropped off when the order came for them to strip once more. When Hessel protested at this senseless procedure the Kapo replied, looking at him out of glazed unlighted eyes which seemed to have seen so much sorrow that they could no longer reflect either joy or misery:

'Just obey orders, my friend. Don't ask any questions, my friend. This is a very dangerous place and the less that you will talk the better it will be for you. There are stool pigeons everywhere. Here you have no friends, my friend. Beware, my friend; continually beware.'

But this time the process was not without purpose. As soon as they had undressed they were marched into a large room fitted with shower baths, beneath which they washed themselves with a gritty, latherless soap. When they had dried themselves with rags they were moved on into another room, from whose ceiling a number of electric clippers hung on long wire. Under each clipper was a stool and behind each stool stood a striped barber, himself completely shorn except for a long tuft of hair running from his brow to the back of his head. Soon the prisoners were shorn too; from their heads to their feet the clippers were ploughed, removing every particle of hair on their bodies. From unshaven bandits with monster beards and moustaches they were transformed into meek-looking, egg-headed tonsured monks. Their bellies and their genitals were then painted white with an astringent liquid which stung their testicles for several days afterwards.

Looking more like savages now in their phosphorescent woad, they were taken to the quartermaster's store, where they were issued with their prison uniforms, multiform in their incongruity: Tommy received a pair of blue and white striped underpants with long lacing legs, a pair of old grey trousers tailored for a man six foot tall and weighing twenty stone, a faded blue mechanic's jacket with sleeves which came down to his elbows and a back which barely reached his waist, a striped forage cap, a pair of wooden clogs and a white nightshirt trimmed with red round the neck; Hubble got a too-short jacket and pair of trousers which made him resemble Larry Semon; and the rest were attired in other varieties of ill-fitting reach-me-downs. The only similar item in their outfit was their wooden clogs. As they made fun of one another's weird appearance the Lagerschutze looked on in silence, with unamused spectral faces.

A fellow Briton had also been watching their mirth with no trace of amusement on his face: he was Perkins, one of Colonel Buck-master's officers, and he warned the prisoners in much the same terms as the Kapo.

'You have little to laugh about,' he told them. 'This is one of the worst concentration camps in Germany. I just can't tell you how bad it is, but you'll soon find out for yourselves. The treatment is terrible and deaths can't be counted any more. For heaven's sake watch your step.' And he added another admonition: 'And don't let on that you are officers. And if any of you held any executive position in peacetime keep it to yourselves. The internal administration of the camp is in the hands of Communists, and they don't like either officers or capitalists.'

An opportunity for practising this reticence occurred almost at once, when they were paraded in front of a middle-aged and shifty-eyed Schreiber who filled out their identity forms in accordance with their answers to his questions. But Yeo-Thomas, Hubble, Southgate, Kane, Frager, Hessel, and a few others made no attempt to conceal their rank from the scrivener, who was manifestly disgusted by their admission. When he had noted their particulars this registrar issued them with number tapes and red triangles to sew on their jackets and trousers; Yeo-Thomas was given the number 14,624.

It was broad daylight by the time these processes were accomplished. As they were marched across the camp the prisoners had their first glimpse of their fellow inmates, and it was anything but reassuring. The compound was filled with emaciated, hairless wretches shuffling wearily round and round in heavy wooden clogs. The eyes of those listless sub-human creatures were mean with terror. On the faces of many of them a sticky stream of yellow rot oozed from purulent sores set in the middle of purple weals. Others were so weak that they staggered as they walked. Even when their clothes were too short for them they were too wide because of the thinness of the frail bodies which they covered. The same grim question occurred simultaneously to all the thirty-seven as they beheld this gruesome spectacle: 'how long is it going to be before we look like them?'

The new prisoners, too, had difficulty in walking, because they were not used to their loose-fitting clogs, and they stumbled and staggered across the rough stony ground. They were glad when they were halted before and then marched into a hut surrounded by barbed wire. On the outside of the hut was the number 17.

This hut was really not so much a hut as a block with wings. At the entrance was a small corridor, with a washing-room with troughs and a circular basin on one side and a lavatory with urinals and latrine pans on the other. The room in which the Blockältester took their names and numbers had also the appearances of public-school comfort: fitted with rows of lockers and furnished with a number of trestle tables, it had a partitioned-off cubicle – for the Blockältester. But their own dormitory, which was situated in another wing of the block, was much less luxurious and consisted of three tiers of long rows of bunks set two by two. Two men were to sleep in each bunk. The palliasses were only half-filled with straw and the blankets, of which there was only one to each bunk, were dirty and long enough to cover only half a man.

But even in this filthy flop-house they were not allowed to linger: during the day they had to remain outside the block. Within a minute of their exit they were surrounded by a mob of other prisoners, talking every man in a different tongue, in Russian, Polish, German, Rumanian, Spanish, Italian, Czech and French. The questions asked in the languages which they didn't understand were obviously the same as those asked in that which they did: who were they and why had they come to Buchenwald? When the newcomers replied that they were parachutists who had been captured by the Gestapo the impression created was tremendous, and the news of their heroism spread rapidly round the camp. From distant alleys thin bony creatures came tottering to gaze with watery-eyed admiration at those who had dared to strike a blow at the tyranny which was responsible for their own distress. Better-fed prisoners, in the striped livery of their privilege and with KAPO, VORARBEITER or LAGERSCHUTZ on their armlets, also called to pay their respects to the intrepid, and some of them even added the tribute of cigarettes, which the newcomers shared, four men to a cigarette, taking it in turns to have a puff.

Unlike the Lagerschutze who had supervised their initiation the night before, all these prisoners did not wear red triangles: some wore black or green or yellow or pink or violet, and those who wore red often wore also a qualifying F., R., T., P. or S. A Frenchman called Guignard explained the meanings of these markings: the red triangles without letters were worn by Germans and those with F., R., T., P. or S. by Frenchmen, Russians, Czechs, Poles or Spaniards; the black and green triangles denoted criminals condemned for common law offences, the yellow Jews, the pink homosexuals and the violet Jehovah's Witnesses, whose common misery had been brought about by very different misdemeanours.

Guignard also corroborated what Perkins had already told them, adding dismal details of his own. They were, he told them, in the worst camp in Germany. Their chances of survival were practically nil: if they did not starve to death they would be worked to death; and if they were not worked to death they would be executed. Every single day more than three hundred prisoners died from starvation or from being beaten by their guards while working in Kommandos. Each Kommando consisted of hundreds of prisoners quarrying stone, dragging logs or cleaning out latrines under the supervision of Kapos and Vorarbeiter. But the SS guards were also there and so were their Alsatian hounds, and when enough amusement couldn't be derived from bludgeoning a man's brains out there was always the alternative of setting the dogs upon him to tear out his throat.

They soon saw for themselves that these reports were not exaggerated. Walking up and down in the sunlight behind their barbed wire and conversing in makeshift esperanto with the other inmates of the Block, they remarked groups of SS men wandering about the camp. They noticed, too, that the prisoners tried to avoid them and that when they couldn't they politely removed their forage caps. But this salute did not prevent the guards beating up any prisoner whose appearance attracted their displeasure; and their new companions informed the thirty-seven that anyone attempting to resist this attention was punished either by death by shooting or strangulation or, if he were lucky, by twenty-five strokes on the small of the back with the handle of a pickaxe.

A squat black chimney just beyond the Block was pointed out to them. 'That's the crematorium,' they were told. 'It's the surest of all escape routes; most of us will only get out of this camp by coming through that chimney as smoke.'

Their predicament was indeed grave and Yeo-Thomas held a council of the thirty-seven to discuss the possibility of escape. In spite of the protests of the few who were still able to believe that wine, women and song or at least their austerity ersatz of beer, bitches and broadcasting lay just round the corner, a committee to direct the activities of three escape groups was formed: Yeo-Thomas took charge of one group, Southgate of another, and Frager and Benoist of the third. The committee undertook the time-honoured ritual of studying the lay-out of the camp and the measures of control operated by the guards. The findings of an immediate topographical reconnaissance, necessarily restricted to their own compound, which they were not allowed to leave, were pathetic: their Block was in a space between two other Blocks, the back of one of which overlooked the space; the other Block was on a slightly higher level, from which they concluded that the camp was built on a slope; the space itself was bordered at either end by barbed-wire fences; running alongside their own Block were two forlorn flower-beds filled with wilting daisies, most of whose petals had been removed by prisoners who smoked them.

They spent the whole of that day without food, the distribution of which they had missed while being disinfected and clothed. In the late afternoon they received a visit from Perkins and Burney, another 'F.' Section officer, from whom they learned that it was not only the SS whose habits they must study if they wished to escape from the camp. Among the prisoners, their visitors told them, there were all sorts of dissensions and intrigues, the adherents to one faction asking for nothing better than an opportunity to betray to their German masters the adherents to another. The chief civil strife was between the common law offenders and the political prisoners, each of which bodies was anxious to secure for itself the valuable prerogative of controlling the internal administration of the camp. This struggle was incessant, but for the present the Communists had prevailed over the cut-throats, and from the former they, as officers, could expect no help.

Perkins and Burney left before the Appell or evening roll call. For this the 380-odd prisoners in Block 17 were paraded behind their private barbed wire while the Blockältester went through the laborious process of counting them. They were then stood at ease, until an SS man in uniform and jackboots came swaggering into their compound. '*Mützen ab!*'[1] the Blockältester shouted, clicking his clogs and saluting the perky little representative of authority. As the prisoners stood capless before him the SS man passed along the front rank checking the Blockältester's count and punching the face of any prisoner whose appearance displeased him. As they watched this process the thirty-seven understood why their companions had seemed so eager to remain in the rear ranks; it was, on a larger scale, like the competition in the hoary old war to fall in second-from-the-left, but the advantages

1 'Caps off!'

of success were greater than that of never forming fours. When the SS man had finished his inspection the Blockältester shouted '*Mützen auf!*'[1] and the prisoners put on their caps again, and the parade was dismissed. After that delegates were allowed to visit the kitchen, just in case any food might be going.

Because Block 17 was considered a convalescence and isolation hut the thirty-seven had been exempted from the larger and much grimmer Appell which had taken place simultaneously on the main square of the camp. This, too, was a count and not an answering to the calling over of a nominal roll; as there were some 80,000 prisoners to be counted by SS guards with shaky arithmetic, it sometimes took as long as four hours, during which the prisoners were required to stand to attention, *mützen ab*, no matter what the weather. Moreover, so as not to tax the brainless tellers with a reconciliation of the camp state, it was a roll call for the dead as well as for the living. Stiff and cold, the corpses of those who that day had died of exhaustion or been murdered by their guards had to be held up by their feeble comrades who would soon be relying upon others to help themselves to answer the same ghastly '*Adsum*'.

More visitors came that evening to visit the parachutists. Among them was Colonel Manhès, a fire-eating French regular who had been arrested at the beginning of Tommy's first mission in 1943 and who, when he addressed his old friend by his right name, had to be informed that Yeo-Thomas was NOT repeat NOT Yeo-Thomas but DODKIN repeat DODKIN. Similar warnings had to be given to Commandant Julitte and Péry, whom Tommy had known in London and who were also surprised to find him among the terrorists on whom they too had called to leave their cards.

Before they went to bed that night the thirty-seven caused another sensation: after undressing with the others at 10 p.m. and piling their neatly folded clothes on the trestle tables in the so-called living-room they washed themselves from head to foot, and even Jehovah's Witnesses marvelled. Then in their shirts they pitter-pattered like little boys to their bunks and tried to make themselves as comfortable as they could in their beds, because there were two of them in each.

1 'Cape on!'

Tommy and Hubble shared a bunk, and, as both were broad, had to lie on their sides and 'when father said "turn" they all turned'. Their blanket was too skimpy to cover them either sideways or longways, but in spite of their discomfort they were able to fall asleep with a great hope in their hearts: that they would be able to last out until the liberating Allied Armies reached them, when this tyranny would be overpast.

Next morning they discovered that they were again among the privileged, although they did not yet know that their presence among the convalescent and the isolated was merely a precaution that they should not escape the highly unpleasant form of execution already prepared for them. '*Aufstehen*' for the rest of the prisoners, who had to hew stone and cart human dung under the lash of whips and the baying of wild dogs, was at 4 a.m.; for Block 17 there was no shouting until 6 a.m., when the thirty-seven once more astonished the devout and the devious by the thoroughness and the complexity of their ablutions. And even among the privileged the new contingent was privileged: their clothing was so worn and tattered that none of their new friends attempted to steal it.

Once more as they walked again in a new day behind their private barbed wire the daring discussed means of escape. Guignard called again, and Perkins and Burney came with a burly Dutch Naval officer called Peter Cool, who brought bread, which was divided out among all the members of the group. All these visitors considerably compromised their own safety by these visits, because the thirty-seven had already been officially proscribed as terrorists, untouchable even by the normally courageous Communists.

Later in the day, those who had brought bundles were allowed to visit the Effectenkammer and withdrew a few articles for their personal use. Although they naturally found that many of their possessions had already been stolen, Robert Benoist retrieved his razor and a few blades, and Hubble shaving soap, a pullover, a khaki shirt, which he gave to Yeo-Thomas, handkerchiefs, which he shared out among his friends, a pocket knife and his all-important pocket chess set.

To the further astonishment of the companions the thirty-seven celebrated this windfall by shaving in a body, taking it in turns to use Benoist's razor and Hubble's soap. Nor was this all. If cleanliness was next to godliness, a martial bearing, their committee decided, was next to cleanliness. Henceforth, the leaders ruled, when the group moved as a body, they would march in step and in column of fours; they would do, *gloria Monty*, physical exercises every morning and would always act in such a way as to maintain and improve the morale of those with whom they came in contact. All but the usual few dissenters accepted this decision, and soon the Block-altester, a Communist, was holding up the capitalists as an example to proletarian delinquents.

To prevent themselves from brooding, they began a chess tournament in which Tommy started out a likely winner. For those who could not play chess there was bridge, played, as cards were forbidden in the camp, with painted pieces of cardboard, of which they manufactured four packs; this diversion, however, could be indulged in only during the two hours after their scrappy lunch when they were allowed to use their dormitory, on the top bunks and with a couple of men keeping watch.

Close friendships were naturally formed among different members of the group. Hubble, Kane and Yeo-Thomas became almost inseparable and soon knew all about one another: Hubble spoke of his wife and children, Kane of his father, and Tommy, of course, of Barbara. Yeo-Thomas also grew to like very much Pickersgill and McAlister, whose lack of French was such that he had at first concluded that they had been left behind after the Dieppe raid, captured while trying to escape in civilian clothes and treated as spies; he found to his horror that the two Canadians had indeed been parachuted into France as agents in spite of their almost total ignorance of the language.

Thanks to the collusion of Perkins, Burney and Cool, the thirty-seven later, but only occasionally, were all to visit the rest of the camp. Yeo-Thomas, Hubble and Kane eagerly used the first of these opportunities to extend their abortive preliminary reconnaissance. The results were even more depressing: not only was the barbed wire by which the camp was surrounded electrified, but the outside of the enclosure was constantly patrolled; and the Miradors all had machine-guns trained on the camp and powerful searchlights. There appeared to be no hope at all of getting out under the wire; a ruse for smuggling arms into the camp and fighting their way out seemed the only possibility of escape. And escape they must if they were not to become like the skinny, fleshless sub-men they kept meeting, shambling along and gazing at them sideways out of terror-stricken eyes.

The more they examined the camp, the more they realised the urgency of their plight. They saw the Revier (hospital), from which few ever emerged alive. They saw, too, Revier Block 50, where the experimental vaccines were manufactured and the grim appendant Block 46, known as the 'Guinea Pig Block', where, under the super-vision of Sturmbannführer (Major) Ding-Schuler and his Kapo, prisoners were inoculated with typhus and other germs and their reactions, almost always ending in death, under the various vaccines studied.

They visited the main square where the gruesome Appell took place, and the adjacent Pathological Block. Facing this Block, on the other side of the square, was the entrance to the camp surmounted by its tower; on either side of the tower was a wing lined with steel shutters inside which were the Bunkers or punishment cells.

There was also a cinema in the camp where German propaganda films were exhibited and, so that even walls might not escape their turn of tears, prisoners beaten up. The brothel, called the Sonderbau, was the only place where pleasure was unadulterated, perhaps because it was brief: there, for the sum of two marks, Kapos, Vorarbeiter and non-class-conscious SS could find fugitive ecstasy in the sweaty embrace of prostitutes or apathetic volunteers seconded from the concentration camp at Ravensbruck. Perhaps it was of this establish-ment that the Feldgendarmerie officer had been thinking when he had spoken of girl friends. At any rate in one respect he had not lied: there was, indeed, a military band whose musicians, garbed in the gold-braided uniform of the Yugoslav Royal Guard and clogs, tooted out of trumpets *Die Wacht am Rhein* to the greater glory of the thousand-year empire which had only another eight months to run.

Perhaps, because only God could make one, in the whole camp there was only one large tree, called Goethe's tree; the superstitious said that when it fell it would be a sign that Germany was doomed.

But there was an inner circle of misery: if conditions in the main camp were bad those in the lesser camp were worse. In the latter there were no 'permanent' buildings but only long, low, windowless huts and tents. In the huts, instead of bunks, there were three or four tiers of shelves split up into compartments in which three men had to sleep in a space designed, under a norm of cruelty, for one. In the tents there were neither shelves nor floor; and in each of them the space was so cramped that three hundred or more men had to sleep squatting on the ground, which in wet weather was like a quagmire, with their knees drawn up under their chins. Neither in the huts nor in the tents were there enough blankets, and the tenants, who were mostly Jews, were systematically starved: every day hundreds of lean, famished men yelped, squealed and grunted as they kicked and clawed one another in the struggle to get at a few pounds of potato peelings or to scrape the grease from the bottom of a cookhouse canister.

The reconnaissance party was naturally depressed when it returned to Block 17, and fortunately other visitors soon called to cheer them up. The Newton brothers, two Englishmen employed as batmen by their Blockältester, came and, introduced by Commandant Julitte, Professor Balachowski of the Institut Pasteur in Paris, who, with his thick and wavy dark hair, was one of the few unshorn prisoners in Buchenwald. Balachowski owed this privilege to the fact that he worked in Block 50 on the production of anti-typhus vaccines. With him Yeo-Thomas, Kane, Benoist and Hubble became friendly and later, when they had been given the freedom of the camp, were invited by him to Block 50 to partake of rabbit, which tasted none the less delicious for having been previously used in a typhus experiment. Nor was the rabbit the only gift they received from their visitors: an artist came too and drew portraits of Yeo-Thomas and others. And, not to be outdone in courtesy, the three chief internal administrators of the camp called, Lagerältester I and II and the very unoperatic Kapo of the barbers: all were Communists and, from their excessive courtesy, it was quite clear that capitalist officers, who had battened on the misery of sergeants-major and the fatherless, had no help to hope for from them.

Perhaps the Germans knew that none of the thirty-seven could succeed in escaping if Figaro and his colleagues were unfriendly, for soon they were allowed to move about the camp more or less as they liked. When together they marched in step, for this was now the only hymn by which they could honour their calling, but they dispersed at the approach of German soldiers, so as not to be forced to salute them.

From Burney and his friends they obtained thirty-six marks, which they used as a common fund for the purchase of cigarettes and watery beer from the prisoners' canteen. Each cigarette had to be shared among three men and sometimes four, because crafty Ukrainians, under pretext of obtaining a light, often sucked through paper tubes rolled to look like cigarettes a goodly portion of their benefactors' smoke.

But whatever the Germans might think of their chances of escape Yeo-Thomas was determined to explore every possibility. Both the Polish and the Russian prisoners of war, interned in Buchenwald contrary to international convention, had good underground intelligence networks, and with the aid of Kane, who spoke Bulgarian, he got in touch with two Russian colonels: one was a tall, white-haired ex-artillery officer of the Imperial Army and the other a broad, squat rather boorish Mongol from a Tank regiment who, because he was also a Political Commissar, exercised the greater authority. These representatives of the old polite rotten world and the new rude rotten world shared as orderly a slim, handsome young Georgian to whom, as he spoke both French and English, Tommy was able to explain the urgency of their needs. With Kane tackling the high-ups and Yeo-Thomas their lieutenant, they soon managed to elaborate one of those hopeless plans which can be concocted only by the truly desperate. When the Russians agreed that it was not absolutely impossible to have arms smuggled into the camp, Tommy and Kane were convinced that Stens, grenades and sub-machine guns were already in their possession. After two or three meetings, at which the British were invited to share their hosts' more elaborate POW rations, Saxons and Slavs had agreed to divide up their groups into units of ten which, under the command of an officer or NCO, would fight their way out of the camp when the signal was given. In earnest of this pledge the aristocratic Russian colonel presented Yeo-Thomas with an old leather belt so that his too loose trousers might not lend a temporary advantage to the enemy by falling down in public on the day of victory.

From Sasha, the orderly, whom he came to know well, Yeo-Thomas learned of the perhaps not wholly incomprehensible lies current about Britain in Russia.

'You must belong to the nobility and be very wealthy,' Sasha said to him one day.

Tommy, remembering perhaps the days when he had slogged at other people's accounts for fifteen hundred francs a month, laughed.

'What makes you say that?' he asked.

'You are wishing to deceive me. You think that we know nothing in Russia. You are wrong. We know many things in Russia. We know that in England officers must buy their commissions and it is clear, therefore, that you must belong to the privileged classes.'

'That is simply not true,' Tommy said. 'And the proof is that I myself started out in this war as a ranker.'

'I do not wish to be rude to you, but I cannot believe that. That is not what we are told in Russia. And in England the ordinary soldiers are not allowed to walk on the pavements when they pass officers and they must also allow their wives to sleep with the officers if the officers wish.'

And even when Yeo-Thomas had explained all about OCTUs and second-lieutenants being court-martialled for impropriety when they winked at a private in the ATS, Sasha still seemed to prefer to believe the truth which he had learned in Russia.

Poor Sasha, he went to his death shortly afterwards, little shaken, no doubt, in his conviction that the Western democracies were cemented with deceit and privilege instead of riddled with a rather touching stupidity. For this, and not the atom bombs which the Kremlin now possesses, is the strength of Communism: the power to turn decent young men and women into fanatics and martyrs for a wrong cause. And fanatics and martyrs for a wrong cause will never be conquered except by fanatics and martyrs for a right cause, who live not by NAAFI and PX alone but by the rather uncomfortable words which proceed out of the mouth of God. Fanatics are not made by talking threadbare balderdash about 'the British Way of Life', which means anything from tarts on Piccadilly to the litany on Wednesdays and Fridays via football pools and the erudition of the *New Statesman*; and martyrs are not mustered by a call to defend a Christianity in which leading national ecclesiastics themselves claim to have blown holes. 'I like to think of God as a vast oblong blur,' a more than ordinarily nonsensical American clergyman said in the 1920s. Stalin was clever enough to know that men do not willingly die for blurs.

On the afternoon of 24 August Allied aircraft flew in over

Buchenwald on their way to the Gustloff factory opposite the garage of the SS barracks and the Deutsche Rüstungswerke, whose buildings touched the perimeter of the camp. As soon as the air-raid alarm went the prisoners were confined to their Blocks, but the Ältester of Block 17 was indulgent enough to allow the thirty-seven to stand where they could get a good view. Shining like lovely moths in the sunshine, the bombers closed in with an illusory benevolence to drop their deadly load on the factories, which they flattened completely. At first no bombs fell on the camp, but when incendiaries started small fires in several of the Blocks, including Block 17, the SS and the German Lagerschutze panicked and began shouting contradictory commands, now ordering the prisoners to run to the small camp, now ordering them to remain where they were. The thirty-seven, forgetting their own danger, remained where they were, cheering as they saw the bombs fall and the smoke rise in black plumes against the pale blue patience of the waiting sky. Yeo-Thomas, practical even in pleasure, kept a special watch to see if the barbed wire was cut at any point.

The barbed wire was not cut, and the prisoners' jubilation soon changed to sorrow when they saw the dead and wounded among their fellows hoisted on to stretchers, carts and planks. Of the guards about 80 had been killed and 300 wounded, but the prisoners had suffered much more heavily: nearly 400 had been killed and 1,450 wounded, of whom 600 seriously: among the last was Princess Mafalda of Italy, who, there being no women's hospital in the camp, died in the arms of a prostitute in the brothel; her body was then thrown naked on to the stock pile and burned with the others in the crematorium. Once again the just had suffered more than the unjust.

Perhaps the fact that an incendiary had damaged Goethe's tree badly put SS officers and men on edge. 'A British Air Force officer, eh?' the SS Hauptsturmführer with the Totenkopf badges on his sleeves sneered at Yeo-Thomas when he paraded after a medical inspection in the cinema. 'The Luftwaffe sweeps them from the sky.' 'I didn't see anything but flak the other day,' Tommy answered with unwise bravado. The SS men avenged their fright with deeds: one of them, Krautwurst, pushed a particularly frail prisoner into a pit full of faeces from the latrines and, when the poor wretch tried to pull himself out, stamped with his jackboots on his fingers and skull until he drowned.

This savage desire for revenge became more and more evident. The water pipes damaged by the bombardment had scarcely been repaired when more than 170 British and American airmen arrived in Buchenwald and were herded together in the small camp, without food, blankets or shelter. Their senior officer, Squadron Leader Lamason, a New Zealander with the battered-looking nose of a boxer, protested angrily to the Camp Commandant Pister and his assistant Schobert that such treatment was contrary to the rules of war, as they had all been taken in fair fight. But Pister and Schobert would have none of it: the airmen were not airmen but terror-flyers and as such were murderers and liable to summary execution.

These airmen were squatting miserably on the only cobbled space in the small camp when Yeo-Thomas, in search of more allies, called to see them. In spite of having passed a bitterly cold night in the open the newcomers were cheerful. Lamason and Yeo-Thomas hit it off immediately and together they visited the two Russian colonels, who organised among their prisoners-of-war a collection of blankets, clothes and clogs for the airmen.

To Yeo-Thomas the arrival of these new recruits for his army seemed providential. Not only with a potential of more than 200 men at his disposal was he now in a better position to bargain with the Russians, but the fact that the majority were trained flyers appeared little short of miraculous. About twelve miles from Buchenwald, he had recently learned, was a small and poorly guarded airfield called Nohra. Provided they could fight their way out of Buchenwald, he was soon persuading Lamason, there would be little to prevent their attacking the airfield, seizing the bombers and flying back to the Allied lines. The combined forces of themselves and the Russians would be divided up into units of ten, this time not according to nationality, but with a pilot, navigator, air-gunner, engineer and radio operator in each team. Lamason, as hot-headed as Tommy, readily agreed. There seemed to be only two stumbling-blocks: one was the presence in Lamason's group of a so-called American flyer suspected to have been planted there as a stool pigeon, and who would require to be kept in ignorance of their plans and watched; and the other was the lack of arms. But even the latter was not insuperable: there were, Yeo-Thomas had also discovered, arms in the camp, but only the Communist leaders knew where they were concealed, and so far all his attempts to make them divulge this secret had failed.

Then suddenly, on 9 September, the blow fell. Over the camp loudspeaker came the command: '*Achtung! Achtung! Achtung! Die folgenden Gefangenen von Block 17 müssen sich sofort beim Turm melden*.'[1] Hubble, Kane, Benoist, Allard, Defendini, Detal, Leccia, McAlister, Mayer, McKenzie, Garel, Garry, Geelen, Pickersgill, Rechenmann, Steele. *Achtung! Achtung! Achtung! Die folgenden Gefangenen von Block 17 müssen sich sofort beim Turm melden: Hubble, Kane, Benoist . . .*' The sixteen of them were to report to the Tower at once.

At first neither the summoned nor their comrades were greatly alarmed: they thought that it was just some sort of identity check although, in case there might be a search of their persons as well, Hubble left his penknife and his pipe in the care of Yeo-Thomas. The sixteen fell in gaily enough in front of the Block and marched off in column of fours, keeping in step to the greater glory of Great Britain and France, whose very proud sons they were.

When he had watched them right wheel in the direction of the Tower, Yeo-Thomas went back into the living-room. The expression on the Blockältester's face as he sat in his cubicle frightened him and, through Hessel, he asked the man why he thought his comrades had been called to the Tower.

The Blockältester did not beat about the bush. 'I do not think that you will ever see any of them again,' he said. 'When prisoners are called to the Tower in that way they never come back. They are executed. It is always the same for spies and terrorists. Sooner or later all of you will be called to the Tower that way and none of you will come back. I am sorry that it should be so, because you are good men who have done your duty and I like you.'

After that there was nothing to do but go outside and hope, in the mockery of the lovely summer morning sun, that the Blockältester might be wrong. For the present, as they did not wish to alarm the others, Tommy and Hessel kept the bad news secret, telling only Southgate, Frager and Peulevé and, eventually, Lamason.

---

1 'Attention! Attention! The following prisoners from Block 17 must report to the Tower immediately . . .'

Even when the sixteen failed to turn up for Appell in the evening they still went on pretending that there was nothing wrong. That night, even although he had his bunk to himself, Yeo-Thomas could not sleep. He had come to love Hubble and Kane as he had loved Brossolette. Were they too to be taken from him? He prayed that God might be merciful and stay the hand of the enemy and let the sixteen men live.

Next morning there was news: a member of the Polish organisation whom Yeo-Thomas contacted in the small camp told him that the sixteen had been thrown into bunkers after being beaten up but were still alive. In the evening the news was slightly better: the sixteen had been seen out for a walk but had been taken back to the bunkers. But the morning after when Yeo-Thomas again met his Polish friend in the small camp the Pole stood to attention and saluted:

'I am sorry to have to tell you that your sixteen comrades were executed last night. There can be no doubt: one of our organisation has seen their bodies. They were brave men and we grieve for you.' The Pole then told Tommy of the manner of his friends' death: they had been hung by hooks in the wall of the crematorium and allowed to perish by slow strangulation; their corpses had been burned in the furnaces and the chimney had belched smoke all night.

Tommy could not speak. For a few minutes he stood in silence. Then with tears in his eyes he turned and walked back to his Block. On his way he met a prisoner wearing an old British Army cap; in exchange for his own forage cap and a piece of bread he obtained this symbol and stuck it proudly on his head: when his turn came to die by slow strangulation he would go to his doom wearing at least a part of the uniform he loved so dearly.

Balachowski was waiting for him in Block 17: he had brought Hubble's note-book, which had fallen out of his pocket after he was dead, and he had already told Southgate and Frager the sad news. There could no longer be any doubt: the thirty-seven had now become twenty-one. Yeo-Thomas then summoned the others and told them what had happened, and warned them that a similar end almost certainly awaited them all. 'And because we shall have to die slowly it is all the more important that we die bravely,' he said. When they gasped and choked and struggled on the hook their pain would be not only their own pain, but that of Great Britain and France as well, and they must bear it nobly. For this was his ethic, and about it he never cheated or compromised.

In the evening the belongings of the dead were distributed among the quick: Tommy got Hubble's pipe and insisted on keeping also his chess set, just in case he should still manage to escape and be able to carry it home to Hubble's children.

During the next few days, however, it became more than ever clear that neither he nor any of them would be able to escape. In spite of all his efforts he could not obtain any definite information about the arms which he had heard were concealed in the camp. Julitte warned him that his plans were foolhardy and bound to end in failure, the two Russian colonels were fearful and even the doughty Lamason was hesitant. And on the evening of 14 September came the news through the Dutch organisation that further executions were imminent.

Yeo-Thomas knew now that he was going to die, and he wrote farewell letters to Colonel Dismore and Barbara for Balachowski to have smuggled out of the camp. Later, thinking that it was his duty to communicate to his Government the very important information he had found out about Buchenwald and to make one last effort to save them all, he coded one last desperate signal.

It was, perhaps, fitting that a doomed White Rabbit should compose his last official telegram in a cellar lined with hutches in which were other doomed rabbits. For it was in the Pathological Block, in which he and Peulevé had been hidden by Balachowski, that he drafted in his old Seahorse code which would prove the authenticity of his message the following:

INVALUABLE DOCUMENTS CONCERNING LATEST RESEARCH AND DISCOVERIES BACTERIOLOGICAL WARFARE KEPT HERE AT BUCHENWALD STOP ALL PREPARED TO SECURE THEM BUT CAN SUCCEED ONLY PROVIDING RAPID ASSISTANCE ARRIVES JUST BEFORE OR IMMEDIATELY UPON GERMAN CAPITULATION AS CAMP OFFICIALS WILL TRY TO DESTROY ALL STOP VALUE OF DOCUMENTS WARRANTS EVERY EFFORT STOP SPEEDY ARRIVAL AIRBORNE OR PARATROOPS ESSENTIAL WILL FIND ORGANISED ASSISTANCE WITHIN CAMP BUT I HAVE NO ARMS STOP BEARER THIS MESSAGE

TRUSTWORTHY AND KNOWS EVERYTHING WILL FIND ORGANISED
ASSISTANCE WITHIN CAMP ACKNOWLEDGE BY IODOFORM[1] DU
MOINEAU AU LAPIN STOP HAVE EVERYTHING UNDER CONTROL
AND HOPE FOR EARLY VICTORY STOP VINGT CINQ SEPTEMBRE
STOP ALL MY LOVE BARBARA TOMMY STOP CHEERIO DIZZY
ASYMPTOTE

Accompanying this cyphered signal was a letter in clear, counter-
signed by Hessel, to the Intelligence Officers at the Allied Headquarters
to which it was hoped both the signal and the letter would be
delivered.

> Bearer is trusted messenger. We have important and valuable docu-
> ments of considerable value to Allies. Please transmit urgently to
> London attached coded message and convey the reply to bearer for
> onward transmission to me. The matter is of considerable importance
> and delay may mean disaster to us all as well as to documents.

He had drawn a long bow and, as he knew that he would very likely
be dead before the arrow reached its destination, he had made
arrangements for a sort of apostolic succession of Allied Resistance to
be continued at Buchenwald after his execution. The signal and the
letter, bound in the cover of a book, were smuggled out of the camp by
a German called Hans Baumeister who had been imprisoned for
opposing the Nazi regime; but they did not reach the 'trusted
messenger' in Dortmund till December, and he had to await the
arrival of the American troops before he could hand them on.

Then, when Tommy's despair was at its blackest, hope suddenly
dawned once more, through a cluster of very complicated clouds.

Through the agency of Balachowski a meeting was arranged
between Yeo-Thomas and Eugen Kogon, the Austrian Catholic secretary of Himmler's personal friend, Ding-Schuler, the Sturmbannführer
of Block 46, where the typhus experiments were conducted. At this
meeting Kogon agreed to approach his master with the warning that
as an Allied victory was now certain it was time for him to take

---

1 Message in BBC French Service.

precautions for his own safety; and to suggest that, in return for a promise from Yeo-Thomas to testify on his behalf at the war crimes trials, he should agree to save the lives of the remaining twenty-one prisoners in Block 17 by substituting their identities for those of other prisoners who died of typhus in the Guinea Pig Block. Before undertaking this mission, however, Kogon pointed out that it might not be possible to save all twenty-one of them, as the substitutions would have to be staggered and orders for further executions were liable to be given at any time. To this possible modification Tommy gave his consent, stipulating only that salvation should be by juniority, with himself as senior officer bringing up the rear.

Once again it was a shot in the dark, but this time it hit bang on the target. Within half an hour Yeo-Thomas learned that Ding-Schuler had accepted and with great glee in his heart he set about drawing up a nominal roll in order of juniority with his own name last on the list. For security reasons, however, he kept the good news to himself and it was fortunate that he did so, because shortly afterwards Balachowski arrived to tell him that Ding-Schuler had had second thoughts and would agree to save only three men of whom Yeo-Thomas must be one. To Yeo-Thomas's reply that he insisted upon the three men being the three most junior Ding-Schuler countered that Yeo-Thomas was not in a position to make conditions and that if he wished any men at all to be saved he himself, who as senior officer could speak most competently in Ding-Schuler's defence, must be of the number. After further argument Yeo-Thomas was forced reluctantly to yield, but even Balachowski's scheme for saving another three officers by securing their admission to the TB section of the hospital failed to soothe his sense of guilt.

Ding-Schuler made another condition, and that was that the complicity of the Kapo of the Guinea Pig Block, whom he wished to be kept for the present in ignorance of his own part in the plot, be obtained separately. Once again Hans Baumeister, who was friendly with the Kapo, came to the rescue and succeeded, in return for a promise of testimony from the prisoners on his behalf, in persuading him to help. In spite of the fact that he, like his master, was likely to be called to account on the day of judgment, it was surprising that the Kapo should have been willing to take such a tremendous risk: because of his privileged position in Block 46 the Kapo was untouchable and could, if he refrained from frustrating the designs of the Gestapo, survive unharmed until the Camp was liberated by the Allies from whom, as a prisoner who had always acted under authority, he would have very much less to fear than Ding-Schuler.

Kogon then acquainted Yeo-Thomas with the details of the plan: the three prisoners, taking care that nobody observed them entering or leaving, were to go to the Guinea Pig Block where the Kapo would give them each an injection productive of a high fever; returning to their own Block, they would report sick next morning to the hospital, where they would state their symptoms, making a point of adding that they also suffered from lice, which were the greatest carriers of typhus germs; the Kapo would then arrive as though by chance, diagnose typhus, and have them taken to Block 46, from which nobody would expect to see them emerge alive.

Yeo-Thomas was now faced with the very disagreeable task of choosing who were to be his two companions: Southgate and two others were to be saved by Balachowski's TB scheme, which meant that seventeen remained, of whom he had to condemn fifteen to almost certain death. Nor was there any possibility of easing his conscience by drawing lots because on security grounds it was essential that only he himself should know of the plan. With heaviness in his heart he sat in Block 17, looking at his comrades, watching their familiar faces, listening to their familiar voices. From them he had to choose one Briton and one Frenchman, but how could he, knowing the anxieties and the conditions of each one of them, decide who was to be the Briton and who was to be the Frenchman? Which Briton was to see the big red buses running up Regent Street again and which Frenchman change again at the Concorde for the Champs Elysées? And which Britons and which Frenchmen were to twist to death in agony struggling in the noose of a cruelly adjusted rope? Praying that wisdom might be upon him, he began by eliminating the selfish, the grumblers and the unco-operative. Then when those that remained were all of a virtue he played in the silence of his mind a game equivalent to the drawing of lots: and from the invisible twirling wheels the names of Peulevé and Hessel emerged.

Although he intimated this selection to Balachowski, Kogon and

Baumeister, for the present he said nothing to the two men concerned for fear that the Kapo might be double-crossing them and he might arouse false hopes. To make sure that the Kapo didn't revenge an approach which he had every right to regard as an impertinence by injecting the three of them with typhus and killing them, he evolved a stratagem by which, without the Kapo suspecting that he was suspected, he himself should be injected alone first and then, if all were well, the others; it was the nearest he could get to being last man to leave the ship.

And when towards the end of September he bared his arm to the Kapo in the Guinea Pig Block he felt that he had been wise to take these precautions. The man's appearance was frightening: his thin lips, kept grimly shut in a straight line, looked as though they had never smiled; his expressionless face tapered down from a broad forehead into a thin, pointed chin; his eyes were grey and cold and hard; and his shaven skull glistened like a paving-stone under the manipulated surgical light. No words were exchanged between them, because the Kapo had no French or English and Yeo-Thomas no German. The needle of a large syringe containing a colourless liquid was plunged into a vein on the inside of Tommy's elbow, the puncture was dabbed with alcohol and the ceremony was complete. When the Kapo had made sure that the coast was clear the patient left the Block and returned to his own quarters.

It was now time to take Peulevé and Hessel partially into his confidence. Calling them aside, Yeo-Thomas told them, under pledge of absolute secrecy, that he had evolved a plan of escape; they must not be surprised when he disappeared the next day and when he sent them back instructions through Balachowski they were to obey without asking any questions.

Two hours later he broke out in a sweat, and all night long he tossed in his bunk with a raging fever. Next morning he reported sick to the Blockältester, who ordered a Czech doctor prisoner to take his temperature; it was 40.7 centigrade. Alarmed, the Czech suggested that he should take Yeo-Thomas over to the hospital for examination, and the Blockältester readily agreed. And, knowing that, whether the Kapo had or had not double-crossed him, he would never come back. Tommy took his possessions with him: among them was Hubble's chess set.

In the hospital everything happened according to plan. When describing his symptoms Tommy said that he also suffered from lice. While he was being examined the Kapo turned up, looked into his eyes and felt his pulse, diagnosed typhus and ordered his immediate transfer to Block 46. The Czech doctor fled in consternation; and Yeo-Thomas, escorted by the Kapo and avoided by all who deduced his malady from his company, walked the two hundred yards which separated the clean from the unclean.

But whatever might be said about the inmates purdah itself was antiseptic, and much more comfortable than the other Blocks. Instead of dormitories with dirty bunks there were beds with clean sheets and pillows and blue and white coverlets, and in the washing room there were baths. What in Block 17 had been the living-room was here a laboratory with a padlocked mortuary chamber opening out of it, so that even death itself seemed tidy.

The nurses, however, were striped and not starched, male and not female, and their badge of efficiency the green triangle of burglars and assassins. Under the care of two of them Yeo-Thomas was undressed and put into a bath in which he wallowed contentedly while his clothes were taken away to be destroyed; it was his first bath for more than six months, and in spite of his high fever he enjoyed it greatly. He enjoyed also the clean bed in an empty ward into which he was made to climb in a long white nightgown; but he enjoyed it less when one of the nurses told him that the ward on the other side of the passage had twenty patients in it, all of whom had been inoculated with typhus germs and all of whom would probably die. With his teeth chattering, his limbs trembling and the ward swimming before his eyes, Tommy began to be very afraid.

Shortly afterwards the Kapo came in, wearing the white linen ephod of a surgeon. He felt Yeo-Thomas's pulse, took his temperature and shook his head gravely. '*Fleckfieber*,' he murmured to the two attendant orderlies, who immediately rushed out and returned with an india-rubber sheet and an ordinary sheet soaked in icy-cold water. The rubber sheet was inserted under the patient on the bed, and the soaked one wrapped around him and he was left to shiver. He underwent this treatment several times until in the evening his fever had left him; but when the orderlies had gone for a moment the Kapo came back and gave him another injection and soon his temperature was soaring again.

He knew now that the Kapo was not double-crossing him, but was only making sure that the evidences of his distemper should be real enough to convince the orderlies. And so he was not alarmed when the latter, impressed by his new rise in temperature, ran in agitation to fetch the Kapo, who, examining him with concern, ordered a renewal of the soaked-sheet treatment. This he bore with equanimity, even although it continued all that night and all the next day; and when, on the third day, his temperature again normal, the Kapo brought him a note from Kogon to ask if all was well he scrawled across it with the intermediary's pencil: 'OK; the others can come.' Next day Peulevé and Hessel, inoculated in their turn, sweated and shivered beside him in the same ward.

The Kapo then had the two male nurses transferred to other duties in another Block while they were still under the impression that their patients were going to die; in this way he both protected himself and ensured that the bad news would be spread throughout the camp. As soon as the orderlies had gone, Yeo-Thomas, Peulevé and Hessel were smuggled into a large room above the ward. This room, divided into two by a row of cupboards, was used half as an office, half as a bedroom by a Dutchman called Schalker and a Pole called Gadzinski, both of whom worked in the Block and were friends of Kogon and Balachowski; in the bedroom part there were three extra beds, and in these the three fugitives slept.

Here they were kept in close confinement: they could not risk being seen by any of the other inmates of the Block and, in case they might be recognised from outside, had to duck when passing in front of the windows. This last precaution was not without its advantages, for although their room was a room with a view, it was one which would have chilled Mr E. M. Forster: at the back of the Block was the small camp, where the Jews rotted to death in hunger and cold; and on the other side of their private wire was a long low wooden hut in which more than 1,200 emaciated wretches were dying on their feet because there was no room for them to die on the ground.

For part of the day they helped Schalker and Gadzinski to plot the progress charts of prisoners who had been inoculated with disease; the switchbacks of those grim graphs almost always ended in a cross, which was the only symbol of mercy accorded to the sufferers. So that they could keep up with the war news Kogon sent them the not always inaccurate communiqué of Oberkommando der Wehrmacht, and for the rest of the time they played games: bridge, crapette, halma, and an extra-liturgical variant of ludo which they baptised 'silly buggers'. The Kapo also brought them French and English books, and occasionally tobacco and cigarettes.

The Kapo was indeed a strange man, a victim of circumstances perhaps, and through Hessel's interpretations they came to know him better and even to like him. He had already been a prisoner for twenty years and it was perhaps his own familiarity with discipline which led him to be so remorseless with others. For he ruled the Guinea Pig Block with a rod as iron as that with which he himself was ruled: when his masters ordered him to inject a prisoner with typhus or poison he did so and he mercilessly and accurately observed their sufferings, making perhaps a vice of necessity. And yet to Yeo-Thomas, Peulevé and Hessel he always kept his word, and to help them he risked more than his life. He was in love with one of the women in the camp and married her after the war.

Sturmbannführer Ding-Schuler, who had now reached an under-standing with the Kapo, was a youngish man with a weak chin and mouth, and a round, pink, babyish complexion. He was shining and elegant in his SS uniform when Yeo-Thomas went to meet him in the Kapo's office.

'So you are Dodkin?' he asked in English.

'And your senior in rank,' Tommy said.

Sturmbannführer Ding-Schuler clicked his heels and stood to attention before the prisoner in his striped garb; he was making sure of getting into the new disorder on the ground floor.

'I have risked my life to help you, and I hope that you are grateful,' he said.

Tact has never been Tommy's strong point and, forgetting that he was still at Ding-Schuler's mercy, he talked to him just as though he had been an Air Commodore too cushioned in custom to appreciate the potential of French Resistance.

'You would be risking your life even more certainly if you did not help me,' he said. 'You know as well as I do that nothing can save Germany now. You will be tried for your crimes and hanged. But if you help us we shall testify on your behalf, and then perhaps you will be given a lesser punishment. And it's not only for our own safety that I am asking you. I also want you to promise me to save all important documents and information and hand them over to the Allies: results of research on typhus, bacteriological warfare and poisons; plans of the underground factories, the identities of the men you have killed or who have died, everything.'

Ding-Schuler, because he was Ding-Schuler, promised; and Yeo-Thomas, because he was Yeo-Thomas, was not surprised.

It remained now for Yeo-Thomas, Peulevé and Hessel to exchange their identities for those of three prisoners who had died of typhus. This was not as easy as it had at first appeared. Most of the prisoners inoculated with typhus were Russians or Germans and these were unsatisfactory for two reasons; none of the three could speak Russian and only Hessel could speak German, and the Germans so treated were almost all criminals whose misdeeds, obligatorily kept secret in Buchenwald, might later lead to the scaffold those who assumed their identity.

Fortunately there had recently arrived in the camp a convoy of prisoners who had been working on fortifications in West Germany. Many of them had contracted typhus and were now segregated in a special ward in the Revier. On the pretext of preventing an epidemic the Kapo secured their transfer to Block 46: among them three Frenchmen, Maurice Chouquet, Marcel Seigneur and Michel Boitel, were on the point of death, and with them it was arranged that Yeo-Thomas, Peulevé and Hessel should exchange identities.

But the three Frenchmen put up a good fight for their lives, and the candidates for their names were insistent that everything should be done to save them. And on 4 October, while the struggle was still going on, there came over the camp loudspeaker the long delayed and dreaded announcement:

'*Die folgenden Gefangenen von Block 17 müssen sich sofort beim Turm melden: Barrett, Corbusier, Chaignot, Frager, Gerard, Loison, Mulsant, de Seguier, Vellaud, Wilkinson, Peulevé. Die folgenden Gefangenen . . .*'

The situation was alarming: none of the three Frenchmen showed any signs of dying immediately and Ding-Schuler was absent in Weimar. Nor did the pitilessness of the Camp Commandant Ober-führer Pister make matters easier: informed that one of the condemned men was ill with typhus in the Guinea Pig Block, Pister ordered that he should be brought immediately to the place of execution and be destroyed with the others. An appeal for clemency on the grounds that the execution would be an unnecessary cruelty practised on an already dying man was refused. And to his horror the Kapo learned that Pister was sending round an SS NCO to take delivery of the sick man on a stretcher. The danger was immediate, and not only to Peulevé: for even the inexpert eyes of the executioners would see that Peulevé was not suffering from typhus, and their plot would be exposed.

The Kapo, however, was a man of resource: on the arrival of the SS NCO at the Block, he contrived to be out and the NCO, afraid to enter the plague house, went away. Returning as soon as the NCO had gone, the Kapo gave Peulevé a super-injection which sent him flying into a delirium, and had him carried down to the ward where the real typhus cases lay. When the NCO came back again he refused to hand over Peulevé, on the grounds that he could not do so without an order from Sturmbannführer Ding-Schuler, who alone had authority over Block 46 and who was absent in Weimar. In the meantime Kogon and Baumeister telephoned Ding-Schuler, who came rushing back from Weimar on his motor bicycle to find that Pister had now sent an ambulance to fetch Peulevé.

The interview between Ding-Schuler and Pister was stormy: Ding-Schuler protested that it would be inhuman to execute a dying man with a temperature of 41 centigrade. Pister roared back that neither he nor Ding-Schuler were in Buchenwald to practise benevolence, but to carry out the orders of their superiors; these orders were that Peulevé was to be summarily executed and there was no reason why even a dying man could not be brought to the Tower and despatched with a revolver bullet while he lay on his stretcher. Ding-Schuler protested that there was one very good reason against taking such a course, and that was the risk of spreading typhus throughout the camp, even into the Commandant's quarters. This argument impressed Pister, who cancelled the order to remove Peulevé from Block 46 and commanded instead that he should be killed there by an injection from Ding-Schuler himself. Ding-Schuler protested that such an act was outside his terms of reference and suggested a more suitable deputy, Hauptsturmführer Schidlowski, should be delegated to perform the task. To this proposal Pister, now calmer, eventually agreed.

Much time had now been gained, but more still was required if one of the three Frenchmen were to die of his own death soon enough to save Peulevé. Knowing that Schidlowski had had his fill of executions and feared reprisals from the Allies, he persuaded the Hauptsturmführer that he himself should appoint a delegate, an NCO called Wilhelm, whose reputation for sadism was well known and who could therefore be relied upon to carry out such congenial instructions. Wilhelm, however, had a reputation for drunkenness as well as for cruelty and when he arrived at Block 46 the Kapo had a special meal and a bottle of Schnaps waiting in his office for the executioner. Wilhelm did not require much inviting and when he had finished the whole bottle of Schnaps by himself he was so drunk that he could scarcely stand. The Kapo then led him into the typhus ward, showed him a moribund man whom he alleged to be Peulevé and pointed out that it would be a waste of his own valuable medicines and of Wilhelm's energy to give a lethal injection to so obviously dying a man whose corpse would in any case be delivered to the crematorium next morning. Wilhelm, keeping his balance with difficulty, agreed, staggered out and reported to Schidlowski that he had executed Peulevé.

Once again it was only a temporary respite which they had gained: a corpse had still to be produced, and if one of the three Frenchmen had not died by ten o'clock the next morning Peulevé would still have to be sacrificed.

Late that evening it began to be clear that Seigneur had not more than twenty-four hours to live, but Yeo-Thomas and Hessel were adamant that nothing should be done to hasten his end: they knew that Peulevé would not wish to owe his life to a man who *might* have been saved. All that night they lay awake in terror and suspense, listening to the groans of the dying man. At one o'clock they were strong, at two o'clock weaker, at three o'clock stronger again, and four o'clock weaker once more. At five o'clock the Kapo wearied and perturbed, appeared and begged with them to be allowed to give the man a fatal injection. 'It'd be a kindness really,' he pleaded. 'He can't last much longer but it's still just possible that he may live till noon.' Once more Yeo-Thomas and Hessel refused. The dying man's groans became fainter and fainter, and at half-past seven they ceased: Peulevé had been saved by a margin of two and a half hours.

Two days later Peulevé had rejoined them in the upper room, secure under the identity of Marcel Seigneur, No. 76,635. But on 7 October the camp loudspeaker blared again:

'*Die Gefangenen Avallard, Evesque, von Block 17 müssen sich sofort bein Turn melden.*'

On 9 October it blared again:

'*Der Gefangene Rambaud von Block 17 muss sick sofort beim Turm melden.*'

There remained now only six of the original thirty-seven, and of these six Yeo-Thomas and Hessel formed two. Maurice Chouquet and Michel Boitel were still not quite at death's door and if their names were called neither Yeo-Thomas nor Hessel could hope to escape by the same good fortune as Peulevé. There was nothing that they could do except to watch and listen and pray and play 'silly buggers'.

Peeping out of the windows of their room they could glimpse the autumn misery of the cold world from which even a painful death would not have been such an unpleasant escape had there not been another world of laughter and sunshine to which they longed to return: in the small camp they could see their friends the Allied airmen, distinguished by their soldierly bearing in misfortune; they could see the wretched Jewish prisoners, with the cold wind flapping their rags about their fleshless bodies, shuffling, their heads sunk into sockets on their rounded shoulders, to work under the cries and blows of their masters; and in the evening they saw the same prisoners return carrying their dead with them, sometimes as many as sixty a day.

They had visitors too, smuggled into the Block by the Kapot Kogon and Baumeister and, on one occasion, Lamason, whom Yeo-Thomas asked to send back news of them to England when he was transferred to a POW camp. From Schalker they received both the BBC and the OKW communiqués and, because all play and no work makes Jack an even duller boy, helped him and Gadzinski to plot the charts of those in an even deeper despond than themselves. But neither play nor work nor conversation nor contemplation of the horrors they witnessed from the window could keep them from brooding upon their main preoccupation: were Yeo-Thomas and Hessel also going to be saved? Perhaps it was Peulevé who suffered most.

The days passed and there was still no summons from the loud-speakers. The two sick Frenchmen took a turn for the worse, and on Friday, 13 October, Maurice Chouquet died. Because his height corresponded more to Tommy's than to Hessel's, Yeo-Thomas took his identity and number 81,642, and Chouquet's body was sent to the crematorium as Kenneth Dodkin, No. 14,624. This substitution was made in the nick of time: next day Ding-Schuler informed Tommy that the order for his execution had just arrived. Tommy now lived in the same anxiety as Peulevé: was Hessel going to be saved?

So once again they played 'silly buggers', plotted the expiring breath of the doomed, watched the death march from their window, imagined dinners in Soho, imitated Tommy Handley's saying, 'Shine your lamp, Sam', and kept their ears open for the dreaded order: '*Die folgenden Gefangenen müssen sich sofort beim Turm melden . . .*'

The order did not come: on 18 October Michel Boitel died and his corpse was sent to be burned as Hessel's. Yeo-Thomas, Peulevé and Hessel had ceased to exist; and it was Chouquet, Seigneur and Boitel who, peering through their lattice, saw the whole of the Copenhagen police force, arrested in one fell swoop by the Germans, arrive in the camp and carry trunks for the despots, two men to each trunk, keeping in step like guards, until hunger and cold should have worked their way with them too.

The problem which Chouquet, Seigneur and Boitel now faced was only less acute than that which Yeo-Thomas, Peulevé and Hessel had confronted; the loudspeaker could no longer blare their names, but they still had to survive until the Allied Armies arrived in triumph to liberate them. They had now to fear their fellow prisoners almost as much as they had formerly feared the Germans: for the Communists, if they learned that, officers had managed to cheat the gallows, would certainly denounce them. (M. Michelin, the director of the famous tyre company, whom Tommy had seen on several occasions, could have been saved, but was sent to a certain death because his communist fellow-countrymen refused to help a capitalist.) The only solution was for Kogon and Baumeister to have them transferred from Buchenwald to a work Kommando where there would be little chance of their being recognised; and, to prepare for their new duplicity, Chouquet, Seigneur and Boitel set about learning all there was to be known about Chouquet, Seigneur and Boitel.

Kogon and Baumeister arranged these transfers quickly; at the beginning of November Peulevé and Hessel were sent to fill two vacancies which had occurred in a small Kommando attached to an aircraft factory at Schönbeck: Peulevé, because he was technically qualified, as an electrician, and Hessel, because he spoke German, as a clerk. Yeo-Thomas was not left in solitude for long to mourn their departure. On 8 November the Kapo told him that Kogon had arranged for him to be sent to a small Kommando called Kommando Wille at Gleina, where he was to get into touch with a prisoner called Hummelsheim, who had been warned of his arrival and would do all in his power to aid him.

Because the Kapo had risked his life to help them Yeo-Thomas now risked his life to help the Kapo: he wrote out a detailed statement of all that the Kapo had done on their behalf, which he signed with his real name, rank and number and gave to him. Perhaps the risk was less than Tommy imagined because his signature is almost illegible. At any rate this document, while it may have saved the Kapo's life, did not prevent him from being sentenced to a long term of imprisonment by an Allied Court after the war.

On 9 November, carrying among his chattels Hubble's chess set and food and a pair of hobnailed leather boots which the Kapo had given him, and wearing underneath a ragged striped coat a pair of fairly good trousers and a corduroy jacket which were also the Kapo's gifts, Prisoner No. 81,642 Maurice Chouquet made his way through a blinding snowstorm to the gates of Buchenwald. Although the snow caked his clogs and made walking difficult, he blessed the cold misery which bit into his face, because it gave him every excuse for keeping his face down, and the few who were abroad were too busy covering their own faces to spare a glance for the hurrying figure whom fair weather might have enabled them to recognise as Prisoner No. 14,624 Kenneth Dodkin. At the gate about twenty other prisoners were already waiting: three of them were Dutchmen, and the rest Central European Jews.

Their names sounded strange when the SS guards read them out in a roll call, but none sounded stranger than his own, in which he had been made neither a taxpayer nor an inheritor of the kingdom of heaven. The shouts of '*Hinein, schnell*' when the truck drove up were however familiar, as were also the kicks and the blows from the rifle butts. The gates of the prison swung open and they drove out of Buchenwald into the lovely white silence of a snow-covered world.

CHAPTER XV

Gleina and Rehmsdorf

It was bitterly cold in the truck, and the red-nosed, peaky-faced prisoners huddled together for warmth, envying the plutocratic comfort of the guards, who wore jackboots, thick greatcoats and fur-lined gloves. Next to Tommy crouched a Jewish boy, Andreas Weiss, who had succeeded in being sent to Gleina to join his father and who spoke a little French. His lack of spirit and oriental fatalism astounded Yeo-Thomas, who was soon exhorting him as he had exhorted so many others. The sermon which he preached was his old homily about never saying die and going down with one's colours flying; if for most of us such phrases have lost their meaning, it is perhaps because they have been so often used by those who never have themselves known danger and have no intention of doing so. With Tommy these words were like Cinderella's slipper: they fitted and because they fitted they shone. Soon he had the Jewish boy full of fight, and the other prisoners singing and humming, making, as the psalmist had counselled their forefathers, a merry noise in Jacob, which seemed all around them, perhaps because it was so very far away. The guards growled but took no violent action to stop them: they knew that the prisoners would not sing for long.

Even Tommy ceased singing when night fell, cloaking in blackness the sweet white earth which had made him hope. The truck lurched over the frozen ruts and the prisoners were bumped against one another, their frightened faces swinging in the darkness like dim lanterns. On and on they went through invisible avenues of uncharted shadow unwound from and wound up again into the greater shadow of the night. At last they entered a village, with its roofs flung up like ranges of mountains against the high indigo of the sky, with here and there chinks of light shining from behind windows, like stars which had somehow come too near. The truck stopped at a gate in the middle of the village. In front of the gate stood an SS sentry, his buckles and buttons looking like holes punctured in the night.

As the gate was opened and the truck entered the yard inside was floodlit. The square on which the prisoners were ordered to jump down was surrounded by farmhouses. They had arrived at Gleina, and the Rapportführer of the camp, Unterscharführer Otto Möller, was waiting with a sheaf of papers in his hand to call the inevitable roll.

Once more Yeo-Thomas answered to the number and name of 81,642 Maurice Chouquet, and for a moment he had a feeling that the real 81,642 Maurice Chouquet was watching him do so: for around the square were ranged rows of spectral beings with large gleaming eyes who looked like the ghosts of the dead; the old prisoners had come to gaze upon the new.

The Kapo, a tall rugged Dutchman of about forty-five whom they were later to know as Hans Gentkow, then ordered them to file into one of the buildings. On his way in Tommy was stopped by a young good-looking man of about twenty-six.

'Etes-vous français?' the young man asked.

'Oui,' Tommy said.

'If you'll tell me your profession I'll try to see what I can do about putting you with other Frenchmen.'

The real Maurice Chouquet had been described on his identity papers as a carpenter, and Tommy's knowledge of carpentry was sketchy. He answered, therefore, that in civil life he had been the owner of a furniture business but that the SS had insisted on listing him as a carpenter. His new friend said that he would see what could be done to fit him in, and Tommy said nothing more. He wasn't really sure whether his new friend was his new friend or his new enemy; Buchenwald had taught him not to be surprised by the hatred of those with whom a shared misery ought to have bound him in love.

Carrying his pitiful bundle of luggage, he climbed a rickety staircase dripping with moisture to a landing on which there were three doors: the first was ajar, and through it could be both seen and smelt the long wooden trough which was the common urinal; the second opened into a square room filled with bunks and in which a double-check roll call was held. When Yeo-Thomas again answered to the name of Chouquet a young man wearing the red triangle of a German political prisoner stepped forward, had a word with the Kapo, and then introduced himself to Tommy as Hummelsheim. Tommy began to understand that the young Frenchman too was a friend when, after consultation with Hummelsheim and Gentkow, he offered to find him a bed for the night.

But even then it didn't seem that the bed was going to be a very comfortable one. Led by the Frenchman into a room behind the third door, Yeo-Thomas entered a dormitory crammed with bunks three tiers high with a central passage just broad enough for one man to pass. Although the room was only dimly lit by unshaded electric bulbs, what he saw of the occupants of the bunks horrified and frightened him. On each bunk was stretched a burning-eyed, emaciated man whose yellow skin glittered with feebleness and sweat. Most of these brittle bodies were covered with bandages stained with dirt, blood and pus. Stinking of urine, faeces, vomit and rot the frail men lay groaning, moaning, muttering and babbling appeals to God in which the rasp of a curse often mingled with the lonely yell of an unanswered *Eli, Eli, lama sabachthani?*

However, it was not among these storeys of the doomed that Yeo-Thomas was required to sleep. At the end of this long room was another smaller and more brightly lit room with twelve bunks in it, piled as usual in tiers of three. The rest of the furniture consisted of two long narrow benches made of planks and a couple of three-legged stools. Against the wall a makeshift stove constructed out of an old oven propped on bricks and coated with earth and cement gave out a restricted, weakly heat. After the spectacle which he had just witnessed these comforts seemed sybaritic.

It was soon clear that he had landed again in a hospital: his guide turned out to be a French Army doctor called Jean Dulac; of the three men lying in the bunks one was a Doctor Mendel: other Jewish doctors came in almost immediately, Doctor Holosz, Doctor Szekely, and

Doctor Weiss, the father of the boy into whom Tommy had pumped pep in the truck. Among the few laymen were Paul Jacquin, a thickset man called Pierre Fauvage, a stripling of twenty called Foulquier and the registrar of the hospital, Pierre Kaan, a grey-haired man with spectacles. This last man looked puzzled when Yeo-Thomas introduced himself as 'Colonel Maurice Chouquet, de l'Armée de l'Air'. It was not without purpose that Tommy had decided not only to remain an officer but to promote himself: he wished to be in a position of authority if he was ever able to organise a mass escape, and he had already arranged with Kogon that he would be taken back to Buchenwald to lead an armed revolt there if an opportunity arose.

He was grateful when Dr Dulac told him that he could have the last vacant bunk in the cubicle and that he would do his best to have him attached to the hospital staff as an orderly, instead of being sent to work with the others in Rehmsdorf. He handed over the food which the Kapo had given him, and from their ill-stocked larder Fauvage produced a special hot supper of potatoes and onions in honour of the newcomer's arrival. All through the meal Kaan kept looking at him queerly and the others looked at him queerly too when Hummelsheim dropped in and took him away to his room for a private conversation.

Hummelsheim's room was a cubicle partitioned off the store on the top floor. In spite of the rule forbidding the display of religious emblems, on the wall hung a crucifix, that hint of mercy which used to be understood throughout the Christian world, but whose universality progress has replaced by the cocktail shaker and Donald Duck. As the two men talked together an incense of Czechoslovakian tobacco arose to this chink of light in a terrible darkness and perhaps, because part of it was puffed from poor Hubble's pipe, the Lord received it for an odour of sweetness.

Hummelsheim, whom Kogon had not informed of Tommy's British nationality, told Yeo-Thomas that he would do all in his power to help him. Gleina, he said, was really only the Revier or hospital of the Jewish extermination camp, lying outside the main compound but strictly subject to the authority of the Commandant. This man, an SS Obersturmführer, was a sadist whose favourite pastime was flogging prisoners to death. Of the 320 SS guards only three were decent and their clemency was more than cancelled by the brutality of three prisoners in authority: the Polish cook at Gleina; Hans Wolff, the Lagerältester at Rehmsdorf; and a Czechoslovakian who was Kapo of the Revier. There were also feuds among the prisoners because the subterranean quarrel of the world, so very much more deadly than the open, divided the wretched as it was later to divide the victorious. Tommy returned to his quarters feeling that, apart from the removal of the threat of immediate death, he had done little more than exchange the frying-pan for the fire.

'*Aufstehen*' next morning in the fire was at the same time as it had been in Block 17 in the frying-pan: six o'clock. This time he made even the sick forget their agony for a little in their astonishment at the extensive ablutions which he performed with the Kapo's soap at the trough at the end of the ward. When he had dressed he found himself alone for a moment with Pierre Kaan.

'I know now who you are,' Kaan said. 'You're Shelley.'

Tommy was surprised, but not alarmed, because Frenchmen who knew Shelley were his friends.

'Shelley is dead; Chouquet is living,' he said sadly, because it wasn't only Shelley who had died with Shelley; with Shelley had perished also Thierry, Tirelli, Gaonach and Dodkin, each of whom had fought for the cause in his way. It was now his turn to look at Kaan closely, but if the Resistance world was small many brave men crowded it, and although Kaan's face seemed familiar he could not for the life of him remember where he had seen him before.

'You knew me before under the name of Biran, I think,' Kaan said, and then it all came back: it was Kaan who, on the already prehistoric 27 October, 1943, had been the Secretary at a meeting of the Comité Militaire at which Brossolette and he had attempted to resolve the differences between the Regional Military Officers and the Resistance Groups.

Yeo-Thomas told Kaan all that had happened to him since then. Kaan said that Tommy's conversation the night before with a privileged German prisoner like Hummelsheim had aroused the distrust of his colleagues, but that he would dispel all misunderstanding by telling them that Tommy had been a valuable member of French Resistance, without, however, disclosing his British nationality.

Their tête-à-tête was interrupted by Dulac, who informed Yeo-

Thomas that he had obtained for him the double hospital appoint-ment of *Totenträger* and *Pfleger*: he was to work with Fauvage and Foulquier, who would instruct him in his duties both towards the living and the dead.

His sinister task of carrying corpses from the hospital began at once, and during all the time he was at Gleina the routine never varied. First of all the SS Sanitäter, an Oberscharführer, came with a pair of pincers and yanked out any gold teeth there might be in the mouths of those who had died during the night. Then Yeo-Thomas and Foulquier carried the bodies to the small hut which was used as a morgue. There the often dysentery-fouled shirt and trousers were removed from each corpse, which was then piled on top of those already there, many of them already green with decay. Sometimes the morgue was so full that they had to stand on top of the old dead in order to slide in the new dead and under their weight the carcases would often eruct in ghoulish posthumous belches and farts. And yet in all their gruesome grocery they never became callous. They could not, Tommy says, 'administer the last rites', but when they had squeezed each new corpse into position on the common catafalque they bared their heads and stood for a few seconds in silence, honouring the mystery. Often while per-forming this reverence they were cursed and kicked by the supervising guards.

Nor was that the end of their duties to the dead: before they were removed from the morgue the bodies had to be placed in coffins, a clemency which amazed Yeo-Thomas until he learned the reason. Most of the prisoners at Rehmsdorf worked in the 'Brabag' factory at Zeitz, and one of the clauses in the contract of their servitude was that their employers should contribute sixty marks towards the burial expenses of those who died. The mistress of the Camp Commandant was an undertaker who also ran a subsidiary capable of producing thirteen coffins a day at a cost price of fifteen marks each. This meant that provided that there were thirteen deaths a day at Gleina – and there had to be thirteen deaths a day at Gleina – the Obersturmführer and his harlot shared a daily profit of 585 marks.

Tommy's duties towards the living were almost as heartrending. As an orderly he had to nurse the sick in their repulsive maladies. Because of malnutrition most of the patients suffered from carbuncles the size of small melons which, when lanced, spurted pus three feet across the ward, leaving a hole deep enough for him to plunge his fist in. Others had the bones of their arms and their legs laid bare by oedemas. On two occasions the living so closely resembled the dead that he and Foulquier carted them off to the morgue by mistake and, when they found that their hearts were still beating feebly, had to clothe them again in their soiled rags and carry them back to die among the others in whom life still flickered. The plight of the dying was made even more terrible by the fact that the Oberscharführer impounded the scanty medical supplies at their disposal and sold them to German civilians outside the camp.

Those of the patients who could still walk had to stagger through the snow on clogs or on bare feet to collect the scanty meals dished out by the Polish cook. It was part of Tommy's job to bring back the bread. On his first day he found that he could carry a sack of fifty loaves, but when he caught dysentery he quickly dropped to twenty: he took advantage of the extra trips which his disability involved to steal a few more SS rations for distribution among his patients. Between journeys he had to go to the latrine, where he sat on a tree trunk with his bottom bared to the biting winter wind, precariously perched above a trench containing six feet of faeces.

Every day the sick prisoners had to stand for two hours in blinding sleet or snow or in a temperature of 15 below zero centigrade while the Appell took place, in spite of the efforts of Rapportführer Otto Möller to shorten the process. Because of his intercession with authority on behalf of the prisoners Möller made himself unpopular with the Camp Commandant, who was merciless. Others who were humane enough to risk the Obersturmführer's displeasure were Rottenführer Kurt Hebestreit, NCO in charge of the stores, who turned a blind eye to Tommy's larcenies, and Oberscharführer Saurbier, who prevented his colleagues from beating up prisoners while he was present. Both these men had been fighting soldiers before being compulsorily transferred to the SS, and when the Obersturmführer heard of Saurbier's allegiance to the old code he arrested him and sent him to gaol in Buchenwald.

There were no age limits in the call-up for suffering: among the prisoners were many Central European Jewish boys, little older than children. When they fell sick Dulac contrived to keep them in the Revier as long as possible, and some of them he saved from work in the factories by retaining them as orderlies. One of these latter was a boy of fourteen called Ivan, who helped Yeo-Thomas on his ghastly duties. His story was so typical that even those who befriended him did not regard it as especially tragic. The son of a Rabbi, he had been arrested in Budapesth while out for a walk with his grandmother, his mother and his little sister of eight. Without being allowed to bid farewell to their family, they were pushed into a cattle truck and taken to Auschwitz. There, as his grandmother was too old, his mother too ill and his sister too young to work, the three of them were thrown into the incinerator of the crematorium and burned alive. Ivan was sent to Buchenwald and thence to Rehmsdorf, to work in the Brabag factory, where he eventually fell ill. With this boy, whom he took under his protection, Yeo-Thomas formed a deep friendship.

It was natural that Tommy, who still wanted to be fighting with the Allied Armies on the day of victory, should think of escape. On one occasion he succeeded in being sent to Leipzig by Hummelsheim, who, as Schreiber of Gleina, had to keep in contact with the merchants who enriched themselves by selling tainted meat to the camp. There he could have escaped, but if he had done so Hummelsheim would have been executed. He was able, nevertheless, to send a message to Barbara through some British prisoners of war whom he saw carrying steel shutters across a factory yard. Although it had to be passed sentence by sentence to a succession of individual soldiers as they filed past him, the message reached England in its entirety, and Tommy is still grateful to the transmitters for their successful co-operation.

Thanks to Pierre Kaan, however, he had now regained the confidence of his new French friends, and with Dulac and others he had organised a small group of twenty who were on the watch for a suitable opportunity to escape. The physical weakness of the majority of the prisoners made the organisation of a larger body impossible, and there was the added difficulty that the doctors regarded their work among the sick as an apostolate. As escape was for the moment out of the question they kept up their spirits by pranks and tomfoolery. For more serious relaxation Kaan, a Hungarian lawyer called Cazar, Yeo-

Thomas and others played chess on Hubble's set, which was as sacred to Tommy as the tibia of a saint.

At the beginning of December the deaths jumped from round about a dozen a day to thirty or more, and in order to relieve the congestion in the morgue those who had so often shared a bunk had also to share a coffin. One day as Yeo-Thomas and Foulquier were carrying a casket to the truck the flimsily made bottom fell out and two bodies were precipitated on the snow under the eyes of the Obersturmführer, who was supervising the supervisors. The sight of these pitiable corpses lying on the cold earth moved the Camp Commandant neither to pity nor fear of the judgment: unmollified by Foulquier's explanation of the reasons of this duplication, he bellowed with rage at so evident an infringement of his profit, and ordered that the doctors should be beaten if they did not succeed in staggering the deaths of their patients so as not to exceed the statutory daily thirteen.

Although there was snow on the ground at Christmas their celebration was not the white indecency dreamed of in the sugary song. Perhaps happy men as well as rich men cannot hope to enter easily into the kingdom of heaven and perhaps it is only when men are bang up against terror and despair that they can appreciate the warmth once promised. Because of their poverty they were unable to blaspheme hope with paper hats, hooters and gin. As their feast was a poor one it was also a holy one. The candles on their tree were made of margarine threaded with string. Their presents were loose cigarettes and pieces of bread wrapped in chalk-coloured paper. But there was nothing ersatz about their song, which reached back to an age in which faith was not obscured by mathematics:

> *Ergo qui natus*
> *Die hodierna,*
> *Jesus tibi sit gloria:*
> *Patris aeterni*
> *Verbo caro factum!*
> *Venite adoremus,*
> *Venite adoremus,*
> *Venite adoremus Dominum.*

And that night even Israel, weeping by the waters of its most terrible Babylon, believed and honoured the root which had come out of Jesse. With tears in their eyes Jews, Gentiles, and the dying of both dispensations sang hymns and canticles of gladness and, after praising the mercy which seemed so very far from them, they sang to Britain and France and America, whose undeliberately Christian armies had made the tenderness seem a little nearer. And even the floggers of the feeble and the usurers of their bodies a desire for holiness seemed to halo, for over the compound came the voices of the soldiers of the Schutzstaffeln[1] raised in plaintive choir:

> *Stille Nacht! Heilige Nacht!*
> *Alle schläft. Einsam wacht,*
> *Nur das traute, hochheilige Paar –*
> *Holder Knabe in lockigen Haar,*
> *Schlaf in himmlischer Ruh,*
> *Schlaf in himmlischer Ruh!*

'Merry Christmas', Kaan whispered under his breath to Yeo-Thomas, knowing that Tommy was hungry to hear an English word. And an SS guard called to wish them all '*Fröhliche Weihnacht*', weeping tears of emotion which did not seem to be entirely Schnaps. The very next day that same guard beat a prisoner to death; perhaps that is why even the best of Christmases is inevitably a let-down: the world always seems so very much more cruel on the 26 December.

And cruel for them all the world became in the New Year, when the Revier was transferred from Gleina to Rehmsdorf, within the barbed wire of the camp proper. They were now directly under the control of the Obersturmführer and his brutal lieutenant Lagerältester Hans Wolff. The hospital was crowded into two huts, each constructed to accommodate 150 and made to hold 600. The doctors had no longer a cubicle to themselves but had to sleep in bunks among the sick, two deep in tiers of four. Tommy, who occupied a middle bunk, had a foot and a half of space between his head and the boards of the bunk above:

1 SS.

on those boards he pencilled the word BARBARA; it was the nearest he could get to a photograph.

For the 1,200 patients in the two huts there was one thermometer, and one bed-pan. Men dying of dysentery, tuberculosis and pneumonia had to go outside to the latrine until the orderlies installed oil drums behind wooden planking to mitigate their discomfort. Even then many of the patients were so weak that they fell into the drums and had to be pulled out and cleaned. Some collapsed and died on their way back to their bunks. Others fouled their bunks, and their ordures oozed through the boards and dripped on the faces of those underneath, who were generally too feeble themselves to protest. To add to this horror, the Obersturmführer, when he visited the wards, was in the habit of pulling patients out of their bunks by their feet and laughing when their skulls fractured on the stone floor.

Yeo-Thomas, Fauvage and Foulquier worked eighteen hours a day carting out the dead, feeling pulses and taking temperatures. Sometimes they took the temperatures of the dead as well as those of the living; for the patients, crammed three to a bunk, would, to obtain extra rations, slide the thermometer under the armpit of a deceased neighbour and, when Yeo-Thomas wasn't looking, rub the mercury up with their hands. As a result corpses were often stiff with the rigour of death when the orderlies removed them. But, stiff or still pliant, all corpses had to be laid out in a row at the entrance to the hut until the NCO came to prise open their jaws with a piece of wood and extract their gold teeth for the SS regimental funds. This ritual was generally supererogatory because the SS guards, in their greed for this bullion, usually beat to death prisoners with gold teeth before they were ill enough to enter the Revier.

In a makeshift surgery railed off from the rest of the hut Mendel, Dulac and the other doctors punctured carbuncles and phlegmons and dressed oedemas, from which six to seven hundred of their patients were suffering. The few instruments could rarely be sterilised; the iodine was ersatz; there was one pair of scissors and no cotton-wool; and, as the small supply of chlorethyl had to be kept for major operations, there were for most no anaesthetics. Yeo-Thomas and the other orderlies held down the shrieking patients while the doctors lanced and the blood and pus spurted out like geysers.

And all the time that he was carrying out his grim duties Yeo-Thomas was feeling far from well himself. He suffered simultaneously from dysentery, boils on his back and a stone in his kidney which caused him agony until he succeeded in passing it out into his bladder. He dared not report sick for fear of being exterminated.

Yet bad as conditions were in the Revier they were worse in the main camp. It was bitterly cold, and the prisoners, who had no winter clothing, no socks and no gloves, had to work outside from morning till night under the threats and blows of the guards. They had almost no food. There was only one way to get extra rations and that was to be a first-class musician or a singer from the Viennese opera and entertain the SS guards while they sat swilling their potations. This privilege, however, carried its own special risks, for in Rehmsdorf even music had little power the savage breast to charm: if a drunken guard didn't like the way a violinist played *The Blue Danube* or a tenor's rendering of *La Donna è Mobile* the offender was likely to be dragged from the platform and beaten to death.

The Revier was the only real refuge from the brutality of the camp and sooner or later all those who weren't murdered qualified for it. Some, although they weren't technically enough near death to be validly excused from work, were admitted temporarily to the hospital by the doctors in order that they might regain their strength. Naturally their number was limited and their stay had to be short in order that as many as possible might benefit. Among them were a few malingerers, of whom one slept in the bunk under that of Cazar, the Hungarian lawyer.

Cazar suffered from an ailment of the bladder which made it necessary for him to pass water frequently. So as not to disturb his neighbours by frequent nocturnal visits to the oil drums he took to bed with him a tin which he used as a chamber-pot. One night he took by mistake the perforated tin used for watering the hut, and when he had micturated the urine trickled down on to the malingerer's head. Yeo-Thomas, Kaan and those in the vicinity were wakened by a banging on the bottom of Cazar's bunk and a violent protest:

'You swine! What are you doing?'

'What's the matter?' Cazar asked gently. 'Surely it's not *Aufstehen* yet.'

'Stop pissing on my bed!'

'My dear friend, you must be mistaken. I am not pissing on your bed.'

'Yes, you are,' the malingerer roared. 'And what's more I'm soaked.'

'Impossible.'

'Damn you, more is trickling down this very minute. Can't you control yourself, you swine?'

'Really, you're crazy.'

'And you are a dirty pisser!'

'I am a pisser, I admit, but I am a clean pisser: I use my tin.'

'Well, you are not using it now, you lazy bastard.'

'Of course I am not using it now; I used it only a minute ago.'

'You clumsy idiot, you must have upset it.'

'No, I have not; my tin is still upright.'

'Well, you are still pissing. Stop it, you dirty pig.'

'Oh, dear,' said Cazar, after investigation. 'I am so sorry. You see, there is a hole.'

'Of course, there is a hole, you damned fool. I'm soaked.'

'But there is a hole.'

'Curse your hole.'

'Oh, dear, oh, dear, there is a hole. I am so very sorry that there is a hole.'

C. S. Lewis uses man's constant amusement at the incongruity of his physical functions with his dignity as an argument in favour of his immortality. Those who listened to this dialogue had suffered too much to need any such high considerations to make them laugh. Their laughter was deep and loud and from the belly and it cleansed them for a little from their misery.

And for what lay ahead of them as well as for what lay behind them they had need of laughter. In spite of the ever-increasing number of deaths the Revier was always full, and the SS, tired of feeding the unproductive, sent eastwards for extermination those they considered unlikely to recover. An SS officer would come clanking into the hut and order the sick to parade in front of him. Those unable to leave their bunks were sent on the next death convoy and the others, sticking out their bony chests as the merciless eyes passed along their ranks, were divided into those who would be murdered with them and those who would be reprieved for further work before they, in turn, were murdered or died of exhaustion. Many of those ordered to return to work were so weak that they collapsed as soon as they left the hut and were beaten to death by the guards. On two occasions the Revier was completely emptied by these inspections; but within three days both huts were full again.

Among those sent to be exterminated was the Jewish boy Ivan, who had contracted meningitis after leaving Gleina. The night before he was taken away he lay on a couple of boards in the camp washroom, and Yeo-Thomas squatted beside him, holding his hand. The boy was too ill to speak, but his eyes were eloquent with despair. Every time that Tommy moved, Ivan clutched his hand desperately. When the SS guards came for him in the morning they removed the blanket which covered his wasted limbs before carrying him out in a wood-fibre shirt into a temperature of 15° below zero centigrade. Tommy went with him to the gate of the camp, where the guards wrenched Ivan's hand from his and bore away the boy, groaning with despair, to die a brutal lonely death.

Seven thousand six hundred prisoners passed through Rehmsdorf while Yeo-Thomas was there, and such was their condition that he could find among them only forty with spirit enough left to co-operate in a plan for escape. Ten of these were Frenchmen, six Dutchmen and twenty-four Jews.

Their old quarters at Gleina had been turned into a POW camp for British Other Ranks, most of whom were commandos or paratroopers. With the complicity of Gentkow, now in charge of fatigue parties, Tommy entered into communication with the NCO in charge of the camp, Corporal Stevenson of the Leicestershire Regiment, to whom he was able to prove his status through the happy accident of being able to mention the name of a captain in the regiment whom his cousin had married. Detailed by Gentkow for a potato and carrot-peeling fatigue at Gleina, he had an interview with the corporal in the cook-house and, over a hot meal which Stevenson provided for him, arranged one of those desperate schemes whose merit is not only that they are courageous but that they sometimes come off. As the Allied troops advanced towards Leipzig, Stevenson and the British POWs would overpower their guards, seize their arms and march on

Rehmsdorf, from which Yeo-Thomas and his forty men, armed with ten rifles, ten pistols and a few dozen hand grenades which they had managed to secure, would make a sortie to meet them. In earnest of this plan, which was never to come off, Tommy took back to Rehmsdorf a parcel of chocolate, biscuits, sugar and cigarettes to distribute among his patients.

And with the approach of spring Rehmsdorf became more than ever a place to escape from, for sadistic SS guards and blackmailing Kapos were no longer the only people they had to fear: their liberating friends came rushing through the skies dropping bombs with that approximation to accuracy that was so lauded by contemporary newsreel commentators in between their sneers at brave enemy generals and their sniggers at bathing beauties' breasts. A night-bomber raid on the Brabag factory, illuminated by R.A.F. Path-finders, was successful: 80 per cent. of the factory was destroyed and none of the prisoners was hurt, although the patients in the Revier clung to the doctors, screaming with fear. Two daylight raids in March on the same factory were, however, much less precise. In one of them, although a distance of four miles separated the camp from the Brabag, a five-hundred-pound bomb fell on a hut diagonally opposite the hospital, disintegrating it completely. Once again the patients blubbered with terror and smothered the doctors and orderlies, who had to throw them off roughly in order to run to the sundered hut.

Several more bombs landed in the camp while 'Monsieur Jean' and 'Monsieur Maurice' and the others began their work of necessarily rule-of-thumb mercy among rubble spattered with blood and brains. Legs and arms without bodies and bodies without legs and arms were strewn all around. On the top of a neighbouring hut lay the mangled trunk of a prisoner gushing blood from the raw hams of two stumps from which his legs had been blasted. Beneath the smoking ruins lay even greater miseries, and as they had no tools, the doctors and orderlies had to dig with their hands in order to pull out those buried underneath, many of whom were already dead.

In their makeshift surgery the doctors had no cotton-wool and even the ersatz iodine had run out. As the water supply had been cut they had to wash out wounds with substitute coffee diluted with disinfectant. Many died on the table before the paper bandages could be applied to their wounds. There were no proper surgical instruments. One man had his leg shattered below the knee and, after ineffectively doping him with two ampoules of chlorethyl, Yeo-Thomas held him down while Dulac proceeded to an amputation with a knife whose blade was one and a half inches long. As he had no clamps to clip on the arteries Dulac had to ligature them with cotton. At the end of an hour's hacking the shattered portion of the leg came away in Tommy's hand. The patient lived for several days before he expired, comforted no doubt by the thought that he had died for civilisation, for television, for tired housewives, four-course dinners in airliners and *bidets* in all the best hotels.

One advantage, however, seemed to accrue to them from these air raids: the prisoners obtained permission to dig trenches in which to shelter, and Yeo-Thomas and Dulac took care to have them dug in strategic positions where, with their paltry armoury, they could make a last stand if their guards received the expected order to exterminate them.

For a new terror was now tearing at the bowels of the prisoners. As the Allied Armies advanced the Germans were evacuating the concentration camps and killing their inmates: some were locked into their huts and burned to death with flame-throwers; others were murdered as they marched along the road. Rehmsdorf, technically a Jewish extermination camp, could scarcely expect to escape the same fate. The sadists were taking precautions that none of their victims should remain alive to tell of the cruelties which had been practised upon them.

Morale in the camp sank lower and lower as rumour succeeded rumour. As food became scarcer the prisoners began to fight one another for their rations. Even patients so sick that they could not rise from their bunks tried to wrest bread from the grasp of those weaker than themselves. And even among those wrangling skeletons it took all Tommy's waning strength to restore order.

Their fears were justified, but the trenches were useless. On the night of 13 April the order came to evacuate the camp. The murder was to take place all right, but not on the spot. This knowledge gave Tommy hope; and, when he had collected his lighter, Hubble's pipe and chess set, he went to see Dulac.

'I am going to organise an attempt to escape during the evacuation,' he said. 'But you do not need to obey my orders if you don't wish to. You see, I'm not a French officer really. I am a Briton. I should like the others to know this too. Pierre Kaan will tell you who and what I am.'

But by now Dulac had learned to know his Tommy.

'I do not care who or what you are,' he said. 'I shall obey you just the same. And I know that the others will too.'

Then Tommy went and smashed the bedboard with 'BARBARA' written on it: he did not wish anybody else to gaze upon his sanctuary.

CHAPTER XVI

Death Convoy

The exodus was grim. Even the sick and the dying had to be loaded on to the train so that nobody might be left behind to tell tales. Those who were strong enough to walk had to carry the bedridden, and the doctors and the orderlies helped. Hundreds of moribunds, with pus oozing from festering sores and wounds, were packed into the open trucks. They were not allowed to take their blankets with them and wore only their shirts. There was an Appell, too, and the few who attempted to hide in the camp were rounded up and killed by the guards. The Obersturmführer was taking no chances: another murderer and torturer SS Oberscharführer and not the benevolent SS Rapportführer Möller had been put in charge of the convoy. And the SS Oberscharführer wasn't making any mistakes either: in each truck there were three armed guards and at the front and the rear of the train there were covered wagons filled with other guards. While they were waiting to move off a few Allied fighters dived down to bomb and machine-gun the train, but, perhaps because they were aiming badly, nobody was hit.

The train moved off in the early morning of 14 April, but even then their journey was slow and punctuated with many stops. One of their halts was on a siding near a women's concentration camp whose in-mates, herded by female SS in jackboots, waved to them from their enclosure. The gaolers lashed into the women at once with their long whips, and a couple of SS officers threw bricks at them. In a few minutes the women had all been shut up in their huts, and the prisoners in the train could hear them shouting insults at their guards, who were obviously unable to use their whips in the confined interiors of the huts.

Their journey was tortuous too, and within twenty-four hours they were back again in Rehmsdorf, but soon after they were moving eastwards and it became clear that they were heading for Czechoslovakia. Death accompanied them on their trip, and it came brutally as it had come in the camp, without sacraments or aspirations. As the men died of exposure or were murdered the SS guards slung their bodies, naked except for their paper bandages, from the train with words of committal whose unoriginal bestiality derived from the stupid Hitlerian grammar of abuse: 'Another pig dog of a Jew to fertilise the ground.' 'You mean to defile it with his filthy carcase.' 'Let's see how far we can swing this lousy Jewish bastard.' And jeering laughter followed each emaciated corpse as it went flying through the air, arms and legs flapping, eyes and mouth open and frozen fast in death, to land on rocks with a thud or hit a tree before it crashed to the ground and sagged as the miracle seemed to go out of it for the second time.

But 170 deaths in a single night were too much for even these brutal undertakers to handle; and on the morning of 16 April, after puffing up the long, rugged, woodlined slopes of the Bohemian foothills and passing through the small station of Marienburg-Gelobtland, the train stopped in a small clearing to permit of their burial in a common grave. Orders were given for the formation of two working parties: one to dig a deep hole slightly in front of and to the left of the engine; the other to throw the bodies out of the trucks on to the track, collect them, carry them to and throw them into the hole.

It was the opportunity for which Yeo-Thomas had been waiting. While on the right of the train the ground was rocky and difficult to negotiate, on the left it was smooth and merged into woods at about fifty yards from the site picked for the grave. He spoke with Dulac and Kaan and outlined his plan. Those who wanted to make an attempt to escape were to join the corpse-carrying working party. When, two to a body, they picked up a corpse to carry it to the grave they would remain bunched so as to deliver their loads in the hole simultaneously. They would then turn about as though to go and fetch another body, but, on a signal from Yeo-Thomas, would run as fast as they could towards the woods, which they must try to reach before the guards, strung out along the train and facing it, had time to swing round and fire on them. After that, he said, 'it would be a matter of luck'.

He tried, however, to leave as little as possible to luck. With 'Georges', a Belgian member of his group, acting as interpreter, he engineered, in a secluded spot some distance from their truck, a private conversation with Rapportführer Otto Möller, upon whom he tried a variant of the blackmail he had already practised successfully upon Sturmbannführer Ding-Schuler.

'Tell Möller,' he said to the astounded Georges, who had not been informed of Tommy's true nationality, 'tell him that I am a colonel in the British Intelligence Service. Tell him that I have been sent to Rehmsdorf specially in order to check up on the action of the SS. Tell him that I have already sent to the Allies a list of all officers and men in the SS and that this list is now in their hands.'

He watched the Rapportführer's face while Georges repeated what he had said in German. Was Möller going to denounce him or would he consent to bargain? The German's body stiffened slightly at the word '*Oberst*', but otherwise his demeanour did not betray what he was thinking.

'Tell him that I am aware that he himself has never ill-treated any prisoner; on the contrary I know that he has been kind to them,' he went on. 'But the Allies won't know that unless somebody tells them. The mere fact that he is an SS will render him liable to be shot when he's captured. His only chance is to help us.'

'*Fragen Sie ihn, wie ich Ihnen helfen kann!*'[1] Möller asked. Although Yeo-Thomas knew little German, he knew what that meant: Möller was going to play; Möller was asking how he could help.

'Tell him that some of us are going to escape and that if he helps us I will see that no harm comes to him when he is caught.' Tommy then gave details of his plan. He said that he knew that Möller could not prevent the guards from shooting, but suggested that he might purposely misdirect their pursuit. Once they had escaped Möller could, if he liked, join them. They could then march along together

1 'Ask him how I can help him.'

as though he were taking them to a camp. When they approached the Allied lines he could put on civilian clothes and cross into custody under Tommy's protection.

His bluff succeeded. Möller accepted and told him of a small stream, some two miles inside the wood and running north-north-east, where they might meet after the chase had been called off.

The group was immediately alerted. There was no time to make elaborate preparations. They could not load themselves with food and in any case there was little food to take. In the pockets of Tommy's jacket there was room for only two pieces of bread: he took one piece of bread and Hubble's chess set.

They started to unload the dead from the trucks in which they sprawled in the pitiful congelation of their last sad perplexity. While they were laying them down beside the track one of the bearers, a poor miserable scarecrow who was almost dead himself, stooped to pick up a piece of potato peeling. For this dereliction of duty he was shot in the back of the skull by the Oberscharführer who happened to be passing.

The grave was finished by the time all the bodies had been taken out of the trucks. In teams of two they picked up the corpses and slowly tramped towards the hole. Yeo-Thomas and Kaan led the way. Close behind them and keeping well together came the other eighteen members of the group who had agreed to make the attempt to escape. Approaching the grave, Tommy and Kaan threw in their burden and then stopped for a minute, pretending to rest. Dulac, Foulquier, Jacquin, Georges and the others did likewise. Then, when they were all collected together, they turned as though to go back for more bodies, but instead of going to the left went parallel to the train, thinning out on the way. Yeo-Thomas gave a quick glance round: none of the guards seemed to be looking in their direction. 'Go!' he shouted and he and his nineteen companions bounded towards the woods.

At once there were cries of 'Halt!' and 'Zurück', followed by the crack of Sten guns and the whizz of bullets as they sang through the air with piercing and very personal threat. Tommy ran on with his heart pounding and thudding inside him. The trees seemed much further off than when he had first seen them. As he tried to increase his speed bullets whistled past him in increasing number and with screeching velocity. He ducked his head down. The trees still seemed a long way off. He could see a few figures ahead of him, diving into the woods. His breath began to get shorter and the effort of running racked his weakened body. More bullets whined past him. 'How can the sods miss me?' he thought as his legs began to feel wobbly beneath him and to falter and flex. And as he stumbled on the sods did their best not to miss him. Suddenly, on the point of collapse, he felt brambles and other undergrowth clinging to his legs. He had reached the fringe of the wood. He pushed blindly on, through twigs and branches which scratched and lacerated his face. And still the bullets came after him, crashing into the trees and snipping off small branches. It seemed as though he was bound to be hit.

Breathless and puffing, his running degenerated into a faltering trot and the trot into a laboured walk. His chest felt as though it were about to burst. His breath came in gasps and sobs. He was exhausted. Behind him he heard voices shouting in German and heavy footsteps closing in on him. Through bloodshot and streaming eyes he saw a thick clump of trees and threw himself into bushes underneath. He landed on top of Foulquier. Foulquier was panting too, and Tommy began to be afraid that their pursuers would be guided to their hiding-place by the thumping of their hearts.

He buried his head in the ground to silence the gasps which were shaking him. He heard the heavy boots of guards crashing through the undergrowth. Looking up, he saw three pairs of jackboots within five yards of them and heard their wearers talking excitedly. Then, as Foulquier grasped his shoulder in fear, another pair of jackboots came up. Raising his head a little further he saw above them the face of Rapportführer Otto Möller.

'*Habt Ihr jemanden gesehen?*[1] Möller asked.

'*Nein. Niemanden,*'[2] one of the other guards answered.

'*Da sind sie!*'[3] Möller shouted and, firing his pistol, charged off in the opposite direction, followed by the three guards, hallooing wildly. Other pursuers joined them, and soon the firing and the shouting died away into the distance. Otto Möller had kept his word.

1 'Have you seen anybody?'
2 'No. Nobody.'
3 'There they are!'

Yeo-Thomas and Foulquier lay still. As their trembling limbs calmed they slowly regained their breath. When all noises had ceased for some time they made their way cautiously and as silently as they could in what they guessed to be the approximate direction of the stream. This they reached about an hour later. As its banks were bare they lay among the trees and waited for the others. Presently there was a crackling of branches and Dulac, Jacquin, Georges, a Frenchman called André and a Pole turned up. A few minutes later a Dutch boy they had known as Pete and two others arrived. Although they sent out a search party to look for the ten others they found no trace of them and were forced to conclude that they had failed in the attempt.

Among those who had failed was Pierre Kaan, of whose fate Tommy did not learn until the war was over. His glasses having brushed off his nose and lost as he entered the wood, he had been found wandering blindly about by Möller, who had smuggled him back into the train and saved him from the summary execution meted out to the others who had been caught. Suffering from a bad ulcer on one of his legs, he died a few weeks later in hospital after having been liberated by the Allies.

While waiting under cover for Möller to arrive, the ten successful fugitives discarded and buried their striped, badged and numbered uniforms under which they wore a motley of shoddy clothes which they had assembled in preparation for their flight. Tommy wore an old velvet jacket, a pair of frayed grey trousers and the boots which the Kapo had given him when he left Buchenwald and which he had concealed beneath rags wound round his feet. By avoiding contacts with the SS, which would have forced him to salute by removing his headgear, he had managed to grow a little hair, and he now discarded the beret which had hidden it. But it was Dulac who was the dandy of the party; using his privilege as a doctor, he had secured a pair of dark trousers and an overcoat with a red stripe down the middle of the back which he had rubbed out with petrol. The others wore an assortment of ill-matched and threadbare garments and in spite of Dulac's comparative elegance they all looked like a bevy of Wearie Willies and Tired Tims.

When after about three hours there was still no sign of Möller, Yeo-Thomas decided to wait no longer. As ten men moving about together would appear suspicious he divided the group up into three subsidiary teams: André and three others; Jacquin, Foulquier and Pete; and Dulac, Georges and himself. They were to leave at half-hour intervals and space out. As the Oberscharfûhrer would have alerted the military, the Feldgendarmerie and the recently recruited Volkssturm, they were not immediately to take the short cut and go north, as their pursuers would naturally expect weak men like themselves to do; instead they were to walk for the rest of the day in the same direction as the train, turning first eastwards and then northwards after night had fallen. After that their action must be left to the discretion of the leader of each team.

The party of four left first; then Jacquin, Foulquier and Pete; and finally, in the middle of the afternoon, Dulac, Georges and Yeo-Thomas.

As they had no compasses, maps or watches, they set their course as best they could by the sun. They walked at a leisurely pace, both so as to avoid making unnecessary noise and to husband their strength. They moved in silence, keeping a sharp lookout and halting at the slightest suspicious sound. At dusk they stopped for a rest. When night came they were still in the woods. They could scarcely see the stars because of the trees. Fumbling through the darkness they eventually came to a clearing, and from the golden and far-away glory of the sky they plotted a rough bearing and plodded on into the blackness, swallowed up once more by the trees.

The night grew colder and colder. The wind rose and bit through their clothes and made them shiver. Although they would have liked to walk a little faster to keep warm they resisted the temptation and moved on slowly through the trees and through the wind. It was well after midnight when they stopped by a large tree and, flinging themselves down between two of its protruding roots, slept for about four hours under the blanket of Dulac's overcoat. It was still dark when they awoke, stiff and numbed with cold. When they had jumped about for a little to get their circulation going they turned northwards.

It was clear by now that they were in a large forest: they had seen nothing but trees since they started and still the trees went on and on. After a little, however, they came to a stream in which, stripping to the waist, they washed and from which they drank. When each had eaten a small portion of his bread they moved on again, into more trees. The milky sky of dawn melted into the pale blue sky of day but they were still in the forest, with trees all around them.

Towards midday they came to a clearing, stretching horizontally as far as the eye could see and vertically about five hundred yards. Ahead of them they heard the noise of axes being wielded by woodcutters and, keeping under cover of the trees, went westwards until they could no longer hear the axes. Then they made a dash for it; they had got about half-way across when they heard shouts of '*Halt*', and, looking back over their shoulders, saw three men, one armed with an axe, running after them to cut them off. At once they turned left and ran with all their might as they had run the day before, diagonally towards the trees. The shouts of the men behind them helped them to effect a ruse: stopping running and moving laterally for a little, they crept cautiously back in the direction from which they had come and thus shook off their pursuers.

Exhausted, they rested for a little and ate some more bread before resuming their journey. When dusk came again they switched westwards, and when night fell, still kept walking on, steering their course as best they could by the inadequately glimpsed stars. Eventually they came to another clearing, and, crawling to the edge of it, saw a single railway line gleaming like silver in a cutting. Guessing that this was the track on which their train had run the previous day, they crossed it, frightened by the rattle of the ballast stones under their feet, and entered the wood on the other side, to plod on and on through more trees. Gradually the ground rose and walking became harder and, coming to a crest, they saw below them a wide river, dark and shining with night. Following the crest they stopped opposite a long bar of foam that stretched right across the river and looked as though it might be caused by rocks. However, as they climbed down, the steep face of the descent forced them to go at a slant, and when they reached the edge of the river they found themselves almost opposite a bridge whose stanchions spanned the water and threw another darkness upon it. But their luck was out, for reconnaissance soon showed that the bridge was guarded, so, skirting the mighty base of the ledge which reared above them, they walked back to the bar of the foam where after rolling up their trouser legs and removing their boots and hanging them round their necks, they stepped gingerly into the swirling water. The current was cold and strong and nearly swept them off their feet. Tommy, who was leading the closely packed group, slipped and plunged up to his waist into a hole, from which he was pulled by Dulac just in time to prevent him being carried away. Dulac then led the way and after a hazardous and unpleasant journey they reached the opposite bank, shivering with cold.

As there was no cover on the river bank they made across open ground for a clump of trees before drying their feet and putting on their boots. They crossed more open ground and came to another wood which was shallow and whose far side was bordered by a narrow stream, which they forded in the same manner as the river. Walking through more trees they found themselves in a factory yard with huts and buildings and girders all around them. Deciding that it might be more dangerous to retreat than to advance, they tiptoed through the yard and came to a large open gate which gave on to a street. They listened carefully and heard, as they had half-expected to hear, the measured tread of a sentry. Concealing themselves in the shadows, they saw his dark form pass the gate and, as the tramp of his feet diminished, peeped out and saw that the factory was the last building in the street and that beyond the house opposite, about twenty-five yards distant, were more trees; the sentry himself was standing some hundred yards to the left, looking to his right. Removing for the third time that night their boots and the rags that served for socks, they waited until the sentry had trudged past the gate again, and, when he was about fifty yards away with his back still turned, ran across the street to the trees. A couple of dogs barked mournfully, but that was all that happened.

They put on their socks and boots again and took their bearings. In front of their shelter of trees was a deeply furrowed field and beyond it more woods. As they were crossing the field they had to fling themselves flat on their faces in the furrows to avoid being caught in the stabbing white headlights of a car which came racing along the road. The car passed and diminished into a tiny glow moving towards the horizon and finally vanishing in darkness. They got up and, although very tired, pressed on to the trees and through them, desirous of leaving the village well behind them.

In the small hours of the morning they lay down to sleep, again with Dulac's overcoat on top of them. Yeo-Thomas did not sleep well because his dysentery, aggravated by the cold water which he had drunk, was troubling him again. When they woke it was quite light. Before starting out again they ate more of their bread; by now Tommy, who, because he had been unwilling to leave Hubble's chess set behind, had brought only about 1 lb. with him, had almost finished his.

The day was fine, with a bright sun from a blue sky sending shafts of light down into their cool cathedral of trees. They pressed on till they came to a clearing on one side of which was a plantation of young saplings. They ran across and gained the preserve. The saplings, although only six or seven feet high, were planted in orderly rows and afforded good cover. Within a few minutes however they had reached the edge of the plantation and came to a road, on the other side of which was another preserve. It was as well that they were wary, for presently they heard footsteps. Lying flat on their bellies they saw a patrol of about half a dozen Volkssturm soldiers armed with rifles and grenades approaching along the road. The patrol passed, walked a short distance, retraced its steps and passed again. When a couple of minutes later it came back again it was clear that it was on a very short beat indeed, and that a reconnaissance was necessary.

The results of their reconnaissance were not promising: walking parallel to the edge of the plantation, they found that it was almost as short as it was shallow and that the road ran straight on past its border. The only solution seemed to be speed from the most advantageous position at the most opportune moment: to wait at one end of the preserve until the patrol had gone a good distance down the road and then run and hope to reach the next batch of saplings before it turned to come back again. But while they were resting in order to gather strength for the attempt they heard a noise of people coming through the trees behind them. Fearing that they were now caught between two dangers, they lay as flat as they could and prepared for the worst. The danger from the rear, however, turned out to be only a compromising increase to their numbers; those who came walking through the saplings were Foulquier, Jacquin and Pete, who had blundered along much the same route as themselves.

Foulquier and his group, who had already had some narrow shaves, were not unduly alarmed when the situation was explained to them, and agreed with its proposed solution. The six of them went together to the fringe of the copse and waited for the best time to cross. They managed it in small batches of two, but because of the weakness of their undernourished bodies were exhausted by the effort and the excitement.

On the other side the two groups parted company again, Yeo-Thomas and his team moving on only after they had given the others a good start. Although the new plantation was much broader than the one they had left behind, it too ended in a clearing; but this time there was no road and no Volkssturm, and they ran across to the next preserve without danger or incident and repeated the process several times that morning.

Eventually they came to an expanse of open country at least a mile wide; the only shelter before reaching the woods on the other side was a small clump of trees in the middle. Another reconnaissance showed that there was no way round this hazard, and while they were resting before crossing it Yeo-Thomas finished his last piece of bread. His dysentery had by now become acute.

They crossed in what used to be called extended order, Yeo-Thomas on the left, Georges in the middle and Dulac on the right. The ground sloped upwards and the going was hard. When they were within about a hundred yards of the clump of trees they heard voices and saw men coming over the crest of the hill to meet them. Running obliquely to the left, Dulac and Georges outdistanced Yeo-Thomas, whose bowels were wrung with agony. Puffing and staggering, Tommy saw them disappear into the clump and, knowing that he could not reach it before the men saw him, threw himself down at the base of a solitary tree and pretended to be asleep. He lay huddled on his stomach, resting his head on his arms in such a way that he could keep a surreptitious watch out of one eye. The men almost missed him, but one of them saw him and called to him. The man and his companions came close and the man shouted at him again, but Yeo-Thomas did not answer and lay absolutely still. The men laughed together and Tommy gathered that they were upbraiding him for a lazy dog. He remained motionless, terrified that they would shake him and, when his lack of German had betrayed him, hand him over to the authorities. Fortunately after a few seconds they moved on, still laughing heartily.

He waited until they had passed out of sight and then he ran for the clump of trees. Dulac and Georges were nowhere to be seen and, as now only a downwards slope of about three hundred yards separated him from the wood, he gathered that they must have taken advantage of the Germans having passed over the ridge of the hill to run for more secure shelter. He himself was now too ill to run any more. He walked down and entered the wood. Once under cover he looked for Dulac and Georges. He failed to find them. He was alone.

His plight was desperate: he had no food; he was suffering agony in his entrails; and he had still a long journey in front of him. But now that he had come so far he was more determined than ever to succeed. He would go on west-north-west in the hope of striking Chemnitz, whence he knew that he could easily find his way to safety.

So he started out on his lonely trek. Inside the wood the ground continued to slope downwards and he stumbled on until he came to a main road intersecting the trees. He scrambled down the embankment, crossed the road and plunged into the continuation of the forest.

Although the ground still sloped downwards, walking was not easy, for every now and then he had to stop while agonizing gripes twisted his bowels.

It began to rain: at first a drizzle which trickled gently down from the branches and soothed his brow and tempered his fever; then a downpour, which soaked through his corduroy jacket and made it feel as heavy as mail. He became very hungry and very cold. With aching feet, legs and belly, he went on until he came to the edge of the wood and saw that below him was another river. On the other side of the river more woods began at a distance of about three hundred yards from the bank.

Knowing that he could not hope to ford the river alone, he turned blindly to the right, and to his joy came upon a small and apparently unguarded wooden bridge. Then he saw that between the bridge and the wood was a small village, nestling by the side of the river. Circling round the village, he found that there was no way of avoiding it, and as darkness was now beginning to fall he took the risk of walking through it. His luck was in and he met nobody, and soon he was on the other side of the bridge, walking up towards the trees.

But the slope up towards the wood was steep, and the ground was mucky and slippery. The rain was now pouring down in torrents and he was drenched to the skin and cold. A more than usually violent pang of dysentery shook him, and, reeling with nausea, he had to sit on the stump of a felled tree to rest. Then he ploughed on up the hill, stumbling over roots, sliding in the mud, until he reached the trees.

In the wood the rain still fell heavily, pouring down his neck and back in icy streams. Stumbling upon a path he followed it in the hope that it might lead to a woodcutter's hut where he might pass the night. With his feet sloshing about in the slimy mud he slithered, slipped and slid along its winding, oozy track. Then he staggered and fell on something soft and, feeling about with his hands, discovered that he had tumbled into a deep pit of sapling branches; and there, when he had drawn the topmost ones over him as a quilt, he spent the night, sinking at once into a dreamless sleep.

When he awoke it was still raining, but the branches had protected him, and his body, although still damp, was warmer. He was hungry, but as he had no food he could only stagger on. All that day he went on through the trees and the rain, dragging his feet, which were terribly weighted down by the mud. That night he came to a potato field and scratched about all over it in hope, but he found no potatoes. It was still raining and he was wretchedly cold, but he walked on through the blackness until he reached a pile of logs at the foot of a tree, between which he flung himself down and slept.

It was still raining when he woke at dawn. He was racked with pain and hunger and his teeth were chattering with cold. Once again he went on, but his progress became more and more exhausting. Each step that he took sent shooting pains through his groins. Dysentery bent him double and his stomach was raw with hunger. Every bone in his body was sore and every muscle stiff, and his mind was as wrung as his bowels, with the cold biting slaps of despair. He began to talk to himself and to stumble and fall to the ground, and to blubber as he picked himself up, crying his hopelessness to the trees: 'I can't go on. I can't go on. I'll pack up and surrender at the nearest village.' But he thought of Barbara and of Britain, which meant so much more to him than to the loud dissemblers in the market place, and he plodded on, through the rain and through the trees.

That afternoon he came upon a road and, dazed with stupor, attempted to cross it without having looked to see if there was anybody on it. Men shouted at him and he saw a patrol about a hundred and fifty yards away advancing towards him. He turned and fled back into the woods, followed by the noise of running feet, rifle shots and whizzing bullets. Fear lent strength to his tired body and, with bursting lungs, he ran on until his legs crumpled up under him and he fell to the ground, shaking and heaving. He tried to rise, but could not stand because his legs were trembling too much to be able to bear his weight. His head was throbbing and he had stabbing pains behind his eyes. Violently sick, he tried to vomit, but there was nothing in his stomach to bring up; and while he had been running his bowels had emptied themselves, squirting their discharge down over his thighs. But there was neither sound nor sign of the patrol and he gathered that he had shaken it off.

He had to lie for about an hour before he could muster strength to go on again. From now onwards he had to stop frequently, as his legs seemed to be sinking away into his body. Each time that he fell down he thought that he would never be able to get up again, but each time he determined to have another try and succeeded. He was so cold and hungry that he began to be lightheaded and to have hallucinations: he saw rows and rows of steaming hot cups of tea, rows and rows of roast beef and Yorkshire pudding and rows and rows of pumpkin pies, stretching away into the distance and for ever evading his embrace as he tried to catch up with them. And after these phantoms he chased madly, sobbing each time that they eluded his grasp. The reality of the illusion was increased by the fact that he disliked pumpkin pies.

When night came again he still walked on, lost in a trance, falling, picking himself up again, banging his head and his face against trees. Suddenly the earth seemed to open under his feet and he fell through space, landing at the bottom of a pit twelve feet deep, filled with decaying leaves. He lay for a little looking up at the stars, and then tried to pull himself out, but the slope of the pit was steep and slippery and time after time he fell back. Panicking, he subsided and lay at the bottom, panting and sobbing, sure that he was going to die. Again he roused himself by thinking of Barbara and of the Britain he loved so simply, and once again his loyalties aided his endeavour. This time he pulled himself up slowly and carefully and, in spite of many a slither, eased himself up to the edge of the pit, where he lay until he had recovered enough strength to stand up. Too tired to walk any further, he huddled up against the trunk of a tree and slept.

Next morning when he woke the rain had thinned to a drizzle. He had a spasm of dysentery, and his hunger was intense. When he rose to his feet the forest spun round him like a merry-go-round and he crashed to the ground. He got up again and leaned against a tree until he had recovered his equilibrium. Then he went on, slowly and painfully. Every now and then his legs folded up under him, but always he picked himself up and always he went on.

The drizzle stopped and the sun began to shine and its rays refreshed and cheered him, and sent a short warmth through his body; and he stumbled on, with a new and stronger vision before him. But dysentery continued to weaken him and soon the world was swimming again in front of his eyes. When he came to a clearing it was with difficulty that he was able to make out a large copse on the other side. To this he staggered, and in it he found a large pit whose bottom was lined with Red Cross cartons. The cartons, however, were empty and indicated the nearness of purloining Germans rather than of friendly Allies, for with them were several dozen unopened letters addressed to British prisoners of war. Disappointed, he pushed on to the far edge of the copse. As he reached it his legs gave way under him and he lost consciousness.

When he came to he felt that somebody was pulling him up, and supposed that he must have been captured again, but was too weak to care. All that he could see was a blur and the blur moved with him as it raised him from the ground and sat him up against a tree. Then the blur became a man with a kindly, smiling face who spoke to him in a language which was not German. Unable to answer, Yeo-Thomas saw from the markings on his tattered uniform that he was a prisoner of war. Eventually he succeeded in saying a few words in French, and in the same language the man haltingly replied that he was a Yugoslav prisoner working nearby.

'I am a Frenchman trying to escape,' Tommy said when he could get the words out. He did not need to say that he was hungry and exhausted: the Yugoslav could see that for himself.

They smiled at each other with the friendliness born of a shared servitude. Yeo-Thomas tried to rise, but fell back to the ground at once. The Yugoslav shook his head, lifted him and carried him further back into the copse, where he propped him against another tree. '*Moi chercher manger, vous restez ici, pas bouger, reposer,*'[1] he said, and left Yeo-Thomas with the world all streaky in front of his eyes, floating away in wisps of misty trees and blotches of indeterminate sky.

A little later the Yugoslav came back and tapped the still half-fainting Yeo-Thomas on the shoulder. From a haversack slung over his shoulders he produced a half-pound loaf of bread and a bottle of white wine. '*Manger,*' he said when he had cut off a piece of bread, but as soon as Tommy tried to eat it he vomited. The Yugoslav then let him drink a little wine, and the wine sent warmth back into his body and revived him. After that the Yugoslav cut the bread into small cubes, which he stuffed into Tommy's pockets, and from his haversack he took a small linen bag fitted with a sling, into which he put the bottle of wine. '*Pour vous,*' he said, '*Bonne chance!*'

Tommy was too moved and too weak to speak. He shook the man's hand, and the Yugoslav smiled at him. '*Méfier,*' the Yugoslav said. '*Dangereux. Ici beaucoup de soldats allemands.*'[2] In awkward, but understandable French he told Yeo-Thomas to wait until he signalled before starting to cross the field in front, as there were many Germans working nearby. And that was all he said before he left Tommy, but his smile said everything else and told Tommy not to worry about what he himself had been unable to say. An hour later he signalled that all was clear and, strengthened by the wine, Yeo-Thomas set out again. As he reached the trees on the far side of the field he turned to wave to the Yugoslav, who stood against the clouds and the sky and waved back at him. It had been the perfect evangelical encounter.

As he went on, he ate his bread a cube at a time; he had to munch each morsel very slowly before he was able to swallow it. The wine

1 'I go get eat, you stay here, not move, rest.'
2 'Be careful. Dangerous. Here many German soldiers.'

helped him more than the bread, but he resolved to ration himself to three sips a day. Even when the rain came on again and his dysentery dug daggers into his bowels he stuck to this resolution. He kept on walking and, because even a sip of wine maketh glad the heart of man, he was able to think of the simple, silly song about Felix who, in the early 1920s, had kept on walking too. But when night fell and it was still raining there was little courage left in him as he trudged heavily on through the sludgy, squelching mud. He kept on until his strength gave out. He lay down to sleep under a tree through whose leaves the rain continued to fall on his already drenched body.

Next morning he awoke cold and stiff. He was violently sick after eating two cubes of bread, but again the wine restored him. He got up and went on, thinking now of Barbara, now of Britain. His legs were badly swollen, his feet felt as though they had been flayed, his body was sore, his belly was on fire, but all that day he walked on, propelling himself by his loyalties. He was so soaked and cold and tired that, coming upon a temporarily driverless lorry standing in a small lane, he risked resting in the cab for a little and left a pool of water behind him when he got out again.

Gradually it became more difficult to find cover and, as houses increased, he realised that he was entering a thickly populated area. At dusk, after circumventing several villages, he came to a wood traversed by a small stream, in which, after stripping, he washed. But, although refreshed, he felt more frozen than before when he had put on his damp clothes again and, as he was too weak and sore to do any jumping about, he took a drink of wine and curled up to sleep under the shelter of a sapling.

When he awoke it was still dark, but it was no longer raining. He ate a few cubes of bread, drank a little wine and started off, taking his bearings from the waning stars. As dawn broke he descended a steep slope to find himself confronted by a broken wall which seemed to stretch for a long distance. Hearing no sounds, he clambered over and came to the ruins of a factory which had obviously been put out of action by bombing. But the wall on the other side of the factory was intact and, as the gates were locked, he had to climb over, tiring himself terribly and dropping on to a road with a jar which sent sharp pains stabbing through his legs. The road, which was straight and metalled, was obviously a main thoroughfare, and he walked along it in search of a signpost. The signpost, when he found it, read: CHEMNITZ 2 KM. He had aimed far more accurately than he had dared to hope. Now all that he had to do was to keep on going westwards.

Chemnitz was too big for him to lose time by making a detour and, encouraged by the excellence of his navigation, he set out towards it with a new will, determined to get through the town while the light was still dim. As soon as he reached the outskirts he saw that the town had been heavily bombed: everywhere there were ruins; roofless and gutted buildings threw their skeletons like escarpments against the pale, creamy early morning sky; and through the windowless grey streets drab men and women walked with buckets and containers, too set on their search for water to pay any attention to the appearance of a stranger whose outward signs of wretchedness made him one with themselves. He heard French spoken as he walked through those grim dilapidations and saw that among those whom he passed in the dismal streets were both French prisoners of war and French civilian workers, both of whom moved about freely in the sinister shadows.

This observation helped him when, safely through the town and marching boldly along the main road, he heard the clippety-clop and rub-a-dub-dub of a horse and cart coming up behind him. Driving the cart was a French prisoner of war, from whom he obtained a lift, saying that he was a French worker who had been bombed out of his employment and was trying to make his way homewards to France. The prisoner of war turned out to be a Parisian and, to avoid being asked where he had been working, Yeo-Thomas talked to him of the metropolis and of the streets which they both loved. In this way he covered twenty-five kilometres.

It was raining hard again when the prisoner of war set him down, but Tommy was now too elated to care. He ate his last cube of bread, drank almost his last drop of wine and pressed on on foot once more. Soon his legs were sore, his groin aching, his bowels burning, but on and on he went, through the day and far into the night. He slept briefly in a clump of trees.

Next morning it was still raining and he was soaked to the skin. He finished his wine, flung the bottle away, and went on. As he walked he began to get light-headed again and so to see more phantasmal processions of cups of hot tea, roasts of beef and Yorkshire pudding. Apart from these visions he does not remember much of what happened that day. Again he slept in a wood.

He awoke as usual to find that the rain had not stopped. But as he started off a blessed sound came to his ears: the muffled thump of cannon firing in the distance, and to him it was as sweet as the chanting of cherubim to a saint. By early afternoon the muffled thump had become a roar and, if he had any doubt that he was approaching where right and glory led, it was dispelled by the sight of a string of refugees, slopping wearily along the road, pushing their cheap possessions in carts, carrying canaries in cages and kittens in baskets: young girls with the rain plastering their flaxen hair against their cheeks, old men and old women with broken boots and blistered feet, babes in arms blinking at the nonsense of the world into which clergymen said that the love of God had dumped them, all the ragtag and bobtail of human misery called, in the cold classification of the chancelleries, displaced persons.

If his safety increased as he approached danger, his danger also increased as he approached safety: every step he took towards the Allied lines led him more deeply into the centre of the enemy formations, and as he debouched into the wood for concealment he almost ran bang into a Wehrmacht patrol. He lay flat on his belly and looked and listened: the woods were full of German troops combining and permuting in their private pattern of the bigger battle and from ahead came the crack of machine-guns and rifles. A peasant and a small girl came along a path carrying bundles of small branches and the soldiers let them pass. Picking up a few pieces of wood, Tommy tucked them under his arm and set off, head bent down, in the direction of the machine-gun and rifle fire.

But he was weaker than he had imagined and soon he had to throw away the branches. Every step was painful. He dropped to the ground and crawled through the undergrowth. As he came near to the edge of the wood he saw a German machine-gun emplacement. The quick rattle that the gun made when it fired did not sound unfriendly but the bullets that came whistling back in answer were definitely hostile. Yeo-Thomas ducked his head and lay down under cover.

When he had rested he crept nearer the edge of the wood. About two hundred yards to the right of the machine-gun nest there was a second, also firing. Sliding in between the two emplacements he saw, in the open ground beyond the fringe of the wood, a shallow path which crossed a field on the other side of which he guessed the Allied lines must be. Deciding to follow the path when night came, he lay down and waited impatiently for dusk, and passed the time in a lewd contemplation already popular with his compatriots: whoring in his heart after bacon and eggs.

At last dusk fell and then darkness. Because of his dysentery, bending double was now his natural position, and he moved forward in the orthodox position, as though carrying a rifle at the trail. When he reached the edge of the wood he looked left and right. He could see nobody, but he could hear the rumble of armoured vehicles and the sound of gunfire. He waited until he heard only an occasional rifle shot and then, realizing that he must beware of friend as well as foe, moved out into no-man's-land. He had not gone twenty-five yards when he heard a shout: '*Halt!*' He tried to run. A couple of bullets hit the ground near his feet. He made another effort and found that he could not even walk. Stars danced before his eyes as he slumped to the ground. Footsteps came up and he was turned over on his face by a kick in the side. He prepared to receive a shot or a bayonet thrust. But this time it was fighting soldiers he was dealing with, and not the Gestapo: when his captors saw that he could not stand up they dragged him back into the woods. Once again he was a prisoner.

CHAPTER XVII

THE LAST LAP

At first the NCO in charge of the patrol which had captured him thought that Yeo-Thomas was shamming weakness and cursed him for encumbering the men with his weight. But when, in the cover of the woods, he had inspected his prisoner's worn and filthy face, his tone changed and he became compassionate, asking if he was hungry and promising him food when he had been interrogated.

The interrogation took place in a heavily guarded hut about a mile inside the wood and was conducted by a Hauptmann of the Wehrmacht who, when the NCO had told him the details of Tommy's arrest, asked:

'Name?'

'*Maurice Thomas, adjutant-chef de l'Armée de l'Air Française,*' Yeo-Thomas lied quickly, knowing that hesitation would be fatal, since discovery that he had escaped from a concentration camp would entail his being handed over to the SS for summary execution. He went on to say that he had been captured at Tours in 1940 and had escaped while his Stalag in Western Germany was being evacuated on account of the advance of the Allies. He had been trying to live on the country while making his way towards France and had got lost.

'Why did you try to escape?'

'Because it is the duty of every prisoner of war to escape if he can.'

This seemed to satisfy the officer. Yeo-Thomas was then taken to a shed where, under the incurious eyes of about a dozen German soldiers, he was given two pannikinsful of potato soup, which brought back his dysentery. After an escorted visit to the *Abort* he spent the rest of the night in the shed.

Next morning two soldiers marched him to a village some two miles on the other side of the wood. There the officer in charge, after telephoning the authorities for instructions, handed him over to a detachment of Hitler Jugend, who escorted him to a small town another ten miles behind the line. These boys between fifteen and seventeen had none of the chivalry of the combatants and, perceiving that their prisoner walked with difficulty, forced the pace and, when he stumbled, reviled him, kicked him, slapped him across the mouth, spat in his face, hit him with their rifle butts and prodded him with the points of their bayonets.

In the small town the local police took temporary charge of him and locked him in a darkened cell in which he punched a common law offender on the nose for attempting to steal Hubble's chess set. After further interrogation he was put in a truck and driven back to Chemnitz, where he spent the night in the guardroom of the barracks and told the NCO in charge to go to hell when he ordered him to sweep the floor. His strength was returning.

And, in spite of the fact that he was still suffering from dysentery and that his feet were so sore and badly swollen that he could not remove his boots, his mind was as alert as ever. Next morning, when interrogated by a French-speaking colonel at Wehrmacht HQ, he added to the story of his being Adjutant-Chef Maurice Thomas of the French Air Force, captured in 1940, the information that he had belonged to the 34 Bataillon de l'Armée de l'Air, stationed at Le Bourget until its retreat to Tours. In this way, because he himself had served alongside this unit, he was able, when the Colonel asked him for the name, to say that his commanding officer had been Colonel Rubis. After corroborating this statement from a French Air Force List on his desk, the Colonel dismissed him with a homily on the folly of attempting to escape.

The following afternoon, after seeing a Canadian POW beaten up by the guardroom NCO, he was, in company with an assortment of other French and British prisoners, marched to a dilapidated transit camp on the outskirts of the town, where they spent the night. Here no rations were issued to them, and next day, still unfed, they were put on the road again. On their way they met a Russian POW, who gave them a few slices of beetroot flavoured with petrol, but when they reached a French Stalag late that afternoon they were still so hungry that they had to make themselves soup by boiling nettles.

At dawn they were marched on again, and in the middle of the day were split into two parties, one British and the other French, each of which took a different direction. Yeo-Thomas naturally remained with the French, who in turn were whittled down by various splits, until he was left alone with his escort. Towards evening he was delivered to the Stalag for French NCOs at Grunhainigen, which was to be his new abode.

Naturally the French NCOs started asking him questions, and at first all went well: he was able to say where he had lived in France, how he had earned his livelihood before the war and to give particulars of the unit with which he had served. But when he said that he had escaped from Stalag IVB, he saw one of the NCOs look at him suspiciously and then rise and beckon the Senior of the camp to follow him. A few minutes later the NCO came back again and sat down opposite Yeo-Thomas, who was sitting alone at a table, resting his head in his hands.

'There's something about your story that I don't like,' he said. 'I was at Stalag IVB but I never saw you there. How was that?'

Tommy knew that he must tell the truth if he wanted to avoid the risk of being regarded as a stool pigeon.

'Because I was never there,' he said. 'I am sorry I had to lie to you, but if you will be kind enough to go and get the Senior NCO I think that I shall be able to make you understand why. Only I must ask you to keep this information to yourselves because the slightest indiscretion might easily cost me my life.'

'I think perhaps you'd better talk first and we can promise afterwards,' the NCO said as he rose to fetch the Senior man.

The two Frenchmen listened carefully while Yeo-Thomas recounted his story. He told them that he was a British officer who had been captured by the Gestapo while working with the French Resistance. He described the prison at Fresnes and the camps at Compiègne,

Saarbrücken, Buchenwald, Gleina and Rehmsdorf. When he had finished the Senior NCO said:

'It's all possible, of course, but what proof have we that you are not working for the Germans?'

It was a natural enough suspicion in a war in which the Queensberry rules had been thrown overboard, the kick in the testicles called strategy and the greater lie used to outwit the lesser. Tommy had no answer to this question because he had no papers. Then he remembered the relic of his saint, and the relic of his saint came to his rescue. He told them about Hubble, showed them the British trade mark on his chess set and after that they believed him.

And they believed him practically. They helped him to cut the uppers off his boots so that he could remove them and tend his swollen feet. They gave him hot water and salt to wash out the festering blisters, and cloth and sulphonamide powder with which to bandage them. That night, for the first time for three weeks, he slept with a blanket over him. Next morning a third NCO called Albaret, who had been let into his secret, provided him with a false POW identity plaque.

Soon it was no longer a question of believing Yeo-Thomas; it was a matter of following his lead. When he told them that he intended to make another attempt to escape and called for volunteers they at first demurred, saying that it would be foolish to risk their lives unnecessarily when liberation was so near. To this Tommy replied that, as far as he was concerned, the necessity was imperative: he had been silly enough to get captured, therefore it was his duty to escape; and he soon had eleven of the others accepting this not unassailable syllogism. The Senior NCO, however, declined to be of the party, as he thought that he could be of more use if he stayed behind to impede the search which would be made when their flight had been discovered.

But a POWs scanty ration of potatoes did little to restore Tommy's strength, exhausted by exposure and an average of twenty evacuations a day, and so he decided that they would have to escape by train. Circumstances were in his favour. Not only were there trains from Grunhainigen to Chemnitz, but there were also night trains. A POW obtained official-looking papers from a girl in the village. Another, who worked in the local Town Hall, stole a rubber stamp, and within forty-eight hours they had forged documents and Ausweise describing themselves as foreign labourers, dismissed by a factory in Grunhainigen and free to take up employment elsewhere.

During Tommy's third afternoon in the camp the wire stretched across one of the windows was unfastened, and that same night the eleven set out across the fields for the station, walking warily behind hedges. Although the station was blacked out they had to be careful in case any of the local inhabitants recognised them, and so Yeo-Thomas, who was completely unknown in the district, bought tickets for a number of them, while two of the others bought the rest. Then, separating, they waited in the shadows until the train came in, when Yeo-Thomas and Albaret got into a compartment together and the rest into different compartments in the same carriage. It was as simple as all that.

The train was a local which stopped at every station and it was soon crowded. Yeo-Thomas made the mistake of speaking English when he rose to offer his seat to a woman, but the lady was too surprised by the gesture to notice the language, and the other passengers were too busy talking. They reached Chemnitz in the early hours of the morning.

Two by two and keeping a distance between each couple, they walked westwards and by dawn had left the suburbs behind them. By now the battle had moved much nearer and they soon heard gunfire. To avoid being seen by troops or patrols they left the road and walked under cover. This meant much harder going for Yeo-Thomas, who had presumed too much on his strength and was quickly in difficulties. All his old pains came back: his feet felt like open stumps; his stiff legs sank like pistons into his pelvis; and his bowels were aflame with diarrhoea. Only the desire not to embarrass his companions and the fear, for now they all knew his story, of disgracing his country in their eyes kept him going. Seeing the sweat pouring down his face, Albaret gave him some chocolate and made him rest. But neither helped much and when they moved on again he had to lean on Albaret's arm. And all the time the evidences of conflict kept increasing: the firing became louder and louder, and soon they could hear the clack and the click of automatic arms. While making a detour to avoid some camouflaged tanks Tommy collapsed. Albaret helped him up and he fell down again. The others stopped and grouped themselves around him.

'It's no use,' Yeo-Thomas said. 'I'm done for. You'll just have to go on without me. Leave me a bit of bread though and I'll see what I can do when I've had a rest.'

They all refused, and from their hearts as well as from their lips. They had no need to stretch their mouths in a lying smile or squeeze a glow they didn't feel into their eyes. They meant what they said. They might have known Yeo-Thomas only for four days but already they had come to love him.

'It's an order,' Tommy said. 'Albaret, I order you and the others to go on and leave me here.'

'You don't seem to know much about the French after all,' Albaret said. 'We Frenchmen aren't always awfully good at obeying our own officers, so I'm damned if we're going to obey a British officer.'

'Once and for all, Albaret, I won't have the rest of you risking your lives for me.'

But with the genius for disobedience of all Gaul they declined to listen to him. Hoisting his arms around their shoulders and linking their hands behind his back, two of them carried him. For hour after hour they progressed like this, the men relaying one another as bearers.

In the late afternoon they came to a wood. Although there were both sniping and shelling they could see no troops and the greater part of the firing seemed to come from their flanks. They passed through the wood and lay down in the fringe. In front of them stretched an open field: Yeo-Thomas was back on the edge of no-man's-land again

Most of them wanted to wait for nightfall before attempting to cross, but Yeo-Thomas remembered his previous failure. If they crossed in darkness there was the additional risk of falling into an Allied ambush and being shot at as Germans, whereas if they crossed in daylight their friends would be able to see that they were unarmed and that they were not wearing enemy uniform. The absence of troops in their part of the wood and the fact that the firing came from either side of them seemed to prove that the sector in which they were was not strongly held. With luck they could get more than half-way across before the Germans saw them and such fire as they attracted would be diagonal. He made his decision, and this time even the piddlers against

Defense D'uriner notices had to obey: they would cross by daylight, as soon as an opportunity offered.

As everything in the vicinity was quiet they made the attempt at once. Yeo-Thomas left cover first, with Albaret and another man on either side of him, assisting him; the others followed behind, in single file. Because of Tommy's weakness it cannot have been a very speedy dash for it and in any case it was also a short one: they had only got about a quarter of the way across when they saw two GIs in American battle bowlers emerge from the wood opposite and point sub-machine-guns at them.

Yeo-Thomas mustered all his strength and shouted:

'Don't shoot. Escaping prisoners of war. Prisoners of war. Don't shoot.'

It was the turn of the transatlantic disobeyers to obey, and fortunately they did so. They shouted something back which Yeo-Thomas could not catch, and he and his companions went on until they reached the wood. There they were surrounded by more American soldiers, all covering them with Tommy guns.

'Who the hell are you?' their leader asked.

It was a little difficult to be coherent in such circumstances but Yeo-Thomas managed to get across the gist of their innocence:

'I am a British Air Force officer, escaped from a concentration camp. The others are French POW.'

'Well, you guys are goddam lucky; you've just crossed a minefield.'

But Yeo-Thomas was too overpowered by happiness at the knowledge that he was at long last back among friends to be surprised by this last stroke of good fortune or to feel grateful for it.

Escorted back to a village called Hondorf, Yeo-Thomas had to tell their story all over again to a young American lieutenant:

'I am a British Air Force officer captured on secret service in German-occupied territory. I escaped from a concentration camp. I was captured again and landed in a French Stalag. I escaped from the French Stalag and these French soldiers came with me.'

But there lived more doubt in honest faith than faith in honest doubt.

'How do I know that you are telling the truth? What papers have you got?'

'How can I have any papers after having been in a concentration camp?' Tommy was reminded of the Air Commodore who had expected him to read Air Ministry Orders while dodging the Gestapo in Paris, but he was patient with the Lieutenant because he knew that scepticism was part of his duty, and because he was not puffed up. 'Listen. I worked with your OSS[1] in London. Take me to your Commanding Officer and I'll tell him how to prove my identity.'

'What about those other guys?'

They have POW plaques and French identity discs. You can easily check on them.'

The Lieutenant began to be convinced that Yeo-Thomas was telling the truth and that, in spite of his scruffy appearance, he really was a British officer.

'OK' The Lieutenant turned to a top sergeant. 'Check on the Frogs and have them looked after and sent back. In the meantime I'll have a talk with this Englishman.'

But before Tommy could either listen or explain he had to be refreshed. He declined a carton of American rations as being too substantial and chose instead two oranges and a cup of coffee, which did the trick. When he had told the Lieutenant his story he was taken to a Major, who consented to see him only under protest. Standing to attention in his rags before the Major, Yeo-Thomas told his name, rank, number and story, said that he had valuable information for GHQ and prepared to be doubted again.

And he was doubted, precisely, coldly, officially:

'Very interesting. But what means have I of verifying your *bona fides?*'

He had Hubble's chess set in his pocket, but this time he thought that more substantial proof was needed.

'If you will wireless to Major-General C. McV. Gubbins of SOE in London you will get immediate confirmation.'

But because of the smallness of the Resistance world the message never required to be sent. As the Major was explaining the difficulty of communicating with London from so advanced a position Lieutenant Javal, whom Yeo-Thomas had known in London, but whom he did

1 Office of Strategic Services

not immediately recognise and who certainly did not recognise Tommy, walked into the Major's office.

'For crying out loud!' the Major said. 'You're the very fellow we want. This guy says he's a Britisher who worked with French Resistance. Says he speaks the lingo like a native. Check up on him, will you?'

Javal turned to Yeo-Thomas.

'*Vous parlez français, parait-il?*'

'*Mais oui, Lieutenant, je parle français.*'

Javal looked at him closely.

'Your voice is familiar. I seem to know you, but I'm not sure. What's your name?'

Tired and weary. Tommy drew himself up as he stated his brief but tremendous title to trust:

'Yeo-Thomas, better known to the Resistance as Shelley.'

Javal was wild with emotion and delight.

'*Mais naturellement je vous connais.* We've all been moving heaven and earth to find you. You know me too. I'm Javal.'

They did not immediately kill the fatted calf. First the Major got out his maps and Yeo-Thomas showed him the route which he and the others had followed, and pointed out the enemy troop and battery locations. The Major decided to do a cleaning-up action that night, using light tanks and infantry. Yeo-Thomas, to his regret, was refused permission to take part in it.

Instead he was given a bath, clean linen and the first pair of socks which he had worn on his sore feet since Buchenwald. Then, lost in an outsize black suit which had belonged to the Bürgemeister of Hondorf, he had a light meal with the Major and drank three-quarters of a bottle of Napoleon brandy while news of the operation which his information had initiated was coming in.

Next morning he was driven back in a jeep to Divisional Head-quarters. They had to keep him there for three days because he was so weak. Then he was taken to Weimar and, while trying to find the British Liaison Officer, fell in with another old Resistance friend, Colonel Fourcauld and his FANY wife, who, startled by his appearance, insisted on driving him back to Paris. There, after being fired on on the way by a pocket of resisting Germans, he arrived very appropriately on 8 May and celebrated VE day by dining with Major Thackthwaite and José Dupuis in the British Officers' Club in the rue du Faubourg St Honoré.

His father said little next morning when Tommy called to see him. That brave old man kept his shock for those who were able to bear it: 'My son has returned, but he looks like an old man of seventy.'

But it was with a light heart that, later that same day, the old man of seventy, still wearing the Bürgermeister's baggy suit, climbed into the plane for London. This time there was no flak over the French coast and the aircraft sailed calmly over the hyphen of sea towards the gentle green fields. The plane landed at Croydon, and carried an undefeated man into an undefeated city.

Colonel Dismore was waiting on the airstrip, and behind him stood Barbara, wearing a very wobbly smile. The White Rabbit had returned to his hutch again, but instead of the now archaic iodoform the Third Supplement to the *London Gazette* of 12 February, 1946, carried these words:

'The King has been graciously pleased to award the GEORGE CROSS to Acting Wing Commander Forest Frederick Yeo-Thomas, MC (89215), Royal Air Force Volunteer Reserve.'

Military Classics

The Great Escape © Tempe and Timothy Brickhill 1950
This Military Classics edition published 2002

The right of Paul Brickhill to be identified as the author of this work has been
asserted by him in accordance with the Copyright, Designs and Patents Act 1988.

The White Rabbit © Sheila E.B. Farrar and Mark Seaman 1952
This Military Classics edition published 2002

The right of Bruce Marshall to be identified as the author of this work has been
asserted by him in accordance with the Copyright, Designs and Patents Act 1988.

ISBN 0-304-36629-3

Printed and bound in Great Britain